Selecting MPLS VPN Services

Chris Lewis

Steve Pickavance

Contributions by:

Monique Morrow

John Monaghan

Craig Huegen

Cisco Press

800 East 96th Street
Indianapolis, IN 46240 USA

Selecting MPLS VPN Services

Chris Lewis

Steve Pickavance

Contributions by:

Monique Morrow

John Monaghan

Craig Huegen

Copyright © 2006 Cisco Systems, Inc.

Published by:
Cisco Press
800 East 96th Street
Indianapolis, IN 46240 USA

Printed in the United States of America   1 2 3 4 5 6 7 8 9 0

First Printing February 2006

Library of Congress Cataloging-in-Publication Number: 2003116871

ISBN: 1587051915

Warning and Disclaimer

This book is designed to provide information about selecting MPLS VPN services. Every effort has been made to make this book as complete and accurate as possible, but no warranty or fitness is implied.

The information is provided on an "as is" basis. The author, Cisco Press, and Cisco Systems, Inc. shall have neither liability nor responsibility to any person or entity with respect to any loss or damages arising from the information contained in this book or from the use of the discs or programs that may accompany it.

The opinions expressed in this book belong to the author and are not necessarily those of Cisco Systems, Inc.

Trademark Acknowledgments

All terms mentioned in this book that are known to be trademarks or service marks have been appropriately capitalized. Cisco Press or Cisco Systems, Inc. cannot attest to the accuracy of this information. Use of a term in this book should not be regarded as affecting the validity of any trademark or service mark.

Corporate and Government Sales

Cisco Press offers excellent discounts on this book when ordered in quantity for bulk purchases or special sales.

For more information, please contact U.S. Corporate and Government Sales at 1-800-382-3419 or corpsales@pearsontechgroup.com.

For sales outside the U.S., please contact International Sales at international@pearsoned.com.

Feedback Information

At Cisco Press, our goal is to create in-depth technical books of the highest quality and value. Each book is crafted with care and precision, undergoing rigorous development that involves the unique expertise of members of the professional technical community.

Reader feedback is a natural continuation of this process. If you have any comments about how we could improve the quality of this book, or otherwise alter it to better suit your needs, you can contact us through e-mail at feedback@ciscopress.com. Please be sure to include the book title and ISBN in your message.

We greatly appreciate your assistance.

Publisher	John Wait
Editor-in-Chief	John Kane
Executive Editor	Brett Bartow
Acquisitions Editor	Michelle Grandin
Cisco Representative	Anthony Wolfenden
Cisco Press Program Manager	Jeff Brady
Production Manager	Patrick Kanouse
Development Editors	Dan Young, Sheri Cain
Senior Project Editor	San Dee Phillips
Copy Editor	Gayle Johnson
Technical Editor	Tim Szigeti
Editorial Assistant	Raina Han
Cover Designer	Louisa Adair
Composition	Fast Pages
Indexer	Tim Wright

CISCO SYSTEMS

Corporate Headquarters
Cisco Systems, Inc.
170 West Tasman Drive
San Jose, CA 95134-1706
USA
www.cisco.com
Tel: 408 526-4000
    800 553-NETS (6387)
Fax: 408 526-4100

European Headquarters
Cisco Systems International BV
Haarlerbergpark
Haarlerbergweg 13-19
1101 CH Amsterdam
The Netherlands
www-europe.cisco.com
Tel: 31 0 20 357 1000
Fax: 31 0 20 357 1100

Americas Headquarters
Cisco Systems, Inc.
170 West Tasman Drive
San Jose, CA 95134-1706
USA
www.cisco.com
Tel: 408 526-7660
Fax: 408 527-0883

Asia Pacific Headquarters
Cisco Systems, Inc.
Capital Tower
168 Robinson Road
#22-01 to #29-01
Singapore 068912
www.cisco.com
Tel: +65 6317 7777
Fax: +65 6317 7799

Cisco Systems has more than 200 offices in the following countries and regions. Addresses, phone numbers, and fax numbers are listed on the
Cisco.com Web site at www.cisco.com/go/offices.

Argentina • Australia • Austria • Belgium • Brazil • Bulgaria • Canada • Chile • China PRC • Colombia • Costa Rica • Croatia • Czech Republic
Denmark • Dubai, UAE • Finland • France • Germany • Greece • Hong Kong SAR • Hungary • India • Indonesia • Ireland • Israel • Italy
Japan • Korea • Luxembourg • Malaysia • Mexico • The Netherlands • New Zealand • Norway • Peru • Philippines • Poland • Portugal
Puerto Rico • Romania • Russia • Saudi Arabia • Scotland • Singapore • Slovakia • Slovenia • South Africa • Spain • Sweden
Switzerland • Taiwan • Thailand • Turkey • Ukraine • United Kingdom • United States • Venezuela • Vietnam • Zimbabwe

About the Authors

Chris Lewis has more than 18 years of experience in networking, with enterprises, a service provider, and Cisco. He is employed as a technical projects systems engineer in the Cisco Worldwide Service Provider Technical Operations group. He wrote *Cisco TCP/IP Routing* (McGraw Hill, 1997) and *Cisco Switched Internetworks* (1999). He was a contributing editor to *Network Computing* from 1994 to 1996.

Steve Pickavance has more than 14 years of experience in designing, building, and deploying systems, solutions, and IP and network services in the enterprise. Steve was the lead architect for the Cisco Systems EMEA IT Network, where he has led the Cisco adoption of IP VPNs within Cisco. He helped identify opportunities for IP VPN services, advising Cisco customers based on the experience of the Cisco IT network, in both the enterprise and service provider arenas. Today, Steve works in the Cisco Advisory Services EMEA consulting practice where he is an enterprise architect working with its largest customers on their service-oriented network architectures.

About the Contributing Authors

Monique Morrow, CCIE No. 1711, is a distinguished consulting engineer at Cisco Systems, Inc. She has more than 20 years of experience in IP internetworking, including design, implementation of complex customer projects, and service development for service providers. She cowrote *Designing IP-Based Services: Solutions for Vendors and Service Providers* (Morgan-Kaufmann, 2002) and *MPLS VPN Security* (Cisco Press, 2005). She is vice chair of the newly formed industry forum IPSphere Forum. She is active in both the IETF and ITU-T SG 13, with a focus on OAM. She has a master's degree in telecommunications management and an MBA.

John Monaghan is a technical leader in the Cisco Network Management Technology Group. He specializes in the design and specification of network management systems for MPLS networks.

Craig Huegen, CCIE No. 2100, has more than ten years of experience in designing, building, and operating IP-based communications networks for enterprises and small network service providers. For the last six years, he has served as chief network architect for the Cisco Systems global network in the Cisco Information Technology department, delivering significant employee productivity increases through the development of the Cisco global infrastructure.

About the Technical Reviewer

Tim Szigeti, CCIE No. 9794, has specialized in QoS technologies since 1998. He helps define and drive strategic QoS solutions across Cisco technology groups while working with many Fortune 500 companies, providing QoS design expertise. He recently wrote *End-to-End QoS Network Design* (Cisco Press).

Dedications

Chris Lewis: My work on this book is dedicated to the memory of my mother, Winifred Lewis.

Steve Pickavance: My work on this book is dedicated to my girls: Louise, Lucy, and Robyn.

Acknowledgments

Chris Lewis: I need to thank each of my family for their understanding of my absence from family life while completing this work. My wife Claudia, son Ben, and daughter Lian all accepted my commitment to this project without complaint, and for that I am truly thankful. I also want to thank two other people. First, Brandon Brooks, for helping me find the time on the weekends, and second, Master Paik of Paik's USA Tae Kwon Do, for providing the perfect outlet for dealing with writer's block and improving my focus. Thanks to you both.

Steve Pickavance: I want to thank my wife and my girls for their patience in putting up with my work and constant travel. I would also like to give a huge thank-you to all the folks who contributed to this work—Tim Szigeti, John Evans, Clarence Filfils, Michael Anderson, Dipesh Patel, and Harry Watson, to name but a few. I'm sure we've forgotten to mention the many others who make the network real every day and who helped by providing their input and expertise to get us here in the first place.

This Book Is Safari Enabled

The Safari® Enabled icon on the cover of your favorite technology book means the book is available through Safari Bookshelf. When you buy this book, you get free access to the online edition for 45 days.

Safari Bookshelf is an electronic reference library that lets you easily search thousands of technical books, find code samples, download chapters, and access technical information whenever and wherever you need it.

To gain 45-day Safari Enabled access to this book:

- Go to http://www.ciscopress.com/safarienabled
- Complete the brief registration form
- Enter the coupon code 44GG-26EF-CE8V-3JFS-NUTN

If you have difficulty registering on Safari Bookshelf or accessing the online edition, please e-mail customer-service@safaribooksonline.com.

Contents at a Glance

Contents

Icons Used in This Book

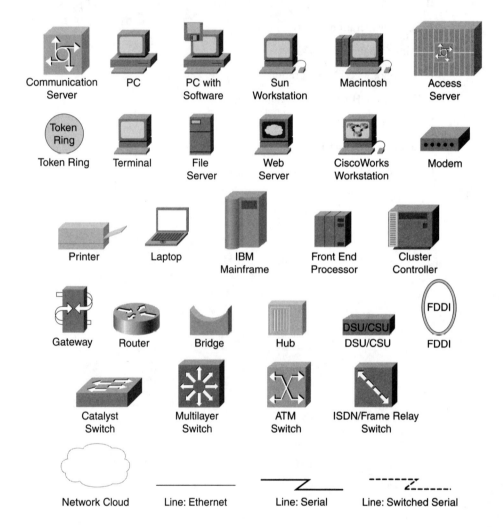

Command Syntax Conventions

The conventions used to present command syntax in this book are the same conventions used in the IOS Command Reference. The Command Reference describes these conventions as follows:

- **Bold** indicates commands and keywords that are entered literally as shown.
- *Italic* indicates arguments for which you supply actual values.
- Vertical bars (I) separate alternative, mutually exclusive elements.
- Square brackets ([ ]) indicate an optional element.
- Braces ({ }) indicate a required choice.
- Braces within brackets ([{ }]) indicate a required choice within an optional element.

Introduction

Selecting MPLS VPN Services addresses the following major objectives:

- Empowers network designers and engineers to investigate the options and benefits of IP/MPLS VPN migration.

- Provides enterprise network engineers with an objective framework for evaluating competing IP/MPLS VPN service offerings.

- Covers the business rationale for implementing IP/MPLS VPNs.

- Includes detailed configuration examples showing the steps necessary for full IP/MPLS VPN operation.

- Presents detailed case studies illustrating key migration issues.

Major service providers worldwide are ramping up VPNs over IP. Since 2002, migrating from Layer 2 connections to Layer 3 IP MPLS/VPNs is the fastest-growing service, indicating that IP MPLS/VPNs are the primary growth vehicle for service provider-to-enterprise connections. IP MPLS/VPNs are attractive to both parties. For enterprises, they enable right-sourcing of WAN services and yield generous operational cost savings. For service providers, they offer a higher level of service to customers and lower costs for service deployment. With migration come challenges, however. Enterprises must understand key migration issues, what the realistic benefits are, and how to optimize new services. Providers must know what aspects of their services give value to enterprises and how they can provide the best value to customers. This book helps enterprise network engineers analyze migration options, anticipate migration issues, and properly deploy IP/MPLS VPNs. Detailed configurations illustrate effective deployment, and case studies present migration options and walk you through selecting the best option for the sample network.

Part I addresses the business case for moving to an IP/MPLS VPN network, with a chapter devoted to the business and technical issues that you should review when evaluating IP MPLS/VPN offerings from major providers. Part II includes detailed deployment guidelines for the technologies used in the IP/MPLS VPN.

Who Should Read This Book?

The primary audience for this book includes networking professionals at service providers and enterprises, including network engineers, architects, and designers; technical managers; and technical consultants. This book assumes that you have a basic understanding of IP routing, IGP and BGP operations, and Layer 3 VPN technology, such as MPLS.

How This Book Is Organized

This book draws from the authors' direct experience with migrating the Cisco internal WAN from Frame Relay and ATM connectivity to a provider-provisioned MPLS VPN. It is organized as follows:

- **Chapter 1, "Assessing Enterprise Legacy WANs and IP/VPN Migration"**—Analyzes strengths and weaknesses of time-division multiplexing (TDM) and Layer 2 WAN services for use by enterprises and makes the business case for IP/VPNs.

- **Chapter 2, "Assessing Service Provider WAN Offerings"**—Defines the primary business and technical issues to address when evaluating IP and MPLS VPN offerings from major providers.

- **Chapter 3, "Analyzing Service Requirements"**—Clearly articulates the needs of the VPN service delivered by the provider to make the migration from Layer 2 to Layer 3 service valuable to the enterprise.

- **Chapter 4, "IP Routing with IP/MPLS VPNs"**—Describes the IP/VPN's addressing, routing, load balancing, convergence, and IP services capabilities. This chapter shows architectural needs with respect to the addressing mechanisms needed and expands this through the routing requirements.

- **Chapter 5, "Implementing Quality of Service"**—The need for quality of service (QoS) is a reality in today's real-time networks, where you seek to operate voice, video, and data. The aim is to provide a usable enterprise QoS policy and implementation guidelines when deploying this over an IP/VPN service. This chapter also tells you what to ask of the service provider.

- **Chapter 6, "Multicast in an MPLS VPN"**—IP Multicast is an essential service to deliver scalable e-learning, live executive broadcasts, media messaging, and high-quality corporate communications while using the network efficiently. With the introduction of IP/VPNs, you must consider IP Multicast needs in this environment. Ensuring transparency is key to the enterprise's achieving scalable support for multicast services.

- **Chapter 7, "Enterprise Security in an MPLS VPN Environment"**—Describes the benefits and drawbacks of implementing various security mechanisms at different locations within the network from the perspective of the enterprise and service provider.

- **Chapter 8, "MPLS VPN Network Management"**—Service provider monitoring and reporting are key to ensuring that the services employed by the enterprise are used properly. You also must plan for the future, resolve service issues, and receive timely support for the enterprise infrastructure.

- **Chapter 9, "Off-Net Access to the VPN"**—Defines the options and technical implementation for the various means to provide remote access, Internet access, and extranet connectivity to the VPN-supported intranet.

- **Chapter 10, "Migration Strategies"**—Provides a clear and concise set of steps to undertake the correct planning and execution of a network migration from the existing ATM/Frame Relay/leased-line network to an IP/VPN.

- **Appendix A, "Questions to Ask Your Provider Regarding Layer 3 IP/MPLS VPN Capability"**—Provides a checklist and Request for Proposal (RFP) template for enterprises to use with providers.

Business Analysis and Requirements of IP/MPLS VPN

This chapter covers the following topics:

- Reviewing the current state of enterprise networks
- Reviewing the evolutionary change of enterprise networks
- Exploring the Acme scenario: a global manufacturing example
- Evaluating and comparing new WAN technologies
- Evaluating and comparing convergence services

CHAPTER 1

Assessing Enterprise Legacy WANs and IP/VPN Migration

This chapter frames the current state of enterprise networks, identifies shifting business and application requirements, and describes options that the enterprise network architect can use to optimize the network for business requirements.

Current State of Enterprise Networks

Enterprise networks as implemented today are largely unchanged from the mid-1990s. The IT application requirements of a typical enterprise have been based largely on client/server data applications from a small set of primary data centers, centered on access to data used in business processes. For example, a typical data access pattern for a manufacturing enterprise includes components such as sales order entry, order status, accounts receivable, service history, and manufacturing and shipping information.

Using Frame Relay or Asynchronous Transfer Mode (ATM), these enterprise networks are based largely on a traditional hub-and-spoke model. Network architects establish a very limited number of hub location(s) at the corporate headquarters (HQ), regional HQ, or major data center, and they connect branch offices to these hubs using point-to-point connections. This type of network is very easy to design and implement, is relatively cost-efficient, and does not present any significant infrastructure management concerns.

Figure 1-1 shows a map of a typical U.S.-based enterprise network, based around its corporate HQ location in San Francisco. Note that almost every connection from a field office connects to the corporate HQ location, even when another backbone site is nearer.

Figure 1-1   *Typical Hub-and-Spoke Enterprise Network*

A drawback of the hub-and-spoke model is its inability to adapt to changing application requirements. As business trends shift, global enterprises are looking to increase their productivity, hoping to drive revenues up while keeping operational expenses down. Enterprise IT departments are expected to deliver many of the enhancements needed to drive productivity growth. For the network architect, this shift drives many changes to the enterprise network.

The typical enterprise IT department once approached different voice, video, and data delivery from separate angles. Voice networks were typically built using private branch exchange (PBX) nodes connected to the public switched telephone network (PSTN). Videoconferencing networks were also built on PSTN technology, using Integrated Services Digital Network (ISDN) BRI. Video delivery networks, where used, were built with satellite delivery mechanisms. Typically, each of these had separate IT organizations engineering and maintaining these services.

In an effort to drive down costs, enterprises have been calling for convergence of these technologies, asking for a single communications network that can carry all application types, whether voice, video, or data. Although this can be accomplished in a traditional hub-and-spoke network, other factors are driving a shift in network architecture.

The desire for increased productivity is changing how the typical employee performs his or her job. The use of collaboration technologies to bring together a diverse and dispersed global organization is strongly influencing the development of the enterprise communications network.

For example, a typical enterprise sales force may have once relied only on a top-down sales strategy and local expertise and knowledge to address customers' requirements. This approach is inherently inefficient, because global teams may not be able to collaborate on a unified global strategy. Also, employees with expertise in each region may not be able to regularly share their experiences and knowledge with each other. These increased requirements for collaboration and knowledge sharing have driven a significant number of applications, both asynchronous and real-time, to integrate these groups more tightly as a global pool of resources. This places "real-time" importance on the network: The enterprise network architect must ensure that the network latency between two locations is optimized for this new suite of applications.

Finally, enterprises are recognizing a change in application distribution between data centers. The resiliency in today's enterprise network is an absolute requirement to guarantee the productivity levels in case of a major (or even minor) failure of any component in the network. In the traditional hub-and-spoke network, this typically means that the addition of another data center requires that the number of permanent virtual circuits (PVCs) in the network be doubled.

Evolutionary Change of Enterprise Networks

These shifting business climates have forced the enterprise network architect to look at new architectures for the network. What was once a simple star architecture based from the corporate HQ location now needs to address peer-to-peer applications. Instead of almost every user endpoint in the network communicating with a central resource, user endpoints are now talking to each other in the form of voice over IP (VoIP), videoconferencing, instant messaging (IM), and document sharing.

To address these demands, the architect must look at alternative network designs that optimize the network. Imagine a scenario in which an enterprise is based in Washington, D.C., and has branch offices in San Francisco and Los Angeles. With a traditional network, the enterprise would likely have a Frame Relay PVC between Washington, D.C. and Los Angeles and between Washington, D.C. and San Francisco. A user in Los Angeles communicating with a user in San Francisco would result in a communications path from Los Angeles, across the U.S. to Washington, D.C., and back across the U.S. to San Francisco, which may result in lower-quality communications. To address this, the enterprise network architect must look at how to optimize latency such that the communications traffic from the Los Angeles office to the San Francisco office can take a much shorter path.

Typical enterprise networks have been built without the quality of service (QoS) capabilities necessary to support delay-sensitive and drop-sensitive traffic, such as VoIP and videoconferencing. The architect must ensure that his or her network can provide support for these real-time applications. This requires increased focus on the part of the enterprise network architect, ensuring that the network has not only optimal latency, but also the proper QoS guarantees.

The typical enterprise would like to be able to reduce the amount of effort and time it takes to build an optimized network. To reduce and optimize latencies, as previously mentioned, the enterprise architect must work with the service provider to understand the basic backbone network, or fiber paths, that the service provider uses. With a map in hand, the enterprise architect can lay out a series of small hubs located where fiber maps meet, form a backbone between the hubs, and then connect each branch office into one of these hubs based on the service provider's access.

For example, the map shown in Figure 1-2 shows how the enterprise architect for the network shown in Figure 1-1 may reorganize his or her network to optimize latency. Note that in contrast with Figure 1-1, in which each site connects all the way back to corporate HQ in San Francisco, each satellite office is now connected to its nearest hub location.

Figure 1-2 *Latency-Optimized Network Architecture*
In this case, the enterprise IT department may find that there is considerable bandwidth

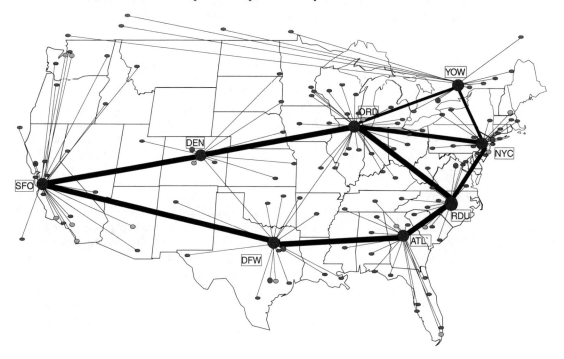

savings or very little additional bandwidth cost in optimizing the network in this way. In this specific example, the average length of a circuit was reduced to 15 percent of its original value, and the bandwidth was increased by 500 percent. In a real-world pricing scenario, this was all accomplished with a very minimal (less than 5 percent) price increase.

The number of hubs, their locations, and their interconnection points depend on the service provider capabilities, the number of enterprise branch offices that may be connected to a hub, and the equipment and circuit costs to establish a hub location. Facilities for hub locations must be considered, whether the hub is established in local branch offices or the enterprise leases space in service provider facilities.

The process of studying fiber maps, establishing hub locations, determining hub facilities, mapping branch offices, and identifying bandwidths can be overwhelming and time-consuming.

One option the architect has is to look at outsourcing the network design to a systems integrator or the professional services organization within his or her chosen service provider. Although this addresses any potential lack of technical skills in the enterprise's IT department, it requires the outsourcer to spend some time understanding the enterprise's business objectives and requirements. The outsourcers may not be able to fully understand the enterprise's business goals and therefore may not be able to play a strategic part in advancing the enterprise's business. Once the learning process is complete, the outsourcer can build a custom, optimized network for the enterprise based on the enterprise's locations and service provider's fiber paths.

Another alternative is the use of IP/MPLS virtual private network (VPN) technology. IP/MPLS VPNs allow enterprises to outsource, effectively, the network's core. Instead of requiring you to spend significant time building a plan for hubs and branches, the technology allows the enterprise to leverage a network with built-in latency optimization. As service providers build out their IP/MPLS network, all enterprise customers using the IP/MPLS VPN service take advantage of the build-out. It also fully meshes the sites on the network, which optimizes for latency beyond a regionally distributed hub-and-spoke network.

The net result is a significant economy of scale, from network engineering to core network capacity planning to managing and monitoring customer networks.

This book describes key enterprise aspects of IP/MPLS VPN technology and how Acme, Inc., a sample global manufacturing enterprise, can leverage IP/MPLS VPNs to reduce its operational expense and increase capabilities for its applications on the enterprise network. This and subsequent chapters discuss the general issues that an enterprise network manager needs to consider. Recommendations specific to Acme are identified and justified in the Summary section at the end of each chapter.

Acme, a Global Manufacturer

Acme is the sample enterprise. Acme makes machine tools for the global manufacturing industry.

Acme's Global Span

Acme's corporate HQ is located in Chicago. It has regional HQ locations in London, Tokyo, Hong Kong, and Melbourne for the regions of EMEA (Europe, Middle East, and Africa), Japan and Northern Asia, Southeast Asia, and Australia, respectively. Acme has approximately 300 branch offices located around the globe.

Business Desires of Acme's Management

From a business perspective, Acme is looking to improve its business by increasing productivity and raising customer satisfaction. Acme executives hope to achieve this through global standardization of business processes. This will allow Acme to pool global resources and offer greater knowledge transfer between regions of the globe, ultimately reducing operational expenses. Common processes and enhanced knowledge share will also increase customer satisfaction by ensuring that customers have access to all of Acme's resources, not a limited subset.

In addition, Acme is focusing on cost-reduction efforts by challenging managers and contributors alike to focus on *core* efforts—items that deliver direct value to Acme. To do this, Acme is actively identifying areas of its operations that can easily be standardized and outsourced to other organizations that can perform the tasks with the same or better quality at a lower cost to Acme. These areas are called *context* efforts.

Acme's IT Applications Base

Acme has a well-established base of applications it uses to manage most existing business processes. It has a few regional implementations of SAP business process software to manage business administration, sales, and service. Acme IT is looking to consolidate these regional implementations as business processes are unified globally.

Acme Engineering has a fairly extensive CAD/CAM implementation for its engineers who design the machines and tools for its manufacturing customers. This CAD/CAM system is heavily integrated with the manufacturing process carried out by its partner manufacturers, which make the physical goods that Acme produces.

Acme IT is preparing to support a handful of new collaboration tools to address Acme's business goals:

- Acme is actively searching for an e-learning application suite to manage training and employee development for its global workforce.

- Videoconferencing is an important part of Acme's strategy to bring global groups together. Acme wants to upgrade its existing room-based system to leverage its IP network and is investigating desktop videoconferencing. Acme also wants to leverage videoconferencing technology to collaborate with its extranet partners and external customers where appropriate.

- Document sharing and IM are also key parts of enabling the type of global collaboration that Acme executives are looking to achieve. Acme is investigating a number of solutions to assist global groups in collaborating on solutions for customers.

- Acme also wants to enable a higher level of resiliency through distributed data centers that lower latency time to critical applications. It also wants to provide a failover location in case of a major disaster at their primary facility.

Acme's IT Communications Infrastructure

Acme's communications infrastructure consists of five major components:

- An intranet data network consisting of private line links between regional HQ locations and ATM and Frame Relay from regional HQ locations to branch offices.

- A voice network of PBXs. In regional HQ locations, these PBXs are interconnected through VoIP trunks provisioned over the data network. Branch offices have voice connectivity to the PSTN only.

- Videoconferencing based on H.320 ISDN technology. All regional HQ offices and key branch sites have room-based videoconferencing equipment, connected via ISDN BRI lines to the PSTN.

- An extranet data network consisting of private-line, Frame Relay, and VPN links to approximately 100 partner businesses. These 100 businesses represent a very wide range of outsourced tasks for Acme, from corporate administration tasks such as payroll and benefits administration to core business functions such as component suppliers and contract manufacturers.

- An Internet-facing demilitarized zone (DMZ) network built to offer its customers online access to sales and service with Acme in a secure fashion.

Acme IT is studying how it can converge these applications to reduce cost. It wants to make this a key point in its investigation into a new WAN. Acme's IT management team also wants to identify the context areas of operation and search out partners or service providers that can offer those context services at a better value to Acme.

Because employees in any office in Acme or its partners will use many of these applications, it is important that latency be optimized in Acme's network.

Acme's Intranet: Backbone WAN

Acme's global backbone WAN, as mentioned previously, is made up of private-line links between regional HQ locations. Acme has purchased DS-3 (45-Mbps) private lines from a global service provider to interconnect the regional HQ locations and the corporate HQ.

Figure 1-3 shows Acme's global backbone WAN.

Figure 1-3 *Acme's Global Backbone WAN*

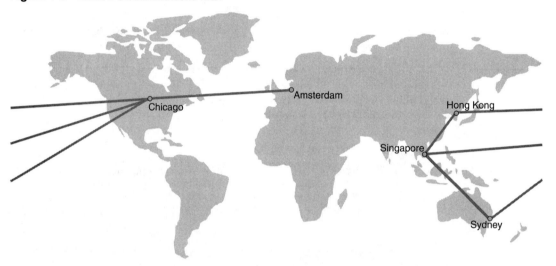

Acme has provisioned backup connectivity between these sites by purchasing redundant private lines from a second global carrier.

One of the challenges that Acme IT is concerned about is the granularity of these leased lines. In several locations, Acme is beginning to see high bandwidth utilization. However, to upgrade, Acme must justify a cost increase for three times the bandwidth, jumping from T3/E3 to OC-3/STM-1 speeds and installing new circuits. This represents a significant cost increase in Acme's budget for bandwidth. Acme would like the opportunity to scale bandwidth more easily. While ATM could provide the granularity of bandwidth that Acme is looking for, Acme IT has found that ATM pricing above approximately 20 to 30 Mbps was not competitive with leased-line pricing. In addition, Acme was concerned about the overhead of IP over ATM, also known as the *cell tax*, which can range from 25 percent to 35 percent of the total link bandwidth.

Acme's Intranet: Regional WANs

To connect branch offices with the regional HQ locations, Acme purchases Frame Relay or ATM connectivity from regional service providers. At the region's HQ location, Acme purchases ATM service on a DS-3 port and an individual PVC to each branch site, which receives T1, E1, or *n*xT1/E1 access ports.

Branch sites receive between 256 Kbps and 8 Mbps of bandwidth, depending on the business function the branch office serves. Engineering sites receive 6 to 8 Mbps of bandwidth to support CAD/CAM functionality, while sales sites typically receive between 256 Kbps and 4 Mbps of bandwidth, depending on size and bandwidth cost. When bandwidth to a branch office is between 256 Kbps and T1/E1 (1.5 to 2 Mbps), Frame Relay is used; when speeds greater than 1.5 to 2 Mbps are needed, Inverse Multiplexing for ATM (IMA) is used.

New WAN Technologies for Consideration by Acme

Acme's current business priorities are certainly not uncommon. As Acme becomes more close-knit as a global enterprise, its IT department must be prepared to handle a dramatic shift in its application load. The network architect at Acme should consider several technologies to achieve the business goals that Acme has set out.

Acme should start by considering Layer 3 (L3) IP/MPLS VPNs. This technology allows Acme to effectively outsource the core of its WAN; eliminate the effort necessary to plan and build a complex, distributed-hub architecture; and take advantage of a service provider's network scale. This type of service typically brings significant cost savings for a full-mesh network, the cornerstone of large-scale enterprise collaboration. Without L3 IP/MPLS VPNs, Acme may find itself working very hard to manage an optimum-latency network.

L3 IP/MPLS VPNs permit the SP core to perform traffic routing based on the customer's IP routing information.

Another technology that Acme could consider is the use of Layer 2 (L2) VPN services. These services, when built on an IP/MPLS network, let Acme retain complete control over the L3 routing within its network, because the service provider does not exchange IP routing information. Acme has its choice between a couple of L2 VPN services, a point-to-point service based on Virtual Private Wire Service (VPWS), and a multipoint emulated LAN based on Virtual Private LAN Service (VPLS). Acme may look to consolidate some metropolitan-area sites into a VPLS-based metropolitan-area network (MAN) and then uplink the MAN into the L3 IP/MPLS VPN WAN.

The following sections contain more-detailed descriptions of these services.

Layer 3 IP/MPLS VPN Services

Acme's network architect believes that L3 IP/MPLS VPN services are precisely what it wants to provide a foundation for its enterprise WAN and to support its business initiatives.

The IP/MPLS VPN solution is based on IETF RFC 2547. This mechanism has wide industry support for network-based VPNs and is quickly becoming a common standard across the globe for IP connectivity.

IP/MPLS VPN Service Topologies and Provisioning

L3 IP/MPLS VPN virtualizes the core of the service provider network, allowing the network cloud to route traffic to its destination based on the enterprise's IP routing table, shared with the SP network. This means that the enterprise is no longer required to design and maintain a mesh of hub locations and interconnecting links. Instead, every site is an end site on the cloud, and the enterprise needs to manage only a single port to the cloud. L3 IP/MPLS VPN also simplifies the capacity planning that an enterprise must perform on its network.

Figure 1-4 shows the enterprise's role in engineering networks based on existing time-division multiplexing (TDM), ATM, or Frame Relay technology. Figure 1-5 shows the role in L3 IP/MPLS VPN-based networks. The dashed, curved portions of the network detailed in Figure 1-4 represent PVCs that the enterprise must engineer, provision, and manage for capacity. In contrast, this requirement of the enterprise is eliminated in the L3 IP/MPLS VPN, where intelligent routing takes the place of the PVC provisioning. Also note the bandwidth provisioning; instead of determining point-to-point capacities, the enterprise network staff needs to maintain only capacity planning on a site-by-site basis.

Figure 1-4   *Layer 2 Network Provisioning*

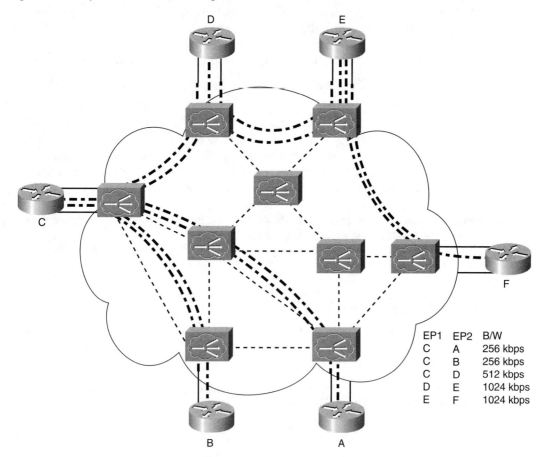

EP1	EP2	B/W
C	A	256 kbps
C	B	256 kbps
C	D	512 kbps
D	E	1024 kbps
E	F	1024 kbps

Figure 1-5 *Layer 3 IP/MPLS VPN Network Provisioning*

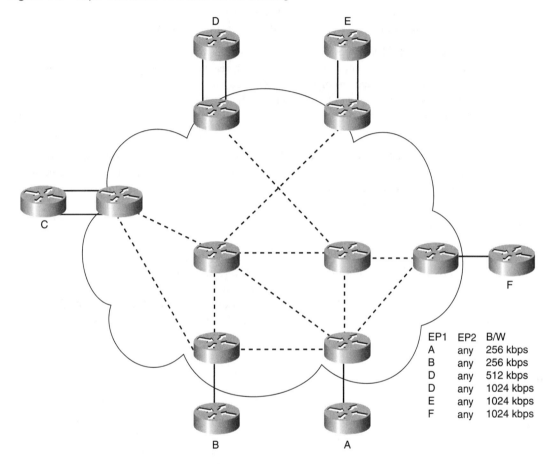

EP1	EP2	B/W
A	any	256 kbps
B	any	256 kbps
D	any	512 kbps
D	any	1024 kbps
E	any	1024 kbps
F	any	1024 kbps

To the enterprise network engineer, the connection from a site to the L3 IP/MPLS VPN cloud looks like a connection to another router in the enterprise's network. External routing protocols such as BGP, or internal routing protocols such as OSPF, RIP, or EIGRP, exchange routing information with the service provider's provider edge (PE) router. The routes are then carried across the service provider's IP/MPLS network in multiprotocol BGP.

In addition, many of the required enterprise network capabilities, such as QoS and IP multicast, can be supported by the IP/MPLS VPN service. These services are provisioned natively, like routing protocols, and appear as if another enterprise router were on the other side of the link.

The key difference between this technology and a typical outsourced WAN is that a single service provider network built once with L3 IP/VPN technologies can be sold many times to many customers, as opposed to a service provider or outsourcer designing an individual WAN for each customer. This results in an economy of scale, which translates into higher value and overall lower WAN costs to the enterprise customer.

Access to the L3 IP/MPLS VPN service can be via any Layer 2 technology. Between the customer edge (CE) router located at the enterprise site and the PE router at the service provider, traditional technologies such as leased line, ATM, and Frame Relay may be used. Alternatively, newer access technologies such as metro Ethernet may be used. The availability of Frame Relay or ATM access to an L3 IP/MPLS VPN service provides a very smooth migration path from an existing network to L3 IP/MPLS VPNs.

The L3 IP/MPLS VPN service also eliminates the enterprise's need to lease facilities and rack space for network equipment in hub locations. Because the intelligence is built in to the service provider network, the enterprise need not interconnect point-to-point PVCs or circuits on its own network equipment and key routing points in the network.

IP/MPLS VPN: A Foundation for Network Services

L3 IP/MPLS VPN technologies offer a better integration capability for advanced network services. Instead of designing special connectivity for a service provider-offered service, such as VoIP gateways to the PSTN, a service provider may be able to integrate the service simply by importing the enterprise routes to and from the customer's VPN into the service VPNs.

IP/MPLS VPN Transparency

One of the most important aspects that must be considered in an L3 IP/MPLS VPN service is its transparency. Enterprises such as Acme that have operated a network for some time have established key parameters for the operation of their networks. Items such as classes of service and their associated Differentiated Services Code Point (DSCP) values, the routing protocol used across the network, and IP multicast capability are required in Acme's network, and the introduction of L3 IP/MPLS VPN service should not force Acme to reengineer its network to make the service fit. One could say that there is a good reason to call it a virtual *private* network—the idea that it needs to look very much like Acme's own private network.

IP/MPLS VPN Network Management and SLAs

In Layer 2-based networks, enterprises have control over the entire L3 network, allowing unrestricted troubleshooting capability across the network. In L3 IP/MPLS VPN services, there is now a shared responsibility for the L3 aspects of the network between the enterprise and service provider, which can make management and monitoring more complex.

One of the hottest topics between enterprises and their service providers today is the service-level agreement (SLA). As enterprises grow increasingly dependent on a converged communications infrastructure, the enterprise network manager expects more from his service providers. Technologies such as voice, video, and storage networking place strict demands on certain characteristics of a data network, such as delay and jitter. Before the IP network adopted these traffic types, delay and jitter requirements were fairly loose. Because L3 IP/MPLS VPN focuses on delivering QoS, the proper capabilities and toolsets for managing SLAs with these characteristics are available and are a key part of the network service.

Finally, enterprises must consider the management of the service. In most cases, the service provider offers a *fully managed* service or an *unmanaged* service or both. In the case of the fully managed service, the service provider supplies and fully manages the configuration, monitoring, and troubleshooting of the CE router and attached WAN connectivity using its tools and procedures. An unmanaged service allows the enterprise to maintain the configuration and management of the CE routers, leaving the service provider to manage only the PE routers. The former (fully managed service) is slightly less flexible to the enterprise but allows the service provider to offer a more complete SLA, having control over the entire wide-area portion of the network. The latter allows the enterprise more control to use its measurement and monitoring tools. Later chapters discuss the differences between the models and introduce some hybrids between the two, depending on enterprise and service provider requirements.

Enterprise Vendor Management Approach

The selection of L3 IP/MPLS VPN will most likely change an enterprise's approach to vendor selection, or the choice of multiple vendors versus a single vendor. An enterprise leveraging L3 IP/MPLS VPNs essentially pushes some of the tasks formerly performed by the enterprise into the service provider cloud. Working with a single service provider within an L3 IP/MPLS VPN environment is more advantageous than working with multiple service providers.

L3 IP/MPLS VPN technologies are designed to allow for some interprovider communication for VPNs; however, service providers must address the major impacts associated with sharing customers in a multiprovider mesh:

- Who is responsible for being the customer's primary contact?
- How can the service providers partner without risking future business?
- How will multiple providers agree on common handling of specific QoS types across the multiprovider mesh?
- How many provider interconnects are necessary to maintain an optimal network mesh?

The challenges of engineering the number and location of physical meet points, as well as the QoS and other handoff parameters, make it difficult for service providers to offer provider interconnection points as a general-purpose service. In most cases, these interconnection points require the same, or even additional, overhead when compared to an enterprise site performing the handoff between networks. As service providers begin to conquer some of the business challenges facing them with regard to interprovider IP/MPLS VPNs, a solution for a global, multiprovider IP/MPLS VPN mesh may be viable and may be the best choice for the enterprise.

Extranet Integration in IP/MPLS VPN Networks

IP/MPLS VPN services also let a service provider offer an extranet service for enterprise networks. This service can be extremely valuable in the integration of enterprises participating in communities of interest. For example, Acme is one of many machine and tool manufacturers participating in a parts supply exchange operated by key manufacturing customers. The L3 IP/MPLS VPN allows Acme's network to interconnect with others in the community of interest and exchange data securely. The security of this arrangement must be carefully engineered, however, so that partners (who may be competitors) on the same network cannot access each other's networks through the VPN service.

Layer 2 IP/MPLS VPN Services

In addition to the L3 IP/MPLS VPN service targeted for large-scale WAN deployments, IP/MPLS networks also enable two Layer 2 VPN services: VPWS and VPLS. Depending on enterprise requirements, these services can be used for point-to-point requirements or metropolitan-area aggregation.

The technology used by the service provider that offers VPWS- and VPLS-based services is usually hidden from the enterprise customer. To the enterprise, these services look like other standard interconnection technologies: private-line, ATM, Frame Relay, or Ethernet.

One of the primary benefits of VPWS- and VPLS-based services is that they allow the service provider to converge its independent networks. Instead of maintaining separate ATM, Frame Relay, Synchronous Optical Network (SONET), and IP networks and maintaining customer interfaces to each network, service providers can now focus on a single IP/MPLS network as a base infrastructure and offer many different customer services from that network. This results in a lower cost for the service provider infrastructure and ultimately is reflected in the service price to the customer.

VPWS

A service based on VPWS technology offers point-to-point connectivity, much like leased line, ATM, and Frame Relay. VPWS-based services can be delivered in any number of common Layer 2 methods: direct high-level data link control (HDLC) or PPP (emulated private line), ATM or Frame Relay, or Ethernet VLANs.

An additional advantage of the flexibility of VPWS-based services is that the access method used on one side of the service does not have to be the same as the other. For example, an enterprise's HQ location may utilize metro Ethernet as an aggregation technology to connect many branch sites that use HDLC or PPP encapsulation on T1s.

An enterprise typically uses VPWS-based services in the same fashion it would use other WAN technologies. After all, to the enterprise network administrator, the service is transparent and actually looks like a leased line, ATM, Frame Relay, or Ethernet trunk.

The enterprise's primary benefit (cost) is indirectly realized through an economy of scale offered to the service provider. Service providers now can build a single IP/MPLS network to offer these services that formerly required independent dedicated networks. However, this technology does not offer any reductions in the effort required to manage and operate the enterprise network. Because these services are presented to the enterprise like any other WAN technology, the enterprise must still focus on laying out a WAN topology design and perform capacity planning with point-to-point circuits or virtual circuits.

Figure 1-6 shows possible uses of VPWS-based services by an enterprise.

Figure 1-6 *Sample Enterprise Use of VPWS-Based Services*

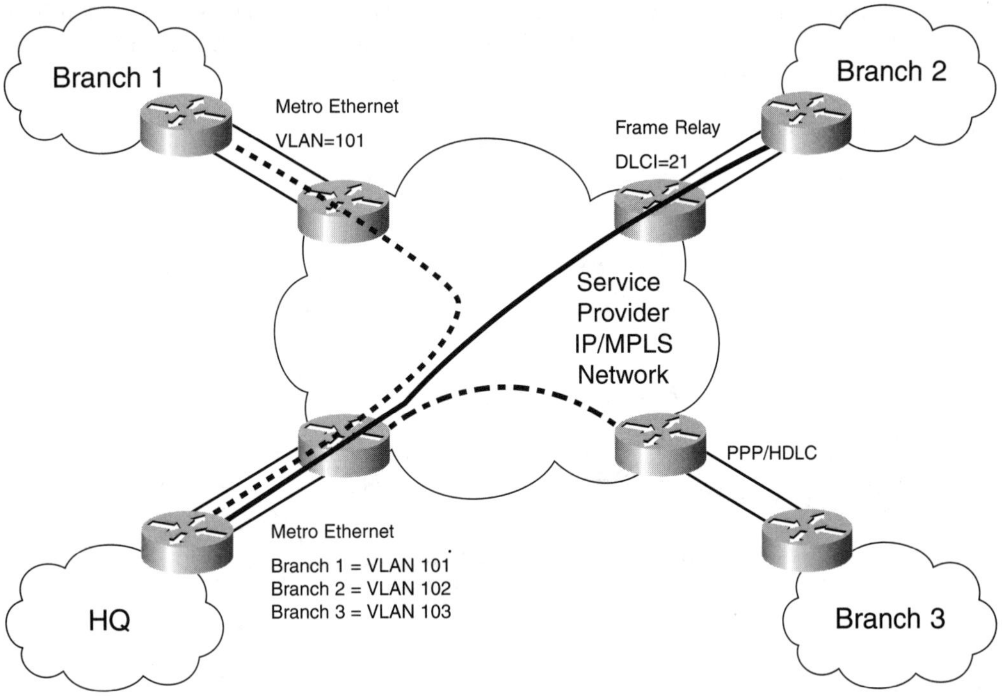

Some service providers are looking at offering *provisionless* VPWS-based services, where the network automatically generates a full mesh of VCs between endpoints in a service. This removes the need for the service provider to implement a specific enterprise's VC layouts. Instead, the service provider offers all remote locations in individual VLANs, DLCIs, or ATM VCIs, and the enterprise is responsible for building and configuring a hub-and-spoke, partial-mesh, or full-mesh topology. It offers unlimited flexibility in network layout for an enterprise; however, this can lead to suboptimal networks.

One immediate concern is the number of routing protocol adjacencies created on individual subinterfaces for a full-mesh VPWS network. Most IGP routing protocols face scalability problems as the number of locations grows in such a network. One local route update may quickly multiply into tens or even hundreds of route updates into the VPWS cloud as each remote CE neighbor is notified, affecting router CPU and QoS queues and possibly even dropping route update packets.

Additionally, if an enterprise does not understand its service provider's fiber paths and topology, it may choose to establish backbone links between two locations that are not well connected in the service-provider topology. Consider Figure 1-7. In this topology, you can see that the enterprise has built a backbone link for its network from San Francisco to Boston. The path for this VPWS service across the service provider network, however, is from San Francisco to Los Angeles to Atlanta to Boston. When the enterprise connects its branch office in San Diego to the San Francisco backbone site, and its branch office in Miami to the Boston backbone site, the traffic experiences significant backhaul latency. Traffic between San Diego and Miami must flow over the service provider network from San Diego to San Francisco via Los Angeles, from San Francisco to Boston via Los Angeles and Atlanta, and from Boston to Miami via Atlanta. Much of the traffic takes the same route twice.

Figure 1-7 *Enterprise Provisioning Paths*

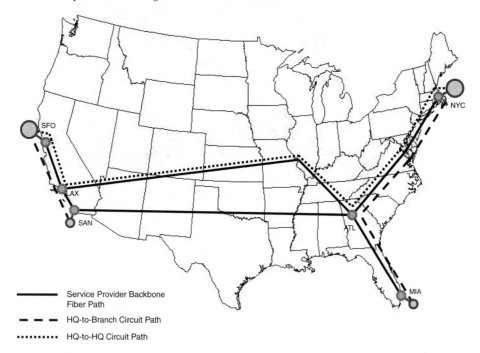

——————	Service Provider Backbone Fiber Path
— — —	HQ-to-Branch Circuit Path
··········	HQ-to-HQ Circuit Path

VPLS

VPLS-based services extend the functionality of VPWS to create a multipoint network, emulating LAN functionality to the enterprise. VPLS-based services are used to create a virtual LAN among the sites attached to the service. The service provider network PE routers make forwarding decisions based on Layer 2 addresses (for example, MAC addresses on Ethernet).

VPLS services offer the enterprise some of the same benefits as L3 IP/MPLS VPNs. Because it is a multipoint architecture, the enterprise need not be concerned with the capacity management or provisioning of individual point-to-point links. Adding a site to a network is as simple as turning a new site's port into the VPLS-based service.

However, the scalability of VPLS-based services is fairly limited, for a few reasons:

- Because VPLS-based services emulate a Layer 2 segment between sites, routing protocols such as RIP and EIGRP require all enterprise routers attached to the service to form routing protocol adjacencies with each other. As the number of routers grows, some routing protocols can experience higher route convergence times. This can have a noticeable impact on real-time applications.

- Because VPLS-based services are a full-mesh emulation of a Layer 2 multiaccess network, a failure of an individual pseudo-wire can result in a split topology or a loss of connectivity to a site on the network.

- IP multicast across the emulated Layer 2 mesh is broadcast to all sites on the service, not just those that want the traffic. Because VPLS services rely on an automatically generated full mesh of VPWS connections as transport for the traffic, each service provider PE router must send multicast and broadcast packets n times for n sites, resulting in wasted bandwidth.

- The service provider network uses Layer 2 (MAC) addresses to decide where traffic should be forwarded. In some designs, the number of MAC addresses used by an enterprise may overwhelm the service's capabilities (such as when a VPLS-based service is used to bridge remote LANs containing workstations and servers). If the service provider limits MAC addresses to a maximum number, the enterprise might experience intermittent connectivity or have difficulty troubleshooting the problem. In addition, the enterprise may find it has to pay surcharges for the service provider to accept a larger number of MAC addresses. In addition, there is no way to indicate MAC addresses that may be of a higher priority, and the network drops traffic indiscriminately.

For these reasons, it is anticipated that VPLS-based services will be used on a limited basis. Enterprises will likely use these services primarily in MANs where a smaller number of enterprise sites are connected and bandwidth is plentiful and inexpensive. L3 IP/MPLS VPNs will be used for larger networks because of their scalability.

Convergence Services

The business case for L3 IP/MPLS VPNs is not limited to IP connectivity. Rather, the VPN service is a solid foundation on which service providers can offer many other services. Because the enterprise network's IP routing table is shared with the service provider network, adding a service can be as simple as injecting additional routes into the enterprise's VPN.

Internet Access

One of the simplest services to deploy in an L3 IP/VPN is Internet access. A service provider can deploy this service fairly easily, especially if it already hosts its Internet connectivity across its IP/MPLS backbone. A default route to the Internet can be injected into the VPN, drawing traffic that does not go to a specific location on the enterprise's network. A managed firewall then screens traffic and may provide Network Address Translation (NAT) if required. By using this service, the enterprise can eliminate the need to carry Internet-bound traffic back to its regional HQ sites and send that traffic on its external Internet connectivity.

Security is a very common concern with Internet access service. Chapter 9, "Off-Net Access to the VPN," discusses Internet access services on L3 IP/MPLS VPN services, common enterprise requirements, and security concerns.

Mobile Access and Teleworker Access

Another service that most service providers are considering for deployment in conjunction with their VPN services is remote access for teleworkers. By coupling the L3 IP/MPLS VPN service with an IPSec VPN service, service providers can offer direct access to the enterprise network for travelers or telecommuters, eliminating the need for the enterprise to operate its own remote access infrastructure. To implement this service, service provider VPN concentrators terminate the IPSec VPN tunnels, and traffic for authenticated users from a particular enterprise customer is directed into the enterprise's L3 IP/MPLS VPN. We will look at this service in more depth in Chapter 9.

Voice Services: Service Provider Hosted PSTN Gateway

Beyond basic connectivity services, the first area that service providers are focusing on for expansion of IP/VPN capabilities is integrating their voice networks with the PSTN. Today, IP telephony installations in enterprise networks consist of an IP call agent server, such as Cisco CallManager, IP telephony endpoints (typically telephone handsets and a PC-based software phone application), and IP telephony gateways that connect to the PSTN through plain old telephone service (POTS) or ISDN PRI. Outsourcing the IP/PSTN gateway functionality to the VPN service provider removes the need for the enterprise to connect multiple PRIs or POTS lines at the branch office and allows the traffic to be hosted in the IP/MPLS VPN service instead.

Voice Services: Service Provider Hosted IP Telephony

Expanding on PSTN gateway service, hosted IP telephony takes the outsourcing of IP telephony one step further by outsourcing the call agent server and its operations to the service provider, leaving only IP-based telephones and a basic POTS gateway functionality for emergency calling. This removes the need for enterprises to manage call agent servers in branch offices. Instead, it only requires users to plug in an IP telephone to the IP network they are already accustomed to for their data connectivity.

Summary

This chapter explored changing business climates and their impacts on network architecture, noting that more than ever there is a need and desire for higher productivity from business. IT departments are looking to outsource capabilities that are not core to the company's business.

This chapter also discussed how the trend of convergence is driving new applications onto the IP network and how the requirements and characteristics of the IP network are changing in response. Optimizing the network latency between sites is now very important for collaboration applications including VoIP, videoconferencing, and data collaboration. These applications are also critical in the pursuit of productivity as companies look to create global processes.

Technologies such as Layer 2 and L3 IP/MPLS VPNs allow service providers to develop and scale a single IP network for all services they want to offer (including some legacy services, such as ATM and Frame Relay). Enterprises using these technologies take advantage of the service provider's economy of scale. In addition, choosing L3 IP/MPLS VPN service lets the enterprise effectively outsource the effort required to engineer, operate, and manage capacity in its network core.

Finally, these IP/MPLS VPN services provide a foundation for the convergence of voice, video, and data services. Service providers can now offer services such as remote access, Internet access, hosted IP telephony, IP-based PSTN gateway, content distribution, and storage in a relatively scalable fashion without having to build a custom infrastructure for each customer.

Acme is actively pursuing L3 IP/MPLS VPNs for the following reasons:

- It will not have to invest in a very large engineering effort to redesign its global backbone and regional WAN networks.

- L3 IP/MPLS VPNs will reduce or remove the overhead in managing an interconnecting mesh of circuits in the middle of the network.

- L3 IP/MPLS VPNs will provide a QoS-enabled, latency-optimized foundation for new collaboration applications used on Acme's network.

- Convergence of Acme's Internet connectivity, some extranet connectivity, PSTN voice access, and IP videoconferencing will likely reduce the network access costs associated with individual circuits into each branch office.

Chapters 2 and 3 discuss Acme's key requirements as it evaluates service providers and their services.

This chapter covers the following topics:

- Evaluating service provider VPN solutions to make them fit enterprise needs
- What to watch out for when reviewing service-level agreements
- Nontechnical issues to consider when comparing different service providers
- Services to consider for future use that may not be part of the initial deployment

CHAPTER 2

Assessing Service Provider WAN Offerings

This chapter advises and assists the enterprise network administrator in assessing and selecting service providers while matching their offerings to the enterprise's requirements. Appendix A, "Questions to Ask Your Provider Regarding Layer 3 IP/MPLS VPN Capability," lists a set of specific questions that you should ask providers competing for your WAN business. These broad concepts are the topic of this chapter.

Enterprise/Service Provider Relationship and Interface

In today's typical private-line, ATM, and Frame Relay networks, the responsibility for specific portions of the network is very clear-cut. The enterprise is responsible for the end-to-end network at Layer 3 and above of the OSI reference model, controlling all aspects of the IP network. In an unmanaged service (meaning the customer premises equipment [CPE]), IT staff generally owns and operates IP routers connected to the WAN service. The IT staff determines the endpoints of private-line circuits, or ATM and Frame Relay virtual circuits (VCs), through its orders placed with the service provider. The service provider is then responsible for setting up the VCs and delivering the traffic sent by the enterprise.

In Layer 2 IP/MPLS virtual private network (VPN) services, this relationship does not change. As shown in Chapter 1, "Assessing Enterprise Legacy WANs and IP/VPN Migration," this is because most Layer 2 IP/MPLS VPN services look like existing private-line, ATM, Frame Relay, or Ethernet connections.

However, in Layer 3 IP/MPLS VPN services, the relationship between the service provider and the enterprise changes to a shared relationship. These Layer 3 services require an integration of the two network environments at the network layer. This means that the service provider and enterprise must share the same common set of capabilities required by the enterprise, which makes the service's demarcation point slightly more complex. However, the benefits of the service generally outweigh the additional complexity.

It is possible to argue that there is no net gain in efficiency by outsourcing Layer 3 to a service provider. This generally has not been a successful argument. By building a service provider-managed core supporting multiple customers, the job of WAN optimization has to be performed only once, and that is good for all customers. Building separate WANs for each customer means that the same problems have to be solved by each enterprise to optimize WAN connectivity.

Investigation Required in Selecting a Service Provider

With private-line, ATM, or Frame Relay services, the selection of a service provider typically is based on "speeds and feeds," or an evaluation of service providers based on the network's bandwidth, coverage, and cost.

In Layer 3 IP/MPLS VPNs, selecting a service provider is far more complicated than a simple "speeds and feeds" evaluation. This is because these VPN services require a stronger integration of the enterprise network and the service provider's network.

In addition, many enterprises want to ensure that their WAN can handle more than just enterprise data. Voice and video integration with data, whether performed by the enterprise or offered as a service by the service provider, place more stringent requirements for data delivery on the network.

Coverage, Access, and IP

The typical discussion of network coverage between the enterprise and service provider changes with the adoption of real-time services, such as voice and video. When network latency is less of a concern, many enterprises do not ask about density of transfer points or IP access nodes in the network.

Consider the simplest of examples, as shown in Figure 2-1. This service provider offers an IP/MPLS VPN service in the U.S. Although it offers access via private line to almost any location in the U.S., its only IP access node is in Chicago. At a minimum, traffic from one site to another must travel through the Chicago IP access node to reach the other site. Although this does not add significant latency for traffic from Los Angeles to New York, it does add a fairly significant amount of latency to the path between Los Angeles and San Francisco.

Enterprises must now be concerned not only with where they can get access to the network, but also with where these "transfer points" exist. Therefore, they must evaluate how traffic will likely flow between any sites on the network given a service provider's access coverage and IP access node coverage.

When planning Layer 2 WANs, the enterprise network manager needs to take care of the placement of hubs in the topology to minimize latency and to optimize traffic paths. This job is removed in IP/MPLS Layer 3 VPNs, but it is wise to perform a once-off check of the provider network to assure yourself that enough transfer points exist within the provider network to offer optimized routing. These transfer points are where the IP intelligence resides. Some service providers still maintain extensive Layer 2 access networks before traffic hits an intelligent IP node. Figure 2-1 shows the worst-case scenario, in which only one location has IP intelligence and all traffic is backhauled over Layer 2 to reach that IP intelligence.

Figure 2-1   *Layer 2 Network Access to a Single IP Node in Chicago*

- - - Layer 2 Access Circuits

Financial Strength of the Service Provider

An enterprise's move to use IP/MPLS VPN services also changes some of the considerations that must be made about the service provider's financial strength.

In traditional private-line, ATM, or Frame Relay networks, these services are a commodity for the most part. Because they are generally simple point-to-point dedicated or virtual circuits, it is simple to mix and match multiple network service providers to protect against the case where a service provider might fail, whether for technical or business reasons.

Because Layer 3 IP/MPLS VPN services are more integrated with enterprise networks, it is no longer possible to mix and match the network's components at will; instead, a holistic network service is chosen. It is for this reason that selecting a service provider is more of a strategic choice than selecting an inexpensive commodity service.

Additionally, because there is a higher level of integration, and there are many more factors to consider in selecting a service provider, enterprises are no longer at a point where they can call another service provider on very short notice and have a replacement service put into place.

Following the Internet bubble burst, many service providers suffered hardship, declared bankruptcy, or in some cases shut down, leaving customers scrambling to find other service providers.

For these reasons, the enterprise must know the service provider's financial strengths and weaknesses. Enterprise procurement departments already investigate many of the basic fundamentals of financial strength (cash flow, profit, and sustainability), but an enterprise network administrator must also ask about service-specific items.

First, an enterprise must ask about the service provider's commitment to the IP/VPN services that are being offered. Many Layer 2 IP/MPLS VPN services offered by service providers are still in their infancy. Consequently, the enterprise should ask questions about the "health" of the service offering.

Here are some questions that an enterprise might ask:

- How many customers are using a particular service from the service provider?
- Are there any other customers in the same vertical business segment with a similar-sized deployment?
- What is the road map for enhancing the service or expanding its deployment?
- Which customers will deploy the features listed on the road map when they are delivered?

It is quite simple for a service provider representative to concoct misleading answers to these questions. This can lead the enterprise network manager to conclude that there is strong commitment to the service, when in fact it is an experiment as far as the service provider is concerned. However, verification of road map items and willingness to deploy them when available with a reference customer should be good validation if it is available.

Convergence

Many enterprises today are looking to consolidate communications providers to reduce the costs of managing vendors and to take advantage of the aggregation of services into a single delivery mechanism. It may be desirable for the enterprise to use a single service provider for many communications service needs, including data transport, voice over IP (VoIP) access to the public switched telephone network (PSTN), and "IP Centrex" services.

Service provider IP/MPLS VPN offerings usually include the ability to connect a site to the Internet, with or without managed security, including firewalls and intrusion detection. This may be valuable to an enterprise that wants to offload traffic to and from the Internet using its intranet WAN.

Many of the converged voice offerings from service providers are undergoing development. It may not make sense for an enterprise to undertake a significant replacement of its voice infrastructure and data infrastructure at the same time. This is especially true if the enterprise already has significant investment in older voice PBX technologies.

However, enterprises such as Acme, Inc., should look at the current and planned service offerings from potential service providers and keep these capabilities in mind when selecting its service provider. In Acme's case, it has a fairly extensive PBX infrastructure that can connect to the PSTN via traditional ISDN PRI-based connectivity. However, Acme believes that in the future it will move toward IP-based voice on its network. Therefore, it wants to ensure that the service provider it selects will offer services compatible with that converged offering. More specifically, Acme believes that its transition toward IP-based voice in its network will require a service provider that offers a Session Initiation Protocol- (SIP-) based service. This service would allow Acme to configure its IP-based voice network to send VoIP directly to the network cloud for access to the PSTN.

In addition, on the horizon are a variety of other service offerings that service providers are looking at for development. Content distribution services would allow the enterprise network to distribute data securely throughout the service provider's network. They also would allow remote offices to pull data from the closest node, reducing latency and enhancing application performance. Disaster recovery services can use that same framework to offer secure short-term and long-term storage and hosting of critical business data in case of a disaster in a primary data center.

Transparency

Transparency of the IP/MPLS VPN service is the single most critical technical issue to consider when planning a migration from time-division multiplexing (TDM) or ATM/ Frame Relay. The benefits of simplified WAN capacity planning, design, and so on from the enterprise perspective have been defined, but they are not free. On more than one occasion, problems have arisen when an enterprise believed that the IP/MPLS VPN service could be deployed as a direct replacement for legacy WAN technologies and the result was not as expected.

The three main issues related to transparency that will be examined in depth from a technical perspective are as follows:

- Quality of service (QoS) markings, class of service (CoS), and MPLS/DiffServ tunneling modes
- Routing protocol transparency, including load balancing and redundancy issues
- Treatment of multicast traffic

Each issue has its own chapter to address the technical considerations pertinent to the role of that technology in delivering overall service in the IP/MPLS VPN. Here, examples taken from real-world deployments will give you an overview of why each of these issues is important.

Taking QoS first, it is a simple matter to understand that most enterprises establish their own marking schemes for traffic and that it is highly likely that many enterprises will come up with schemes that are different from each other. Many well-known applications have standard markings, such as Differentiated Services Code Point (DSCP) value 46 for voice. However, there are no such standards for how an application requiring a given amount of loss, latency, and jitter to work properly should be marked. There are moves within the Internet Engineering Task Force (IETF) to standardize which application types should be marked with what DSCP value. The moves would help, but for now, you can safely assume that many enterprises will select different markings for perfectly legitimate reasons.

Given that a service provider is faced with many different marking schemes from its multiple customers, it is not possible to define a single matching QoS scheme within the provider that matches all possible enterprise marking schemes. So clearly, there has to be some translation or matching when the enterprise seeks to use a QoS-enabled VPN service from a service provider. Where this translation or matching takes place is a matter for negotiation within the definition of the service. For scalability concerns, providers may want to distribute the marking of traffic from the provider edge (PE) to customer edge (CE) device, because it reduces the processing load on their PE device. Typically, the PE is configured with a specific number of classes that require a specific marking for traffic to gain entrance into each class. To accommodate this, each CE device can be configured to map traffic to each of the service provider-defined markings to gain access to the required CoS in the service provider's network.

This is fairly straightforward in concept but requires some care in real-world deployment. The first hurdle to overcome is that enterprises tend to define more classes within their networks than service providers. The reason for this is that enterprises define multiple classes for application separation, whereas service providers define classes based on service type.

Application separation in enterprises is implemented so that traffic from one application does not consume bandwidth provisioned for another application, typically by the use of bandwidth allocation within a class in the QoS configuration. For service provider scale networks, it is not feasible (or even technically possible) to define a separate class and queue for each possible application that any enterprise would want to provision bandwidth for. Instead, providers configure classes based on the type of service (ToS) they deliver— typically a low-latency service operated with priority queuing, an assured bandwidth class to offer bandwidth guarantee, and a best-effort class. The thinking is that if the priority and bandwidth assurance classes are sized to meet the aggregate demand of the edge classes requesting that service, the more granular commitments made on a per-application basis are met. For example, if an enterprise needs 256 kbps for Oracle, 128 kbps for FTP, and 128 kbps for Telnet traffic, the enterprise network can be configured with three classes that assure bandwidth for each application. Each of these classes requires the same service (assured bandwidth) and can be placed in the same service provider class if that class reserves the sum of bandwidth allocations (512 kbps).

Clearly, some planning needs to go on to ensure that these types of mappings provide the desired result. This is not the end of the story, however. Service providers typically police these classes to ensure that enterprises get only what is paid for. In the case of the voice class, if an enterprise transmits more traffic than is subscribed to, traffic is normally dropped, so it is not much of an issue. However, in the data class case, it is common practice to have excess traffic re-marked in some way, which can be a source of problems. There are two prime sources of problems related to this re-marking practice. The first problem relates to how TCP operates; the second problem relates to the capabilities of the service provider's PE equipment and its impact on enterprise marking schemes.

Taking the TCP issue first, if the enterprise transmits more traffic for a class than is subscribed to, the provider may mark this down in priority to a DSCP value that will admit this excess traffic to a lower-priority class. For example, there may be a high-priority data class and a best-effort class. If the provider marks down exceeding traffic from the high-priority marking to the best-effort marking, and those packets become a service from the best-effort queues in the network, out-of-sequence packet reordering is likely to occur. Out-of-sequence packet reordering has dramatic effects on TCP throughput. If a host has to reorder packets in a TCP stream before passing them to an application, the number of packets that are sent is reduced substantially while the host waits for the out-of-sequence packets.

The reason out-of-sequence reordering occurs in this case is that a class is associated with a queue. Thus, different queues drain at different rates, so if packets from the one flow are in different queues, reordering is highly likely to occur. This does not mean that a service provider should not be able to mark down exceeding traffic. A common practice is to change the DSCP marking of exceeding traffic to a value that keeps it in the same class and therefore avoids the packet reorder issue. However, the new marking identifies the packet as the first to be dropped should congestion occur via the use of Weighted Random Early Detection (WRED) configuration. Clearly, you need to understand this point when you are selecting VPN services, because the provider configuration can have a significant impact on the throughput you can obtain over the WAN links.

NOTE   If you are unfamiliar with this concept, http://www.faqs.org/rfcs/rfc2597.html is a good place to start. It discusses the reasons for keeping traffic from a specific flow within the same class.

The second issue related to re-marking is driven by the capabilities of the PE router used by the provider. For a VPN to be private, the enterprise needs to have the flexibility to mark packets any way it sees fit and for the service provider not to change those markings. TDM and Frame Relay/ATM networks do not change IP QoS markings, so neither should an IP/MPLS VPN. This should be achievable. As in IP/MPLS VPNs, the provider appends a header to the packets coming from the enterprise. That way, the service provider can mark the packets any way it wants to for treatment within its network, leaving the enterprise marking untouched.

The issue arises when there are limitations in how PE devices can police and mark traffic in combination. In some PE devices, the only way to set the EXP field in the MPLS header (which is the field used for QoS policies in an MPLS VPN network) is to copy that value from the IP precedence field in the original IP packet sent from the enterprise CE. This is fine until a packet needs to be re-marked if it is exceeding the contracted rate. With the restriction just described, the PE device has to mark down the IP precedence field in the IP packet and then copy that value to the MPLS EXP field. As soon as the packet has traversed the provider network and the MPLS header is stripped off, the packet no longer has the IP precedence field marking it was sent into the VPN with. It also is not treated appropriately after it is back in the enterprise QoS domain. Clearly, a good understanding of how the service provider treats exceeding packets is necessary when designing the end-to-end QoS scheme. A full discussion of this concept is given at http://www.faqs.org/rfcs/rfc3270.html.

RFC 3270 discusses the options for how DSCP values can be mapped to the MPLS experimental bits to preserve DiffServ behavior over the MPLS portion of the WAN. Figures 2-2 and 2-3 show the two main modes of this RFC: Uniform mode and Pipe mode.

Figure 2-2 *Uniform Mode MPLS Tunneling*

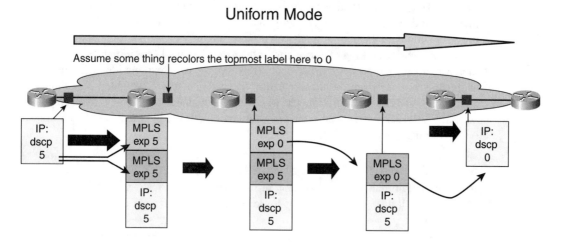

From the enterprise perspective, the primary issue to coincide is how the QoS marking is affected in the original packet by service provider operations. The Uniform mode of Figure 2-2 shows that a mark-down action within the provider cloud affects the DSCP value of the IP packet transmitted from the egress PE back toward the enterprise. This often is not what an enterprise wants to see, because what was a differentiated packet on entry to the MPLS VPN is now unmarked.

Figure 2-3   *Pipe Mode MPLS Tunneling*

Pipe Mode

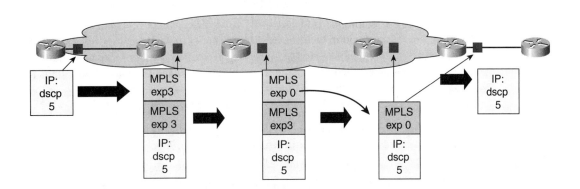

Figure 2-3 shows Pipe mode, which allows the provider to mark down the MPLS EXP field for exceeding traffic, queue within the egress based on this marked-down value, and transmit the packet with its original DSCP intact.

IP Version 6

Although predominantly U.S.-based, Acme does have operations in other regions of the world. Therefore, IP version 6 (IPv6) is a technology being planned for in the current WAN migration. The reasons for this geographic diversity regarding IPv6 importance are several; however, one of the main reasons is the distribution of existing IP version 4 (IPv4) address space. For example, at one point, the Massachusetts Institute of Technology (MIT) had more IPv4 address space assigned to it than all of China. Additionally, applications that are popular in Asia do not lend themselves so well to the use of Network Address Translation (NAT), and they require dedicated IP addresses. An example of this is the use of the buddy-finder mechanism in Japan. A mobile phone can be programmed with the user's interests and can alert him to the presence of like-minded people in a public setting, effectively making introductions. This type of direct peer-to-peer communication is difficult to support in a scalable way if handsets are being dynamically assigned IP addresses. Beyond these types of applications, IP-enabled appliances are becoming a reality, putting further pressure on the number of IPv4 addresses available. Currently, the main driver for IPv6 deployment is mobile data access, but it is expected that over time, IPv6 importance for other applications will grow.

Migrating to an IP/MPLS VPN gives Acme the opportunity to have IPv6 supported over the same network connection delivered by the service provider. Just as transparency issues were a concern for IPv4-based communications over a VPN, similar issues arise when you look at how any provider will support IPv6 services. The rest of this section reviews how service provider networks are being built to support IPv6 in a VPN environment so that the enterprise can better understand the capabilities of providers offering IPv6 support. Chapter 4, "IP Routing," contains a case study of how Acme implemented a tunneling scheme to support IPv6 traffic in the absence of native IPv6 support within the service provider network.

When looking at the requirements to support IPv6 services from a service provider perspective, stability and return on investment (ROI) are of prime concern. IPv4 backbones with MPLS support are now very stable in the major providers, but this did not come without significant investment. The thought of adding dual-stack IPv4 and IPv6 routers to this stable backbone is not attractive. Equally, the drive to support more services over the same infrastructure to improve ROI is very strong for service providers.

Service providers that have deployed MPLS in their core networks are well positioned to offer IPv6 services using that same infrastructure. From the enterprise perspective, the service offerings to look for are 6PE and 6VPE.

6PE (which refers to a version 6-capable PE router) can be thought of as using MPLS tunnels to transport native IPv6 packets. As such, 6PE is useful to both service providers and enterprises, but it does not offer the separation of a VPN service. To offer a similar level of separation between different enterprises using the same provider backbone, 6VPE (which refers to a version 6 VPN-capable PE router) is required. It supports the concept of IPv6 addresses within a service provider-operated virtual routing/forwarding instance (VRF) in the PE router. It is expected that 6VPE will become the more dominant model in terms of deployment. To help you understand these service provider offerings, a brief overview is given here. Also, Figure 2-4 shows the main components of a 6PE service within a provider network.

In the network shown in Figure 2-4, the MPLS core infrastructure is unaware of IPv6. The only upgrades necessary are on the edge PE routers. Enterprise CE routers exchange IPv6 routes directly with the provider PE routers, just as is done with IPv4 in regular VPN. The difference here, though, is that IPv6-enabled interfaces on the PEs are separate from the IPv4 VPN-enabled interfaces. The reason for this is that for regular IPv4 VPN, the customer-facing interface on the PE is made a member of a VPN by putting the interface into a VRF. With plain 6PE, the VRF is not IPv6-aware, so any IPv6 traffic must come into the PE on a different interface.

From the perspective of forwarding traffic over the core, though, the same concepts that are used in MPLS forwarding of IPv4 still hold. With reference to Figure 2-4, this means that the regular Interior Gateway Protocol (IGP) used by the service provider identifies labels that transport packets to their destination over the core. Multiprotocol Border Gateway Protocol (BGP) is used to exchange labels that associate IPv6 destinations with IPv6 next-hop values derived from IPv4 destinations. The exact mappings of label values to next-hop destinations are not important to understand from an enterprise perspective. The main point is that with 6PE, IPv6 reachability can be provided for the enterprise over the stable IPv4 provider network, but only via a separate interface.

Figure 2-4 *Overview of 6PE*

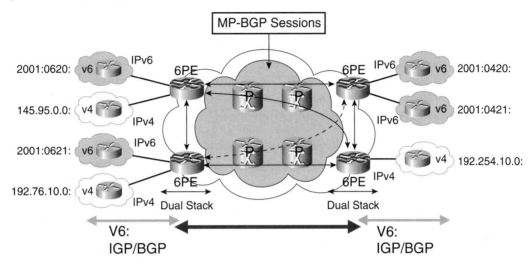

Taking IPv6 service from a service provider that supports only 6PE is better than not having the service at all. However, it requires more work from the enterprise perspective when compared to 6VPE, which is examined next.

6VPE is different from 6PE in that a 6VPE router maintains separate routing tables on a per-enterprise basis to maintain separation as in regular IPv4 MPLS VPN deployments. In regular MPLS VsPN, route distinguishers were added to enterprise routes to ensure that overlapping addresses could be supported. It is the same for IPv6 in a 6VPE environment. IPv6 routes are made into VPNv6 routes within the PE node itself. The route target extended community is used to advertise those unique VPNv6 routes via multiprotocol BGP to other 6VPE nodes. As soon as VPNv6 information is distributed between the 6VPE-capable routers within the provider network, the 6VPE router adds labels to forward these packets based on label values rather than IPv6 addresses across the core.

When running 6VPE, the provider delivers more functionality to the enterprise than a 6PE provider, because each interface on a 6VPE router has both IPv4 and IPv6 stacks and has a VRF membership for each on it. So the 6VPE service may be charged at a higher rate to reflect the greater functionality and cost of operation from the provider's perspective.

The transparency issues raised for IPv4 VPN service concerning routing protocol, QoS, and multicast still need to be considered for IPv6; however, there are a few additional considerations:

- The minimum IPv4 transmission unit is 68 bytes, whereas in IPv6, the minimum needs to be 1280 bytes. Under most conditions, this is not an issue because Ethernet links generally present an MTU of 1518 bytes within the network. This is clearly above the 1280 minimum value that IPv6 expects to see. However, if any dial links exist, you need to carefully consider the MTU values for IPv6 transport, because dial links can have lower MTU values than IPv6 expects.

- IPv6 has the concept of link-local addresses that are used by routing protocols to form adjacencies. These addresses are separate from the global IPv6 address that is assigned to an interface. The link-local addresses are not propagated across the provider network, as the global ones are. Care must be taken with link-local addresses if the access medium between the CE and PE is a multiaccess network of some kind, such as is the case with Frame Relay and ATM. If that is the case, you must create separate mappings for the link-local address across the Layer 2 data-link connection identifier (DLCI) or permanent virtual circuit (PVC) for the link-local address for routing protocol adjacency to form.

Provider Cooperation/Tiered Arrangements

For Acme, a key issue is how the new WAN can deliver service across diverse geographic regions when no one service provider offers a network covering all of them. Can service providers cooperate to provide seamless service? Can services be maintained if they traverse the public Internet?

Additionally, as has been stated, due to the more intimate nature of the relationship between enterprise and service provider required by IP/MPLS VPNs, it is preferable from the enterprise perspective to have to invest in only one of those relationships. So should Acme arrange a "prime contractor" relationship and have its preferred service provider negotiate service in regions where it does not have a presence and be responsible for organizing the delivery of service there?

At a technical level, there are no impediments to service providers being able to interconnect their networks to provide seamless connectivity for enterprises. The reality, though, is that differences in operational practice, design philosophies, and political issues currently typically keep that level of cooperation between service providers from being pervasive across the globe.

For Acme, the choice is clear. It establishes a preferred vendor of choice for each major region in the globe. It also provides separate handoffs from the internal network in each geography to these preferred regional vendors. This typically breaks down into a VPN provider for America, one for Europe, and one for Asia Pacific, with Acme providing the interconnect between these service providers.

This provides Acme with the flexibility to control addressing, QoS marking, and multicast traffic between service providers in a way that suits their needs, rather than expecting service providers to cooperate to achieve the desired result.

Enhanced Service-Level Agreement

As soon as the jump has been made to integrate Layer 3 IP operations with a service provider, the SLAs that exist for the service can be enhanced and made more specific. With Frame Relay or ATM, SLAs typically refer to some sort of availability, the committed rate, and perhaps some bursting above the committed rate. This is for any traffic traversing the link. It is not specific to any application that may need better or worse treatment than other applications during congestion time. With Layer 2 services over the WAN, the practice has been to shape traffic outbound from the CE router to the committed rate and have that CE perform all queuing and drop functions. This does not take advantage of burst within the service provider's network.

With the VPN being a Layer 3 service, it is now possible for the service provider's devices to understand which packets are voice, high-priority, or best-effort and which SLA parameters can be written for each of these across the WAN. The major benefit of this change is that bandwidth can be more efficiently allocated for access links. In the case where the service provider's network is unaware of which packets are voice, high-priority, or best-effort, all packets need to be treated as if they are high-priority, meaning low loss, latency, and jitter. For many data or best-effort applications, the low latency delivered is not required. It is not bad to give an application better service than it needs to operate, just wasteful and expensive as far as resources.

The enhanced SLAs available from providers delivering Layer 3 VPN service provide the granularity needed for enterprises to consider purchasing different types of bandwidth. This means a given amount of low-latency bandwidth, a given amount of assured bandwidth, and a given amount of best-effort bandwidth to more accurately reflect the needs of the enterprise traffic. The benefit here is that only the minimum amount of expensive low-latency bandwidth needs to be purchased, resulting in a lower overall bill for bandwidth from the service provider. Chapter 5, "Implementing Quality of Service," discusses how to determine the different amounts of bandwidth required. Chapter 3, "Analyzing Service Requirements," addresses some of the specific performance requirements for traffic of different types.

Customer Edge Router Management

One of the first issues to resolve when considering a Layer 3 VPN service is who will own and operate the CE router. This is not a straightforward question, because both alternatives have pros and cons.

Consider the case in which the enterprise decides to own and operate the CE router, which is the more common model in the U.S. The enterprise has the freedom to upgrade to different Cisco IOS versions when required and make use of new features as they become available. It does, however, make the service more complex to support from the enterprise perspective, because it now has to resolve access circuit issues in cooperation with the service provider. Additionally, it is impossible for the service provider to offer service guarantees covering the access circuit when the provider does not manage the CE. This issue is worthy of more examination.

The most common place for congestion to occur on a network is over the access link between the campus LANs and the service provider backbone, which is the most constrained bandwidth link. The performance of that link in terms of the loss latency and jitter it provides to the applications that use it is almost totally dependent on the amount of traffic sent to the link by the enterprise. Of course, this is not under the control of the service provider in the unmanaged CE case, so it is not a simple matter to offer performance guarantees from a provider perspective. As a simple example, suppose the enterprise subscribes to a 256-kbps access link service and sends 2 Mbps to the egress interface toward the provider. Queues fill, packets are dropped, and latency grows, even though the provider has done nothing to generate that poor network performance.

Generally, unmanaged CEs have not had performance guarantees attached to them for the access link, but managed CEs have. We will look at this issue again in the section "Customer Reports and SLA Validation."

For the case in which the service provider manages the CE, more specific guarantees for access link performance can be given, because the provider owns, operates, and controls the CE. Therefore, it can be configured to not attempt to send too much traffic over the access link. It also can report back to the provider if queues fill up because too much traffic was sent to that egress port. In some cases where the provider offers BGP only as a CE-to-PE routing protocol, this can also offload the BGP configuration from enterprise to provider. The downside is that the CE is now upgraded only according to the provider's schedule and for releases it approves of, which may or may not match the enterprise service needs. Having ownership of the CE also lets the provider set up probes and report on performance from a CE-to-CE perspective, a much more relevant measurement than the more usual PE-to-PE measurements provided in the unmanaged case.

In the case of Acme, a one-off agreement was reached with the service provider such that Acme would own and manage the CEs, but the provider would be given one-off access to the device to set up probes and provider reports on network performance from a CE-to-CE perspective. This is not a usual service offering from providers, but it might be open to negotiation, depending on the contract's size.

Service Management

Beyond managing the CE router, you also need to consider managing additional services delivered as part of the VPN service. These additional services could include the following:

- Content distribution and web cache service
- Firewall
- Intrusion detection
- Voice services
- Denial of service (DoS) protection
- Internet access

When crafting SLAs, it is typical to create different metrics for different aspects of the VPN, including hardware, bandwidth, and any services provided. Clearly, the network connectivity has to be there for any service to run on top of it, so bandwidth availability has to be greater than or equal to service availability. Beyond simple availability, each service requires specific metrics or service characteristics relevant to the service operation. An example might be support required for Survivable Remote Site Telephony (SRST) to enhance voice service availability.

The negotiation of service management is typically specific to each enterprise's needs. It can be pivotal in deciding whether the service is continually managed by the enterprise or outsourced to the service provider.

Customer Reports and SLA Validation

Regular reports from the service provider form the basis of service validation and potentially rebates for nonperformance. Reports should provide measurement of metrics that are important to the enterprise, such as per-site performance on a per-class basis, per-site availability reports, and so on.

The reports available should be defined in the initial service agreement, with care taken to negotiate how availability, loss latency, and jitter are calculated.

The service provider's advertised performance for loss latency and jitter on its networks typically refers to PE-to-PE measurements that are averaged over groups of devices for a long period of time. As such, it is quite difficult to map those to what they mean for performance of a voice class at a particular location, for example. Care must be taken to ensure that the basis of SLA measurement and reporting of that measurement make sense from the enterprise perspective.

One of the issues discussed earlier in this section was that of the enterprise's remaining operational control over the CE device and the difficulty that poses in the provider offering CE-to-CE performance guarantees. One way to mitigate those difficulties is to request given loss latency and jitter characteristics, as long as the utilization on a per-class basis remains below a given level—say, 70 or 80 percent. This protects the service provider, because if the enterprise puts too much traffic into the class, the provider is not responsible. However, if the class's performance is poor during times that the enterprise is not overloading the class, the provider is to blame, and penalties can be claimed.

How performance of the class is measured can be contentious. The recommended best practice is for active monitoring, such as the Cisco IP SLA probes, to be sent for each class. This lets per-class statistics for loss, latency, and jitter be collected. Typically an enterprise wants the provider to collect the results of these probes and format them into a regular report. However, it is common practice for enterprises to perform random verification of these reports with their own probe mechanisms.

Summary

This chapter looked at some of the concepts you must consider when assessing service providers that may be supplying a VPN service for an enterprise WAN. These issues broadly fall into two categories—technical and nontechnical.

The technical issues covered are as follows:

- IP footprint and location of IP transfer points
- Transparency of QoS service and SP classes of service
- Transparency of multicast service
- Transparency of routing protocol support
- Method of supporting IPv6

The nontechnical issues covered are as follows:

- Financial stability
- Experience with delivering Layer 3 services
- Commitment to the VPN service
- SLA negotiation and reporting

Appendix A lists more-specific questions you might ask when constructing a Request for Proposal (RFP) for providers to bid on.

This chapter covers the following topics:

- Application/Bandwidth Requirements
- Backup and Resiliency
- Enterprise Segmentation Requirements
- Access Technologies
- Security Requirements
- Multiprovider Considerations
- Extranets
- Case Study: Analyzing Service Requirements for Acme, Inc.

CHAPTER 3

Analyzing Service Requirements

This chapter's objective is to define the Layer 2 to Layer 3 migration requirements that a service provider must deliver for the enterprise customer to perceive the Layer 3 virtual private network (VPN) offering as valuable. This chapter retains the fictional Acme, Inc. as a reference for the overall discussion. This chapter looks at application and bandwidth requirements that help drive services, such as videoconferencing and data collaboration, that are a basis for enterprise loss and jitter targets. The chapter further examines access technologies such as Frame Relay, ATM, time-division multiplexing (TDM), and Metro Ethernet, in addition to the associated quality of service (QoS) concerns from the enterprise customers. Chapters 1 and 2 introduced these technologies, and this chapter describes the applications that are commonly used with them. The chapter concludes with a case study on an enterprise organization that migrated from a Layer 2-centric service to a Layer 3-centric service as input to Acme for consideration as it embarks on its own journey.

Application/Bandwidth Requirements

Enterprise IT managers must continually manage costs and maintain reliable WAN infrastructures to meet their business goals. But, success in today's business climate also depends on the ability to overcome a more complex set of challenges to their corporate WAN. Enterprise IT managers are faced with the following:

- Geographically dispersed sites and teams that must share information across the network and have secure access to networked corporate resources.

- Mission-critical, distributed applications that must be deployed and managed on a network-wide basis. Furthermore, IT managers are faced with a combination of centralized hosted applications and distributed applications, which complicates the management task.

- Security requirements for networked resources and information that must be reliably available but protected from unauthorized access.

- Business-to-business communication needs, for users within the company and extending to partners and customers. QoS features that ensure end-to-end application performance.

- Support for the convergence of previously disparate data, voice, and video networks resulting in cost savings for the enterprise.

- Security and privacy equivalent to Frame Relay and ATM.

- Easier deployment of productivity-enhancing applications, such as enterprise resource planning (ERP), e-learning, and streaming video. (These productivity-enhancing applications are IP-based, and Layer 2 VPNs do not provide the basis to support these applications.)

- Pay-as-you-go scalability as companies expand, merge, or consolidate.

- Flexibility to support thousands of sites.

Which services and applications indeed drive bandwidth requirements? You can deconstruct service categories as follows:

- Interactive

- Noninteractive

- Interactive and noninteractive

- Regulated

Examples of interactive services include the following:

- Real-time conversational voice services

- Point-to-point interactive multimedia services, including interactive real-time voice, video, and other media (video telephony, interactive gaming, whiteboarding, and so on)

- Point-to-multipoint interactive multimedia services (videoconferencing, video chat, and interactive gaming)

- Push to Talk

- Instant messaging (IM) and messaging services (Short Message Service [SMS], multimedia messaging service [MMS], and so on)

- Group messaging

- Existing public switched telephone network (PSTN)/ISDN services (PSTN/ISDN emulation)

- Data communication services (data file transfer, fax, electronic mailbox, chat, and so on)

- Data-retrieval applications (telesoftware)

- Online applications (online sales for consumers, e-commerce, online procurement for commercials, and so on)

- Speech-enabled services

- Web browsing

- Transaction services (high-priority, e-commerce, and so on)

Content-delivery services, also referred to as noninteractive services, include the following:

- Audio and video streaming
- Music and video on demand
- Digital TV channel distribution
- Financial information distribution
- Professional and medical image distribution
- E-learning
- Electronic publishing
- Sensor network services
- Push services
- Remote control/teleaction services, such as home application control, telemetry, alarms, and so on
- Broadcast/multicast services
- Over-the-network device management

Some of the interactive and noninteractive services are as follows:

- VPN services
- Hosted and transit services for enterprises (IP Centrex and so on)
- Information services (movie ticket information, highway traffic reports, advanced push services, and so on)
- Location-based services
- Presence and general notification services (display of peers that a user can contact, their current status, and any service-related notifications)

Proceeding with bandwidth requirements, let's look at an example under interactive services for audio (voice messaging) that is primarily unidirectional.

NOTE   Voice—specifically, voice over IP (VoIP)—is symmetrical when provisioning the service. Two-way VoIP will be discussed shortly.

A typical data rate is between 4 and 13 kbps. Web browsing via HTML requires about 10 kbps; with e-mail (server access), it takes approximately < 10 kbps. Table 3-1 summarizes these data rates and performance targets for interactive services.

Table 3-1   *Performance Targets for Interactive Services*

Medium	Application	Degree of Symmetry	Typical Data Rate/ Amount of Data	Key Performance Parameters and Target Values		
				One-Way Delay (Response Time)	Delay Variation	Information Loss
Audio	Voice messaging	Primarily one-way	4–13 kbps	< 1 sec for playback < 2 sec for record	< 1 msec	< 3 percent packet loss ratio
Data	Web browsing—HTML	Primarily one-way	~ 10 kbps	< 4 sec/page	—	0
Data	Transaction services— high-priority (for example, e-commerce and ATM)	Two-way	< 10 kbps	< 4 sec	—	0
Data	E-mail (server access)	Primarily one-way	< 10 kbps	< 4 sec	—	0

In determining bandwidth for streaming services, the amount of bulk data transfer/retrieval and synchronization information is approximately < 384 kbps. A movie clip, surveillance, or real-time video requires 20–384 kbps, as shown in Table 3-2.

Table 3-2   *Performance Targets for Streaming Services*

Medium	Application	Degree of Symmetry	Data Rate/ Amount of Data	Key Performance Parameters and Target Values		
				Start-Up Delay	Transport Delay Variation	Packet Loss at Session Layer
Audio	Speech, mixed speech and music, and medium and high-quality music	Primarily one-way	5–128 kbps	< 10 sec	< 1 msec	< 1 percent packet loss ratio
Video	Movie clips, surveillance, and real-time video	Primarily one-way	20–384 kbps	< 10 sec	< 1 msec	< 2 percent packet loss ratio

Table 3-2   *Performance Targets for Streaming Services (Continued)*

Medium	Application	Degree of Symmetry	Data Rate/ Amount of Data	Key Performance Parameters and Target Values		
				Start-Up Delay	Transport Delay Variation	Packet Loss at Session Layer
Data	Bulk data transfer/ retrieval, layout and synchronization information	Primarily one-way	< 384 kbps	< 10 sec	—	0
Data	Still image	Primarily one-way		< 10 sec	—	0

Finally, bandwidth requirements for conversational/real-time services, such as audio and video applications, include videophone, which is 32–384 kbps; Telnet, about < 1 KB; and telemetry, approximately < 28.8 kbps. (See Table 3-3.)

Table 3-3   *Performance Targets for Conversational/Real-Time Services (Audio and Video Applications)*

Medium	Application	Degree of Symmetry	Typical Data Rates/ Amount of Data	Key Performance Parameters and Target Values		
				End-to-End One-Way Delay	Delay Variation Within a Call	Information Loss[1]
Audio	Conversational voice	Two-way	4–25 kbps	< 150 ms preferred[2] < 400 ms limit[2]	< 1 ms	< 3 percent packet loss ratio

(continues)

[1]   Exact values depend on the specific codec, but this assumes the use of a packet loss concealment algorithm to minimize the effect of packet loss.

[2]   Assumes adequate echo control.

  Note that the values for VoIP depend on the codec in use as well as the Layer 2 overhead. For example, G.729A over 802.1Q/ P Ethernet requires 37 kbps, whereas G.722 requires 322 kbps plus Layer 2 overhead. You need to factor in Layer 2 overhead in assessing the VoIP values.

Table 3-3   *Performance Targets for Conversational/Real-Time Services (Audio and Video Applications)*
            (Continued)

Medium	Application	Degree of Symmetry	Typical Data Rates/ Amount of Data	Key Performance Parameters and Target Values		
				End-to-End One-Way Delay	Delay Variation Within a Call	Information Loss[1]
Video	Videophone	Two-way	32–384 kbps	< 150 ms preferred < 400 ms limit Lip-synch: < 100 ms		< 1 percent packet loss ratio
Data	Telemetry two-way control	Two-way	< 28.8 kbps	< 250 ms	—	0
Data	Interactive games	Two-way	< 1 KB	< 250 ms	—	0
Data	Telnet	Two-way (asymmetric)	< 1 KB	< 250 ms	—	0

Service providers tend to bundle (propose multiple services with a target) to prevent customer churn. An example is a triple play where voice, data, and video may be offered as a bundle, perhaps over a single transport link. Bandwidth requirements for cable modem may be approximately 1 Mbps upstream to the provider and 3 Mbps downstream to the subscriber. You can additionally have prioritized traffic for VoIP—two VoIP phone lines, per-call charging, and broadcast video MPEG 2, one-half D1, with one channel per set-top. Table 3-4 further illustrates service bundles with bandwidth requirements.

Table 3-4   *Triple-Play Service Bundles*

Service Bundle	Service Elements
Internet with video on demand (VoD) Turbo Button	Broadband digital subscriber line (DSL) access pipe—128 kbps up and 640 kbps down Turbo Button bandwidth on demand—3 Mbps down Access control list (ACL)-based firewall Uncached VoD MPEG 2, one-half D1 **Wholesale Layer 3 VPN access**
Triple Play	Maximum transmission unit (MTU)-based ETTx—10 Mbps bidirectional Best-effort transport Two VoIP phone lines, prepaid calling Broadcast video MPEG 2, one-half D1, one channel per home **Residential grade Internet access**

Table 3-4   *Triple-Play Service Bundles (Continued)*

Service Bundle	Service Elements
Triple Play Plus	Cable modem—approximately 1 Mbps up and 3 Mbps down
	Prioritized transport: VoIP stream
	Two VoIP phone lines, per-call charging
	Broadcast video MPEG 2, one-half D1, one channel per set-top
	Residential grade Internet access
Quadruple Play Platinum Service	Fiber to the Home (FTTH)—10 Mbps bidirectional (up to 32 Mbps downlink)
	Residential gateway router with wireless
	Prioritized transport: VoIP stream and gaming
	Four VoIP phone lines, one emergency POTS line, unlimited calling
	Mobile phone integration with 802.11
	Deep packet inspection network-based firewall
	Uncached VoD, MPEG 2, one-half D1 and MPEG 4, High-Definition Television (HDTV) 12 Mbps
	Broadcast video, MPEG 2, one-half D1 and MPEG 4, HDTV 12 Mbps
	Per-subscriber session Layer 3 VPN access

The next section identifies requirements for backup and resiliency that are pivotal to Layer 3 services.

You cannot assume that all interactive applications (especially those bundled into a service package) are equal in terms of priorities as negotiated by the customer with the service provider. Specifically, the fact that an application may be interactive does not mean it will be a high priority for a business. Customers negotiate priorities as part of the service-level agreement (SLA) discussions with a service provider.

Backup and Resiliency

Circuit failure protection requires the traffic load to be split across multiple circuits or requires an unloaded backup circuit to be in place for redundancy. The most common forms of circuit protection use redundant links and multihoming.

For the purposes of incremental bandwidth and link-level redundancy, multilink PPP (MLP) provides an effective bundling solution. MLP requires all links to be originated and terminated on the same physical customer edge (CE) and provider edge (PE) routers and requires the links to be fairly similar in bandwidth and latency characteristics. Also note that Frame Relay Form 16 (FRF.16) (when supported by the service provider) can offer the same benefit as MLP. Load redistribution during circuit outages is automatic. If applications sensitive to packet missequencing will be deployed, such as VoIP, flow-based load balancing (rather than packet-based) should be used.

Note that a flow here is a source- and destination-based construct at Layer 3. Flow-based load balancing automatically occurs at Layer 2 with MPLS or FRF.12. There is a caveat when implementing VoIP over MLP over multiple physical links. In these cases, VoIP uses Compressed Real-Time Transport Protocol (cRTP), because packet reordering may occur (over the separate physical links) because only fragmented packets are encapsulated with MLP. Therefore, we recommend that Multiclass Multilink PPP (MCMP) be used in this case.

For a backup circuit to be effective, detailed research into the physical circuit path is required. In many cases, separate physical facilities for entering the building are required to avoid the possibility that both circuits are disrupted at the same time, which is commonly called "backhoe fade."

NOTE   In many cases, circuit providers share physical facilities. Purchasing circuits from separate providers does not guarantee that they will be built on separate physical facilities.

Resilient protection against link and PE failure requires multihoming the CE router to different PE routers. Additionally, protection against CE router failure requires multiple CE routers homed to multiple PE routers (to the same PE routers). The CE-to-PE routing protocol and the CE and PE hardware platforms affect the multihoming implementation. If Border Gateway Protocol (BGP) 4 is used for the CE-to-PE routing protocol, BGP multipath load sharing is preferred for multihoming the CE router. If multiple CE routers are required, or other routing protocols are used on CE-to-PE links, designs using Gateway Load Balancing Protocol (GLBP) and the Globally Resilient IP (GRIP) architecture should be considered. Resiliency options depend on service provider support. Not all service providers support all options. Virtual Router Redundancy Protocol (VRRP) is a standards-based alternative to GLBP (see RFC 3768). Some service providers offer the option of contracting a port on an alternative node as part of a backup service. The port is accessed through ISDN or another switched circuit service in the event of a circuit failure on the primary node. Backup ports are sometimes offered at a reduced rate, because the primary and backup ports cannot consume bandwidth concurrently.

Survivable Remote Site Telephony (SRST) is recommended for subscriber sites with IP telephony. As enterprises extend their IP telephony deployments from central sites to remote offices, one of the factors considered vital in deployment is the ability to provide backup redundancy functions at the remote branch office. However, the size and number of these small-office sites preclude most enterprises from deploying dedicated call-processing servers, unified-messaging servers, or multiple WAN links to each site to achieve the high availability required.

Enterprise Segmentation Requirements

Why segment the enterprise network? The main driver is security to mitigate worms and provide virus containment that reduces global service impact. There are three types of VPNs:

- Server VPNs for business-critical applications
- User VPNs for standard production
- Global VPNs for guest access and VoIP

Enterprise virtualized network services for Acme includes firewalls, intrusion detection, and VPN service modules such as IPsec and load balancers. VLAN "awareness" also comprises an enterprise virtualized network service. So when exploring enterprise segmentation requirements, it is important to note what capabilities will be applied to the designated service segments, as shown in Figure 3-1.

Figure 3-1   *End-to-End Enterprise*

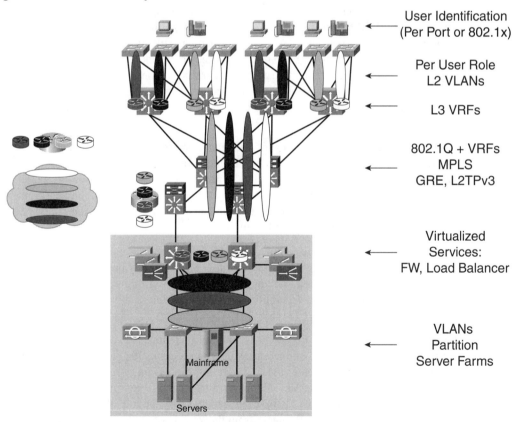

Traditionally, the most common approach to designing campus networks has been one that is both hierarchical and modular. Hierarchy is defined by network roles assigned from the center of the network toward the edge: core, distribution, and access. Modularity is defined by grouping distribution switches to provide modular access to the core for entire physical network areas. Additionally, some smaller enterprises have collapsed distribution and core layers to a single core/edge layer.

One key element of providing scalability and high availability in a campus network is restraining the reach of Layer 2 failure domains by deploying a Layer 3 (routed) core and distribution, which keeps the surrounding Layer 2 domains isolated from each other in terms of failure propagation. The net result of this type of design is a network that leverages IP routing in its core and bridging toward its edge. The size of the Layer 2 and Layer 3 domains is debatable. Some engineers advocate the use of Layer 3 switching everywhere (even in the wiring closet), and others preach the benefits of using Layer 2 switching over most of the network, except for the core.

There is an option to use virtual routing/forwarding (VRF) to extend VPNs in cases where the platform at the edge of the Layer 3 domain does not support Multiprotocol Label Switching (MPLS). This is discussed at Cisco.com under the heading of multi-vrf CE. All the points discussed so far for VLAN-to-VPN mapping still apply. In this case, the edge of the Layer 3 domain acts as a CE, so two issues need to be addressed. One is the segmentation of the PE-CE link to transport the traffic for the different VPNs separately, and the other is the updating of the routing information between PE and CE, or PE-CE routing. The first issue is handled in the campus by means of 802.1Q trunking over an Ethernet link.

Whatever the case, any segmentation of traffic achieved over the Layer 2 switching domain by means of VLANs is lost in the routed Layer 3 core. In many cases, it is desirable to preserve such segmentation over the routed core and create closed user groups while centralizing network services (Internet access, DHCP, and server farms) and enforcing security policies. MPLS VPNs provide a scalable manner of segmenting the routed portion of the network to achieve the desired result.

Deploying MPLS VPNs in the campus should be approached as a nondisruptive enhancement to the existing routed infrastructure. This is largely because MPLS VPNs are simply overlaid onto the routed domain, thus preserving existing services and scalability while adding the benefits and versatility of a network virtualized by means of Layer 3 VPNs.

Overlaying MPLS Layer 3 VPNs onto a hierarchical campus network involves expanding the roles of the access, distribution, and core switches to include the VPN responsibilities of provider (P), PE, and, in some cases, CE. For this discussion, assume that the switch that is the first Layer 3 hop (where VLANs are terminated and IP routing starts) plays the PE role. Thus, in this example, the distribution switches play the role of PE routers, and the core switches play the role of P routers from the VPN perspective. Because the access switches are Layer 2 devices, no CE role is to be played in this network.

Mapping VLANs to VPNs in the Campus

Because virtualization is achieved by means of VLANs in the Layer 2 portion of the network, although MPLS VPNs virtualize the routed portion of the network, you must map the VLANs to the VPNs and vice versa to obtain end-to-end virtual networks.

Mapping of VLANs to VPNs happens in the PE router for full MPLS VPN deployments or on the CE router for VRF-lite extended deployments. To achieve a mapping, it is sufficient to include a Layer 3 interface that belongs to the VLAN in the VRF corresponding to the desired VPN. Thus, no specific commands are necessary to map VLANs into VPNs. A VLAN is mapped into the VPN after it is made a subnet within the corresponding VRF at the edge of the routed domain. The VLAN acts as a logical interface associated with a given VRF. Therefore, any attribute learned from that interface becomes part of the VPN.

A switched virtual interface (SVI) can be used as the Layer 3 interface for VLAN 100, for example. The use of SVIs as the point of routing for a given VLAN (default gateway) is a well- established practice in campus switching deployments. This approach allows the aggregation of traffic from many wiring closets onto a single virtual Layer 3 interface.

NOTE   Aggregating traffic from different wiring closets connected to a VLAN and forwarding that aggregated traffic to an SVI is called local switching.

Because any given VLAN cannot be associated to multiple Layer 3 interfaces, you can only cater to traffic from a single switch connected to the PE router by a dot1q trunk. For example, if multiple (Layer 2) switches with VLAN 100 traffic are connected to the PE router, you must insert an aggregation switch in front of the PE to be able to map all traffic onto the red VPN with the preceding configuration. Alternatively, the network engineer could choose to use several separate VLAN IDs and map them to a single VPN. Managing this scheme becomes more complex as the number of subnets and VLAN IDs increases. The main advantage of such an approach is that it can potentially eliminate the use of spanning tree.

In general, the best practice is to use SVIs and rely on local switching to aggregate the different switches. This approach has the advantage of being able to map a single VLAN to a VPN. Care must be used when designing the access redundancy in this scenario. This is the well-studied situation in which a common VLAN exists on many access switches. To provide effective redundancy, the topology must include a Layer 2 link between the distribution switches, which are acting as PEs or multilite VRF CEs. Such links allow spanning tree and HSRP (Hot Standby Router Protocol) to operate together properly. Without this alteration in the topology, the convergence times of spanning tree could put HSRP in a state that will cause packets to be black-holed.

One of the most important aspects of deploying MPLS VPNs in a campus is that it allows every VPN to use services and policies that are centrally available, yet private to each VPN. Thus, by defining the VPN routing such that there is a single point of access into and out of the VPN, security policies that used to be distributed across the campus and were therefore hard to manage can now be enforced at this single point of access and are much simpler. This method also allows different VPNs to share a common firewall appliance that provides individualized policies by associating a separate virtual firewall to each VPN.

The key to centralizing services in the campus is to provision the routing within each VPN in such a way that there is a single, common point of ingress and egress among all of them. In service provider terms, this equates to the Internet. In campus terms, this could or could not be associated to the Internet (though it generally is). Thus, the Internet is a transit zone for VPNs to communicate with each other. To reach this transit zone, all traffic must go through a firewall in which security policies are enforced. Services could reside in the transit zone. However, if the transit zone is actually the Internet, an extra firewall is required, and services are better off placed in a Services VPN.

NOTE   Firewalls are actually inserted outside of each VPN (on the VLAN that is mapped to the VPN). So at this point, this is equivalent to a problem of traditional IP routing between different networks that have a firewall at the headend.

Access Technologies

Layer 2 technologies include private circuit constructs, Frame Relay/ATM, and emerging Ethernet. This section describes various Layer 2 services available to customers.

Private circuit mechanisms typically are delivered over SONET/Synchronous Digital Hierarchy (SDH) and have been popular for the past several years. The reliability inherent in SONET/SDH is because of the Automatic Protection Switching (APS) element, which provides recovery within 50 ms. The lack of bandwidth flexibility actually makes a private circuit service less interesting for customers today because customers must select between fixed bandwidth, such as T1 (1.5 Mbps) and T3 (45 Mbps) in North America and E1 (2 Mbps) and E3 (34 Mbps) in Europe and elsewhere. The bandwidth and price differences between T1 and T3 and E1 and E3 are so significant that customers tend to remain with their T1 and E1 links and seek ways to reduce usage on these links. More importantly, an equipment upgrade is required for both the service provider and the customer to increase from one rate to another.

Frame Relay

Frame Relay was designed as a telecommunications service for cost-efficient data transmission where traffic can be intermittent between an enterprise LAN and distributed between WAN locations. As a packet-switching protocol, historically, Frame Relay was developed as a result of WAN requirements for speed and, consequently, for LAN-to-LAN and LAN-to-WAN internetworking. Frame Relay inserts data in a variable-size unit called a frame, where the error-correction function (retransmission of data) is the responsibility of the endpoints. The service provider typically provides a PVC for most services and results in the customer's possessing a dedicated virtual connection without being charged for a full leased line. An enterprise can select a level of service quality by prioritizing some frames to primarily transport data over Frame Relay. Service providers offer CIR as an option to a customer that permits an allocated minimum capacity and allows for traffic bursts when required. Voice and video applications are adequately provisioned over Frame Relay networks. The hub-and-spoke configuration is a common topology used for Frame Relay deployments. Although full-mesh implementations are supported, they are rare. They can be costly due to the price of individual circuits. Furthermore, operational complexities associated with the maintenance of the N^2 connections in such a configuration also poses significant challenges, as stated earlier in this chapter. Typical applications of Frame Relay include LAN interconnections, client/server, e-mail, terminal-to-host, and host-to-host, such as file transfers between mainframe computers.

ATM

ATM defines cell switching with a packet adaptation layer, which permits high-speed transmission of data through the use of small, fixed-length packets (cells) rather than the frames used in Frame Relay. ATM was originally developed as a key component of broadband ISDN (B-ISDN) and is a derivative of Frame Relay. ATM was designed to integrate voice, data, and video services by transporting these multiple channels over the same physical connection. A customer can order a PVC with a specific ATM QoS characteristic, such as voice via CBR, transactional applications via variable bit rate (VBR), and noncritical applications via unspecified bit rate (UBR). The CoS elements of ATM provide QoS assurance for the various service types, such as voice and data. ATM benefits include dynamic bandwidth capability and CoS support for multimedia service classes. Typical business applications include videoconferencing, voice, real-time audio, and high-bandwidth data such as medical imagery. Frame Relay and ATM offer connection-oriented services, whereas the IP is connectionless.

Customers generally want the lowest-cost portfolio of WAN services that meets their quality objectives and connectivity requirements. Total cost of ownership factors include staff training, equipment, service charges, and service exit fees incurred when subscribing to an alternative service. For these customers, WAN connectivity costs are high due to the multiplicity of protocols implemented by the service providers. Because legacy services are expected to be matched by new service offerings, Ethernet interface for WAN connectivity is attractive for customers due to the potential cost savings that are attributed to the removal of the protocol, unlike Frame Relay, for example. Transparent Layer Service (TLS) originates from Metro Ethernet at the access. Multicast-aware VPN-based service is an example of an enhanced service offering needed to support IPTV, videoconferencing, and push applications such as stock market quotes. Internet access and secure firewall services broaden the service provider's portfolio for enhanced services, all of which can be deployed over IP/MPLS. Layer 2 MPLS services may lower TDM switching costs by emulating existing Frame Relay and ATM services. MPLS traffic engineering (TE) and fast reroute (FRR) can replace Synchronous Digital Hierarchy (SDH) for network resilience under failure scenarios. Layer 3 VPNs offer any-to-any connectivity, with support of data, voice, and video intranet applications via differentiated CoS mechanisms.

Two major factors in the selection of the CE-to-PE link access technology are cost and the density of the service provider MPLS core network. Many service providers supplement the MPLS core by using existing Frame Relay and ATM networks to provide transport from locations without a PE router, or to lower port costs by using existing ATM equipment to provide access ports.

Although ATM and Frame Relay are cost-effective to "backhaul" or "multiplex" traffic to a PE MPLS node, additional consideration is required in the network design using these access technologies.

NOTE   CE-to-PE link access is described in this section. Queuing for the link is discussed in Chapter 5.

Dedicated Circuit from CE to PE

This is the simplest form of access, but it requires the service provider MPLS network to have a high penetration of PE routers in locations where subscriber service is required. With a dedicated circuit between the CE and PE routers, high-level data link control (HDLC)/ PPP encapsulation is used on the link, and all the normal queuing functions are required.

MLP may be used to combine multiple low-speed links for greater bandwidth when MLP is used with stream-oriented applications, such as VoIP.

If VoIP is deployed, the Link Fragmentation and Interleaving (LFI) capability of MLP should be used on low-speed links (< 768 kbps) to fragment large data packets and reduce latency and jitter for VoIP packets. If multiple low-speed links are combined with MLP, LFI and flow-based load balancing should be configured on all links. The LFI fragment size can be configured in milliseconds and should be configured to acceptable VoIP packet delay for a site.

LFI is not supported by HDLC or PPP, which is why MLP is required for slow-speed links that transport VoIP. Note further that if multiple slow-speed links are bundled and the VoIP is compressed by cRTP, we recommend using MCMP.

ATM PVC from CE to PE

Normally, this type of access is used in locations where the service provider has an ATM presence but not an MPLS PE node.

One of the characteristics of ATM is to break IP frames into 48-byte cell payloads and an additional 5 bytes that comprise ATM headers. A 64-byte packet requires two cells to transport, which is 106 bytes and, therefore, 1.6 times the original bandwidth. Cell padding can add wasteful overhead if the MLP LFI fragment sizes are not optimally selected.

The effect to the access design is when a dedicated circuit in the existing hub-and-spoke network is replaced with an ATM link to access the MPLS network. Thus, the bandwidth needs to be increased to achieve the equivalent performance.

The ATM link should be limited to a single PVC configured as VBR, and the CE router should be configured to shape the traffic to the sustainable cell rate (SCR) of the PVC.

CAUTION   Overprovisioning the SCR of the CE router results in cell loss and poor link performance and is not recommended.

If the ATM link is a low-speed link and VoIP is deployed, MLP LFI should be configured to fragment large data packets and reduce latency and jitter for VoIP packets. ATM (AAL5) cannot support interleaving (that is, when all cells arrive in order), whereas a method of fragmentation and interleaving is required on slow-speed (< 768 kbps) links to reduce serialization delays for VoIP. Therefore, MLPoATM can offer a solution, because MLP supports MLP LFI and can be deployed over another Layer 3 protocol, such as ATM and Frame Relay. An alternative solution is ATM PVC bundling, where voice and data are assigned dedicated PVCs. (Although the second alternative is technically suboptimal, it may be economically attractive.)

Although some service providers have developed designs using a PVC for access to the subscriber VPN and a separate PVC for access to an "Internet VPN," the approach recommended in this chapter is to use a single PVC on the CE-to-PE ATM link. This is especially important in designs with latency-sensitive applications, such as voice and video, and in hardware with a single output queue.

Frame Relay PVC from CE to PE

Some service providers use Frame Relay to supplement access to the MPLS core in a manner similar to ATM.

Although the overhead requirements imposed by Frame Relay are less than ATM, additional bandwidth may still be required (versus IP over a dedicated circuit). Frame Relay frames are variable-length (not fixed, as in ATM cells). An additional 6 or 7 bytes of Frame Relay headers are added to each IP packet for transmission across the link. The size of the IP packets varies, so the additional bandwidth required for Frame Relay headers also varies.

As with ATM, a single PVC is recommended with traffic shaped at the CE router to the CIR of the Frame Relay PVC.

CAUTION Overprovisioning of the CIR in the CE router results in frame loss and poor link performance and is not recommended.

If the Frame Relay link is a low-speed link, and VoIP is deployed, we recommend using FRF.12. FRF.12 can fragment large data packets and reduce latency and jitter for VoIP packets. However, if the option exists to change the media type from Frame Relay, we recommend using MLP.

Metro Ethernet

Metro Ethernet can be described in several constructs, such as point-to-point or multipoint-to-multipoint.

Ethernet single point-to-point connectivity provides a single, port-based Ethernet connection between two physical data ports provided across an MPLS network that is the foundation for Virtual Private Wire Service (VPWS). The port may operate in a direct Ethernet Advanced Research Projects Agency (ARPA) encapsulation mode or in an 802.1Q encapsulation format, but all traffic entering that physical port is transported to a remote end without alteration. Generally, such a design is used with a Layer 3 customer network, where the typical WAN serial links are replaced with higher-speed point-to-point facilities. Alternatively, the customer network may comprise a Layer 2 domain where the customer wants to interconnect various LAN islands into a larger whole using the service provider's Layer 2 services. In either case, the Layer 2 VPN network is a transport for customer frames in a similar manner as a set of dedicated links.

Multiple Ethernet point-to-point connectivity builds on the previous scenario by allowing for subinterface (VLAN)-based point-to-point connections across the WAN cloud. VLANs defined on the physical port may be switched to different destination endpoints in this model. Typically, the customer network is a Layer 3 entity and the customer is seeking a service from the service provider analogous to a traditional Frame Relay or ATM offering.

Although efforts are under way in various vendor communities and standards bodies to provide multipoint mesh Layer 2 VPN connectivity, these mechanisms are not yet generally available. The previous two scenarios simply provide one or more point-to-point connections to allow for the desired degree of network meshing. In the future, this meshing (or bridging) will use the service provider network resources to provide true multipoint connectivity. That is, from the CE's perspective, a single connection into the service provider network will have the appearance of a LAN interconnect (or bridged interconnect) to some or all of the customer's other CE gear. This approach is frequently called TLS, which is the foundation for Virtual Private LAN Service (VPLS).

VPLS is a VPN technology that enables Ethernet multipoint services (EMSs) over a packet-switched network infrastructure. VPN users get an emulated LAN segment that offers a Layer 2 broadcast domain. The end user perceives the service as a virtual private Ethernet switch that forwards frames to their respective destinations within the VPN. Ethernet is the technology of choice for LANs because of its relative low cost and simplicity. Ethernet has also gained recent popularity as a MAN (or metro) technology.

A multipoint technology allows a user to reach multiple destinations through a single physical or logical connection. This requires the network to make a forwarding decision based on the packet's destination. Within the context of VPLS, this means that the network makes a forwarding decision based on the destination MAC address of the Ethernet frame. A multipoint service is attractive because fewer connections are required to achieve full connectivity between multiple points. An equivalent level of connectivity based on a point-to-point technology requires a much larger number of connections or the use of suboptimal packet forwarding. In its simplest form, a VPLS consists of several sites connected to PE devices implementing the emulated LAN service. These PE devices make the forwarding decisions between sites and encapsulate the Ethernet frames across a packet-switched network using a virtual circuit or pseudowire. A virtual switching instance (VSI) is used at each PE to implement the forwarding decisions of each VPLS. The PEs use a full mesh of Ethernet-emulated circuits (or pseudowires) to forward the Ethernet frames between PEs.

VPLS uses a Layer 2 architecture to offer multipoint Ethernet VPNs that connect multiple sites over a MAN or WAN. Other technologies also enable Ethernet across the WAN, including Ethernet over MPLS, Ethernet over Layer 2 Tunneling Protocol version 3 (L2TPv3), Ethernet over SONET/SDH, and Ethernet bridging over Any Transport over MPLS (AToM). Even though most VPLS sites are expected to connect via Ethernet, they may connect using other Layer 2 technologies (ATM, Frame Relay, or PPP, for example). Sites connecting with non-Ethernet links exchange packets with the PE using a bridged encapsulation. The configuration requirements on the CE device are similar to the requirements for Ethernet interworking in point-to-point Layer 2 services.

VPWS makes integrating existing Layer 2 and Layer 3 services possible on a point-to-point basis across a service provider's IP/MPLS network. Implementation examples include

AToM and L2TPv3. Both AToM and L2TPv3 support the transport of Frame Relay, ATM, HDLC, and Ethernet traffic over an IP/MPLS core.

The key attribute with VPLS and VPWS is the concept of an Ethernet virtual circuit (EVC). VPLS and VPWS constructs may be summarized as port-based and VLAN-based. The port-based example is point-to-point for deployment of an Ethernet wire service (EWS), which is deployed with a private line replacement via a router or a bridge. A point-to-point Ethernet service may interconnect with ATM and Frame Relay. Another port-based example is multipoint-to-multipoint for an EMS, where each location acts as if it is connecting to a switch. Ethernet Relay Service (ERS) is an example of a VLAN-based construct where you could have multiple EVCs per port. This service may be used as a Frame Relay replacement, where an EVC is similar to a Frame Relay PVC in function. Ethernet Relay Multipoint Services (ERMS) is another example of a VLAN-based construct for multiple EVCs per port. Finally, at Layer 1, there is the concept of Ethernet private line, such as over SONET/SDH. Together, these service types comprise the Metro Ethernet architecture.

QoS Requirements

The service requirements or the QoS guarantee provided by the network are the terms of the network's performance. Bandwidth, packet delay, jitter, and packet loss are some common measures used to characterize a network's performance. The QoS requirements vary depending on the applications' requirements. For VoIP or IP Telephony, packet delay, jitter, and packet loss are important. For applications that involve bulk data transfer, bandwidth is a QoS requirement. Additionally, for bulk data, the requirement is to constrain bandwidth (that is, not to permit a few TCP sessions to adversely dominate a link to the detriment of interactive applications).

Bandwidth

Bandwidth describes the throughput of a given medium, protocol, or connection. It describes the size of the pipe that is required for the application to communicate over the network. An application requiring guaranteed bandwidth wants the network to allocate a minimum bandwidth specifically for it on all the links through which the application's data is transferred through the network. Depending on the type of network, the bandwidth guarantee can be provided at the IP layer or the data link layer. Guaranteed bandwidth at the IP layer depends on the type of data-link network. Not all data-link networks support guaranteed bandwidth when several IP connections share the same data link network.

Packet Delay and Jitter

Packet delay or latency at each hop consists of the following:

- **Serialization or transmission delay**—How long it takes a device to send the packet at the output rate. This depends on the packet's size and the link bandwidth. A 64-byte packet on 4-Mbps line takes 128 μs to be transmitted. The same 64-byte packet on a 128-kbps line takes 4 ms to be transmitted.

- **Propagation delay**—How long it takes a bit to be transmitted by the transmitter and to be received by the receiver. This is a function of the media and the distance and is independent of the bandwidth.

- **Switching delay**—How long it takes a device to start transmitting a packet after it receives the packet. This depends on the network's status and the number of packets in transit at this hop.

End-to-end delay for a packet belonging to a flow is the sum of all these types of delays experienced at each hop. Not all packets in a flow will experience the same delay. It depends on the transient delay in each hop in the network. If the network is congested, queues are built at each hop, and this increases the end-to-end delay. This variation is in the delay and is called jitter.

Queuing mechanisms at each node can be used to ensure that the delay of certain flows is minimized and that the delay jitter has an upper bound, which is a defined binding of a degree of variation, as in delay and jitter.

Packet Loss

Packet loss specifies how many packets are lost in the network during transmission. Packet loss can be caused by corruption in the transmission medium, or packets can be dropped at congestion points in network due to lack of buffer space in the incoming or outgoing interface. Packet loss caused by drops should be rare for a well-designed network that is correctly subscribed or undersubscribed. Packet loss caused by faulty transmission media can be avoided by building good physical networks.

NOTE   Packet loss during noncongestion is a function of network availability, such as designing a network to be highly available. (Five-nines is a target, meaning that the network has less than 5 minutes downtime/drops per year.) The loss due to congestion is inherent with networks that are based on oversubscription and speed mismatches. QoS design scope addresses loss caused by congestion via congestion-avoidance mechanisms.

Enterprise Loss, Latency, and Jitter Requirements

VoIP and video applications are sensitive to delay and jitter. Delay is the amount of time taken by the IP network to deliver the packet from the source to the destination. Jitter is the variation in the delay. Unlike traditional IP-based applications that depended on best-effort services, VoIP applications have strict delay and jitter requirements. Packets from these applications must be delivered to the destination with a finite delay (about 150 ms). Videoconferencing has a built-in VoIP component (typically G.711) and therefore has the same delay and jitter requirements as traditional VoIP. Note that the 150-ms end-to-end target is an ITU-T specification, G.114. VoIP and videoconferencing require guaranteed end-to-end bandwidth, meaning that at any time, the IP network can guarantee a minimum throughput (measured in kbps) from the source to the destination. In the world of data communication, the need for communication is to access data or to exchange data. Data may be located in a central location or may be located in several locations. Depending on the nature of the data and the type of applications that require the data, the QoS requirements of the data communication can vary.

Traditionally, IP networks have provided best-effort service. Best-effort means that the packet may eventually be delivered to the destination. There is no guarantee that the packet will be delivered within a given time period or even be delivered at all. However, there is an implied "good-faith" guarantee that best-effort traffic will be delivered. IP provided the means for delivering data from a source to one or multiple destinations. The Internet is a classic example of this type of IP network. The transport layer (TCP) provided QoS such as the following:

- Guaranteed delivery in case of packet loss (retransmission)
- Delivery of packets in the correct order (reordering of packets)
- End-to-end flow control in case of congestion in the end systems or in the service provider network

In addition to best-effort, some of the additional requirements are as follows:

- Delivery on time (low latency)
- Delivery of packets with minimum loss (low loss)
- Delivery of a minimum number of packets in a given time period (guaranteed bandwidth)
- Data security

The first two requirements can be fulfilled using the transport layer (TCP), but the other requirements depend on IP and the lower layers used by IP to deliver packets. Delay is how long it takes the packet to reach the destination. Delay variation refers to the difference in delay for each packet that is delivered to the same destination. Packet loss means that not all packets are delivered to the destination.

Delay depends on the queuing mechanisms IP uses to deliver packets when there is congestion on the network. It is possible to compute the minimum delay to deliver a packet from the source and destination based on the information about the physical media and Layer 2 services and the delays in the intermediate nodes in the network. However, congestion in the network can result in additional delays in the intermediate nodes and can increase the end-to-end delay.

NOTE   End-to-end delay is how long it takes the packet to be delivered from the source to the destination. It also includes the time taken to retransmit the packet if the packet gets lost in an intermediate node. Several factors affect delay, such as fixed packetization, fixed propagation, variable serialization, and variable queuing.

Some of the reasons for packet loss are faults that occur at Layer 2, faults that occur at Layer 1, and network congestion. Network congestion can occur because of lack of resources such as memory to buffer incoming packets, and also when the sum of bandwidth for all the incoming interfaces exceeds the bandwidth of the outgoing interface. IP depends on the QoS offered by the lower layers in providing this QoS to the application layer services. Overall, you can expect network congestion due to natural oversubscription that is integrated into networks, such as speed mismatches.

QoS at Layer 2

Depending on the QoS requirements, QoS functions are available at the data link layer (Layer 2) and network layer (Layer 3) of the Open System Interconnection (OSI) reference model. Guaranteed bandwidth as a QoS requirement can be provided by several Layer 2 technologies, such as Frame Relay and ATM, when the physical medium is shared simultaneously by several Layer 3 connections. ATM can also meet other QoS requirements, such as delay and jitter. Furthermore, guaranteed bandwidth can be provisioned on Layer 2 protocols via InterServ QoS, such as Resource Reservation Protocol (RSVP). DiffServ does not provide explicit bandwidth guarantees, but rather per-hop behavior constructs. Layer 2 protocols in themselves do not provide bandwidth guarantees. For example, it is possible to oversubscribe both Frame Relay and ATM and cause drops.

QoS is an important aspect of any IP service offering. QoS helps define an important component of the SLA—packet delivery. When it comes to delivery of business-critical traffic, in most cases, best-effort delivery is no longer sufficient. Many applications require bandwidth guarantees, and some of them also require delay and jitter guarantees. Any service delivered with Layer 3 must also be able to deliver QoS to meet the needs of business-critical applications. Applications such as voice and video have stringent requirements with respect to jitter and packet loss. These days, highly efficient codecs can mask some delay and jitter with appropriate buffering, encoding, and decoding techniques. Nevertheless, despite these efficient codes, bandwidth, delay, and jitter guarantees are still needed from the network for better quality of experience (QoE). Because a large number of enterprises and services are considering IP/MPLS for network convergence, the expectations for an IP/MPLS network are very high. Many times, we have seen a comparison between a Frame Relay or ATM network and Frame Relay or ATM QoS. Enterprises are used to the bandwidth models of Frame Relay committed information rate (CIR) and ATM constant bit rate (CBR) (also called guaranteed bit rate service). They use these commonly as access circuits into the provider network, even for IP access. They have an expectation of peak and sustained information rate based on the connection-oriented nature of Frame Relay or the ATM network.

The QoS delivered by the subscriber network results from the network design. In migrating to an MPLS VPN, problems in the design of the subscriber network are more likely to affect QoS than issues in the service provider backbone.

SLAs are contracts with the service provider guaranteeing the level of service the VPN core will deliver. Effective SLAs include quantifiable measurements of service levels and remediation requirements.

The subscriber network design and the backbone SLA are tightly coupled in a subscriber MPLS VPN. In legacy networks based on dedicated circuits or permanent virtual circuits (PVCs), QoS and SLAs by definition were designed and enforced on a site-to-site basis. In an MPLS VPN, the link from each site to the core contracts QoS individually. Mismatches in the traffic load may cause unacceptable performance in the subscriber network, while the core is meeting all the QoS requirements.

The full mesh of PVCs, and sometimes multiple PVCs for differing levels of QoS in the existing subscriber network, is replaced with a single link at each site. With bandwidth dynamically shared across all classes of service (CoSs), efficiency and economy are optimized in the subscriber network. Frequently, MPLS VPNs perform so well that attention to network design gradually diminishes. Migrating or adding new sites is reduced to ordering a new link with the same characteristics as existing sites.

Designing and maintaining the QoS in a subscriber MPLS VPN requires understanding the volume, characteristics, and patterns of each of the traffic load classes, as well as vigilance in expanding the network for additional applications.

IP QoS implementation can be divided into the following categories:

- **Classification**—The use of Differentiated Services Code Point (DSCP) or the first 6 bits of the Type of Service (ToS) field classifies traffic based on customer requirements. As soon as the packets are properly classified, they can be accordingly handled by other QoS mechanisms, such as congestion management and policing and congestion avoidance to properly implement end-to-end QoS requirements. Packet classification typically is done on the edge of the network. Sometimes, packets are reclassified in the core network by remarking certain fields in the packet. This reclassification is required when traffic is aggregated. However, the network must ensure that the original value of the DSCP field in the IP packet is restored at the edge of the network when the packet is delivered to the customer. This can be done in an MPLS network because two fields are available.

- **Congestion management**—This involves creating queues, assigning packets to the proper queues, and scheduling the queues and the packets within the queues. The number of queues depends on the customer requirements and the number of CoSs offered by the network. Assigning packets to queues and scheduling policies depend on the type of QoS services offered to the customer. For example, high-priority traffic such as VoIP requires preemptive queue mechanisms that ensure that VoIP packets are scheduled and transmitted before other packets. RFC 3246 describes this mechanism in detail.

- **Congestion avoidance techniques**—Congestion avoidance is achieved by dropping the packets. Which packets have to be dropped are determined based on the drop policy. Congestion avoidance mechanisms are activated when congestion is detected (that is, to the point when congestion buffers reach capacity). Congestion avoidance techniques do not ensure that the network is congestion-free; rather, they obviate TCP slow-starts and TCP synchronization by randomly dropping packets when queuing buffers fill. Each queue has Weighted Random Early Detection (WRED) thresholds. Drops commence when these thresholds are exceeded. If substantial traffic is offered to a queue with a guaranteed bandwidth via class-based weighted fair queuing (CBWFQ), for example, it could trigger WRED drops before the WRED threshold is exceeded on the best-effort queue. Each WRED mechanism is queue-dependent and therefore is independent of other queues.

- **Policing and shaping mechanisms**—These mechanisms ensure that each CoS (based on the marked IP packet) adheres to the service contract. The service contract can include several issues, such as bandwidth, burst size, and delay. A policer typically drops or remarks out-of-contract traffic, and a shaper delays excess traffic.

- **QoS signaling**—This is used between nodes in the network to signal the QoS requirements of each class and also to reserve resources. RSVP is a QoS signaling protocol that can be used to reserve resources such as bandwidth. QoS signaling mechanisms also depend on the routing protocols to determine the best path between the source and the destination.

Implementing QoS in an IP network is a challenging task. It requires a good understanding of queuing theory and the customers' requirements to determine the parameters for the queuing policies. Some of the challenges are communication between the signaling plane (QoS signaling protocols, such as RSVP) and the data-forwarding plane (congestion in network) to ensure that resource reservation for an application can be done correctly. For example, RSVP uses bandwidth as the resource to do reservation. In addition to bandwidth, other network resources, such as queue buffers on the network devices, are also important resources that are required to guarantee QoS. Congestion in the network device due to lack of queue buffers must be communicated to RSVP so that it can use alternative paths (between the source and destination) that have enough network resources (bandwidth, queue buffers, and so on) to meet the QoS requirements of the application making the RSVP request.

Subscriber Network QoS Design

Designing the subscriber MPLS VPN usually starts with understanding the fundamental characteristics of the existing subscriber network. Baselining the current network provides a starting point for requirements for migrating to Layer 3 VPN. Baselining the network and applications is discussed in the next few sections.

Baselining involves measuring and profiling the volume and type of traffic on the network. Network traffic is divided into classes based on a number of characteristics:

- **Real-time traffic**—Traffic highly sensitive to delay and delay variation, such as IP telephony and VoIP.

- **Delay-sensitive business traffic**—Interactive and transactional traffic highly sensitive to delays. Transactional traffic may involve several request-response round trips in a single transaction. A small increase in delay is multiplied several times in each transaction. Applications using transactional databases frequently are included in this category.

- **Non-delay-sensitive business traffic**—Critical applications that tolerate variations in delay and occasional packet loss. This is the normal class for most business applications.

- **Bulk background traffic**—Traffic with a higher tolerance of delay and packet loss and non-business-critical traffic. E-mail, FTP, and similar traffic are frequently included in this category.

Some network baselines provide finer resolution (more categories) of traffic. At a minimum, traffic should be profiled based on the preceding categories. The traffic profile should then be further analyzed to find the volume based on source and destination for each class. Any areas of the network with excessive delay, packet loss, or high utilization should also be noted.

Baseline New Applications

In most cases, completing the migration of existing applications to the MPLS VPN before implementing new applications is recommended.

In some situations, adding new applications during the migration is unavoidable. Baselines should be established for new applications comparable to the baseline for the existing network applications.

Develop the Network

The information previously gathered provides the starting point for the network design.

Some traffic patterns are apparent immediately. For example, e-mail host locations and hosts with other business applications that are frequently accessed present clear patterns.

Comparing the traffic matrix with bandwidth utilization between locations highlights problem areas and anomalies in routing and other areas of the network.

In developing the subscriber network design, the critical information to recognize is the peak traffic per class for each source and destination pair, and the relationship between the peak hours for the various traffic classes.

The CE-to-PE link bandwidth for a given location is based on the peak traffic and the subscriber policy for noncritical traffic classes. In some locations, multiple applications reach individual peaks concurrently. For example, many people check voice mail and e-mail in the morning. IP telephony is a real-time CoS, whereas e-mail is frequently considered batch traffic. CE-to-PE link bandwidth may also be affected by the underlying technology used for the access link.

After you determine the bandwidth for the subscriber CE-to-PE link, the QoS policy for managing traffic on the link needs to be determined. The QoS policy determines the allocation of traffic to classes, and the treatment of the traffic in each of the classes, under congested conditions. QoS policy has no effect in uncongested conditions. The QoS policy involves marking, policing, fragmentation, interleaving, and compression functions (to name a few), all of which are active policies with or without congestion.

The four classes described for profiling the existing network are frequently defined as classes for the QoS policy. Networks without VoIP or IP telephony may define as few as three traffic classes. If the enterprise has the business objective of supporting VoIP, only then is a three-class model sufficient. However, if an enterprise has many applications with unique service-level requirements, applying unique classes of service (up to 11, for example) may be appropriate. Ultimately, business requirements dictate the CoS implementation model.

After determining the required traffic classes, handling of each class is defined based on the traffic characteristics. If either VoIP or IP telephony traffic is supported, low-latency queuing (LLQ) is recommended. LLQ provides a priority queue that is serviced exhaustively before other queues are serviced. A bandwidth limit can be configured for the LLQ to prevent starvation of other queues. A bandwidth limit (enforced via an implicit policer) is always present with LLQ. Other queues are serviced based on the CBWFQ policy defined. Unless otherwise specified, taildrop is used to discard packets in excess of the bandwidth assigned to the class under congested conditions.

If VoIP or IP telephony traffic is not supported, modular QoS CLI (MQC)-based LLQ is recommended for defining QoS policy for the allocation and treatment of traffic classes under congested conditions.

Each traffic class is marked based on the QoS policy. DSCP specifies how traffic is handled in the service provider network.

Most service provider networks recognize four levels of service at a minimum. The levels are usually divided along the lines of the traffic classes recommended for baselining the network. The premium CoS is usually reserved for LLQ ToS and is recommended for voice applications. The larger packet sizes associated with video applications generally are better suited to the second CoS.

The IP Precedence or DSCP bits are mapped to the experimental field of the MPLS label at the PE router. The experimental field is a 3-bit field, allowing a maximum of eight levels of service to be supported in an MPLS VPN core network. Although the field is 3 bits, most service providers support a maximum of four levels of service.

NOTE   Three bits (offering eight levels) lets EXP bits indicate whether traffic for a class is within or out of contract (two states per class equals eight values).

QoS has a significant role in the enterprise network when it comes to offering network services. With the advent of applications, such as videoconferencing and VoIP, it becomes essential to ensure that the network can offer services such as end-to-end bounded delay and guaranteed bandwidth to end-user applications. Without these sorts of QoS features, it can't meet the requirements of these applications without compromising the quality of the video or the voice services.

With QoS in place, the enterprise network can assure its users that its network can meet the requirements of the user applications. This also helps the enterprise distinguish between different types of users: one set of users who require services with a certain guarantee (such as end-to-end delay or bandwidth), and others who are satisfied with best-effort services. This distinction between types of users also helps the enterprise charge these users (for network services) based on their requirements.

Security Requirements

In any network, security considerations devolve into essentially two types of issues. Compromises are either accidental; occur through misconfigurations, growth, or unanticipated changes in the network; or deliberate attacks by some entity bent on causing havoc. The risk vectors are either external issues (driven by events external to the network in question) or internal problems (which are sourced from within the network itself). Additionally, most security-related problems fall into the categories of denial of service (DoS) or intrusion. DoS events may be intentional or accidental, whereas intrusion issues by definition are intentional. It is essential to harden the network components and the system as a whole to minimize the likelihood of any of the preceding scenarios. However, as with all resource-consuming features, a balance must be struck between maximizing security and offering the performance and usability that the service is intended to provide. Clearly, a wholly disconnected host or router has total security; however, its ability to forward data or provide services is substantially compromised.

The state of the network from an availability and security viewpoint may also differ with respect to the perspective of the interested party. That is, the concerns of the service provider and the customer are an intersecting, but not completely overlapping, set of needs. Indeed, the two parties might have different perspectives on the network's current status.

Topological and Network Design Considerations

Clearly, the type of physical network selected to interconnect the CE and PE offers differing levels of resilience to intrusion and redirection. A serial point-to-point facility is very difficult to subvert, and intrusions usually are quite noticeable. When a serial connection of this nature is interrupted, alarms are raised very quickly, and the two endpoints are difficult to masquerade.

PVC-based networks, such as Frame Relay and ATM, are somewhat less resistant because they generally are controlled by software-based virtual circuit switching and can be readily misswitched or duplicated. However, even these facilities typically use a serial point-to-point connection between the CE and the telco central office, making intrusion difficult outside the telco realm.

Ethernet-based facilities are most readily compromised in that it is relatively easy to insert a promiscuous monitoring device somewhere in the path.

NOTE   The physical links from the CE to the central office remain directly cabled. Consequently, intrusion still generally requires telco access.

Of course, it is possible to insert equipment into these physical plants, but the level of expertise required to identify the correct facility, access the physical structures, and unobtrusively insert illicit systems is very high and is not readily performed by any but a determined and well-funded attacker.

The more significant issues with shared physical interface accesses (PVC-based or VLAN-based) would be managing the offered traffic loads so that one VPN cannot affect the operational characteristics of other VPNs being terminated on the same port. To guarantee the performance of the VPNs per SLA agreements, it is necessary to either provision much greater bandwidth on the access port than the expected load or to manage the bandwidth available using policing and shaping mechanisms.

Typically, this is done by offering a limited set of performance options (say, four or five classes) to the customers when they request the service. Policing controls are then applied to the interfaces based on these predefined classes of service to meet the customer's expectations. In an unmanaged VPN where different entities control the CE and PE, and consequently, neither can be guaranteed to stay within the expected operational characteristics, these controls need to be applied to both routers to ensure that offered loads do not affect the applicable networks.

In general, MPLS/VPN implementations may be characterized in five sets, which present differing requirements with respect to the CE-PE arrangements.

SP-Managed VPNs

In the SP-managed VPN, the service provider's control extends all the way out to the point of presence within the customer's Interior Gateway Protocol (IGP).

As such, the service provider has full control of the CE configuration, including the following:

- Access to the router itself
- Interaction with the rest of the customers' IGP
- Interaction with the service provider's PE routing mechanism
- Openness to customer statistics gathering
- Management requirements specific to the service provider's operation

This model gives the service provider the greatest degree of control over the potential impact on the customers' operations on the service provider's network itself. It also offers greater control over issues that may affect other service provider customer VPNs.

In converse, this arrangement implies some degree of trust on the part of the customer:

- The customer allows another company (the service provider) to have access to its IGP.
- The customer trusts the service provider to map its network communications solely to endpoints approved by the customer.
- The customer assumes that the service provider will provide the majority of fault analysis and resolution activity (because its own access is somewhat limited).

The challenge presented in migrating from the existing network infrastructure to an MPLS VPN is to capture all the requirements accomplished as a result of the Layer 2 network infrastructure within the Layer 3 VPN model.

Unmanaged VPNs are distinguished by the notion that the CE router is owned and controlled by the customer. Although the term "unmanaged VPN" is, strictly speaking, a misnomer (and perhaps indicative of a more service provider-centric perspective), it is widely accepted to mean a network where the customer rather than the service provider manages the CE router. In this scenario, the demarcation point between the service provider and the customer is usually the data set at the customer premises. (But, it is quite possible that the communication facility provider may not in fact be the Layer 3 MPLS VPN provider.) The customer has full control over the configuration of the CE router and interacts with the service provider's network over some mutually agreed-on arrangement between the service provider and the customer.

In this situation, the service provider's network operation might be exposed to the customer's configurations of the CE router. As such, the service provider needs to take additional steps to ensure that its network operations are not disturbed by changes in the customers' network environment or CE router setups.

However, this operative mode may be more palatable to customers who want to maintain the following:

- Complete control over their IGP
- Additional fault analysis/troubleshooting information access
- Minimized exposure of their network to the service provider
- The ability to manage their Layer 2 and Layer 3 exposures to the service provider

From the service provider's perspective, the unmanaged VPN environment changes the span of control significantly. This approach affects the service provider in a number of ways:

- Need to protect Layer 3 interconnect between the CE and PE
- Possible need to protect the Layer 2 interconnect (if shared)
- Requirement for clear definition of SLA-affecting responsibilities due to changes in span of control and the need to closely interact with the customer in the event of problems
- Additional level of security awareness at the PE router because the CE is no longer under its explicit control

Multiprovider Considerations

Most enterprise requirements are within the scope of a single MPLS VPN service provider. However, some circumstances require multiple regional MPLS VPNs. For example, a large multinational corporation may require high densities of service in North America, Europe, and the Asia Pacific regions. Based on either cost or density, it may be decided that more than one service provider is required.

In the best case, the service providers support an interconnection with appropriate routing and QoS, and the result is offered to the subscriber as a single seamless solution.

In the more likely case, the subscriber network is required to interconnect to both (or multiple) service providers. Designing the interconnection of subscriber VPNs is greatly simplified by limiting the interconnection between any two VPNs to a single location.

Within a subscriber VPN, all CE routers appear to be only one hop away from all other CE routers. If subscriber VPN A touches subscriber VPN B at more than one location, routing metrics are required to determine which gateway should be used for which locations. Difficulties in advertising routing metrics in the CE-to-PE routing protocols cause additional complexities in this design.

The following example illustrates the situation just described: LargeCo is a multinational corporation with many locations in Europe and North America. For density and economy, LargeCo selects service provider Eurcom to provide MPLS VPN services to sites in Europe and Northcom to provide MPLS VPN services to sites in North America. LargeCo wants two interconnections between the subscriber networks for redundancy. One interconnection will be between Paris and New York, and a second connection will be between London and Washington, D.C. Because all sites in each VPN appear to be only one hop away, all sites are advertised through both gateways at equal cost, causing routing problems.

Resolving this problem requires one of the following:

* A limitation to a single interconnection
* Routing metrics to be adjusted to reflect costs for VPN paths

Subscriber routing metrics are passed through the MPLS VPN without modification. The MPLS label-switched path (LSP) nodes are not reflected in the routing path metrics. Routing metrics may require adjustment to reflect appropriate costs and provide appropriate routing. This approach requires a highly detailed understanding of routing protocols and the network topology.

Extranets

For the purposes of this section, extranets are defined as the intersection of the subscriber network with networks outside the subscriber network that have been merged into the subscriber VPN.

Extranets are very useful to meet specific communications requirements. For example, large corporations (such as Acme) with many subsidiaries frequently view MPLS networks as an opportunity to take advantage of economy of scale. By combining their network purchasing power into a single network with a single service provider, companies can realize significant savings. The parent corporation gains economy of scale in contracting with the service provider, and each of the subsidiaries retains autonomy over its own VPN.

Although each subsidiary is autonomous, they all have requirements to communicate with the parent corporation and, to a lesser degree, with other subsidiaries. Extranets enable this communication with no additional infrastructure requirements for any of the subsidiaries. Acquisitions and mergers can also be integrated into the corporate communications infrastructure initially through extranets. Over time they can be migrated to the appropriate industry subsidiary VPN or retain their own VPN.

A more limited application of extranets is enabling e-commerce by interconnecting suppliers, vendors, and customers for electronic exchange of ordering, billing, and other supply-chain transactions.

Extranets in Layer 3 require security design considerations similar to extranets in an existing network. An extranet connection between a supplier and a customer in an existing network would be "fenced in" with firewalls and other security measures to ensure that access is limited to the hosts and applications required by the partner for business transactions.

Although extranet access is limited by the extranet Layer 3 VPN routing construct, similar security precautions are required in a Layer 3 extranet. Firewalls and security measures are required to isolate the hosts and applications and to limit the business partner's access.

Case Study: Analyzing Service Requirements for Acme, Inc.

Acme has decided to look at an enterprise case as a reference that has already migrated from Layer 2 to Layer 3 to analyze the service requirements further.

This case study evaluates MPLS network service providers and the issues faced by an enterprise customer in transitioning from a circuit- and Layer 2-based network to a service provider MPLS network. It is based on the experiences of a large enterprise customer in the aerospace and defense industries.

The purpose of the case study is to provide a template for other enterprise customers facing similar evaluations and to provide insight into implementation issues that came to light during the transition phase.

A secondary goal is to allow service providers to better understand the criteria that enterprise customers typically use when evaluating an MPLS network. DefenseCo Inc. has a large national and international network in place, consisting of more than 300 sites in more than 25 countries. The core of the network is a combination of Layer 2 technologies. Within the U.S. the majority of the network is Switched Multimegabit Data Service (SMDS)-based, with smaller segments based on ATM and Frame Relay.

DefenseCo distributed a request for proposal (RFP) to 15 network service providers. The responses to the RFP were evaluated, and three service providers were selected to be tested during the technical evaluation. DefenseCo's primary goal is to replace the SMDS network, which will expire in 18 months. Secondary goals include moving video from ISDN to the MPLS network, reducing network costs, and improving the network return on investment (ROI).

Layer 2 Description

DefenseCo's current network is composed of Cisco routers, including 2600s, 3600s, 7200s, and 7500s in various configurations. Major hubs within the U.S. are in a full-mesh configuration. SMDS is provided by the current service provider between hub nodes. Branch offices are connected to hubs by Frame Relay in a hub-and-spoke configuration. Certain sections of the network have an ATM backbone, resulting from the integration of acquisitions, and are used for other special requirements. The current network provides data transport between all sites but does not provide voice or video capabilities.

Existing Customer Characteristics That Are Required in the New Network

DefenseCo's backbone is essentially a fully meshed backbone between all major hubs. Because of the nature of SMDS, routing in the backbone can be influenced by configuring paths between hubs. SMDS constructs a Layer 2 network that determines the neighbors at Layer 3. In a number of instances, DefenseCo uses this capability to segment parts of the network or to provide special routing in areas of the network. Layer 3 routing within the DefenseCo backbone is based on Enhanced Interior Gateway Routing Protocol (EIGRP) and uses private addressing. One instance requiring special routing is Internet access. DefenseCo's backbone has three Internet access points in three different regions.

Because of the fully meshed nature of the SMDS backbone, remote sites are always within one hop of the nearest Internet access point. A specific default route in the remote site configuration points to the nearest Internet access point. Internet access points in the DefenseCo backbone translate from private to public addressing and provide firewall protection between the backbone and the public Internet. The same Internet access points are retained with the MPLS backbone. However, in the MPLS network, routing distances change. In some cases, the default route points to the wrong Internet point of presence (PoP) for a remote site. The capabilities to direct traffic to a specific Internet PoP and to provide redundancy in the event of an Internet PoP failure are required in the new MPLS backbone.

Acquisitions also require special routing. DefenseCo has acquired a number of other companies, each of which has its own network and access to the Internet. In a number of cases, the IP addressing of the acquired company overlaps the address space of the DefenseCo corporate backbone. DefenseCo is in the process of integrating these network segments into the corporate backbone. Using SMDS, these network segments retain their private addressing until they are incorporated into the corporate backbone. The same capability for retaining private addressing space until segments can be incorporated into the corporate backbone must be retained.

DefenseCo's Backbone Is a Single Autonomous System

The same single autonomous system (AS) is required in the new MPLS backbone. DefenseCo's backbone has less than 100-ms round-trip delay between any two sites and very minimal jitter due to the SMDS backbone. In the MPLS backbone, both the delay and jitter characteristics must be maintained or improved for the real-time traffic class. For other traffic classes, the maximum delay parameters must be maintained. DefenseCo's requirements are as follows:

- Access to the Internet at three major points, with a need to maintain ingress and egress through these same points
- Private addressing, potentially overlapping due to acquisitions
- Single autonomous system across the MPLS backbone
- Special routing due to acquisitions
- Maximum of 100-ms round-trip delay, with minimum jitter for the real-time traffic class
- Maximum of 100-ms round-trip delay for all other traffic classes

Reasons for Migrating to MPLS

The first priority for DefenseCo was to find a replacement for the SMDS backbone.

The SMDS technology was nearing the end of the product cycle for the service provider, and DefenseCo received notice that the service would be terminated within 18 months. In evaluating replacement technologies, DefenseCo looked at several critical factors. The SMDS backbone economically provided a full-mesh configuration. With full routing updates exchanged between DefenseCo's CE routers and the MPLS service provider backbone, DefenseCo was able to economically retain a fully meshed network. Furthermore, by categorizing traffic into four levels of service, DefenseCo was able to take advantage of the benefits of QoS and at the same time gain maximum benefit by dynamically allocating the total bandwidth. The equivalent solution in an ATM or Frame Relay network would have incurred higher costs for a full mesh of PVCs and might have required multiple PVCs between sites for differing levels of QoS. Bandwidth between sites would have been limited to a static allocation configured for each of the PVCs, thus further reducing network efficiency. Ongoing operational expenses for adding and deleting sites, and keeping bandwidth allocations in balance with traffic demands, would also have increased. The total cost of ownership for the network would have increased significantly. Finally, almost all of DefenseCo's sites are equipped for videoconferencing. In the legacy network, videoconferences were set up using ISDN and a videoconference bridge. DefenseCo plans to move to H.323 videoconferencing using QoS across the MPLS backbone. Although some router upgrades are required, the cost savings of converging video with data on the MPLS backbone, compared to the current videoconferencing costs, will drive a significant ROI benefit from the network.

Evaluation Testing Phase

DefenseCo's goal in evaluating service providers was to understand, in as much detail as possible, how the service provider network would support the projected traffic load and how the network would react under various adverse conditions of failure and congestion. Each of the three service providers on the short list provided a network for evaluation. The test networks were constructed using Los Angeles, New York, and Dallas as hub cities. Each hub had a T1 connection from the service provider edge router to the CE router.

To evaluate network capabilities, DefenseCo profiled the projected traffic mix and then simulated as closely as possible real network traffic conditions. A baseline network performance was established, and then various congestion and failure conditions were simulated to determine deviation from the baseline and time to recovery after service was restored. Details on the packet size and traffic mix are included in the "Evaluation Tools" section later in this chapter.

In evaluating service provider networks, DefenseCo found two models for the MPLS backbone. In the first model, used by most of the MPLS service providers, DefenseCo provided the customer premises equipment (CPE) router that served as the CE router. In this model, DefenseCo installed, configured, and maintained the CE router. DefenseCo also was responsible for the first level of troubleshooting within the network. The service providers called this model the unmanaged service because DefenseCo was responsible for managing the CE router. Sample configurations with location-specific data were provided to DefenseCo to coordinate the configurations between the PE and CE routers. In the second model, the service provider installed and maintained the CE router. DefenseCo's interface to the network was through an Ethernet port. In this model, the service provider was responsible for all network installation, configuration, and troubleshooting. The service providers called this model the managed service because the service providers were responsible for managing both the PE and CE routers. DefenseCo preferred the first model, in which it supplied the CE router. The benefits of lower cost and greater visibility into the network, along with the ability to quickly resolve problems through DefenseCo's own IT staff, were viewed as critical factors. DefenseCo required all the sites within the network to function as a single AS.

Routing information is exchanged between the DefenseCo CE router and the service PE router using Exterior Border Gateway Protocol (eBGP). To allow DefenseCo to use a single AS for all sites, the service provider BGP configuration required the **neighbor AS-override** command to be enabled. This command allows routers to accept routing updates from EBGP peers that include routes originated in the same AS as the receiving router. Without the **neighbor AS-override** command in the PE router, these routes would be dropped. This worked well in the model with DefenseCo supplying the CE router. However, Interior Border Gateway Protocol (iBGP) and additional configuration were required in the model where the service provider supplied the CE router. The following sections provide details on the tests DefenseCo performed, an overview of the results, and some insight into DefenseCo's final vendor selection.

The results presented in this section are typical of the actual results DefenseCo encountered in the test networks. The actual test sets were run over an extended period of time and provided a more extensive set of data, including some anomalous results that required further investigation. The test results included in this section are typical for their respective tests and are derived from the actual DefenseCo data. The anomalous results have not been included. The tests were conducted over a period of 60 days. In response time tests, and other similar tests, data was collected for the entire period. Tests run under specific test conditions were run multiple times for each service provider.

Routing Convergence

DefenseCo tested convergence times to determine the expected convergence in the event of a link failure. Convergence tests were performed by examining routing tables in the CE router. One of the three sites in the test network was then disabled by disconnecting the circuit and disabling the port. The routing tables were again examined to ensure that the disabled site had been dropped from the routing table. The site was then reenabled, and the time for the route to appear in the routing table was measured. Routing convergence tests were run under both congested and uncongested conditions. All three service provider networks were found to converge within an acceptable period of time under both congested and uncongested conditions. The differences between the managed and unmanaged service models caused disparities in conducting the convergence tests. In the unmanaged service model, DefenseCo supplied the CE router. The EBGP routing protocol was used to exchange routing information between the CE and PE routers. In the managed service model, the service provider supplied the CE router. The IBGP routing protocol was used to exchange routing information between the DefenseCo network edge router and the CE router managed by the service provider. Under uncongested, best-case conditions, convergence times ranged from less than a minute to slightly less than 2 minutes. Under congested, worst-case conditions, all three service provider networks converged in less than 2 minutes. The results of this test were within acceptable limits for all three service providers. No further comparisons were considered because of the disparity in the service models.

Jitter and Delay

The first step in the delay tests involved a simple ping run between sites with the network in a quiescent state. A packet size of 64 bytes was used to keep packetization and serialization delays to a minimum and to expose any queuing or congestion delays in the service provider networks. In the existing SMDS network, the delay between Los Angeles and New York was on the order of 100 ms round trip (r/t). The delay between New York and Dallas averaged 70 ms r/t, and the delay between Dallas and Los Angeles averaged less than 60 ms r/t. These numbers were used as the maximum baseline permissible in the service provider network. The users of the current network experience these delays in interactive transactions and in batch transactions such as system backups. A small change in delay could significantly affect the time required for backing up a system and extend the backup beyond the specified window.

After establishing the minimum baseline response time, DefenseCo started a more complex set of tests that required the Cisco IP SLA to generate traffic streams that simulate VoIP and voice and video over IP streams and measure the delay and jitter of the streams under various network conditions. The packet sizes and traffic mixes for these streams, and more details on the Cisco IP SLA, are provided in the "Evaluation Tools" section. The remainder of this section examines the testing methodology and the results of the vendor networks being tested. The goal of this objective set of tests was to determine if network performance would meet the requirements for voice and video quality under heavily congested conditions.

Three test scenarios were developed to ensure that the objectives were met. The Cisco Service Assurance Agent (SAA) generates traffic in both directions—source to destination and destination to source.

In the first scenario, the IP SLA was used to establish a baseline with a typical mix of voice and video streams in an uncongested network and without QoS enabled. The IP SLA measured both delay and jitter in each direction.

In the second scenario, an additional traffic load was added to the network such that the load exceeded the capacity in the source-to-destination direction, causing congestion at the egress port. It should be noted that the port speed of the egress port was reduced to exacerbate this condition. The New York site was the destination under test. Although one network appeared to perform better than the others, none of the networks provided acceptable results under congested conditions (without QoS enabled).

In the third scenario, the networks again were tested with a baseline voice and video traffic load and an additional traffic load so that the network capacity was exceeded. The traffic load was identical in all respects to the preceding scenario. The difference in this scenario was that QoS was enabled in the networks.

Congestion, QoS, and Load Testing

QoS and load tests were designed to objectively test the service providers' networks under oversubscribed conditions. The goals of the tests were to measure the benefits of enabling QoS capabilities and to provide objective metrics for comparing the service provider networks. Test Transmission Control Protocol (TTCP) generated and measured the data streams for the objective load tests. (See the "Evaluation Tools" section for more details on TTCP.) It was established during the previous test phases that all three of the service provider networks functioned with essentially zero packet loss when tested within normal subscription parameters. Most service provider networks offer three or four CoSs. The CoS within the service provider network is determined by the amount of service a given queue receives relative to other, similar queues. For example, traffic in the silver CoS is in a higher-priority queue and receives more service than traffic in the bronze CoS, a lower-priority queue. If three CoSs are offered, they are frequently called the silver, bronze, and best-effort classes. If a fourth class is offered, the gold class, it is usually reserved for real-time traffic such as voice and video. The gold class, or real-time traffic, requires LLQ in which the queue is serviced exhaustively (within configurable limits) before other queues are serviced. The silver, bronze, and best-effort queues are serviced based on WFQ methods.

Queuing and the use of CoS to differentiate between traffic priorities are meaningful only when the network is operating under congested conditions.

First Scenario

DefenseCo's first test scenario was used to establish a baseline without QoS in an uncongested network for each of the service providers. Three TTCP streams were generated between Los Angeles and New York. As expected, none of the streams received priority queuing, and all three streams finished with a very minimal difference in transfer time. All three service provider networks performed similarly.

Second Scenario

The second test scenario tested the benefit of QoS with traffic differentiated into two CoSs between two locations. Two TTCP streams were enabled between Los Angeles and New York. QoS was enabled in the service provider networks to give one of the TTCP streams a higher priority. As expected, the TTCP stream with the higher priority finished significantly ahead of the lower-priority stream.

Third Scenario

The third test scenario introduced additional congestion at the network's egress port. To accomplish this task, the second test scenario was rerun with an additional TTCP stream generated between Dallas and New York. The total bandwidth of the three TTCP streams (two from Los Angeles to New York and one from Dallas to New York) exceeded the egress bandwidth in New York. The TTCP stream from Dallas to New York was configured as best-effort and was generated primarily to ensure that the egress port in New York would be tested under highly congested conditions and with the best-effort CoS in the traffic mix. One of the TTCP streams from Los Angles to New York was configured to be in the silver priority queue. The second stream was configured for the bronze priority queue. Although the results varied between the service provider networks, all three networks clearly demonstrated the benefits of QoS for the two streams from Los Angeles to New York.

Subjective Measures

The objective tests previously performed were designed to test the service provider networks under specific conditions of failure, congestion, and adverse conditions. In some cases, the traffic mix was selected to resemble a typical mix of voice and video traffic. In other cases, it was selected to stress the QoS environment. Traffic-generation tools were used to ensure that the tests were homogenous across service providers, to allow the tests to be set up and performed quickly, and to provide accurate measurements that could be compared between the service provider networks. The subjective tests had several purposes. Simulations of real traffic are not a perfect representation, and subtle differences may cause undetected flaws to surface. Voice and video equipment requires signaling that is not present in load simulations to set up and tear down connections. Finally, ensuring interoperability of the voice and video equipment with the service provider networks was a critical concern.

The subjective tests used actual voice and video equipment in configurations as close as possible to the anticipated production environment. IP telephony tests were implemented with a variety of equipment, including gateways and telephones, all using the G.711 codec. Video testing was based on the H.323 standard, using one Polycom Viewstation codec at each of the test locations. The video bandwidth stream was limited to 128 kbps. Each of the service provider networks was again subjected to three test scenarios.

First, the network was tested without QoS enabled and with no test traffic other than the voice and video. This test established a baseline for voice and video performance in the service provider network. In this test scenario, two of the three service provider networks performed well, with video jitter measured in the 60-ms range. The third service provider network experienced problems resulting in unacceptable video quality.

In the second test scenario, QoS was not enabled, and in addition to the voice and video traffic, the network was subjected to a heavy simulated traffic load. This test ensured that the offered load would congest the service provider network. As expected, this test scenario resulted in unacceptable video quality in all three service provider networks. Although audio quality was acceptable in one of the service provider networks, it was less than business-quality in the remaining networks. Video jitter appeared to remain constant at approximately 60 ms, but all networks experienced heavy packet losses resulting in poor quality for the Real-Time Transport Protocol (RTP) streams.

In the third test scenario, QoS was enabled, and the service provider networks were subjected to both the voice and video traffic and a heavy simulated traffic load.

This test compared the performance of voice and video in a congested network with QoS enabled to the performance established in the baseline tests. In the final test scenario, all three service provider networks demonstrated the benefits of QoS. However, there were notable differences. One service provider network performed very close to the baseline established in the uncongested network tests. Another service provider displayed a slight degradation in quality but was within acceptable levels. The final service provider network appeared to perform well but failed on multiple occasions. Without further investigation, these differences were attributed to the tuning of QoS parameters in the service provider networks and differences in the internal design of the service provider networks.

Vendor Knowledge and Technical Performance

In addition to the evaluation tests and subjective tests, DefenseCo also rated each of the service providers' technical performance. The rating for technical performance was based on the service providers' ability to make changes in their network when moving from a non-QoS configuration to one that provided QoS. It also was based on the ability to resolve problems and provide technical information when problems occurred. In rating the three service providers, DefenseCo found that one clearly exhibited superior knowledge and had more experience in working with MPLS network design. Although it was more knowledge-able and experienced, this particular service provider's backbone performance was less robust than other providers and did not fully satisfy DefenseCo's requirements. Additionally, this service provider's business model was based on providing an end-to-end managed service and did not meet DefenseCo's needs for cost-and-service flexibility. Of the two remaining service providers, one demonstrated a slightly higher level of technical expertise and was also significantly more proactive in meeting DefenseCo's requirements. Both in troubleshooting network problems and in explaining possible network solutions, this service provider was more responsive to DefenseCo's requests. In addition, this service provider's network provided an additional CoS (see the earlier section "Congestion/QoS and Load Testing" for more details) and performed slightly better for voice and video when QoS was enabled. This service provider was selected to enter contract negotiations.

Evaluation Tools

This section describes the tools DefenseCo used in evaluating the test networks. The test results presented in the previous sections were based largely on the tools described here. The Cisco IP SLA is an integral part of Cisco IOS. The IP SLA can be configured to monitor performance between two routers by sending synthesized packets and measuring jitter and delay. Synthesized packets of specified sizes are sent at measured intervals. The receiving end detects variations from the specified interval to determine deviation caused in the network. Some tests also require the network time between the routers to be tightly synchronized, based on the Network Time Protocol (NTP). NTP is required for calculating network performance metrics. The IP SLA must be enabled in the routers on both ends of the network under test.

To use the IP SLA for testing, DefenseCo first profiled the actual network traffic. Three specific streams were considered: VoIP, the audio stream from an H.323 session, and the video stream from an H.323 session.

To simulate these streams using the IP SLA, DefenseCo first monitored the actual RTP streams for voice and video over IP. After some calculations to smooth the streams and determine an average, DefenseCo determined that the following packet sizes and intervals were the most appropriate for simulating its traffic loads:

- **VoIP**—64-byte packets at 20-ms intervals
- **H.323 voice stream**—524-byte packets at 60-ms intervals
- **H.323 video stream**—1000-byte packets at 40-ms intervals

The IP SLA synthesized streams were used to produce audio and video test streams and to collect test measurements for objective test phases measuring delay and jitter outlined in this chapter. Actual audio and video test streams were used for subjective test phases. After selecting a network service provider, DefenseCo continued to use the Cisco SAA at strategic locations in the network to monitor network performance and to ensure that the service provider met the SLAs. The continued IP SLA monitoring also provides the IT staff with a troubleshooting tool for rapidly isolating problems within the enterprise area of the network.

TTCP

TTCP is a downloadable utility originally written by Mike Muuss and Terry Slattery. Muuss also authored the first implementation of ping. The TTCP program, originally developed for UNIX systems, has since been ported to Microsoft Windows as well. TTCP is a command-line sockets-based benchmarking tool for measuring TCP and User Datagram Protocol (UDP) performance between two systems. For more information on the TTCP utility, see http://www.pcausa.com/Utilities/pcattcp.htm. TTCP was used to generate TCP streams for QoS differentiation testing. Although it is recognized that under normal operating conditions QoS would frequently be applied to UDP streams, transferring the same file using multiple concurrent TTCP streams at differing levels of QoS provided a measurable way of testing and verifying QoS operation in the service provider's network.

The TTCP tests are essentially a "horse race." Multiple streams are started concurrently. Without QoS, they should finish in a fairly even "race." When QoS is introduced, the "horses" are handicapped based on the QoS parameters applied to the stream. If QoS is functioning properly, the "horses" should finish in "win," "place," and "show" order, with the "margin of victory" based on the parameter weights for each of the selected streams. DefenseCo used TTCP to first establish a baseline for the vendor network without QoS enabled. The vendor was then asked to enable QoS, and the baseline tests were rerun and the differences measured.

Lessons Learned

At the conclusion of the testing, the primary lessons learned were in the areas of "engineering for the other 10 percent" and how to handle the transition and implementation. When engineering for the other 10 percent, all large networks have a small percentage of traffic that requires special handling. In the DefenseCo network, special traffic resulted from two main categories:

- Traffic routed based on the default route (Internet destinations)
- Extranet traffic (from acquisitions and vendor network interconnections)

In the SMDS network, routing for these problems was resolved with Layer 2 solutions. Although the traffic requiring special handling was a small percentage of the overall traffic, an economical, manageable, low-maintenance solution was required.

Default route traffic was a problem because DefenseCo had multiple connections to the Internet through different Internet service providers (ISPs).

Multiple Internet connections were required to ensure redundancy to the Internet and to maintain adequate response time for users. The specific problem was how multiple default routes could be advertised into the MPLS network. The PE router would include only one default route in its routing table, and the selection would be unpredictable. Traffic from a given source might be routed to the most expensive egress to the Internet. Extranet traffic presented a different issue. Extranet routes are advertised in the DefenseCo intranet. However, because of certain contractual restrictions, not all sites within the DefenseCo intranet can use the extranet routes to the extranet site. DefenseCo sites with these restrictions are required to route to extranet sites through the Internet. A deterministic capability for different sites to take different routes to the same destination was required. To resolve special routing issues, DefenseCo solicited input from the selected service provider, Cisco, and its own engineering staff. After considering and testing several potential solutions, DefenseCo decided on a solution using one-way generic routing encapsulation (GRE) tunnels.

The Internet hub sites in the DefenseCo network act as a CE to the MPLS network and provide firewall and address translation protection for the connection to the Internet. The solution uses one-way GRE tunnels, which are configured at each remote site, pointing to one of the Internet hub site CE routers. The tunnels are initiated at the remote-site CE routers and terminate at the hub-site CE routers. Remote sites have static default routes pointing into the tunnel. The tunneled traffic is unencapsulated at the hub-site CE router and is routed to the Internet based on the hub-site default route. Return-path traffic (from the Internet) takes advantage of asymmetric routing. It is routed directly onto the MPLS backbone, not tunneled, and it follows the normal routing path to the destination IP address.

This solution has several advantages for DefenseCo. It has a minimal cost. The GRE tunnels through the MPLS backbone add very little cost to the backbone. The CE routers and the Internet hub-site routers are configured and maintained by DefenseCo. Routes can be changed or modified without contacting the service provider (as multiple MPLS VPNs would require). Finally, performance through the GRE tunnels is predictable, based on the three centralized Internet hub sites. The major disadvantage of this solution is that the GRE tunnel interface does not go down. Route flap can occur if the route to the Internet hub site is lost. The switchover to the backup tunnel requires manual intervention. Although this solution efficiently solves DefenseCo's problem with default routing, it is not an ideal solution. DefenseCo would have preferred a native MPLS solution to building GRE tunnels through the MPLS network. GRE tunnels appeared to be the best compromise. DefenseCo is actively reviewing alternatives and other special routing requirements.

Transition and Implementation Concerns and Issues

DefenseCo signed a contract with the service provider selected through the evaluation process. An aggressive transition schedule was executed. After four months, DefenseCo has transitioned approximately 25 to 30 percent of its U.S. sites from the SMDS network to the MPLS network.

During this period of aggressive installations, most problems resulted not from the MPLS network, but from lower-layer problems. Missed dates for circuit installations, faulty circuit installations, and problems at Layer 2 when Frame Relay or ATM was used for access all contributed to delays during this critical period. DefenseCo also found that the operational support from the service provider was much less reactive than the engineering team assigned during the evaluation process.

Post-Transition Results

Thus far, the MPLS network has met DefenseCo's expectations. DefenseCo is moving forward with plans to migrate and expand videoconferencing and other services on the MPLS network. In retrospect, QoS was a major focus during the evaluation phase.

Given the experience of working with the service providers, going through the evaluation, and understanding the results, the DefenseCo engineers felt that if they faced a similar evaluation today, they would allocate more time to the following areas:

- The transition from a Layer 2 network to a Layer 3 network severely limited DefenseCo's control in influencing neighbors and routing. During the transition, rapid solutions were devised for "oddball" routing situations. DefenseCo believes that more of the "oddball" routing situations should have been addressed during the evaluation period, and perhaps more optimal solutions designed.

- As an enterprise, DefenseCo had limited exposure to BGP before the transition to and implementation of the MPLS network. During the evaluation, DefenseCo determined that BGP was superior to static routes and Routing Information Protocol (RIP) in its ability to control routing. Understanding how to influence Layer 3 routing using BGP metrics while transitioning to the MPLS network introduced additional complexity during this critical period. DefenseCo believes that closer examination of this area during the evaluation phase would have been beneficial.

- The MPLS network has capabilities that exceed DefenseCo's requirements. Understanding these capabilities may lead to better-optimized and lower-cost solutions. DefenseCo believes that more focus on these areas during the evaluation may have been beneficial.

DefenseCo gained unexpected benefits from the transition in several areas:

- In the SMDS network, the core backbone architecture was almost a full-mesh environment. DefenseCo was running EIGRP.

- Given the scale of the DefenseCo network, frequent changes occurred in the backbone due to circuit failures and other outages. Requiring DefenseCo to migrate to a core distribution architecture would have been cost-prohibitive for the customer because the service provider is providing the core routers. A key lesson is to minimize IGP convergence issues in the backbone as part of the service migration strategy.

  This factor requires that the service provider understand the customer network. In the MPLS network, each CE router has only the PE router as a neighbor. BGP peering has greatly improved routing stability. The customer truly benefited from migrating to an MPLS-based solution. The underlying transport for the MPLS network is a high-speed all-optical backbone. By doing some network tuning during the transition phase, the service provider was able to significantly reduce response time and jitter and improve service well beyond the capabilities of the SMDS network.

Summary

In this chapter, you learned about the requirements that facilitate a migration from Layer 2 to Layer 3 services. These requirements range from understanding applications and bandwidth to security and enterprise segmentation for MPLS VPN service constructs. Exploring QoS implications as a basis for defining service classes also was covered. Finally, the case study captured the essential requirements and issues that are associated with a Layer 2 to Layer 3 service migration. It introduced technologies for Acme to consider, such as MPLS and routing factors that are further discussed in Chapter 4.

References

RFC 791, *Internet Protocol*

RFC 2474, *Definition of Differentiated Services*

RFC 2475, *An Architecture for Differentiated Services*

RFC 2547, *BGP/MPLS VPNs*

RFC 2597, *Assured Forwarding PHB*

RFC 2917, *A Core MPLS IP VPN Architecture*

RFC 3768, *Virtual Router Redundancy Protocol*

Cisco QoS Solution Reference Network Design
http://www.cisco.com/go/srnd

Deployment Guidelines

This chapter covers the following topics:

- Introduction to Routing for the Enterprise MPLS VPN
- Network Topology
- Addressing and Route Summarization
- Site Typifying WAN Access: Impact on Topology
- Site Typifications and Connectivity Standards Routing Between the Enterprise and the Service Provider
- Case Study: BGP and EIGRP Deployment in Acme, Inc.

CHAPTER 4

IP Routing with IP/MPLS VPNs

This chapter's objectives are to define the options and technical implementations for the various routing mechanisms available to enterprises for typical IP virtual private network (VPN) deployments. Routing is the cornerstone of every IP network. Without a properly designed IP routing schema, a network is in danger of suffering from severe stability and scaling issues.

In this chapter, you will learn about the requirements for supporting the converged world of Multiprotocol Label Switching (MPLS) VPNs and how they influence the addressing and routing policies applicable in the enterprise. The aim is to provide a deployable approach that the enterprise can use as a guideline, as well as to show you how to address these policies to the service provider. Specifically, Acme, Inc.'s foundation routing and addressing needs are covered in the case study section.

This chapter introduces the concept of routing between the customer edge (CE) and the provider edge (PE). To assist with this, we will use Acme's intranet WAN as the proof point for the basis of the MPLS VPN service.

Introduction to Routing for the Enterprise MPLS VPN

Routing is the cumulative process that discovers paths through the network toward specific destinations, comparing alternative paths and creating a table that contains IP forwarding information.

In a traditional WAN, whether it be Frame Relay, Asynchronous Transfer Mode (ATM), or leased line, the connectivity is typically built on a point-to-point basis with an Interior Gateway Protocol (IGP) or Exterior Gateway Protocol (EGP) providing the necessary routing information to destinations across the WAN.

This changes the any-to-any world of Layer 3 MPLS VPN, because the routing is carried out between the CE and PE. The PE receives from the local CE the route information of the CE connected site and provides route information to the local CE about routes available via the MPLS VPN. This can be achieved in many ways, as covered later in this chapter. These mechanisms are

- Static routing
- IGPs
- Exterior Border Gateway Protocol (eBGP)

Selecting the correct protocol is key. It largely depends on what the enterprise in question uses as its current IGP or what the service provider supports. In most cases, the common approach is to use static routing when a stub site is behind the CE. Then, the static routing information is redistributed at the PE toward the rest of the MPLS/VPN service provider network into Border Gateway Protocol (BGP) for advertisement across the multiprotocol internal BGP (iBGP) session that connects the PE routers or route reflector depending on the service provider network. The service provider will map the static route for each network at the local site, or summary route, to the correct virtual routing/forwarding (VRF) instance on the PE router that connects the site.

This approach has a drawback. Static routing can cause issues when a failure occurs on the CE router or other elements on the forward routing path. The manually created static route has no way of updating itself, unlike dynamic IGPs.

Other options involve the use of dynamic routing protocols, such as BGP, Open Shortest Path First (OSPF), Routing Information Protocol (RIP), or Enhanced Interior Gateway Routing Protocol (EIGRP), between the CE and PE. In this particular case, you will look at gaining additional benefit by using EIGRP between the CE and PE to gain IGP transparency across the service provider network.

Transparency can be important to consider in a large enterprise where the enterprise wants to retain a level of control over internal IGP routes to influence path selection. More importantly, it can greatly ease the migration to a service provider-based MPLS VPN because the redistribution of routing information takes place at the PE and there is no need to introduce BGP onto the CE. Of course, a balanced approach is often called for. You will see some of the trade-offs that need to be made later in this chapter.

NOTE   BGP/MPLS VPNs are described in detail in RFC 2547. The more current draft-ietf-l3vpn-rfc2547bis-03 describes the method by which a service provider may use an IP backbone to provide IP VPNs for its customers. This method uses a "peer model," in which the CE routers send their routes to the service PE routers. No "overlay" is visible to the customer's routing algorithm, and CE routers at different sites do not peer with each other. Data packets are tunneled through the backbone so that the core routers do not need to know the VPN routes.

It's useful to consider the foundations of routing protocol selection. The design implications of EIGRP, OSPF protocol, and BGP are

- Fixed network topology
- Addressing and route summarization
- Route selection
- Convergence

- Network scalability
- Security

EIGRP, OSPF, and BGP are routing protocols for IP. An introductory section outlines general routing protocol issues. Subsequent discussions focus on design guidelines for the specific implementation considerations.

Implementing Routing Protocols

The following discussion provides an overview of the key decisions you must make when selecting and deploying routing protocols. This discussion lays the foundation for subsequent discussions about specific routing protocols. It also lays the foundation for migrating from traditional network topologies to the Layer 3 IP VPN, as well as the need to understand the fundamental implementation and operation of routing.

Network Topology

An internetwork's physical topology is described by the complete set of routers and the networks that connect them. Networks also have a logical topology. Different routing protocols establish the logical topology in different ways.

Some routing protocols do not use a logical hierarchy. Such protocols use addressing to segregate specific areas or domains within a given internetworking environment, as well as to establish a logical topology. For such nonhierarchical, or flat, protocols, no manual topology creation is required.

Other protocols can support the creation of an explicit hierarchical topology by establishing a backbone and logical areas. The OSPF and Intermediate System-to-Intermediate System (IS-IS) protocols are examples of routing protocols that use a hierarchical structure. A general hierarchical network scheme is illustrated in Figure 4-1.

Figure 4-1   *Sample OSPF Hierarchical Scheme*

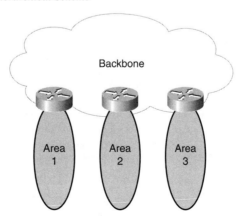

If a hierarchical routing protocol such as OSPF is used, the addressing topology should be assigned to reflect the hierarchy. If a flat routing protocol is used, the addressing implicitly creates the topology. There are two recommended ways to assign addresses in a hierarchical network. The simplest way is to give each area (including the backbone) a unique network address. An alternative is to assign address ranges to each area.

Areas are logical collections of contiguous networks and hosts. Areas also include all the routers that have interfaces on any one of the included networks. Each area runs a separate copy of the basic routing algorithm. Therefore, each area has its own topological database.

Addressing and Route Summarization

Route summarization procedures condense routing information. Without summarization, each router in a network must retain a route to every subnet in the network. With summarization, routers can reduce some sets of routes to a single advertisement, reducing both the load on the router and the network's perceived complexity. The importance of route summarization increases with network size.

Figure 4-2 illustrates route summarization. In this environment, R2 maintains one route for all destination networks beginning with B, and R4 maintains one route for all destination networks beginning with A. This is the essence of route summarization. R1 tracks all routes because it exists on the boundary between A and B.

Figure 4-2   *Route Summarization*

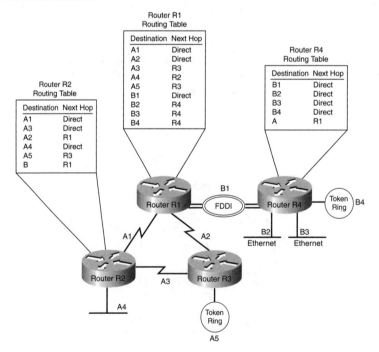

The reduction in route propagation and routing information overhead can be significant. Figure 4-3 illustrates the potential savings. The vertical axis shows the number of routing table entries. The horizontal axis measures the number of subnets. Without summarization, each router in a network with 1000 subnets must contain 1000 routes. With summarization, the picture changes considerably. If you assume a Site Type B network with 8 bits of subnet address space, each router needs to know all the routes for each subnet in its network number (250 routes, assuming that 1000 subnets fall into four major networks of 250 routers each), plus one route for each of the other networks (three), for a total of 253 routes. This represents a nearly 75 percent reduction in the size of the routing table. If an individual subnet becomes unavailable, that change is not propagated beyond the summarizing router. This prevents subnets from flapping and adversely affecting routing stability.

Figure 4-3   *Effects of Route Summarization*

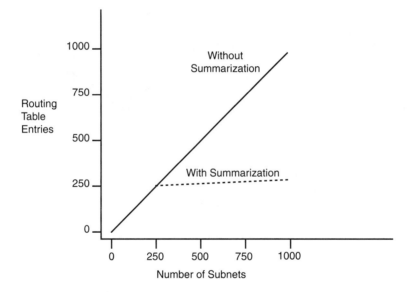

The preceding example shows the simplest type of route summarization: collapsing all the subnet routes into a single network route. Some routing protocols also support route summarization at any bit boundary (rather than just at major network number boundaries) in a network address. A routing protocol can summarize on a bit boundary only if it supports variable-length subnet masks (VLSMs).

Some routing protocols summarize automatically. Other routing protocols require manual configuration to support route summarization.

Route Selection

Route selection is trivial when only a single path to the destination exists. However, if any part of that path should fail, there is no way to recover. Therefore, most networks are designed with multiple paths so that there are alternatives in case a failure occurs.

Routing protocols compare route metrics to select the best route from a group of possible routes. Route metrics are computed by assigning a characteristic or set of characteristics to each physical network. The metric for the route is an aggregation of the characteristics of each physical network in the route. Figure 4-4 shows a typical meshed network with metrics assigned to each link and the best route from source to destination identified.

Figure 4-4   *Route Metrics*

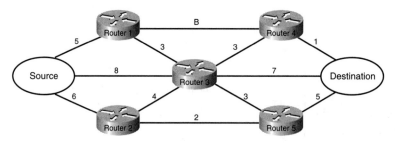

Routing protocols use different techniques to assign metrics to individual networks. Furthermore, each routing protocol forms a metric aggregation in a different way. Most routing protocols can use multiple paths if the paths have an equal cost. Some routing protocols can even use multiple paths when paths have an unequal cost. In either case, load balancing can improve the overall allocation of network bandwidth. Some protocols even support unequal-cost path load balancing, such as EIGRP.

When multiple paths are used, there are several ways to distribute the packets. The two most common mechanisms are per-packet load balancing and per-destination load balancing. Per-packet load balancing distributes the packets across the possible routes in a manner proportional to the route metrics. With equal-cost routes, this is equivalent to a round-robin scheme. One packet or destination (depending on switching mode) is distributed to each possible path. Per-destination load balancing distributes packets across the possible routes based on destination. Each new destination is assigned the next available route. This technique tends to preserve packet order. The Cisco implementation supports source and destination load balancing.

NOTE   Most TCP implementations can accommodate out-of-order packets. However, out-of-order packets may cause performance degradation.

When fast switching is enabled on a router (the default condition), route selection is done on a per-destination basis. When fast switching is disabled, route selection is done on a per-packet basis. When Cisco Express Forwarding (CEF) is enabled, the default is per-destination.

Convergence

When network topology changes occur, network traffic must reroute quickly. The phrase "convergence time" describes how long it takes a router to start using a new route after a topology changes. Routers must perform three actions after a topology changes:

1 Detect the change.

2 Select a new route.

3 Propagate the changed route information.

Some changes are immediately detectable. For example, a router can immediately detect WAN line failures that involve carrier loss. Other failures are harder to detect. For example, if a serial line becomes unreliable but the carrier is not lost, the unreliable link is not immediately detectable. In addition, some media (Ethernet, for example) do not provide physical indications such as carrier loss. When a router is reset, other routers do not detect this immediately. In general, failure detection depends on the media involved and the routing protocol used.

After a failure has been detected, the routing protocol must select a new route. The mechanisms used to do this are protocol-dependent. All routing protocols must propagate the changed route. The mechanisms used to do this are also protocol-dependent.

Network Scalability

The capability to extend your internetwork is determined, in part, by the scaling characteristics of the routing protocols used and the quality of the network design.

Network scalability is limited by two factors: operational issues and technical issues. Typically, operational issues are more significant than technical issues. Operational scaling concerns encourage the use of large areas or protocols that do not require hierarchical structures. When hierarchical protocols are required, technical enhancements are geared toward optimizing along the lines of greater flexibility through modular design and deterministic failure domains that improve overall scalability. Finding the right balance is the art of network design.

From a technical standpoint, routing protocols scale well if their resource use grows less than linearly with the growth of the network. Routing protocols use three critical resources: memory, CPU, and bandwidth.

Beyond this lies the operational and technical scaling considerations needed when assessing the sizing of the WAN and how this applies to the scalability of the selected design. The number, location, and accessibility of sites, and the number of users and applications required, are all key factors that affect the sizing. This will be discussed more in the case study section near the end of this chapter.

Memory

Routing protocols use memory to store routing tables and topology information. Route summarization cuts memory consumption for all routing protocols. Keeping areas small reduces the memory consumption for hierarchical routing protocols. For example, OSPF, which is a link-state protocol, builds multiple databases of all routes, versus distance vector protocols, such as RIP, which store only received and advertised routes.

CPU

CPU usage is protocol-dependent. Some protocols use CPU cycles to compare new routes to existing routes. Other protocols use CPU cycles to regenerate routing tables after a topology change. In most cases, the latter technique uses more CPU cycles than the former. For link-state protocols, keeping areas small and using summarization reduces CPU requirements by reducing the effect of a topology change and by decreasing the number of routes that must be recomputed after a topology change.

NOTE   These three issues also affect CPU usage.

Distance vector protocols, such as RIP and Interior Gateway Routing Protocol (IGRP), broadcast their complete routing table periodically, regardless of whether the routing table has changed. When the network is stable, distance vector protocols behave well but waste bandwidth because of the periodic sending of routing table updates, even when no change has occurred. Extensions to RIP, which are detailed in RFC 2091, add triggered RIP updates that were designed to allow RIP to run over lower-speed circuits. Only when a route changes does RIP send a routing update, thereby minimizing the number of calls required to maintain the routing table. When a failure occurs in the network, distance vector protocols do not add excessive load to the network, but they take a long time to reconverge to an alternative path or to flush a bad path from the network. Despite the lack of excessive load by delay variance (DV) protocols, they remain fairly CPU-intensive.

NOTE   If you're using IGRP in your network, it is advisable to consider changing either to an EGP between you and the service provider or to a supported IGP, such as EIGRP, OSPF, or RIP.

Link-state routing protocols, such as OSPF and IS-IS, were designed to address the limitations of distance vector routing protocols (slow convergence and unnecessary bandwidth usage). Link-state protocols are more complex than distance vector protocols, and running them adds to the router's overhead. The additional overhead (in the form of memory utilization and bandwidth consumption when link-state protocols first start up) constrains the number of neighbors that a router can support and the number of neighbors that can be in an area.

When the network is stable, link-state protocols minimize bandwidth usage by sending updates only when a change occurs. A hello mechanism ascertains neighbors' reachability. When a failure occurs in the network, link-state protocols flood link-state advertisements (LSAs) throughout an area. LSAs cause every router in the failed area to recalculate routes.

EIGRP is an advanced distance vector protocol that has some of the properties of link-state protocols. EIGRP addresses the limitations of conventional distance vector routing protocols, such as slow convergence and high bandwidth consumption in a steady-state network. When the network is stable, EIGRP sends updates only when a change in the network occurs. Like link-state protocols, EIGRP uses a hello mechanism to determine the reachability of neighbors. When a failure occurs in the network, EIGRP looks for feasible successors by sending messages to its neighbors. The search for feasible successors can be aggressive in terms of the traffic it generates (such as updates, queries, and replies) to achieve convergence.

In WANs, consideration of bandwidth is especially critical. For example, Frame Relay, which statistically multiplexes many logical data connections (virtual circuits) over a single physical link, allows the creation of networks that share bandwidth. Public Frame Relay networks use bandwidth sharing at all levels within the network. That is, bandwidth sharing may occur within the Frame Relay network of Enterprise X, as well as between the networks of Enterprise X and Enterprise Y.

Two factors have a substantial effect on the design of public Frame Relay networks:

- Users are charged for each permanent virtual circuit (PVC), which encourages network designers to minimize the number of PVCs.

- Public carrier networks sometimes provide incentives to avoid the use of committed information rate (CIR) circuits. Although service providers try to ensure sufficient bandwidth, packets can be dropped.

Overall, WANs can lose packets because of lack of bandwidth. For Frame Relay networks, this possibility is compounded because Frame Relay does not have a broadcast replication facility. So, for every broadcast packet that is sent from a Frame Relay interface, the router must replicate it for each PVC on the interface. This requirement limits the number of PVCs that a router can handle effectively.

Security

Controlling access to network resources is a primary concern. Some routing protocols provide techniques that can be used as part of a security strategy. With some routing protocols, you can insert a filter on the routes being advertised so that certain routes are not advertised in some parts of the network.

Some routing protocols can authenticate routers that run the same protocol. Authentication mechanisms are protocol-specific and generally weak. In spite of this, it is worthwhile to take advantage of existing techniques. Authentication can increase network stability by preventing unauthorized routers or hosts from participating in the routing protocol, whether those devices are attempting to participate accidentally or deliberately.

Although they vary in the strength of the authentication they offer, nearly all routing protocols support some form of message authentication. Two principal types of authentication are used in routing protocols today: plaintext password and Message Digest 5 (MD5).

Plaintext Password Authentication

Plaintext password authentication is just what it sounds like. A password is attached to the routing update and is sent in the clear along with the routing update. The passwords have specific length requirements as defined by the routing protocol in use. Plaintext password authentication should be considered specious security because anyone who sees a single routing update on the wire sees the authentication information if it is in use. From this point on, the attacker can appear to be a member of the trusted routing domain. The plaintext password does offer some benefit in that it prevents routing protocol changes when an invalid router is accidentally introduced into a production routing environment.

MD5 Authentication

MD5 works by creating a 16-byte hash of the routing message combined with a secret key. Therefore, the 16-byte value is message-specific, so if an attacker modifies the message, he or she invalidates the 16-byte digest appended to the message. Without the secret key, which the routing protocol never sends over the wire, the attacker is unable to reconstruct a valid message. It is worth noting that the MD5 option provides authentication and packet integrity, not confidentiality.

MD5 passwords should have the same properties as other critical passwords in your network. They should follow the password-creation guidelines in your security policy. If you choose a weak password, an attacker can use brute-force guessing to determine your digest password, thereby allowing him or her to become a trusted member of the routing domain.

Site Typifying WAN Access: Impact on Topology

You should carefully consider site typifying access to the new service. Typically, you would think about business need, location, and the number of users and applications or services required for a given site. As discussed in Chapter 3, "Analyzing Service Requirements," many elements must be considered beyond these basic tenants. For the purposes of this discussion, we will concentrate on the following topological needs:

- Performance
- Availability
- Flexibility

Site typification becomes important to define the characteristics of operational and technical implementation to be delivered, by both the internal operations teams and the service provider.

If you take Acme, Inc. as an example, four site types have been created:

- **Site Type A**—This site type describes "core" business sites, such as data centers, headquarters sites, or sites of large user populations. Typically, these require the highest degree of availability and performance.

- **Site Type B**—Largely high-population sites where few or no data center facilities require a high degree of availability and performance.

- **Site Type C**—This site type tends to be medium to large in terms of user populations and complexity of services and applications required, but it has no data center facilities. Availability and performance are important but not as important as with Site Type A or Site Type B sites.

- **Site Type D**—Smaller sites ranging from several to dozens of users, typically requiring connectivity for a limited set of services and applications.

Aside from support for corporate applications, such as e-mail, collaboration tools, Customer Relationship Management (CRM), and Enterprise Resource Planning (ERP), all sites have a requirement to support voice over IP (VoIP), and most require video over IP.

When considering performance characteristics, you can divide these into categories based on the number of users, application traffic volume, and profile and interactive traffic (voice and video) to derive the needs.

Availability is the point we're concerned with. In the context of routing between the service provider and Acme, there will be differing needs based on the site typifications. These can be divided into the following areas:

- High availability with low convergence times and equal-cost paths for primary and secondary connectivity to the service provider
- High availability with unequal-cost paths for primary and secondary connectivity to the service provider
- High availability via private, Internet xDSL, or dial backup

---

NOTE   xDSL refers to ADSL-, HDSL-, SDSL-, and VDSL-type connections.

Flexibility is a further consideration that must be examined, specifically when it comes to ease of migration. Ease of migration can be addressed through the standardization of access model. A standardized access model applied across the site typification models (Site Types A, B, C, and D) will aid the migration greatly.

Site Type: Topology

Site Type A typically constitutes large data centers, major campus sites, or core operational facilities in the Acme network. They need high-speed access to the MPLS VPNs—in this case, via dual connections to the service provider MPLS VPN. This can create challenges for connectivity, so this needs to be addressed carefully if an IGP is between the CE and PE. Mainly caused by the presence of connectivity via dual links to the MPLS VPN, this can create what is known as a "backdoor link." This will be addressed later, with the dual CE/dual PE connection model. Figure 4-5 shows the topology.

Figure 4-5   *Site Type A—Connectivity to the Service Provider*

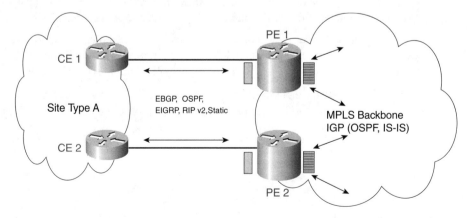

Site Type A has the following characteristics:

- Data center facility, delivery of services to most other sites

- High availability, business requirements for highest service availability

- Very high performance for centralized services, such as call processing for voice, Internet, VPN, and business-critical applications

- Extranet access services, providing supply chain integration to business partners and third-party networks

These core sites also act as the gateway to other Acme international sites, which may not be part of the MPLS VPN. Diversity of service provider access is a key requirement with high site level service-level agreements (SLAs) required. Low convergence times are key.

Site Type B is largely similar to Site Type A sites in their mode of connection to the MPLS VPN, with the same requirements to have diverse connections to the service provider network. With this site type, connectivity may not need the same level of separation, but diversity is still a requirement. Figure 4-6 shows Site Type A and B connectivity options.

Figure 4-6   *Site Types A and B*

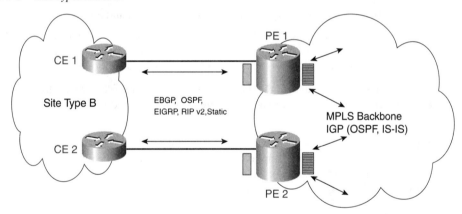

Site Type C sites are the majority of locations, mainly using services at central sites and generating the bulk of the inbound traffic toward the Site Type A or Site Type B sites. Figure 4-7 shows Site Type C/dual CE/single PE.

Figure 4-7   *Site Type C—Dual CE, Single PE*

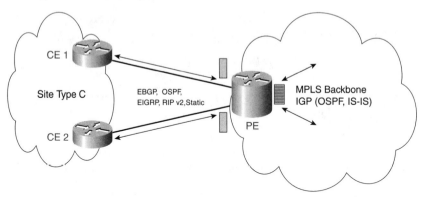

Type C sites have the following characteristics:

- Sales or engineering sites of varying sizes
- Medium or high performance
- Access to central site services such as voice, Internet, and applications

Efficiency of the access mechanism, bandwidth, and site service levels will vary for this site type because of the locations involved. The characteristics are balanced against economic cost factors, some of which may require compromises because of cost.

These sites may also "bundle" the dual links to use multilink PPP (MLP) to provide live link resilience between the CE and PE where terminating on dual PEs is cost- or operationally prohibitive.

Type D sites are typically the smaller field sites, mainly for sales staff, that use a limited set of central services in terms of applications. However, they may be using voice and, as such, still require high performance in the real-time site type and low convergence common to all other sites. Figure 4-8 shows Site Type D connectivity.

Figure 4-8   *Dual Home Site Type D—Single PE*

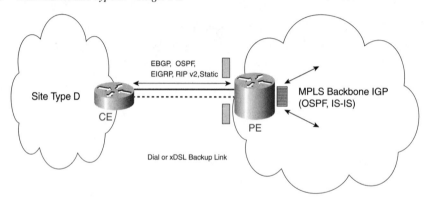

Type D sites have the following characteristics:

- Typically smaller field sites
- Cost/economics of connectivity main factor
- High availability implemented on limited SLA
- Site-based metrics for connectivity SLA
- Low or medium performance requirements (may increase to high performance where cheaper high-speed access to MPLS VPNs exists)
- Access to central site services, such as voice, Internet, and applications

WAN Connectivity Standards

Various connection options are required to service the generic site models of the four site types. These models derive varying site-level SLAs that can provide alignment against the level of criticality to the business.

Although you can select many permutations, Acme has categorized its requirement model as shown in Figure 4-9.

These provide the characteristics that can be used to derive the SLA delivery for sites against

- Performance
- Availability
- Flexibility
- Economic factors

Acme's needs require it to be translated to the service provider connectivity options, matching against Layer 2 transport to connect to the MPLS network. It also derives the performance assurances the service provider will deliver through its SLA. Examples of these can be seen in Chapter 8.

The importance of these topologies plays on the routing elements, which in turn derive aspects of the SLA when it comes to convergence and availability aspects of the topologies employed. Where redundancy is applied in the chosen topology, you must consider the CE-PE routing in the MPLS VPN environment, especially where potential routing loops are concerned.

Figure 4-9 *Connectivity Option Overview*

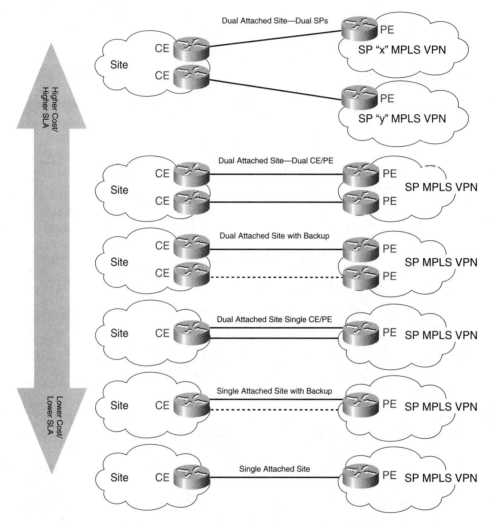

Site Type A Attached Sites: Dual CE and Dual PE

Establishing the connectivity for the most critical sites within Acme follows the model of dual CEs and dual PEs—diversity of connectivity. (Diversity is the complete service provider resilience of Layer 1, Layer 2 connectivity to the service provider—no common duct/trunking, a separate service provider carrier office [CO] facility, and so on.) This provides protection from link-level failures to PE and CE failure protection, as shown in Figure 4-10. This presents some challenges:

- **Correct routing**—bidirectional route exchange, avoiding routing loops, and delivering fast convergence times
- **Load sharing or load balancing challenges**
- **Effective utilization of equal-cost paths**

Figure 4-10 *Dual-Homed Connectivity (Diverse)*

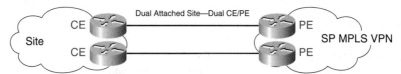

Extending this redundancy option would be connecting to a second service provider MPLS VPN to increase resilience and avoid complete service failure from one service provider. This introduces other challenges in the form of route exchange, if required, between two service providers—through back-end inter-autonomous system (AS) VPN peering arrangements or through managing eBGP connectivity between multiple service provider autonomous systems on the enterprise side. Figure 4-11 shows an overview of this model.

Figure 4-11 *Dual-Attached Site—Dual Service Providers*

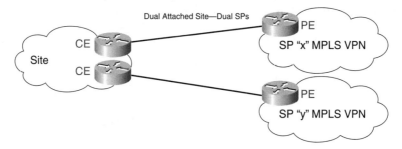

Backdoor links need to be guarded against in the multihomed scenarios just shown. Loops don't occur when a site is only a stub, but in the multihomed environment, these can be prevented through the application of Site of Origin (SoO) by the service provider.

A backdoor link or route is a connection that is configured outside the VPN between a remote site and a main site. An example is a WAN leased line that connects a remote site to the corporate network. Backdoor links are typically used as backup routes between EIGRP sites if the VPN link is down or unavailable. A metric is set on the backdoor link so that the route through the backdoor router is not selected unless a VPN link fails.

The SoO extended community is defined on the backdoor router's interface. It identifies the local site ID, which should match the value that is used on the PE routers that support the same site. When the backdoor router receives an EIGRP update (or reply) from a neighbor across the backdoor link, the router checks the update for an SoO value. If the SoO value in the EIGRP update matches the SoO value on the local backdoor interface, the route is rejected and is not installed to the EIGRP topology table. This typically occurs when the route with the local SoO value in the received EIGRP update is learned by the other VPN site and then is advertised through the backdoor link by the backdoor router in the other VPN site. SoO filtering on the backdoor link prevents transient routing loops from occurring by filtering out EIGRP updates that contain routes that carry the local site ID.

If this feature is enabled on the PE routers and the backdoor routers in the customer sites, and SoO values are defined on both the PE and backdoor routers, both the PE and backdoor routers support convergence between the VPN sites. The other routers in the customer sites only need to propagate the SoO values carried by the routes, as the routes are forwarded to neighbors. These routers do not otherwise affect or support convergence beyond normal Diffusing Update Algorithm (DUAL) computations.

Site Type B/3 Dual-Attached Site—Single CE, Dual PE

The option of connecting a site with a single CE to two PEs provides protection against service provider failures at either the PE level or the link level. You must take into consideration routing loops and convergence times. Load sharing can be achieved on a per-destination basis or by weighting links so that they operate a primary/backup mechanism. Figure 4-12 provides an overview of this option.

Figure 4-12 *Dual-Attached Site—Single CE, Dual PE*

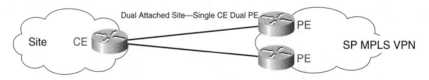

Site Type B/3 Dual-Attached Site—Single CE, Single PE

Where demand for link protection is a necessity, the option of connecting with dual paths between the CE and PE provides a simple solution. This protects against carrier link failures. Load balancing can be done either per-destination or by distributing based on equal-cost paths. CEF can deliver the per-packet or per-destination solution. The per-destination, which is the default mechanism, is typically the preferred option. Figure 4-13 provides an overview of this option.

Figure 4-13 *Dual-Attached Site—Single CE, Single PE*

Site Type D Single-Attached Site—Single CE with Backup

Where the option for a single attached site is pursued for smaller field sites, consideration should be given to recovery in the event of link loss or service provider failure. As soon as the link or service is restored, the backup service should cease. There are multiple ways to do this. The most common is ISDN-based dial between the CE and the service provider network, with the service provider network initiating the call to the CE on failure detection.

ISDN is being replaced by xDSL connectivity either direct to the service provider network or as an Internet-based VPN service in many enterprise implementations. However, this can be more complex to implement. Acme pursued the option of Internet-based VPN where available on a cost basis. An example of how this was implemented is discussed later in this chapter.

Figure 4-14 shows a single-attached site with backup via ISDN or Internet.

Figure 4-14 *Single-Attached Site with Backup Via ISDN or the Internet*

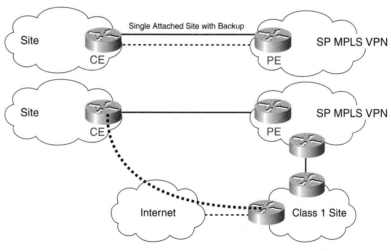

Convergence: Optimized Recovery

Convergence, in routing terms, is the time taken to converge to a new path when a path fails or a new route is introduced within the network. Table 4-1 documents the mechanisms of provider convergence, which the enterprise needs to be aware of.

Table 4-1   *Mechanism of Provider Convergence*

Service Provider Convergence Event	Value
PE router receipt of a routing update from a CE router	Worst case on a new route is 30 seconds, based on the default advertisement timer. This can be tuned by the service provider.
PE router loss of link to the CE router	Failure of the directly attached peer: Interface failure would cause an immediate down condition on the eBGP session.
PE router detects loss of routes behind the CE router	Failure of nondirectly attached peer: 60 seconds based on the next-hop validation timer (default scan-time timer).
Import of local routing information or change into the corresponding ingress VRF	Immediate.
Receipt of local route/update into BGP on the PE router	Redistribution is immediate.
Advertisement of route/update to MP-BGP peers or route reflector (RR)	Variable: 5 seconds when there is no RR; assume RR. Check with the service provider.
Receipt of advertised route/update into BGP on PE	Immediate: BGP routes are immediately processed.
Import of newly received route/update into local VRF	Worst case is 15 seconds—default scan time. This can be tuned by the service provider.
Advertisement of route/update to CE routers	Worst case is 30 seconds—default advertisement timer. This can be tuned by the service provider.
Processing of updates by CE router	Immediate.

When assessing how convergence will impact the network recovery, keep in mind these two main elements:

- **Service provider backbone recovery elements, as shown in Table 4-1**—These depend on tuning and mechanisms employed by the service provider from the physical to the MPLS, BGP, and IGP convergence variables they employ.

- **VPN site-to-site**—This is a factor of the underlying recovery by the service provider and the reaction of the CE/PE to updates or removals of routes and failures within the network.

Although the service provider is responsible for optimizing the recovery of its backbone network, it is the joint collaboration between the service provider and the enterprise that improves edge convergence times.

IP Addressing

The addressing within the enterprise is maintained when implementing an MPLS VPN; however, it is strongly advisable to take the time to allocate site-based blocks that can be easily summarized—thus reducing the need to announce unaggregated addresses toward the service provider. This streamlines routing tables and improves the network's operational support. When it comes to the links between the service provider and the enterprise, the service provider should provide the enterprise with address space to facilitate this. Typically, the addresses are delegated from public address space by the service provider. In some cases, the service provider may prefer to use unnumbered PE-CE links.

Addressing can be a key point that drives whether it will be possible to integrate the IGP between the CE and PE. For example, if unnumbered links were to be used, the implication is that the service provider is sharing the loopback address on its PE with multiple customers to optimize address allocation. This also makes it easier for the service provider to secure the PE, because the policies are based on PE loopback addresses and not IP interface addresses.

Other alternatives to this are as follows:

- **Using customer-allocated address space**—This is unsuitable, because administrative responsibility to address allocation is beyond the service protocol control.

- **Using RFC 1918 private address space**—This is a commonly employed mechanism, typically managed by the service provider. It needs close collaboration to prevent overlap with customers' use of RFC 1918 address space.

Where shared network management is taking place (that is, when ownership of the CE still resides with the enterprise but the service provider is given management access for SLA purposes), careful allocation of address space is a necessity. Typically, this is RFC 1918 address space.

To ensure that management options are not restricted, it is advisable to use IP numbered interfaces between the CE and PE, with an RFC 1918 address assigned to loopback interfaces. Where shared management is required, it is important to align with the service provider the use of these blocks to ensure consistency.

Routing Between the Enterprise and the Service Provider

As you will see in the case of Acme, two mechanisms can be employed to route between the service provider and the enterprise. The more common of these is the use of BGP between the CE and PE. However, this sacrifices some aspects of routing information, such as route metrics, while adding the need to operate and support multiple routing protocols. Some enterprises are not geared to such change. In any event, it is often a required balance.

Multihomed sites, or sites with multiple service provider demarcations, may benefit from the use of BGP as the routing protocol between the CE and PE. The simplification to be gained by running the IGP between the CE and PE reduces the change needs for the greater number of sites. Any use of IGP between the CE and PE must be able to provide the same, or similar, security as delivered by BGP, as well as be able to handle multiple route policies.

In the case of Acme, the use of BGP was maintained in the Site Type A sites while all other sites were delivered using EIGRP between the CE and PE. This allowed for maintenance of routing metric information that would otherwise have been lost.

Using EIGRP Between the CE and PE

The EIGRP IP network routing solution is well known to enterprise customers, who take advantage of its greater optimization of path routing, fast convergence, and lower CPU usage benefits. EIGRP allows service providers to more rapidly and cost-effectively deploy IP VPN services for their customers. In turn, enterprise customers can more quickly enjoy affordable, efficient, and secure managed VPNs.

IP/MPLS VPNs deployed using site-to-site EIGRP—rather than external BGP or static routes—eliminate the need for enterprise network staff to learn new protocols. By integrating the capabilities of link-state and distance vector protocols, EIGRP greatly increases operational efficiency in networks of all sizes. It is highly scalable for large networks, giving bigger enterprises the confidence they need to implement managed services offered by service providers.

Why do service providers support EIGRP as PE-CE?

- **Already in enterprises**—There is a large installed base of enterprises with EIGRP.

- **Customer preference**—Enterprises that are moving toward buying VPN services from an MPLS provider prefer to run EIGRP all the way to the service provider's boundary rather than deploying eBGP. In this scenario, customers do not have to learn any other protocol and can preserve the routing environment they are used to.

How EIGRP MPLS VPN PE-to-CE Works

EIGRP MPLS VPN support allows native EIGRP to run on PE-CE links, requiring no upgrade of existing enterprise customer equipment or configurations. All necessary equipment or configuration changes are consolidated to the PE routers, as shown in Figure 4-15. BGP redistributes routes into EIGRP using route type and metric information extracted from BGP extended community information.

Figure 4-15 *Redistributing EIGRP into BGP*

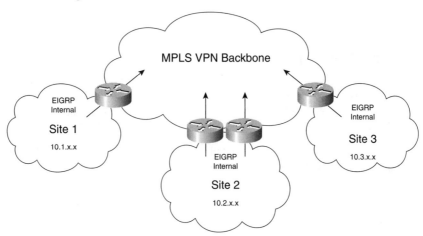

Without EIGRP PE-CE support, normal redistribution of EIGRP into BGP (and vice versa at the PE) would result in intersite EIGRP routes appearing as external routes in the target CE cloud. The loss of the original route attributes would result in all routes traversing the MPLS VPN backbone becoming less preferable than the routes that do not traverse the MPLS VPN backbone.

To solve this problem, redistribution of EIGRP metrics are preserved across the MPLS VPN backbone through the use of MP-BGP extended community attributes. The EIGRP route type and vector metric information is encoded in a series of well-known attributes. These attributes are transported across the MPLS VPN backbone and are used to re-create the EIGRP route when received by the target PE router.

The MPLS VPN backbone is treated as another transport to pass EIGRP route information from one customer site to its peering site. EIGRP routes are redistributed into BGP with extended community information appended to the BGP route. BGP then carries this route over the MPLS VPN backbone, with the EIGRP-specific information encoded in the BGP extended community attributes. The EIGRP route information appears as any other MPLS label-encapsulated data within the VPN backbone. Routing protocols within the MPLS VPN backbone have nothing to do with the enterprise routes.

After the peering enterprise site receives the route, BGP redistributes the route into EIGRP. EIGRP then extracts the BGP extended community information and reconstructs the route as it appeared in the original enterprise site.

PE Router: Non-EIGRP-Originated Routes

On the PE router, if a route is received via BGP and it has no extended community information for EIGRP, it is advertised to the CE router as an external EIGRP route using the default metric. If no default metric is configured, the route is not advertised to the CE router.

PE Router: EIGRP-Originated Internal Routes

If a route is received via BGP and it has extended community information for EIGRP, the route type is set to "internal" if the source's AS matches. If the source AS fails to match the configured AS for the given VPN VRF Cisco IOS route table instance, the rules for non-EIGRP-originated routes hold.

The internal route is then reconstructed and advertised to the CE router as an internal EIGRP route using the extended community information.

EIGRP supports internal and external routes. Internal routes originate within an EIGRP AS. Therefore, a directly attached network that is configured to run EIGRP is considered an internal route and is propagated with this information throughout the EIGRP AS. External routes are learned by another routing protocol or reside in the routing table as static routes. These routes are tagged individually with the identity of their origin.

External routes are tagged with the following information:

- Router ID of the EIGRP router that redistributed the route
- AS number of the destination
- Configurable administrator tag
- ID of the external protocol
- Metric from the external protocol
- Bit flags for default routing

Route tagging lets the network administrator customize routing and maintain flexible policy controls. Route tagging is particularly useful in transit autonomous systems, where EIGRP typically interacts with an interdomain routing protocol that implements more global policies, resulting in very scalable, policy-based routing.

PE Router: EIGRP-Originated External Routes

If a route is received via BGP and it has extended community information for EIGRP, the route type is set to "external" if the source AS matches. If the source AS fails to match the configured AS for the given VRF, the rules for non-EIGRP originated routes hold.

The external route is then reconstructed and advertised to the CE router as an external EIGRP route using the extended community information.

Multiple VRF Support

On a PE router, one instance of EIGRP can support multiple EIGRP MPLS VPN VRFs. Support for each VRF translates into its own EIGRP process. The number of EIGRP processes depends on the available system resources and the number of supported VRFs on a given platform. An EIGRP process is always created for the default routing table.

Extended Communities Defined for EIGRP VPNv4

No EIGRP adjacencies, EIGRP updates, or EIGRP queries are sent across the MPLS VPN backbone. Only EIGRP metric information is carried across the MPLS VPN backbone via the MP-BGP extended communities.

The PE router is part of the EIGRP network; therefore, all EIGRP protocol-specific behavior with MPLS VPNs is no different than with any other regular EIGRP network. As mentioned before, the MPLS VPN backbone is treated as a transport.

For EIGRP to re-create metrics derived from the originating enterprise site, the PE router encodes the original metric in MP-BGP extended communities. BGP may then transport these extended communities across the MPLS VPN backbone.

Metric Propagation

The PE router re-creates routes and sends them to the CE router as an EIGRP route, as shown in Figure 4-16. The same route type and cost bases as the original route are used to re-create the EIGRP route. The metric of the re-created route is increased by the interface's link cost. You can make the MPLS VPN backbone or the backdoor link the preferred path by adjusting the metrics.

Figure 4-16 *EIGRP Between the CE and PE*

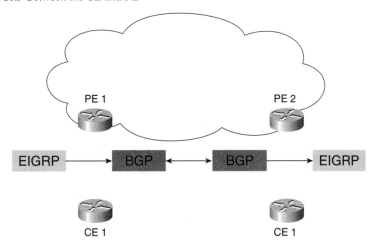

For a given Network X, in the CE 1 router, the following things happen:

- CE 1 advertises Network X to PE 1 via EIGRP.
- PE 1 EIGRP (VRF) redistributes Network X to BGP (VRF).
- PE 1 BGP (VRF) requests external attributes from EIGRP (VRF).
- PE 1 BGP sends Network X to PE 2 with attached extended community attributes.
- PE 2 BGP (VRF) redistributes Network X to EIGRP (VRF).
- PE 2 EIGRP (VRF) requests external attributes from BGP (VRF).
- PE 2 EIGRP (VRF) rebuilds the route as a native EIGRP route.
- PE 2 advertises Network X to CE 2 via EIGRP.
- CE 2 receives Network X from PE 2 as a native EIGRP route.

NOTE   At this point, CE 2 has the same information as CE 1 for Network X.

Configuring EIGRP for CE-to-PE Operation

Configuring EIGRP operation on the CE router requires little change over the normal operations of EIGRP for the enterprise. Example 4-1 provides a sample configuration.

Example 4-1   *Configuring EIGRP Between the CE and PE*

```
Interface Serial 1/0
    Description CEx_to_PEx_SP :: CCT ID 001 :: S/N x45
    Ip address 10.1.1.1 255.255.255.252
    IP summary-address EIGRP 100 10.1.1.0 255.255.255.0
Router EIGRP 100
    Network 10.0.0.0 255.255.0.0
    Distribute-list prefix OUTBOUND out serial 1/0
    Distribute-list prefix INBOUND in serial 1/0
    No auto-summary
!
IP prefix-list OUTBOUND description permit local address blocks only
IP prefix-list OUTBOUND seq 5 permit 10.1.1.0/24
!
IP prefix-list INBOUND description permit exact ACME ranges only
IP prefix-list INBOUND seq 5 permit 0.0.0.0/0
IP prefix-list INBOUND seq 10 permit 10.48.0.0/13
```

In the preceding Acme CE EIGRP routing example, a simple policy is applied to do the following:

- Permit only local sites' routes to be sent from the CE to the PE.
- An implicit deny of 0/0 (the default route) is sent from remote/stub sites to the MPLS VPN.

- Inbound permit of only the default route and known address block—in this case, 10.48.0.0/13.
- An EIGRP summary is placed on the outbound serial interface toward the service provider PE.

This policy services the needs of all the Acme sites that are using EIGRP between the CE and PE. In the case where there are multiple interfaces toward the service provider PE, the same policy can be applied to the additional interfaces under the EIGRP router configuration.

The permit of the default route ensures reachability to the Internet. In the case of Acme, this is generated from the Internet connection point of presence (PoP) in the Site Type A site. The implicit deny that is incorporated into the OUTBOUND prefix list ensures that sites cannot resend a default toward the network and cause routing anomalies.

Using BGP Between the CE and PE

Configuring BGP (eBGP) between the CE and the PE requires that the local site redistribute its local routes into BGP and learn through redistribution external routes from BGP.

CE routers need to have specific policies applied to ensure that the correct routes are being learned from BGP and that the correct routes are being injected into the MPLS VPN BGP process from the local site.

Example 4-2 shows the configuration required to do this.

Example 4-2 *Configuring BGP Between the CE and PE*

```
Router bgp 65535
    Bgp log-neighbor-changes
    Neighbor PE_peer_address remote-as SP-AS
    Neighbor PE_peer_address update-source CE_peer_address
    Neighbor PE_peer_address ebgp-multihop ! only required if peering with PE
  loopback rather than PE /32 of local connect
!
Ip route PE_peer_address 255.255.255.255 CE-PE (sub~)_interface
```

This provides the basics of the BGP configuration. The policy needs to be set. This is handled as shown in Example 4-3.

Example 4-3 *Setting the Redistribution Policy on the CE*

```
Interface Serial 1/0
    Description CEx_to_PEx_SP :: CCT ID 001 :: S/N x45
    Ip address 10.1.1.1 255.255.255.252
Router EIGRP 100
    Network 10.0.0.0 255.255.0.0
    Redistribute bgp 65535 subnets route-map BGP-TO-EIGRP ! only VPN routes
    Redistribute static subnets route-map static-to-EIGRP ! next hop address for
                                                          ! iBGP sessions
```

continues

Example 4-3 *Setting the Redistribution Policy on the CE (Continued)*

```
      Passive-interface serial 1/0
      No auto-summary
 !
Router BGP 65535
    Bgp log-neighbor-changes
    Network 10.2.1.25 mask 255.255.255.255
    Redistribute eigrp 100 route-map BGP:EIGRP>BGP
    Neighbor PE_peer_address prefix-list BGP-prefix-filter out
    Neighbor PE_peer_address prefix-list BGP-prefix-filter in
Neighbor PE_peer_address filter-list AS-path-filter in
Neighbor PE_peer_address send-community
 !
IP prefix-list BGP-prefix-filter deny 0.0.0.0/0
IP prefix-list BGP-prefix-filter deny 0.0.0.0/8 le 32
IP prefix-list BGP-prefix-filter permit 0.0.0.0/0 le 32
 !
Ip as-path access-list AS-path-filter deny_SP_AS$
IP as-path access-list AS-path-filter permit .*
 !
Route-map SetCommunity permit 10
    Set community VPN:site
Route-map BGP:EIGRP>BGP deny 20
    Match tag 4445
Router-map BGP:EIGRP>BGP permit 30
    Description permit all else
```

Route filtering is employed, as before in the EIGRP example, to ensure that no bogus or unintentional routes are introduced into the MPLS VPN. The policy is a simple one that can be extended to include specific routes within the enterprise domain.

As in the EIGRP example, these are used to do the following:

- Control which routes are advertised from the site to the VPN. The first part ensures that the default route is not propagated (where not desired) from a local site.
- Filter the routes originated by the service provider from being redistributed.
- Add a community value to "color" routes for more granular filtering.

This filter could be extended to include the filtering of undesired RFC 1918 address blocks (10.0.0.0/8, 172.16.0.0/16, 192.168.0.0/16), provide granular filtering based on lengths (le) of address blocks greater than a certain desired size, and deny any subnet originated by the service provider (other than those desired for management purposes). The final aspect is to permit all other routes.

Securing CE-PE Peer Sessions

Through the use of encrypted passwords for neighbor authentication, either with EIGRP or BGP, the use of MD5 is preferred. When neighbor authentication is enabled, the receiving router authenticates the source of the routing updates by using a shared key that the source and the receiver have been set up with.

MD5 authentication ensures that no plaintext sending of the key occurs—where the key is sent in the clear and is open to compromise. MD5 creates a hash by using the key and the message.

Example 4-4 demonstrates this for BGP.

Example 4-4   *Configuring MD5 Authentication for BGP Peers*

```
router BGP 65535
    neighbor PE_peer_address password BGP-Secret
```

Improving BGP Convergence

You might need to tune the BGP convergence parameters. This applies to CE-PE recovery times when losing a link and improving the BGP advertisement times. This applies to the CE side configuration. The PE side is the responsibility of the service provider. However, enterprises are encouraged to work with service providers to test and validate the correct alignment of convergence needs to ensure operational integrity.

When you use a directly connected interface for the eBGP session between the CE and PE, a link failure causes the eBGP session to go down immediately. Failure detection for nondirectly connected eBGP peers depends greatly on the BGP hold timer. The holdtime timer defaults to 180 seconds for nondirect peers. The BGP next-hop validation time (known as the scan-time timer) defaults to 60 seconds. From this it could, in worst cases, cause longer convergence times, depending on the peer mechanism employed and the configured parameters for the holdtime and scan-time timers. eBGP sessions don't go down immediately when a transit interface fails.

There are mechanisms to fine-tune these. Principally, these depend on the peer mechanism employed. BGP fast-external-failover applies only to directly connected eBGP sessions, for example. Thus, when peering indirectly, BGP relies on keepalive and holdtime timers or BGP scan-time to check activities.

Scan-time can be tuned from its default of 60 seconds to 30 seconds. However, this can affect where static routes are employed, thereby pointing to a false or unavailable peer when no end-to-end signaling capability exists. Low scan-time configurations also affect the CPU when a large number of routes are present.

Adjusting the keepalive and holdtime values from their defaults on the CE causes BGP to select the smaller of the two hold times—for example, changing to 10 seconds for keepalive and 30 seconds for holdtime.

Tuning can also be done on the advertisement interval. The default advertisement interval is 60 seconds; this can be tuned to 0. On the CE side, this can be lowered to 15 seconds, but you should ensure that the PE side is also 15 seconds. It is critical to work with your service provider to ensure that tuning is matched to its configured parameters. Example 4-5 is a sample of the required CE side configuration.

Example 4-5 *Tuning CE Configuration Timers*

```
router BGP 65535
    neighbor PE_peer_address timers 10 30
    neighbor PE_peers_address advertisement-interval 15
```

Case Study: BGP and EIGRP Deployment in Acme, Inc.

Having established the basis for routing between the service provider and the enterprise, this section brings together the four site types with practical examples. These cover the following topology models:

- **Small site (Site Type D)**—Single-homed, no backup
- **Medium site (Site Type C)**—Single-homed with backup
- **Medium site (Site Type C)**—Dual-homed (a single CE dual-linked to a PE)
- **Large site (Site Type B)**—Dual-homed (dual CE, dual PE)
- **Very large site/data center (Site Type A)**—Dual service provider MPLS VPN

Small Site—Single-Homed, No Backup

Sites of this type generally are small and require a moderate number of services and receive a moderate amount of traffic from other sites.

Site Type D can be described as follows:

- Sites are relatively small; they mainly use services from other sites (low importance and not highly business-critical). They do not offer any important services to other sites.
- Traffic profile: Incoming traffic is several times larger than outgoing traffic.
- Acme guidelines for site design: The economic factor of the performance characteristics is the key factor when designing a WAN for this site type.
- The performance, availability, and flexibility requirements for this site type are in most cases low or medium.
- In some countries and regions, these site types may even have higher performance characteristics due to the low cost of high-speed access.
- An xDSL connection may be a cost-effective replacement for the primary and backup connections to the service provider. High availability is implemented on a best-effort basis. (Some sites may have parallel links, other sites may rely on dial backup, and still other sites may not have any backup path.)

- Quality of service (QoS) mechanisms must be used on backup links (where available) of sites where the backup path has lower speed than the primary site. Flexibility of Layer 2 technology (such as modifying access speed) is a requirement that needs to be specified.

- Connectivity is via a single attached site with a permanent connection to one service provider. Figure 4-17 shows Acme Site Type D connectivity.

Figure 4-17 *Acme Site Type D Connectivity*

The service provider should evaluate the Acme request for connecting the Site Type D site while considering the bandwidth and service level requested. For the service provider and Acme, the cost of the bandwidth is the most important parameter when determining the WAN solution. The service provider then ensures that the selected solution is in accordance with its policy through offering the SLA.

For Site Type D, common configurations are to provide connectivity either with EIGRP or via a static configuration using eBGP, as shown in Example 4-6.

Example 4-6 *Site Type D Configuration for the CE*

```
ip route site_network_address mask mask Interfacex/x(.x)
!
!
interface Loopback0
 description ACME Management Loopback
 ip address CE-1-management-loopback 255.255.255.255
!
interface Loopback10
 description ACME BGP Connectivity Loopback for SP
 ip address CE-1-peer-loopback 255.255.255.255
!
interface Serialx/y(.z)
 description ACME CE-PE (sub-)interface
 ip unnumbered Loopback10
 ip verify unicast reverse-path
!
router EIGRP 100
 redistribute bgp CE_AS subnets route-map BGP-to-EIGRP(VPN routes)
 network site_network_address mask
 passive-interface Serialx/y(.z)
 no auto-summary
!
router bgp 65535      !Site AS num
 no synchronization
```

continues

Example 4-6 *Site Type D Configuration for the CE (Continued)*

```
bgp log-neighbor-changes
aggregate-address site-aggregate mask summary-only
redistribute connected/static route-map Site_prefix_permit
neighbor PE-1-peer-loopback remote-as PE-AS    !SP AS num
neighbor PE-1-peer-loopback password BGP-secret
neighbor PE-1-peer-loopback ebgp-multihop 2
neighbor PE-1-peer-loopback update-source Loopback10
neighbor PE-1-peer-loopback timers 10 30
neighbor PE-1-peer-loopback advertisement-interval 15
no auto-summary
!
ip route PE-1-peer-loopback 255.255.255.255 Serialx/y(.z)
```

Medium Site—Single-Homed with Backup

For a single-attached site with a dialup backup, the solution characteristics are as follows:

- Lower cost
- Limited recovery in the event of a link failure
- Solution applicability: Site Type C/D

In a setup with a permanent primary link and a dialup backup link, dynamic routing should not be used over the dialup link because dynamic routing keeps the dialup connection up. The solution is to divert the backup eBGP session over the primary link so that the eBGP session over the backup is pre-established. Otherwise, the process of dialing the line, establishing a link-level connection, establishing the eBGP session, and then finally exchanging routes takes too much time. Figure 4-18 provides an overview of this connection type.

Figure 4-18 *Site Type C/D with a Backup Link*

The alternative solution of using floating static routes over the dialup connection has been dropped, because the default routing is not allowed and would require configuring static routes matching the routes received dynamically.

The BGP peers have their TCP session already established, and the BGP routes have already been exchanged. This is accomplished by using the eBGP multihop feature and the static routes directing both BGP sessions over the primary link, as shown in Example 4-7.

Example 4-7   *Configuring eBGP Multihop*

```
interface Loopback0
 description ACME Management Loopback
 ip address CE-1-management-loopback 255.255.255.255
!
interface Loopback10
 description ACME BGP Connectivity Loopback for SP
 ip address CE-1-peer-loopback 255.255.255.255
!
interface Serialx/y(.z)
 description ACME CE-PE (sub-)_interface
 ip unnumbered Loopback10
 ip verify unicast reverse-path
!
!
interface dialer0
 ip unnumbered Loopback10
 ip verify unicast reverse-path
!
router EIGRP 100
 redistribute bgp CE_AS subnets route-map BGP-to-EIGRP(VPN routes)
 network site_network_address mask
 passive-interface serial x/y(.z)
 passive-interface dialer0
 no auto-summary
!
router bgp 65535
 no synchronization
 bgp log-neighbor-changes
 neighbor PE-1-peer-loopback remote-as PE-AS
 neighbor PE-1-peer-loopback password BGP#1-secret
 neighbor PE-1-peer-loopback ebgp-multihop 2
 neighbor PE-1-peer-loopback update-source Loopback10
 neighbor PE-1-peer-loopback timers 10 30
 neighbor PE-1-peer-loopback advertisement-interval 15
 neighbor PE-2-peer-loopback remote-as PE-AS
 neighbor PE-2-peer-loopback password BGP#2-secret
 neighbor PE-2-peer-loopback ebgp-multihop 3
 neighbor PE-2-peer-loopback update-source Loopback10
 neighbor PE-2-peer-loopback timers 10 30
 neighbor PE-2-peer-loopback advertisement-interval 15
 no auto-summary
!
ip route PE-1-peer-loopback 255.255.255.255 Serialx/y(.z)
ip route PE-2-peer-loopback 255.255.255.255 Serialx/y(.z) 201
```

When the primary link fails, the primary eBGP session goes down, and the dynamic routes between the backup eBGP peers are lost. There must be an additional floating static route on the CE side toward the service provider's backup edge router, PE-2. This route directs the outgoing packets to the dialer interface. As soon as the packets reach the dialer interface, the call is placed. When the PPP session is established, the router receiving the call installs a host route to the caller. The eBGP session runs uninterrupted over the dialup link.

All previously received eBGP information is still valid. The next-hop attribute is the same, but the address now can be reached over the dialup link and not, as it used to be, over the primary link.

Due to the pre-established session, the eBGP session continues uninterrupted if the dialup session is established within 30 seconds. The traffic is black-holed for the time the call is placed and the PPP session is established.

The main difference is the backup scenario, when typically, much less bandwidth can be distributed between the available classes of traffic. The implementation should use the following guidelines:

- IP telephony (if/where used) should be rerouted to a fixed telephone network (such as the dedicated ISDN ports).
- Business-critical traffic is guaranteed a percentage of the bandwidth.
- Best-effort traffic is guaranteed a percentage of the bandwidth.

MLP can provide additional benefits:

- Multiple links double (multiply) backup bandwidth.
- Link fragmentation and interleaving can minimize serialization delay on this slow link.

Medium Site—Single CE Dual-Homed to a Single PE

Solution characteristics for a single CE dual-homed to a single PE are as follows:

- Low cost
- Improved performance and availability by using identical parallel links
- Improved SLA and recovery capability
- Solution applicability: Site Type C

Suppose you have a limited budget or you cannot purchase a link with higher performance characteristics. You still can enhance performance by deploying multiple permanent connections between a single CE router on the Acme side and a single PE router on the service provider side. This setup is simplified by having EIGRP run between the CE and PE, thus removing the need to have BGP configured on the CE. Figure 4-19 provides an overview of the connection model.

Figure 4-19 *Single CE to Single PE—Dual Paths*

Load sharing can be performed depending on the CEF switching mode. The recommendation is to use Cisco default per-source-and-destination load balancing, where all packets with the same source/destination address pair are forwarded on the same link. Alternatively, an MLP bundle can be created, thus creating one logical link over which traffic is automatically load-shared. Example 4-8 shows this configuration.

Example 4-8 *Configuring a Single CE to a Single PE with Dual Paths*

```
interface Loopback0
 description ACME Management Loopback
 ip address CE-1-management-loopback 255.255.255.255
!
interface Serialx/y(.z)
 description ACME CE-PE#1 (sub-)interface
 ip address 10.10.10.1 255.255.255.252
 ip verify unicast reverse-path
!
interface Serialx/z(.w)
 description ACME CE-PE#2 (sub-)interface
 ip address 10.10.10.6 255.255.255.252
 ip verify unicast reverse-path
!
Router EIGRP 100
  Network 10.0.0.0 255.255.0.0
  Distribute-list prefix OUTBOUND out Serialx/y(.z)
  Distribute-list prefix INBOUND in Serialx/y(.z)
  No auto-summary
!
IP prefix-list OUTBOUND description permit local address blocks only
IP prefix-list OUTBOUND seq 5 permit 10.1.1.0/24
!
IP prefix-list INBOUND description permit exact ACME ranges only
IP prefix-list INBOUND seq 5 permit 0.0.0.0/0
IP prefix-list INBOUND seq 10 permit 10.48.0.0/13
```

In the single-CE setup, the link-level procedures should detect the link failure and place the interface in a down state. Recovery occurs via the EIGRP feasible successor, and all traffic is immediately forwarded on the remaining path.

Large Site—Dual-Homed (Dual CE, Dual PE)

Dual-homed solution characteristics are as follows:

- High availability (emphasis on link and device protection)
- The site is a critical business site
- Solution applicability: Site Type B

As shown in Figure 4-20, the solution with multiple permanent connections between different routers in both the Acme network and the service provider network increases redundancy. It also covers the lost link and failures in the routers. The route selection policy is primary/backup, which is achieved by CE-2 and PE-2 assigning low local preference values on backup links, as shown in Example 4-9.

Figure 4-20 *Dual-CE-to-Dual-PE Connectivity*

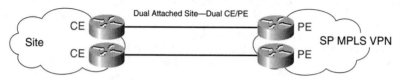

Example 4-9 *Configuring Dual-CE-to-Dual-PE Connections*

```
! CE-1 Configuration
router EIGRP 1000
 redistribute bgp CE_AS subnets route-map BGP-to-EIGRP !(VPN routes)
 network site_network_address wildcard_mask
 !For BGP connectivity include also loopback interfaces as host routes
BGP routing
interface Loopback0
 description ACME Management Loopback
 ip address CE-1-management-loopback 255.255.255.255
!
interface Loopback10
 description ACME BGP Connectivity Loopback for SP
 ip address CE-1-peer-loopback 255.255.255.255
!
interface Serialx/y(.z)
 description ACME CE-PE (sub-)interface
 ip unnumbered Loopback10
!
router bgp CE-AS     !Site AS num
 no synchronization
 bgp log-neighbor-changes
 neighbor CE-2-peer-loopback remote-as CE-AS !iBGP session
 neighbor CE-2-peer-loopback update-source Loopback10
 neighbor PE-1-peer-loopback remote-as PE-AS          !SP AS num
 neighbor PE-1-peer-loopback password BGP#1-secret
 neighbor PE-1-peer-loopback ebgp-multihop 2
```

Example 4-9 *Configuring Dual-CE-to-Dual-PE Connections (Continued)*

```
 neighbor PE-1-peer-loopback update-source Loopback10
 neighbor PE-1-peer-loopback timers 10 30
 neighbor PE-1-peer-loopback advertisement-interval 15
 aggregate-address site-aggregate mask summary-only
 !
 ip route PE-1-peer-loopback 255.255.255.255 Serialx/y(.z)
```

```
 ! CE-2 Configuration
 interface Loopback0
  description ACME Management Loopback
  ip address CE-2-management-loopback 255.255.255.255
 !
 interface Loopback10
  description ACME BGP Connectivity Loopback for SP
  ip address CE-2-peer-loopback 255.255.255.255
 !
 interface Serialx/y(.z)
  description ACME CE-PE (sub-)interface
  ip unnumbered Loopback10

 !
 router bgp CE-AS     !Site AS num
  no synchronization
  bgp log-neighbor-changes
  neighbor CE-1-peer-loopback remote-as CE-AS           !iBGP session
  neighbor CE-1-peer-loopback update-source Loopback10
  neighbor PE-2-peer-loopback remote-as PE-AS           !SP AS num
  neighbor PE-2-peer-loopback password BGP#2-secret
  neighbor PE-2-peer-loopback ebgp-multihop 2
  neighbor PE-2-peer-loopback update-source Loopback10
  neighbor PE-2-peer-loopback timers 10 30
  neighbor PE-2-peer-loopback advertisement-interval 15
  neighbor PE-2-peer-loopback route-map LP-backup in
  aggregate-address site-aggregate mask summary-only
 !
 ip route PE-2-peer-loopback 255.255.255.255 Serialx/y(.z)
 !
 route-map LP-backup
  set local-preference 50
 BGP route propagation router bgp CE-AS
  network site_prefix mask mask
  no auto-summary
```

In the event that the BGP configuration on the service provider PE assigns no particular preference to north or south connections, CE routers CE-1 and CE-2 can influence the return path selection by assigning multiexit discriminator (MED) values on outgoing updates, as shown in Example 4-10.

Example 4-10 *Configuring the MED to Influence Path Selection*

```
! CE-1 Configuration
! Announcing MED for return path selection
router bgp CE_AS
 neighbor PE-1-peer-loopback route-map MED-primary out
 !
route-map MED-primary permit 10
 set metric 50

! CE-2 Configuration
! Announcing MED for return path selection
router bgp CE_AS
 neighbor PE-2-peer-loopback route-map MED-backup out
 !
route-map MED-backup permit 10
 set metric 100
```

If the primary link or primary router fails, only one of the connections is lost. The other connection is still available. The third event type deals with breaking the connection between the CE routers in the Acme network.

The following are the essential high-availability issues theoretically assessed with presumptive failures:

- **Primary link failure**—With this type of failure, CE-1 takes up to the default holdtime (adjusted to 30 seconds) to detect that the PE-1 loopback address (the address used for the BGP peering) has gone. As soon as the lack of reachability has been identified, the router CE-1 removes all the routes from that neighbor, withdraws them from the CE-2 BGP table, and then must perform a path selection identifying CE-2 as a winner for the VPN routes.

- **CE router failure scenario**—Router failure is detected either by the iBGP holdtime or by IGP removing the route to the peering loopback and the BGP scan process verifying the next-hop reachability. The first requires fine-tuning of the BGP scan process. The latter is considered more suitable by adjusting the BGP keepalive and holdtime timers.

- **Failure inside the Acme network**—As soon as the link failure has been detected and the site iBGP session is torn down, both CE routers withdraw lost and start advertising reachable subnets. It is important that aggregation is turned off, or at least done architecturally adequately, so as not to attract the traffic to unreachable subnets.

Load Sharing Across Multiple Connections

The objective that Acme wants to achieve at WAN speeds greater than E1/T1, for specific sites where the cost of a T3 or E3 is prohibitive, is load balancing. With this approach, the two access links actively share the traffic load from and to the branch. With the fallback port solution, one of the access links is the primary, and the other is the backup.

The load sharing occurs on the two links so that the following things happen:

- The traffic from Acme toward the service provider is shared between the two access lines by configuring Hot Standby Router Protocol (HSRP) or Gateway Load Balancing Protocol (GLBP) on the two CE routers or, alternatively, on two routers or Layer 3 switches on the LAN, behind the CE.

- Load sharing from the service provider toward Acme is achieved by using iBGP multipath and eventually is combined with multipath load sharing for both eBGP and iBGP in an MPLS VPN feature on a particular PE router.

When HSRP is used to provide default gateway redundancy, the backup members of the peer relationship are idle, waiting for a failure event to occur for them to take over and actively forward traffic. GLBP protects data traffic from a failed router or circuit while allowing packet load sharing between a group of redundant CE routers, such as alternating between the multiple default gateways. HSRP may use multiple HSRP groups on a single interface to alternate between the multiple default gateways, but it is not optimal from a configuration or maintenance perspective.

Very Large Site/Data Center—Dual Service Provider MPLS VPN

Dual service provider MPLS VPN solution characteristics are as follows:

- High availability (emphasis on link and device protection and even partial path protection)

- Data center site—larger campus locations

- Business-critical

- Solution applicability: Site Type A

The multihomed site has two permanent links to different service providers. The links terminate in different edge routers in the Acme network. Otherwise, one of the major advantages, resilience to router failure, is lost. Figure 4-21 shows the design.

Figure 4-21 *Connecting to Dual Service Providers*

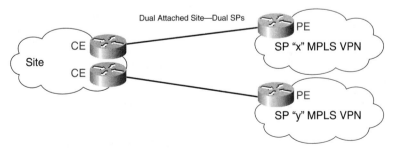

The assignment in this setup is to have one link as primary and the other as backup only. The site can use the local preference configuration to direct all outgoing traffic over the primary link. This configuration is no different from multiple connections running BGP to a single service provider.

Controlling the distribution load of incoming traffic over the links is more difficult in the multihome scenario compared to multiple links to a single service provider. MED cannot be used because the updates are sent to two different autonomous systems. It is done with AS path prepending, extending the AS path attribute of local routes before sending the advertisement to the backup service provider. When the backup service provider receives the advertisement, the AS path is longer.

This solution works in all cases where the default BGP route selection process (based on AS path length) is done, which is almost always the case. Example 4-11 provides an example of the required configuration actions.

Example 4-11 *Configuring the AS—Prepending to Influence Path Selection Between Service Providers*

```
router EIGRP 100
 redistribute bgp CE_AS subnets route-map BGP-to-OSPF !(VPN routes)
 network site_network_address wildcard_mask area area_num
 !For BGP connectivity also include loopback interfaces as host routes


! CE-1 Configuration
interface Loopback0
 description ACME Management Loopback
 ip address CE-1-management-loopback 255.255.255.255
!
interface Loopback10
 description ACME BGP Connectivity Loopback for SP
 ip address CE-1-peer-loopback 255.255.255.255
!
interface Serialx/y(.z)
 description ACME CE-PE (sub-)interface
 ip unnumbered Loopback10
!
router bgp CE-AS    !Site AS num
 no synchronization
 bgp log-neighbor-changes
 neighbor CE-2-peer-loopback remote-as CE-AS    !iBGP session
 neighbor CE-2-peer-loopback update-source Loopback10
 neighbor PE-1-peer-loopback remote-as PE-AS    !SP AS num SP "X"
 neighbor PE-1-peer-loopback password BGP#1-secret
 neighbor PE-1-peer-loopback ebgp-multihop 2
 neighbor PE-1-peer-loopback update-source Loopback10
 neighbor PE-1-peer-loopback timers 10 30
 neighbor PE-1-peer-loopback advertisement-interval 15
 neighbor PE-1-peer-loopback filter-list 10 out
!
ip route PE-1-peer-loopback 255.255.255.255 Serialx/y(.z)
ip as-path access-list 10 permit ^$
```

Example 4-11 *Configuring the AS—Prepending to Influence Path Selection Between Service Providers (Continued)*

```
BGP routing with SP x

! CE-2 Configuration
interface Loopback0
 description ACME Management Loopback
 ip address CE-2-management-loopback 255.255.255.255
!
interface Loopback10
 description ACME BGP Connectivity Loopback for SP
 ip address CE-2-peer-loopback 255.255.255.255
!
interface Serialx/y(.z)
 description ACME CE-PE (sub-)interface
 ip unnumbered Loopback10
!
router bgp CE-AS     !Site AS num
 no synchronization
 bgp log-neighbor-changes
 neighbor CE-1-peer-loopback remote-as CE-AS     !iBGP session
 neighbor CE-1-peer-loopback update-source Loopback10
 neighbor PE-2-peer-loopback remote-as PE-AS     !SP AS num SP "Y"
 neighbor PE-2-peer-loopback password BGP#2-secret
 neighbor PE-2-peer-loopback ebgp-multihop 2
 neighbor PE-2-peer-loopback update-source Loopback10
 neighbor PE-2-peer-loopback timers 10 30
 neighbor PE-2-peer-loopback advertisement-interval 15
 neighbor PE-2-peer-loopback route-map LP-backup in
 neighbor PE-2-peer-loopback filter-list 10 out
!
ip route PE-2-peer-loopback 255.255.255.255 Serialx/y(.z)
!
route-map LP-backup
 set local-preference 50
!
ip as-path access-list 10 permit ^$
BGP route propagation router bgp CE-AS
 network site_prefix mask mask
 no auto-summary
 neighbor PE-2_peer_address route-map AS-prepend out
!
route-map AS-prepend permit 10
 set ip as-path CE_AS CE_AS
```

A dual-homed site with two CEs linked to two service providers creates challenges in the equalization of QoS design. Implementation must follow a consistent policy with both providers. QoS design and implementation on the backup path through service provider Y should follow these guidelines:

- Provide QoS guarantees on the CE-PE link from both ends. Try to enforce the same QoS policy that is used with service provider X to maintain consistency.

- If the other service provider's X SLA differs significantly from the service provider's Y policy, try to translate one of the service provider's policies into the policy of the other by doing one of the following:

  — Use marking as specified by the second service provider.

  — Provide a bandwidth guarantee to business-critical traffic.

  — Provide low latency to VoIP (IP telephony).

  — Reroute IP telephony to the public switched telephone network (PSTN) if a low-delay minimum-bandwidth guarantee is not possible under the SLA of the second service provider.

- The high-availability requirements in this site type are assessed with the following objectives in mind:

  — The communication path at the physical layer needs to be protected against a single point of failure (node, ports, and link).

  — The Layer 3 network must be able to quickly converge in the event of route failure. The convergence of IGP and BGP contributes to the availability of IP.

Site Typifying Site Type A Failures

The following are the essential high-availability issues theoretically assessed with presumptive failures:

- **Link failure scenario**—CE-1 takes up to the default holdtime (adjusted to 30 seconds) to detect that the PE-1 loopback address has gone. The router CE-1 then removes all routes from that neighbor, withdraws them from the CE-2 BGP table, and performs a path selection identifying CE-2 as a winner for the VPN routes.

- **CE router failure scenario**—Router failure is detected either by the iBGP holdtime or the IGP removing the route to the peering loopback and BGP scan process verifying the next-hop reachability. The first requires fine-tuning of the BGP scan process. The latter is considered more suitable by adjusting the BGP keepalive and holdtime timers.

- **Failure inside ACME network**—As soon as the link failure has been detected and the site iBGP session is torn down, both CE routers withdraw lost and start advertising reachable subnets. It is important that aggregation is turned off, or at least done architecturally adequately, so as not to attract the traffic to unreachable subnets.

Solutions Assessment

Table 4-2 summarizes the test results to prove the presented connectivity concepts for Site Type A sites. As stated, high performance and high availability are the key factors when designing WAN for this site type; therefore, the testing is performed with the intention to verify the ability of these features for this site type.

Table 4-2   *Sample Testing Matrix*

Test	Test Observation with Regard to Solution	Pass/Fail/Comments
Failover—service provider X Failover—service provider Y		
BGP routing		
BGP load sharing		
BGP convergence		
Link failure		
CE router failure		
Simulated PE failure		
Failure inside the Acme network		
Load performance on the secondary path during an outage		
Load balancing (internal) end access point access		
Real-time traffic (voice/video) performance during failure		
Recovery time tracking		
IGP routing recovery		
IGP convergence		

Summary

This chapter assessed the need for a solid routing foundation and the implications to the enterprise when using an MPLS VPN-based service. If you create a consistent routing foundation with the appropriate mechanisms, the enterprise can easily scale to very large MPLS VPN implementations.

Consideration for support of existing IGP routing protocols, and their growing support by the MPLS VPN providers, is easing the transition and lessening the need to maintain multiple routing protocols. With the Layer 3 VPN, it is possible to integrate the IGP and thus gain transparency between the service provider and the enterprise.

Convergence times of MPLS VPN networks are constantly improving, as are the connectivity options that ensure that the platform can support the aspects of converged voice, video, and data. Because these business services require high SLAs, especially voice, it is especially important that you be careful when designing the routing for the enterprise. It is the key foundation on which all else relies.

References

RFC 2547, *BGP/MPLS VPNs*
http://www.faqs.org/rfcs/rfc2547.html

RFC 2475, *An Architecture for Differentiated Service*
http://www.faqs.org/rfcs/rfc2475.html

Cisco Products Quick Reference Guide: February 2002
http://www.cisco.com/warp/public/752/qrg/cpqrg2.htm

Cisco Press

Routing TCP/IP, Volume I (CCIE Professional Development) by Jeff Doyle

Routing TCP/IP, Volume II (CCIE Professional Development) by Jeff Doyle and Jennifer DeHaven Carroll

Cisco BGP Routing
http://www.cisco.com/en/US/partner/tech/tk365/tk80/tsd_technology_support_sub-protocol_home.html

Cisco EIGRP Routing
http://www.cisco.com/en/US/partner/tech/tk365/tk207/tsd_technology_support_sub-protocol_home.html

Cisco OSPF Routing
http://www.cisco.com/en/US/partner/tech/tk365/tk480/tsd_technology_support_sub-protocol_home.html

Cisco RIP Routing
http://www.cisco.com/en/US/partner/tech/tk365/tk554/tsd_technology_support_sub-protocol_home.html

Cisco IP Routing Design Guides
http://www.cisco.com/en/US/partner/tech/tk365/tech_design_guides_list.html

Cisco IP Switching
http://www.cisco.com/en/US/partner/tech/tk827/tk831/
tsd_technology_support_protocol_home.html

Cisco MPLS
http://www.cisco.com/en/US/partner/tech/tk436/
tsd_technology_support_category_home.html

This chapter covers the following topics:

- Introduction to QoS
- QoS Tool Chest: Understanding the Mechanisms
- Building the Policy Framework
- IP/VPN QoS Strategy
- Identification of Traffic
- QoS requirements for Voice, Video, and Data
- The LAN Edge: L2 Configurations
- Case Study: QoS in the Acme, Inc. Network
- QoS Reporting

CHAPTER **5**

Implementing Quality of Service

This chapter's objectives are to define the options and technical implementations for the various types of quality of service (QoS) required by enterprises for typical virtual private network (VPN) deployments. Service providers and enterprises typically build parallel networks to support the transport of data, voice, video, and mission-critical and non-mission-critical applications. With the move toward convergence, as well as the use of packet-based IP networks, the shift from circuit-switched division and parallel builds of network resources toward a single IP network is increasing. This chapter covers the requirements for supporting the converged world of Multiprotocol Label Switching (MPLS) VPNs and how this maps to QoS policy applicable in the enterprise. The aim is to provide a deployable set of policies that the enterprise can use as guidelines. You'll also see how to address these policies to the service provider. Specifically, the QoS needs of Acme, Inc. are addressed in the case study.

Introduction to QoS

Although the amount of bandwidth is increasing as higher-speed networks become more economically viable, QoS is not unnecessary. All networks have congestion points where data packets can be dropped, such as WAN links where a larger link feeds data into a smaller link, or a place where several links are aggregated into fewer trunks. QoS is not a substitute for bandwidth, nor does it create bandwidth. QoS lets network administrators control when and how data is dropped when congestion does occur. As such, QoS is an important tool that should be enabled, along with adding bandwidth, as part of a coordinated capacity-planning process.

Another important aspect to consider alongside QoS is traffic engineering (TE). TE is the process of selecting the paths that traffic will transit through the network. TE can be used to accomplish a number of goals. For example, a customer or service provider could traffic-engineer its network to ensure that none of the links or routers in the network are overutilized or underutilized. Alternatively, a service provider or customer could use TE to control the path taken by voice packets to ensure appropriate levels of delay, jitter, and packet loss.

End-to-end QoS should be considered a prerequisite with the convergence of latency-sensitive traffic, such as voice and videoconferencing along with more traditional IP data traffic in the network. QoS becomes a key element in delivery of service in an assured, robust, and highly efficient manner. Voice and video require network services with low latency, minimal jitter, and minimal packet loss. The biggest impact on this and other real-time applications is packet loss and delay, which seriously affects the quality of the voice call or the video image. These and other data applications also require segregation to ensure proper treatment in this converged infrastructure.

The application of QoS is a viable and necessary methodology to provide optimal performance for a variety of applications in what is ultimately an environment with finite resources. A well-designed QoS plan conditions the network to give access to the right amount of network resources needed by applications using the network, whether they are real-time or noninteractive applications.

Before QoS can be deployed, the administrator must consider developing a QoS policy. Voice traffic needs to be kept separate because it is especially sensitive to delay. Video traffic is also delay-sensitive and is often so bandwidth-intensive that care needs to be taken to make sure that it doesn't overwhelm low-bandwidth WAN links. After these applications are identified, traffic needs to be marked in a reliable way to make sure that it is given the correct classification and QoS treatment within the network.

If you look at the available options, you must ask yourself some questions that will inevitably help guide you as you formulate a QoS strategy:

- Do I need to support real-time delay-sensitive applications?
- Do I have mission-critical applications that require special handling?
- Do I know which applications and services are being planned that may affect the strategy?
- Does my selection correspond with what I am being offered by the service provider? If not, how do I make this transparent?
- What current traffic patterns or aggregate application traffic should I take into consideration?

From these questions, you have various options: Define a policy that supports the use of real-time applications and that treats everything else as best-effort traffic, or build a tiered policy that addresses the whole. After all, QoS can provide a more granular approach to segmentation of traffic and can expedite traffic of a specific type when required. You will explore these options in this chapter.

After the QoS policies are determined, you need to define the "trusted edge," which is the place where traffic is marked in a trustworthy way. It would be useless to take special care in transporting different classes of network traffic if traffic markings could be accidentally or maliciously changed. You should also consider how to handle admission control—metered access to finite network resources. For example, a user who fires up an application that consumes an entire pipe and consequently affects others' ability to share the resource needs a form of policing.

Building a QoS Policy: Framework Considerations

Traffic on a network is made up of flows, which are placed on the wire by various functions or endpoints. Traffic may consist of applications such as Service Advertising Protocol (SAP), CAD/CAM, e-mail, voice, video, server replication, collaboration applications, factory control applications, branch applications, and control and systems management traffic.

If you take a closer look at these applications, it is apparent that some level of control over performance measures is necessary—specifically, the bandwidth and delay/jitter and loss that each class of application can tolerate. These performance measures can vary greatly and have various effects. If you apply a service level against these performance measures, it can be broadly positioned into four levels that drive the strategy:

- **Provisioning**—The first step is ensuring that the correct transport is selected. Appropriate allocation of bandwidth ensures the proper start point for network design. Understanding application characteristics is key—what they will use in terms of network bandwidth and their delay, jitter, latency, and loss needs.

- **Best-effort service**—The majority of application data flows fit this service level. Best-effort service provides basic connectivity with no guarantee for packet delivery and handling.

- **Differentiated service**—Traffic at this service level can be grouped into classes based on their individual requirements. Each class is then treated according to its configured QoS mechanism.

- **Guaranteed service**—Guaranteed service requires absolute allocation of specific resources to ensure that the traffic profiled to receive this service has its specific requirements met.

Applying these service levels against the application classes for their required level of service means that you need to understand where in the network they should be applied. The best approach is to define a "trust boundary" at the edge of the network where the endpoints are connected, as well as look at the tiers within the network where congestion may be encountered. After you know these, you can decide on the policy of application.

For example, in the core of the network, where bandwidth may be plentiful, the policy becomes a queue scheduling tool. However, at the edge of the network, especially where geographically remote sites may have scarce bandwidth, the policy becomes one of controlling admission to bandwidth. Basically, this is equivalent to shoving a watermelon down a garden hose—intact! Figure 5-1 outlines the high-level principles of a QoS application in network design.

Figure 5-1 *Principles of QoS Application*

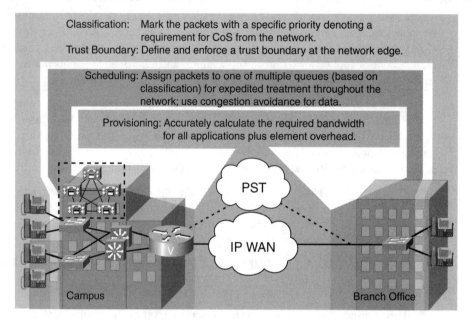

Classification: Mark the packets with a specific priority denoting a requirement for CoS from the network.

Trust Boundary: Define and enforce a trust boundary at the network edge.

Scheduling: Assign packets to one of multiple queues (based on classification) for expedited treatment throughout the network; use congestion avoidance for data.

Provisioning: Accurately calculate the required bandwidth for all applications plus element overhead.

PST

IP WAN

Campus   Branch Office

This design approach introduces key notions to the correct road to QoS adoption. These notions provide the correct approach to provisioning before looking at classification of packets toward a requirement for a class of service (CoS) over the network. Determine where the trust boundary will be most effective before starting such a classification, and then indicate the area of the network where scheduling of packets to queues is carried out. Finally, determine the requirement of provisioning that is needed to ensure that sufficient bandwidth exists to carry traffic and its associated overheads.

After the network's QoS requirements have been defined, an appropriate service model must be selected. A service model is a general approach or a design philosophy for handling the competing streams of traffic within a network. You can choose from four service models:

- Provisioning

- Best-effort

- Differentiated Services (DiffServ)

- Guaranteed Services or Integrated Services (IntServ)

Provisioning is quite straightforward. It is about ensuring that there is sufficient base capacity to transport current applications, with forward consideration and thinking about future growth needs. This needs to be applied across the LANs, WANs, and MANs that will support the enterprise. Without proper consideration to provisioning appropriate bandwidth, QoS is a wasted exercise.

The best-effort model is relatively simple to understand because there is no prioritization and all traffic gets treated equally regardless of its type. The two predominant architectures for QoS are DiffServ, defined in RFC 2474 and RFC 2475, and IntServ, documented in RFC 1633, RFC 2212, and RFC 2215. In addition, a number of RFCs and Internet Drafts expand on the base RFCs—particularly RFC 2210, which explores the use of RSVP with IntServ. Unfortunately, the IntServ/RSVP architecture does not scale in large enterprises due to the need for end-to-end path setup and reservation. The service model selected must be able to meet the network's QoS requirements as well as integrate any networked applications. This chapter explores the service models available so that you can leverage the best of all three.

Implementing QoS is a means to use bandwidth efficiently, but it is not a blanket substitute for bandwidth itself. When an enterprise is faced with ever-increasing congestion, a certain point is reached where QoS alone does not solve bandwidth requirements. At such a point, nothing short of another form of QoS or correctly sized bandwidth will suffice.

QoS Tool Chest: Understanding the Mechanisms

The preceding section discussed the need to apply a QoS policy in the network, where it should be applied, and the models under which you can operate. To help you completely understand the mechanics of QoS, the next section explores the mechanisms available to perform the tasks at hand.

Classes of Service

To provide a mechanism for prioritizing the different types of IP traffic that exist on the network, it is important to adopt a CoS model that is flexible and simple to maintain and that meets the behavioral needs of different applications. Applications can then be categorized into the appropriate classes according to their delivery requirements. Based on this strategy, the following QoS classes of service are defined to address the different forwarding requirements of all traffic while maintaining a small number of classes. Figure 5-2 shows an approach an enterprise could follow, leading toward the mature 11-class IP precedence model. A four- or five-class IP precedence model should be the starting baseline an enterprise should consider. This model allows a migration path as more granular classes are added over time.

Figure 5-2 *How Many Classes of Service Do You Need?*

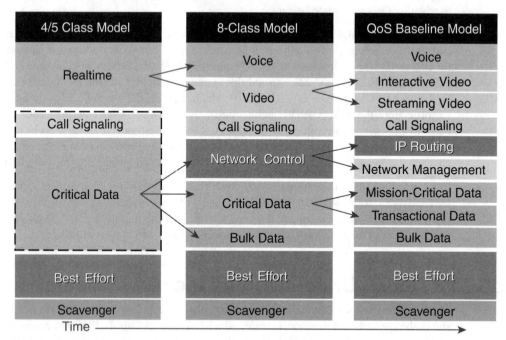

Understanding the deployment needs is a multistep process:

Step 1 Strategically define the business objectives to be achieved via QoS.

Step 2 Analyze the service-level requirements of the various traffic classes to be provisioned for.

Step 3 Design and test QoS policies before production network rollout.

Step 4 Roll out the tested QoS designs to the production network.

Step 5 Monitor service levels to ensure that the QoS objectives are being met.

These steps may need to be repeated as business conditions change and evolve. These steps are derived from the QoS baseline model developed by Tim Szigeti.

The classifications are split into two different areas: Layer 3 classification and Layer 2 CoS. The Layer 3 classifications cover the following:

- IP Precedence (or type of service [ToS]) markings
- Differentiated Services Code Point (DSCP), which provides for markings based on value ranges, where each DSCP specifies a particular per-hop behavior that is applied to a packet

- Per-hop behavior forwarding treatment applied at a differentiated services-compliant node to a behavior aggregate

IP ToS

In general, when referring to the ToS values, there are two methods for specifying QoS information within an IP packet. The first is to use the three most-significant bits (MSBs) of the ToS field in the IP header. These are called the IP Precedence (IPP) values. They allow for up to eight user-definable classes of service. The second method, referring to the 6 MSBs of the ToS field, is an extension of the IPP model, which allows for up to 64 DSCP values.

Based on these classifications, real-time voice bearer traffic is marked as Class 5 with guaranteed expedited delivery using an expedited queuing mechanism for voice traffic to ensure that voice quality is not adversely affected under heavy link utilization. This mechanism alone cannot guarantee protection for voice, so it needs to be used in combination with good capacity planning and call admission control (CAC). You will explore the capabilities available in the upcoming sections.

Traffic marked as Class 2, 3, 4, and 6 is provided guaranteed minimum bandwidth and is serviced via class-based weighted fair queuing (CBWFQ). The minimum bandwidth used should be calculated to account for peak usage for all traffic within each class. Should these classes require bandwidth usage that exceeds the configured minimum amount, this would be allowed, provided that other classes are not fully using their minimum bandwidth allocation.

All traffic marked as Class 0 is guaranteed the remainder of the bandwidth. Class 1 (batch/scavenger) traffic is drop-insensitive, or batch transfers are given a lower-priority treatment than all other classes. Typically, Class 1 should be assigned the smallest possible amount of bandwidth. Therefore, in the event of link congestion, Class 1's bandwidth usage is immediately contained to protect other higher-priority data.

Although the standard direction is to move toward the full adoption of the DSCP model, older implementations used to define the classes of service and perform traffic matching and queuing based on the IPP values. Because the IPP value is based on the first 3 MSBs of the DSCP field, it is possible for each IPP value to cover the full range of DSCP drop precedence values (bits 3 to 6) for each class selector. It should be noted that such mechanisms are now better placed to be moved to DSCP support to allow for the additional benefit of expedited forwarding/assured forwarding (EF/AF) class granularity and scaling of classes supported over time.

Ensure that the correct traffic mapping is carried out. Failing to do so may lead to classification of voice traffic to some value other than the DSCP value of 46 (EF). This may come about as a result of classification errors within the network or at the LAN edge due to incorrect CoS-to-DSCP or DSCP-to-CoS mappings, which can lead to service impact.

Hardware Queuing

QoS-enabled Ethernet switches provide a Layer 2 (L2) queuing mechanism, which allows for ingress and egress queuing. Ingress frames arriving at the L2 switch require buffering before scheduling on the egress port. Therefore, depending on the number of buffers available to each port, it is possible for ingress frames to be dropped instantaneously. If strict priority queues are not used, real-time voice traffic is not guaranteed for expedited delivery. Using the priority queues, if present, for both ingress and egress traffic provides a low-latency path through the L2 device for delay-sensitive traffic. All current Cisco platforms (2950, 2970, 3550, 3750, 4500, and 6500) support the use of internal DSCP to determine QoS treatment. These are derived from either the packets' DSCP trust classification, the trusted CoS markings, or an explicit configuration policy.

Although no standard number of queues is provided, the port capabilities can be determined via Cisco IOS or CatOS. The information is presented separately for both transmit and receive interfaces and is represented in 1PxQyT format. 1P refers to the strict priority queue available, xQ refers to the number of input or output queues available, and yT is the number of drop or Weighted Random Early Detection (WRED) thresholds that can be configured. It is recommended that all future hardware support a minimum of 1P1Q queuing for both ingress and egress.

Software Queuing

Prioritization and treatment of traffic is based on defined CoSs. Where potential network congestion may occur ensures that each class receives the appropriate forwarding priority, as well as minimum reserved bandwidth. If traffic for each class exceeds the allocated bandwidth requirements, depending on the WAN technologies, one of the following actions needs to be taken:

- Drop the excess traffic
- Forward excess traffic without changes to the original QoS information
- Forward the excess traffic with the ToS bits reset to a lower-priority CoS

QoS Mechanisms Defined

The QoS architecture introduces multiple components that form the basis of the building blocks of an end-to-end solution. First, you must understand the various capabilities that are available, as shown in Figure 5-3.

Figure 5-3   *Scheduling Tools: Queuing Algorithms*

These capabilities can be broken into several categories:

- **Classification and marking**—Packet classification features allow traffic to be partitioned into multiple priority levels or CoSs.

  Packets can be classified based on the incoming interface, source or destination addresses, IP protocol type and port, application type (network-based application recognition [NBAR]), IPP or DSCP value, 802.1p priority, MPLS EXP field, and other criteria. Marking is the QoS feature component that "colors" a packet (frame) so that it can be identified and distinguished from other packets (frames) in QoS treatment. Policies can then be associated with these classes to perform traffic shaping, rate-limiting/policing, priority transmission, and other operations to achieve the desired end-to-end QoS for the particular application or class. Figure 5-2 showed an overview of classification for CoS, ToS, and DSCP.

- **Congestion management**—Congestion-management features control congestion after it occurs.

  Queuing algorithms are used to sort the traffic and then determine some method of prioritizing it onto an output link. Congestion-management techniques include Weighted Fair Queuing (WFQ), CBWFQ, and low-latency queuing (LLQ):

  - WFQ is a flow-based queuing algorithm that does two things simultaneously: It schedules interactive traffic to the front of the queue to reduce response time, and it fairly shares the remaining bandwidth between high-bandwidth flows.
  - CBWFQ guarantees bandwidth to data applications.
  - LLQ is used for the highest-priority traffic, which is especially suited for voice over IP (VoIP).

- **Congestion avoidance**—Congestion-avoidance techniques monitor network traffic loads in an effort to anticipate and avoid congestion at common network and internetwork bottlenecks before it becomes a problem.

As shown in Figure 5-4, the WRED algorithm avoids congestion and controls latency at a coarse level by establishing control over buffer depths on both low- and high-speed data links. WRED is primarily designed to work with TCP applications. When WRED is used and the TCP source detects the dropped packet, the source slows its transmission. WRED can selectively discard lower-priority traffic when the interface begins to get congested.

Figure 5-4   *Congestion Avoidance: DSCP-Based WRED*

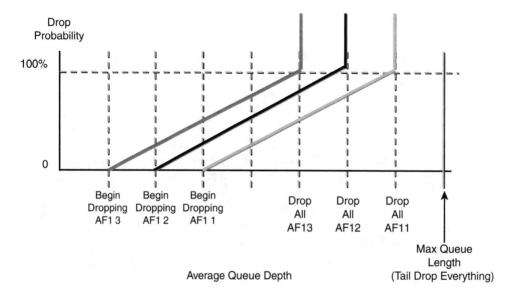

- **Traffic conditioning**—Traffic entering a network can be conditioned (operated on for QoS purposes) by using a policer or shaper.

  Traffic shaping involves smoothing traffic to a specified rate through the use of buffers. A policer, on the other hand, does not smooth or buffer traffic. It simply re-marks (IPP/DSCP), transmits, or drops the packets, depending on the configured policy. Legacy tools such as committed access rate (CAR) let network operators define bandwidth limits and specify actions to perform when traffic conforms to, exceeds, or completely violates the rate limits. Generic traffic shaping (GTS) provides a mechanism to control traffic by buffering it and transmitting at a specified rate. Frame Relay traffic shaping (FRTS) provides mechanisms for shaping traffic based on Frame Relay service parameters such as the committed information rate (CIR) and the backward explicit congestion notification (BECN) provided by the Frame Relay switch.

Policers and shapers are the oldest forms of QoS mechanisms. These tools have the same objectives—to identify and respond to traffic violations. Policers and shapers usually identify traffic violations in an identical manner; however, their main difference is the manner in which they respond to violations:

— A policer typically drops traffic.

— A shaper typically delays excess traffic using a buffer to hold packets and shape the flow when the source's data rate is higher than expected.

The principal drawback of strict traffic policing is that TCP retransmits dropped packets and throttles flows up and down until all the data is sent (or the connection times out). Such TCP ramping behavior results in inefficient use of bandwidth, both overutilizing and underutilizing the WAN links.

Since shaping (usually) delays packets rather than dropping them, it smoothes flows and allows for more efficient use of expensive WAN bandwidth. Therefore, shaping is more suitable in the WAN than policing. Figure 5-5 demonstrates the need for policers and shapers.

Figure 5-5   *Provisioning Tools: Policers and Shapers*

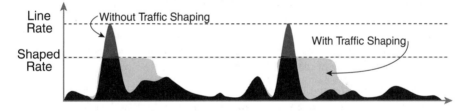

This is especially the case with nonbroadcast multiaccess (NBMA) WAN media, where physical access speed can vary between two endpoints, such as Frame Relay and ATM.

- **Link efficiency mechanisms**—Two link efficiency mechanisms work in conjunction with other QoS features to maximize bandwidth utilization.

  Newer multimedia application traffic, such as packetized audio and video, is in Real-Time Transport Protocol (RTP) packets and Cisco IOS Software. This saves on link bandwidth by compressing the RTP header (Compressed Real-Time Protocol [cRTP]), as shown in Figure 5-6.

VoIP packets are relatively small, often with a G.729 voice packet and approximately 20-byte payloads. However, the IP plus User Datagram Protocol (UDP) plus RTP headers equal 40 bytes (uncompressed), which could therefore account for nearly two-thirds of the entire packet. A solution is to use the Van Jacobsen algorithm to compress the headers for VoIP, reducing the header size from 40 bytes to less than 5 bytes.

Figure 5-6 *IP RTP Header Compression*

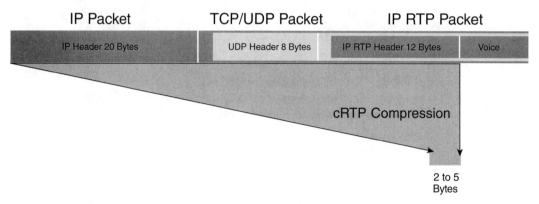

A data frame can be sent to the physical wire at only the interface's serialization rate. This serialization rate is the frame's size divided by the interface's clocking speed. For example, a 1500-byte frame takes 214 ms to serialize on a 56-kbps circuit.

If a delay-sensitive voice packet is behind a large data packet in the egress interface queue, the end-to-end delay budget of 150 ms could be exceeded. Refer to ITU G.114, which defines this measure as "most users being satisfied." Additionally, even a relatively small frame can adversely affect overall voice quality by simply increasing the jitter to a value greater than the size of the adaptive jitter buffer at the receiver.

Link Fragmentation and Interleaving (LFI) tools fragment large data frames into regular-sized pieces and interleave voice frames into the flow so that the end-to-end delay can be accurately predicted. This places bounds on jitter by preventing voice traffic from being delayed behind large data frames. To decrease latency and jitter for interactive traffic, LFI breaks up large datagrams and interleaves delay-sensitive interactive traffic with the resulting smaller packets, as shown in Figure 5-7.

Figure 5-7 *LFI*

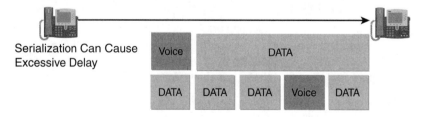

A maximum of 10-ms serialization delay is the recommended target to use for setting fragmentation size. This allows for headroom on a per-hop basis, because it allows adequate time for end-to-end latency required by voice. Two tools are available for LFI: multilink PPP (MLP) LFI (for point-to-point links) and FRF.12 (for Frame Relay links).

While reviewing these capabilities, it is important to keep in mind that the LLQ is in effect a first-in, first-out (FIFO) queue. The amount of bandwidth reserved for the LLQ is variable, yet if the LLQ is overprovisioned, the overall effect is a dampening of QoS functionality. This is because the scheduling algorithm that decides how packets exit the device is predominantly FIFO. Overprovisioning the LLQ defeats the purpose of enabling QoS. For this reason, it is recommended that you not provision more than 33 percent of the link's capacity as LLQ.

The 33 percent limit for all LLQs is a design guideline recommendation only. There may be cases where specific business needs cannot be met while holding to this recommendation. In such cases, the enterprise must provision queuing according to its specific requirements and constraints.

To avoid bandwidth starvation of background applications such as network management services and best-effort traffic types, it is recommended that you not provision total bandwidth guarantees to exceed 75 percent of the link's capacity. This is a subjective area because of the size of the link employed for the connection. It should be applied as a general rule. When a larger link is employed, the 75 percent rule is less relevant—links such as E3/DS3 and above, for example. Figure 5-8 provides an overview of the recommendations for WAN egress design scheduling.

Figure 5-8   *WAN Scheduling Design Principles*

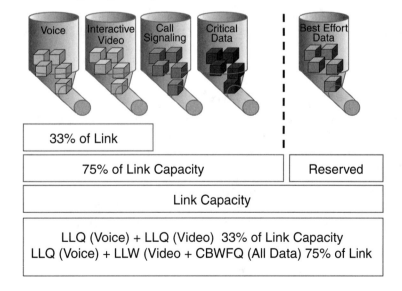

Figure 5-9 blends this all together by demonstrating the relevant tools and how they apply in the context of the network. You will explore how and where these should be applied in the case study later in this chapter.

Figure 5-9   *QoS Tools Mapping*

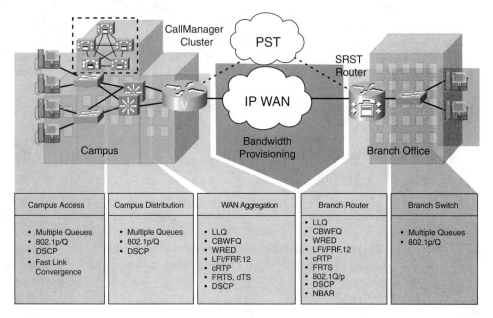

From the tools mapping, you can see that you have various options to use in terms of campus access, distribution, and WAN aggregation, with capabilities that extend through the service provider MPLS VPN and into the branch network.

Pulling It Together: Build the Trust

As discussed earlier, there are many places in the network in which the application of QoS, either marking or classification, occurs. In this section, you will pull this together in some configurations, starting with the trust boundary principle of marking nearest to the end-points on the network.

To apply this, you need to understand the edge marking mechanisms that can be applied. In this case, you will use the notion of trust boundaries. The concept of trust is an important and integral one to implementing QoS. As soon as the end devices have a set CoS or ToS, the switch can either trust them or not. If the device at the edge (in our case, a switch) trusts the settings, it does not need to do any reclassification. If it does not trust the settings, it must perform reclassification for the appropriate QoS.

The notion of trusting or not trusting forms the basis of the trust boundary. Ideally, classification should be done as close to the source as possible. If the end device can perform this function, the trust boundary for the network is at the access layer. This depends on the capabilities of the switch in the access layer. If the switch can reclassify the packets, the trust boundary remains in the access layer. If the switch cannot perform this function, the task falls to other devices in the network going toward the backbone.

In this case, the rule of thumb is to perform reclassification at the distribution layer. This means that the trust boundary has shifted to the distribution layer. It is more than likely that there is a high-end switch in the distribution layer with features to support this function. If possible, try to avoid performing this function in the core of the network.

Frames and packets can be marked as important by using Layer 2 CoS settings in the User Priority bits of the 802.1p portion of the 802.1Q header or the IPP/DSCP bits in the ToS byte of the IPv4 header.

Figure 5-10 gives an overview of the trust boundary states that can be applicable when establishing this capability:

- A device is *trusted* if it correctly classifies packets.
- For scalability, classification should be done as close to the edge as possible.
- The outermost trusted devices represent the trust boundary.
- (1) and (2) are optimal; (3) is acceptable (if the access switch cannot perform classification).

Figure 5-10 *Establishing the Trust Boundary*

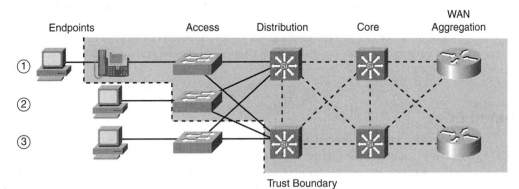

For example, suppose you have a LAN edge that is configured to have the voice traffic sit in an auxiliary virtual LAN (VLAN) and data traffic that transports standard desktop PC connectivity in a standard data VLAN. In this case, you can establish a policy of trust on the auxiliary VLAN where the voice endpoints are connected and there's no trust for the data VLAN. This forms a fundamental design principle of the Differentiated Services model, which is to classify and mark packets as close to the source as possible. To keep users from marking their own traffic, a trust boundary needs to be enforced, which should likewise be as close to the source as possible.

Building the Policy Framework

To achieve a consistent end-to-end network QoS implementation, it is expected that all IP traffic follow a set of defined processes from the source to the destination device. As a strategy, the trust boundary should be established at the LAN edge closest to the connected devices, such as desktop/voice/server L2 switches or lab gateways. All IP traffic that arrives at the LAN edge switch should be classified as either trusted or untrusted.

Classification and Marking of Traffic

As the name implies, trusted devices, such as IP phones, call managers, and unity voice servers, already originate traffic with the desired ToS marked to the appropriate values. Hence, it is simply a matter of trusting and preserving the received ToS values when the packets are subsequently forwarded to the next switch or router in the network. On the other hand, not all traffic originating from devices that are user-/admin-configurable, such as desktop PCs and file/print/application servers, should be trusted with respect to their ToS settings (real-time desktop applications are covered in later sections). Therefore, the traffic from these devices needs to be re-marked with the appropriate ToS values that accurately reflect the desired level of priority for such traffic up to a predefined bandwidth limit.

As soon as the traffic is classified as trusted or is re-marked with the correct ToS settings at the LAN edge into one of the defined classes of service, a trusted edge boundary is established. This enables the traffic to be fully trusted within the network such that it can be prioritized and acted on accordingly at any of the potential congestion points. Typically, these congestion points are at the WAN edge; however, they can also be found at the LAN aggregations.

Trusted Edge

For traffic to be fully trusted within the network core, it is critical that all traffic classification and re-marking at the edge be performed before any frames are forwarded to the next switch or router. This means that the ingress traffic must be inspected to determine whether it is to be trusted or untrusted. If it is considered trusted, the L2 CoS, Layer 3 (L3) IPP, or DSCP values can be derived from the incoming frame/packet and subsequently forwarded to the next device unmodified. Untrusted traffic, on the other hand, should be rewritten to a default DSCP value.

Device Trust

To simplify the edge classification and re-marking operation, the concept of a trusted device needs to be defined. These are devices that are known to correctly provide QoS markings for traffic they originate. Furthermore, these devices also have limited or minimal user QoS configuration capability, such as IP phones, Call Manager/Unity/IPCC servers, and voice/videoconferencing gateways. Whenever these devices are connected to the L2 edge switch, it is easier to trust the L2 CoS or L3 DSCP information on the ingress port rather than to manually identify the type of traffic that should be trusted by means of access control lists (ACLs). For some traffic types, such as RTP streams, it is more difficult to match on specific Layer 4 (L4) ports because the application operates on dynamic port ranges. In such cases, where possible, it is preferable to allow the device or application to correctly classify the traffic and be trusted by the switch.

Application Trust

Although it is possible to establish a trust boundary using ingress CoS or ToS values from devices that are considered trusted, it is important to note that not all devices support the proper QoS marking. Hence, forwarding the traffic without first modifying the ToS value to the appropriate IPP or DSCP can potentially result in erroneous QoS treatment of the traffic for a particular CoS at the WAN edge. By passing all untrusted traffic through an ACL at the LAN edge, it is possible to correctly identify applications that cannot provide correct QoS marking based on the L3/L4 protocol information. Subsequently, these applications can be reclassified and marked to the appropriate classes of service. All other traffic that the ACL does not correctly identify should have its CoS and/or ToS values rewritten to the default/best-effort CoS.

An example of classification by ACL is to re-mark traffic originating Cisco Softphone RTP stream from workstations to Class 5 and associated Skinny (SCCP) packets to Class 3 and non-drop-sensitive batch transfer traffic to Class 1. All other traffic is rewritten to Class 0 regardless of how the original ToS values are set.

By enabling trust for specific real-time desktop applications, such as Cisco Softphone and videoconferencing, it is envisioned that a strategy for ingress traffic policing or rate limiting of traffic belonging to Classes 3, 4, and 5 also be applied at the LAN switch. This would ensure that each attached desktop machine does not exceed a predefined maximum bandwidth value for these priority classes of service. This does not eliminate the need for a comprehensive call admission control (CAC) implementation for voice and video. However, this is yet another level of protection against potential misuse of the QoS classes of service whether it is executed intentionally or unintentionally.

CoS and DSCP

At the L2 edge, Cisco IP phones can VLAN trunk to the Catalyst switches using 802.1Q tagging. Within the 802.1Q tagged frame is a 3-bit CoS field that is commonly referred to as the 802.1p bits. Coincidentally, this is equivalent to the 3 IPP bits within the L3 ToS field. Hence, to maintain end-to-end QoS, it is necessary to ensure that the CoS-to-IPP and IPP-to-CoS are consistently mapped throughout the network. Similarly, CoS values can also be mapped to DSCP to provide the same end-to-end QoS functionality; however, care must be taken to ensure that each CoS value is mapped to a DSCP range of values that has a common 3 MSBs.

By leveraging the CoS setting of the frame coming from the phone, strict priority ingress queuing is possible on Catalyst platforms that support a receive queue mechanism. Because the intelligence of the ingress application-specific integrated circuit (ASIC) on the switch is limited to L2 header inspection, ingress queuing based on L3 ToS values is not possible. For trusted devices that are not capable of 802.1Q trunking to the Ethernet switches, as well as ports configured for edge switch to router uplinks, it is necessary to trust the DSCP values of all incoming IP packets.

Strategy for Classifying Voice Bearer Traffic

Voice traffic traverses the network in the form of RTP streams. The Cisco IP phone originates RTP packets with a DSCP value of 46 (EF) and a CoS value of 5. Based on the device trust model, the DSCP value of voice packets should be preserved across the network. Because MPLS VPN is the WAN transport you are considering, it is common across many service providers to expect RTP traffic presented at the ingress of the provider edge (PE) device to be marked with a DSCP value of 46.

QoS on Backup WAN Connections

Today, WAN services are diverse. Depending on the geographic location of the sites, they may include technologies such as ATM, Frame Relay, ISDN, point-to-point time-division multiplexing (TDM), and network-based VPNs. However, a site is not always provisioned with equal-sized connections. Hence, if a backup connection exists, it is expected to be of a lower bandwidth than the primary link as well as being idle during normal operating conditions. This means that when the site's traffic is required to be routed over the backup connection, potential oversubscription of the link may occur.

To understand how QoS can be applied to back up WAN circuits, it is important to understand exactly how much is allocated for each CoS on the primary connection. However, due to the diverse nature of the types of site locations and sizes of WAN circuits implemented in today's environment, the overall amount of bandwidth required for real-time traffic can vary from one site to another. It is therefore recommended that, for any given fixed-line primary WAN link, no more than 33 percent of the total available bandwidth be assigned to traffic belonging to Class 5. This is consistent with the overall recommendations for provisioning LLQ, as discussed in earlier sections. This can also be overprovisioned.

Shaping/Policing Strategy

There are many cases in which a connection's guaranteed bandwidth is not necessarily the same as the physical port speed. Hence, anything that is transmitted in excess of the available bandwidth is subject to policing and potentially can be dropped by the service provider without regard for the traffic classes. WAN technologies such as Frame Relay, ATM, and L2 and L3 IP/VPN services are good examples of this, whereby it is possible to transmit up to the physical access port speed. However, the service provider guarantees delivery for traffic only up to the contracted bandwidth such as CIR or sustainable cell rate (SCR) in the case of ATM.

The decision of whether excess traffic should be dropped or marked down to a different class depending on the applicable WAN technology should be left to the discretion of the network administrator. Traffic shaping and policing at the WAN edge means that there is more control over the type of excess traffic that should be sent to the provider's network. This avoids the chance that service providers will indiscriminately discard excess traffic that belongs to all classes of service.

A better approach is to treat traffic with a different drop preference, as defined in RFC 2597, *Assured Forwarding Drop Preference*. The reason for this is that different queues are drained at different rates. Therefore, if you mark to a different class, you introduce out-of-sequence packet delivery, which has detrimental effects on the in-profile traffic. DSCP-based WRED is then employed to discard out-of-profile traffic aggressively ahead of in-profile traffic.

Real-time voice traffic is sensitive to delay and jitter. Therefore, it is recommended that whenever possible, excess burst traffic for this class should be policed. By default, real-time voice traffic that exceeds the bandwidth allocated to the strict priority queue (low-latency queuing [LLQ]) is allowed limited bursting.

When using network-based VPN services, such as MPLS VPN, and depending on the service provider offerings, each class can be allocated guaranteed bandwidth across the provider network. By shaping each class at the customer edge (CE), excess traffic could still be forwarded to the provider network but may be marked down to a different CoS or set to a higher drop preference value within the same class selector. This would ensure that if a service provider experiences network congestion, traffic is dropped based on the network administrator's preference rather than random discards by the provider.

NOTE	Providers apply an always-on policer to protect their core capacity planning. This means that even if bandwidth on the link is available, if the EF traffic exceeds allocation, it is dropped within the provider network.

In the case of L2/L3 VPN, it is also possible to have many sites connected to the same service provider network with varying connection speeds. Often, the hub site is serviced by a much larger connection while remote offices are connected at significantly reduced speed. This may cause an oversubscription of the remote WAN connection due to the peer-to-peer nature of L2/L3 VPNs. Egress shaping should be considered on the CE, particularly at the hub location, to prevent this situation from occurring. However, some level of oversubscription of the remote link may still occur, due to the fact that remote-to-remote office traffic patterns are unpredictable and cannot be accounted for. For L2 VPN services that share a common broadcast domain, it is not recommended that these types of technology be adopted due to the difficulty inherent in egress traffic shaping.

Queuing/Link Efficiency Strategy

QoS mechanisms such as LLQ and CBWFQ address the prioritization of L3 traffic to the router's interface driver. However, the underlying hardware that places actual bits on the physical wire is made up of a single transmit ring buffer (TX ring) that operates in a FIFO fashion. The result is the introduction of a fixed delay (commonly called serialization delay) to the overall end-to-end transmission of a packet before it is encoded onto the wire. Depending on link speed and the packet's size, this serialization delay can be significant and can have a severe impact on voice quality.

Small voice packets that are processed via LLQ are still queued behind other packets in the TX ring buffer. In the worst-case scenario, the voice packet would have to wait for a 1500-byte packet to be transmitted first. Hence, serialization delay becomes a major factor in the overall end-to-end latency of the voice packet.

The size of the TX ring buffer represents a trade-off. If the buffer is too large, it is possible that too many data fragments may be placed in the queue before an LLQ fragment. This would result in the LLQ fragment's being delayed, causing higher latency and jitter. A buffer that's too small can keep higher-speed interfaces from failing to achieve line rate. For 2-Mbps circuits, the default depth is two fragments. This means that at the worst there is the potential for up to two low-priority data fragments to be on the TX ring when an LLQ fragment is ready to transmit.

Therefore, fragment sizes must be calculated to account for a transmit delay of up to two fragments. Based on the fragment-sized calculation, the worst-case jitter target for these low-speed links should be approximately 18 ms. MLP fragments in Cisco IOS have 11-byte L2 headers (with shared flags and long sequence numbers). Based on 11-byte overhead and fragment-size multiples of 32, the following calculation is used to derive the fragment size for MLP:

$$FragmentSize = \frac{LinkRate(bps)* \ .009}{8} - 11(Bytes)$$

Then, you round down to multiples of 32, as shown in Table 5-1.

Table 5-1   *Fragment Sizing*

Line Rate (in kbps)	Fragment Size (in Bytes)
128	128
256	256
384	416
512	576
768	864
1024	1152
> 1024	No fragmentation

The overhead of FRF.12 is similar and does not affect the fragment sizes used. As a result, LFI (via MLP or FRF.12) is required for link rates of 1024 kbps or less.

For the low-speed links defined in Table 5-2, LFI techniques such as MLP and Frame Relay FRF.12 can be used to reduce the effect of serialization delay on voice traffic in such an environment. LFI functions by fragmenting larger packets into smaller-sized fragments such that, for a given low-speed link, all packets can be transmitted onto the wire with a serialization delay that is acceptable to voice traffic. For low-speed ATM links, it is inadvisable to use MLP LFI over ATM virtual circuits because of the high overhead associated with encapsulation for small packets. Implementing low-speed ATM links is becoming an uncommon practice. However, if such scenarios exist and if voice is a requirement, it is recommended that the link speed be provisioned above 1024 kbps to avoid serialization delay and the need for fragmentation.

Table 5-2   *LFI Fragment Sizing: Serialization Delay for Link Speeds of 1024 kbps and Below*

Link Speed (in kbps)	Packet Size (in Bytes)					
	64	128	256	512	1024	1500
64	8 ms	16 ms	32 ms	64 ms	128 ms	187 ms
128	4 ms	8 ms	16 ms	32 ms	64 ms	93 ms
256	2 ms	4 ms	8 ms	16 ms	32 ms	46 ms
512	1 ms	2 ms	4 ms	8 ms	16 ms	23 ms
768	0.64 ms	1.3 ms	2.6 ms	5.1 ms	10.3 ms	15 ms
1024	0.4 ms	0.98 ms	2 ms	3.9 ms	7.8 ms	11.7 ms

For WAN services that do not support LFI, such as digital subscriber line (DSL) and cable technologies, it is recommended that manual override of TCP segment size values be configured on the connected router interface. This ensures that large TCP packets are fragmented to reduce the effect of serialization delay on low-speed broadband circuits.

IP/VPN QoS Strategy

Layer 3 VPN technology, such as MPLS VPN, introduces several challenges. One of those challenges is the QoS treatment and handling of traffic across the service provider's IP network, which would likely have a different type and number of QoS CoSs. Given that traffic would be routed by the provider across the IP network, it is imperative that the internal QoS classes of service be handled correctly to ensure that service levels are being met.

In some cases, there may not be a direct one-to-one mapping of enterprise CoSs to those offered by the service providers. In that case, it is necessary at the WAN edge to merge or remap the internal classes so that they may align. To ensure that important and high-priority classes are given the same level of service as if they were traversing the internal private WAN, care must be taken when such actions are carried out.

Enterprises implement more classes of service, because they want to separate applications. However, in the provider's IP core, they aggregate classes based on the service-level agreement (SLA) type. That is, they have priority queuing (PQ) for controlled latency and CBWFQ for guaranteed-bandwidth and best-effort. All CBWFQ applications that are separated at the edge are lumped together. However, as long as the aggregate meets the needs of the sum of the individual guarantees at the edge, it is fine for the service provider core and is of no concern.

Service providers may have different strategies for enforcing QoS classes. Although it may be a common practice for one provider to discard excess traffic marked with higher drop precedence within a class selector, others may elect to drop traffic from lower-priority classes instead. This aspect of the provider's QoS offering must be fully understood and assessed so that the correct merging and/or remapping of an enterprise's internal classes are performed.

For example, if the service provider is offering four levels of QoS—EF, AF1, AF2, and best-effort (BE)—it is not recommended that more than one internal customer class share a common service provider class selector. That is, if traffic belonging to Class 2 is mapped to AF2, only packets that exceed the maximum bandwidth for this class should be marked down to AF22 or AF23, because these represent higher drop preference values within this particular class selector. In this case, no other traffic should be marked as AF22 or AF23, except excess traffic belonging to Class 2.

IP values 6 and 7 are also used for network control traffic (routing protocols). Most of this traffic is link-local, so an individual class of traffic can be set up for this traffic on a WAN port, with minimum bandwidth. On the CE side of the CE-to-PE links, it is recommended that a separate class be used for management traffic. On the PE side of the CE-to-PE link, this tends to vary per provider. This traffic must, at a minimum, be mapped into a high-priority data CoS in the service provider cloud.

Approaches for QoS Transparency Requirements for the Service Provider Network

Any L3 IP/VPN solution implemented in an enterprise network must support QoS transparency. QoS transparency is defined as the ability to recover your original discrete CoSs at the remote end of the IP/VPN network. It is unacceptable for multiple CoSs to be combined into one service provider class such that, at the remote end, the traffic cannot be recovered into the separate CoSs. This transparency can be achieved in one of two ways.

With the first option, the enterprise CE can convert the IP DSCP values to those expected by your service provider's PE, as long as a minimum of five discrete values across the service provider's network preserve the independence of the five CoSs. At the remote CE, traffic can be re-marked back to the appropriate levels for the enterprise network. It is unacceptable for traffic from one class to be re-marked by the network into another class such that it would end up in a different CoS when it was converted back to the enterprise's expected values.

The second option, available in MPLS VPN only, is to leave the IP DSCP markings untouched and use those values to set the MPLS Experimental (EXP) QoS bits to an appropriate level of service based on the markings defined by the enterprise.

RFC 3270 discusses more of the operational aspects with the transport of differing DiffServ implementations. It also classifies these into three effective modes. The Uniform, Pipe, and Short-Pipe modes provide the solution for service providers' flexibility in selecting how DiffServ CoSs are routed or traffic-engineered within their domain.

DiffServ tunneling modes introduce a new Per-Hop Behavior (PHB) that allows differ-entiated QoS in a provider's network. The tunneling mode is defined at the edge of the network, normally in the PE label switch routers (LSRs) (both ingress and egress). You may need to make changes in the P routers, and you must also consider what occurs when the topmost label is removed from a packet due to Penultimate Hop Popping (PHP). It may be necessary to copy the MPLS EXP value from the top label that is being popped to the newly exposed label; this does not always apply to all tunneling modes.

In some cases (for example, a plain non-VPN MPLS network), the PHP action on the final P router can expose a plain IP packet when a packet with only one label is received. When this IP packet is received by the egress LSR (PE), it is not possible to classify the packet based on the MPLS EXP bits because there is no label now. In these situations, you must configure the egress PE router to advertise an explicit-null label. When the PHP action is performed on the P router, a label with a value of 0 is sent. With this special label, you can mark the EXP bits as normally labeled packets, allowing the correct classification on the egress PE router.

MPLS network support of DiffServ specification defines the following tunneling modes:

- Uniform
- Pipe
- Short-Pipe

The next sections examine each tunneling mode and provide examples that show how you can configure each one. The examples include a full mapping of IPP to MPLS EXP bits. It is possible to have a number of different QoS parameters and tunneling modes for each customer.

NOTE   The configuration examples are not specific for MPLS VPN and are applicable for plain MPLS networks and Carrier-Supported Carrier (CsC) networks. It is also possible that your network can vary from another network in which many different QoS parameters and tunneling modes can be used.

Uniform Mode

DiffServ tunneling Uniform mode has only one layer of QoS, which reaches end to end. The ingress PE router (PE1) copies the DSCP from the incoming IP packet into the MPLS EXP bits of the imposed labels. As the EXP bits travel through the core, they may or may not be modified by intermediate P routers. In this example, the P router modifies the EXP bits of the top label. At the egress P router, you can copy the EXP bits to the EXP bits of the newly exposed label after the PHP. Finally, at the egress PE router, you can copy the EXP bits to the DSCP bits of the newly exposed IP packet.

Pipe Mode

DiffServ tunneling Pipe mode uses two layers of QoS:

- An underlying QoS for the data, which remains unchanged when traversing the core.
- A per-core QoS, which is separate from that of the underlying IP packets. This per-core QoS PHB remains transparent to end users.

When a packet reaches the edge of the MPLS core, the egress PE router classifies the newly exposed IP packets for outbound queuing based on the MPLS PHB from the EXP bits of the recently removed label.

Short-Pipe Mode

DiffServ tunneling Short-Pipe mode uses the same rules and techniques across the core. The difference is that, at the egress PE router, you classify the newly exposed IP packets for outbound queuing based on the IP PHB from the DSCP value of this IP packet.

QoS CoS Requirements for the SP Network

The service provider's network must support a minimum of three classes at all interfaces with speeds of OC-12/STM-4 (622 Mbps) and less. These classes must include a real-time class using LLQ, a high-priority data class with CBWFQ "minimum bandwidth," and a best-effort class.

Four or five classes are preferred (with the minimum requirements for an LLQ class and all but one of the remaining classes supporting minimum bandwidth), such that the enterprise classes can map directly to the service provider's network.

WRED Implementations

Whereas QoS and LFI are techniques for congestion management, WRED is a technique used for congestion avoidance. WRED, when implemented, allows for the early detection of network congestion and provides the means for the selective discard of packets based on the IPP or DSCP values. When the average queue depth exceeds a user-defined minimum threshold, WRED begins discarding lower-priority packets (both TCP and UDP) based on the QoS information. The intent is to allow TCP applications to decrease their transmission rate and allow the network utilization to level out. Should the average queue depth increase above the user-defined maximum threshold, WRED reverts to "tail-drop" operation. This means that all packets entering the queue at that point are dropped until the traffic utilization is reduced to below the maximum threshold.

Because all traffic is classified and marked at the LAN edge, it is more useful for WRED to be implemented at the WAN edge routers. This way, when the core of the network experiences congestion, packets can be intelligently discarded. In most cases, WRED is recommended only for WAN edge routers that directly connect to IP/VPN providers that explicitly indicate that they support this feature. Packets that exceed threshold values can have their priority marked down or selectively discarded. An important point to keep in mind is that WRED should not be applied to queues that support voice traffic, due to the potential impact that packet loss can have on voice quality.

Additionally, Explicit Congestion Notification (ECN) is an extension to WRED in that ECN marks packets instead of dropping them when the average queue length exceeds a specific threshold value. When configured with WRED's ECN feature, routers and end hosts use this marking as a signal that the network is congested and slow down sending of packets.

As stated in RFC 3168, *The Addition of Explicit Congestion Notification (ECN) to IP,* implementing ECN requires an ECN-specific field that has 2 bits: the ECN-capable Transport (ECT) bit and the CE (Congestion Experienced) bit in the IP header. The ECT bit and the CE bit can be used to make four ECN field combinations of 00 to 11. The first number is the ECT bit, and the second number is the CE bit. Figure 5-11 gives an overview of ECN application.

Figure 5-11 *ECN Application*

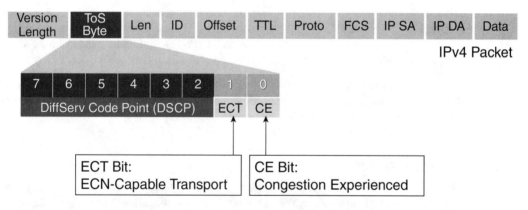

RFC3168: IP Explicit Congestion Notification

ECN is being adopted in a lot of enterprise and service provider networks, which complements WRED. The benefits can be summarized as follows:

- **Improved method for congestion avoidance**—This feature provides an improved method for congestion avoidance by allowing the network to mark packets for later transmission, rather than dropping them from the queue. Marking the packets for later transmission accommodates applications that are sensitive to delay or packet loss and provides improved throughput and application performance.

- **Enhanced queue management**—Currently, dropped packets indicate that a queue is full and that the network is experiencing congestion. When a network experiences congestion, this feature allows networks to mark a packet's IP header with a CE bit. This marking, in turn, triggers the appropriate congestion-avoidance mechanism and allows the network to better manage the data queues. With this feature, ECN-capable routers and end hosts can respond to congestion before a queue overflows and packets are dropped, providing enhanced queue management.

For more information on the benefits associated with ECN, refer to RFC 2309, *Internet Performance Recommendations*.

Identification of Traffic

After the QoS policy and toolsets that can be employed have been defined, the starting point is to understand the profile of traffic that exists in the network. To identify the traffic, several approaches can be taken to identify the current flows and start the work of classification. The easiest way to do this is to first determine the real-time applications that require special handling as they traverse the network. With these, there is a need to identify not just the bearer traffic but also the signaling traffic that may be required as part of the bearer's normal operation.

What Would Constitute This Real-Time Traffic?

Applications, such as VoIP, videoconferencing over IP, and certain business-critical applications or systems processes, can be one such classification. These applications could be categorized and then assigned a specific handling criteria, such as SAP enterprise resource planning (ERP), storage area network (SAN) replications, Citrix applications, CAD/CAM operations, and, of course, those real-time requirements of voice and video.

The treatment of the traffic is, within a framework of QoS policy, done based on its classification. Endpoints that perform this function need to be able to mark their traffic in a specific way to allow the proper handling to be done as traffic traverses the network. When it comes to real-time applications, this requires identifying the bearer and control (signaling) traffic and ensuring that it is placed in the appropriate class. When this occurs, action needs to be taken to understand what happens with the remaining traffic. Thus, a process of identification is required. It is safe to assume that most applications that traverse the network are, for the most part, unclassified or unmarked where no QoS policy is currently in play.

Figure 5-12 takes the simplistic approach of baselining the existing network to determine the makeup of traffic and applications in play. This is useful because it helps serves as the checkpoint from where to start the classification work. It also requires that an audit be done of the existing network infrastructure to assess its ability to support the applicable policies.

Areas such as device capability and Cisco IOS version must be brought to a consistent level to ensure that there is a base level of capability, stability, and ability to execute the policy.

Figure 5-12 *Identifying the Policy Process*

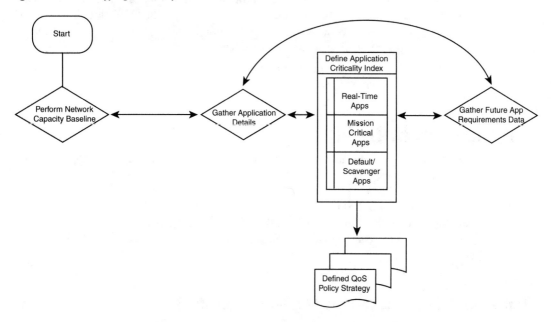

There are many different mechanisms to start to derive the application communications flow, the most useful of which is Cisco NetFlow Accounting. NetFlow provides valuable information about who is using the network, what applications are being used, when the network is used, and where traffic is going on the network. Essentially it is a way to answer the questions of who, where, when, and what. The mechanism extracts the following:

- Source IP address
- Destination IP address
- Source port
- Destination port
- Layer 3 protocol type
- Type of service byte (DSCP)
- Input logical interface (ifIndex)

Using this capability helps you build a scalable mechanism by which to classify application characteristics and start the work of placing these within a classification framework.

QoS Requirements for Voice, Video, and Data

The next step in the process is to identify the detailed requirements for the classes you would create as part of the QoS framework. These characteristics are well defined, and the process involved in their identification is the critical component to ensuring a consistent approach.

To achieve such values, enterprises and service providers must cooperate and be consistent in classifying, provisioning, and integrating their respective QoS solutions.

Additionally, the service provider's network must support a bare minimum of three classes at all interfaces. This is to ensure that the enterprise need not modify or rework its policy to map to the SP policy needlessly or carry the classes within its own classes transparently. These classes must include a real-time class using LLQ, a high-priority data class with CBWFQ's "minimum bandwidth," and a best-effort class.

Four or five classes are preferred, with the minimum requirements for an LLQ class and all but one of the remaining classes supporting minimum bandwidth.

QoS requirements and high-level recommendations for voice, video, and data are outlined in the following sections.

QoS Requirements for Voice

Voice calls, either one-to-one or on a conference connection capability, require the following:

* ≤ 150 ms of one-way latency from mouth to ear (per the ITU G.114 standard)
* ≤ 30 ms jitter
* ≤ 1 percent packet loss
* 17 to 106 kbps of guaranteed priority bandwidth per call (depending on the sampling rate, codec, and Layer 2 overhead)
* 150 bps (plus Layer 2 overhead) per phone of guaranteed bandwidth for voice control traffic

The choice of codec has impacts in many areas. The most important is the capacity planning on the network, because the bandwidth consumed in different codecs varies.

When exploring the details of these needs in their work on tight IP SLA, John Evans and Clarence Filsfils wrote that G.114 states that 150 ms of end-to-end one-way delay does not cause a perceivable degradation in voice quality for most use of telephony.

These targets typically include a U.S. coast-to-coast call (equivalent to a Pan-European call) of 6000 km at a propagation speed of 200.000 km/s—thus, 30 ms.

Some carriers try to push to the 100-ms target (excellent: 70 ms without propagation).

A usual target is 150 ms (good: 120 ms without propagation).

Enterprise VoIP networks tend to have a looser target — 250 ms (a decent limit: 220 ms without propagation).

It is also recommended that you look at the consumption of Layer 2 overhead; an accurate method for provisioning VoIP is to include the Layer 2 overhead. Layer 2 overhead includes preambles, headers, flags, cyclic redundancy checks (CRCs), and ATM cell padding. When Layer 2 overhead is included in the bandwidth calculations, the VoIP call bandwidth needs translate to the requirements shown in Table 5-3.

Table 5-3 *VoIP Bandwidth Reference Table*

Codec	Sampling Rate	Voice Payload in Bytes	Packets per Second	Bandwidth per Conversation
G.711	20 ms	160	50	80 kbps
G.711	30 ms	240	33	74 kbps
G.729A	20 ms	20	50	24 kbps
G.729A	30 ms	30	33	19 kbps

A more accurate method for the provisioning is to include the Layer 2 overhead in the bandwidth calculations, as shown in Table 5-4.

Table 5-4 *VoIP Bandwidth Needs with Layer 2 Overhead*

Codec	801.Q Ethernet + 32 Layer 2 Bytes	MLP + 13 Layer 2 Bytes	Frame Relay + 8 Layer 2 Bytes	ATM + Variable Layer 2 Bytes (Cell Padding)
G.711 at 50 pps	93 kbps	86 kbps	84 kbps	104 kbps
G.711 at 33 pps	83 kbps	78 kbps	77 kbps	84 kbps
G.711 at 50 pps	37 kbps	30 kbps	28 kbps	43 kbps
G.711 at 33 pps	27 kbps	22 kbps	21 kbps	28 kbps

Sample Calculation

The following calculations are used to determine the inputs to the planning of voice call consumption:

total packet size = (L2 header: MP or FRF.12 or Ethernet) + (IP/UDP/RTP header) + (voice payload size)

pps = (codec bit rate) / (voice payload size)

bandwidth = total packet size * pps

For example, the required bandwidth for a G.729 call (8-kbps codec bit rate) with cRTP, MP, and the default 20 bytes of voice payload is as follows:

total packet size (bytes) = (MP header of 6 bytes) + (compressed IP/UDP/RTP header of 2 bytes) + (voice payload of 20 bytes) = 28 bytes

total packet size (bits) = (28 bytes) * 8 bits per byte = 224 bits

pps = (8-kbps codec bit rate) / (160 bits) = 50 pps

NOTE   160 bits = 20 bytes (default voice payload) * 8 bits per byte

---

bandwidth per call = voice packet size (224 bits) * 50 pps = 11.2 kbps

QoS Requirements for Video

The requirements for streaming video, such as IP multicast, executive broadcasts, and real-time training activities, are as follows:

- Four to 5 seconds of latency allowable (depending on the video application's buffering capabilities). No significant jitter requirements.
- Two percent packet loss permissible. Bandwidth required depends on the encoding and the rate of the video stream.
- Video content distribution such as video on demand being replicated to distributed content engines.
- Delay- and jitter-insensitive.
- Large file transfers (traffic patterns similar to FTP sessions).
- Restrict to distribution to less-busy times of day.
- Provision as "less-than-best-effort" data.

The requirements for videoconferencing can be applied as either a one-to-one capability or a multipoint conference.

- ≤ 150 ms of one-way latency from mouth to ear (per the ITU G.114 standard).
- ≤ 30 ms jitter.
- ≤ 1 percent packet loss.
- Minimum bandwidth guarantee is videoconferencing session + 20 percent. For example, a 384-kbps videoconferencing session requires 460 kbps guaranteed priority bandwidth.

I-Frames are full-frame samples, whereas P and B frames are differential (or delta) frames. Videoconferencing shares the same latency, jitter, and loss requirements as voice but has radically burstier and heavier traffic patterns.

A 384-kbps stream can take up to 600 kbps at points rather than provisioning the stream + 60 percent (to accommodate the occasional 600-kbps burst). The video stream includes an additional 20 percent of bandwidth with a burst allowance in the LLQ of 30,000 bytes per 384-kbps stream, as shown in Figure 5-13:

- Provision LLQ to stream + 20 percent.

  For example, 384-kbps stream → 460-kbps LLQ

- Additionally, extend the LLQ burst to capture I frames without requiring additional LLQ bandwidth reservation.

Figure 5-13 *Video Stream Sequence*

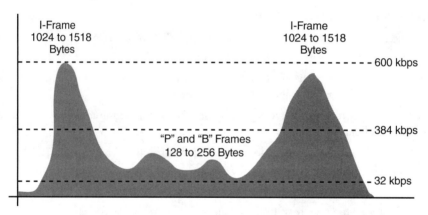

QoS Requirements for Data

Following the earlier discussion about the application of traffic identification, there are a few key points to remember about classifying data traffic:

- Profile applications to get a basic understanding of their network requirements.

- Perform capacity planning to ensure an adequate bandwidth baseline.

- Use no more than four separate data traffic classes:

  — Transactional data (mission-critical)—ERP, transactional, and high-priority internal applications

— Bulk data (guaranteed-bandwidth)—Streaming video, messaging, and intranet

— Best-effort (the default class)—Internet browsing, e-mail, and unclassified applications

— Scavenger (less-than-best-effort)—FTP, backups, and noncritical applications

- Minimize the number of applications assigned to the transactional and bulk data classes (three or fewer are recommended).

- Use proactive provisioning polices before reactive policing policies.

These requirements for the data classes are guidelines. They need to take into account many different factors, including the service provider. They must be able to support the number of classes required by the enterprise. As such, they may affect the decision process in the policy's creation.

Governance plays a key role in identifying and classifying applications. By building a governance checkpoint in the development of new applications, a lot of cycles can be reduced in determining an application's bandwidth needs and its impact on network requirements. The process can pinpoint whether the new application will lead to any network upgrades as well as determine a baseline for the application, which can lead to predictive planning on an incremental yearly basis of adding the application to the network. It allows for better planning, thereby removing the challenge that can be created because of bottlenecks or scaling issues, and the key tenant of running the network as a fairly used business asset.

A critical factor in the service provider delivery is the SLA, affecting the ability to support delay-sensitive classes, as seen in voice and video requirements. In some cases, other factors preclude the service provider's ability to deliver an SLA against these requirements, such as the geographic location of sites and the interconnections over the service provider network.

For example, suppose you have a site in a geographically remote location that has a large propagation delay imposed on it because of its location. It may not be possible to meet the requirements for delivery of real-time services to its location. In such cases, there is a trade-off between what is possible for the majority of the corporate sites and that of the remote geographies and their interconnection capability to the rest of the network.

The LAN Edge: L2 Configurations

Framing this in the context of a sample configuration, the switch device at the edge of the network has the following policy applied:

Depending on the switch model, it may be necessary to first activate QoS using this command:

```
switch(config)#mls qos
```

This command is required on both the Catalyst 3550 and the Catalyst 6500. The Catalyst 2950 has QoS enabled by default.

The trust is configured on the switch port using this command:

```
switch(config-if)#mls qos trust dscp
```

Any ISL or 802.1Q/p frames that enter the switch port have their CoS passed (untouched) through the switch. If an untagged frame arrives at the switch port, the switch assigns a default CoS to the frame before forwarding it. By default, untagged frames are assigned a CoS of 0. This can be changed using this interface configuration command:

```
switch(config-if)#mls qos cos default-cos
```

where *default-cos* is a number between 0 and 7.

The syntax to configure QoS trust switch-wide for IP phone endpoints is all that is required in typical installations:

```
Switch(config-if)#mls qos trust device ciscoipphone
```

Here's the legacy syntax that was required on a per-VLAN basis:

```
Switch(config-if)#switchport voice vlan {vlan-id | dot1p | none | untagged}
```

To instruct the Cisco IP Phone to forward all voice traffic through a specified VLAN, use this command:

```
Switch(config-if)#switchport voice vlan vlan-id
```

By default, the Cisco IP Phone forwards the voice traffic with an 802.1Q priority of 5. Valid VLAN IDs are from 1 to 4096.

An alternative to specifying a particular voice VLAN on the switch is to instruct the switch port to use 802.1P priority tagging for voice traffic and to use the default native VLAN (VLAN 0) to carry all traffic. By default, if enabled, the Cisco IP Phone forwards the voice traffic with an 802.1P priority of 5.

```
Switch(config-if)#switchport voice vlan dot1p
```

In some cases, it may be desirable—indeed, highly recommended—not to trust edge CoS for nonvoice/video endpoints and not to trust any CoS value that may be present in frames sourced from an edge device. For example, an office PC used for general applications, such as web browsing, e-mail, and file and print services, may not require special QoS treatment. Allowing it to request higher levels of QoS may adversely affect applications such as voice and video, which require guarantees of bandwidth and latency.

NOTE   This may not hold true for data center or server-based systems, which need to be given individual consideration based on the prioritization needs of any application they serve.

For this reason, it is possible to use the **override** parameter to tell the switch to ignore any existing CoS value that may be in the frame and apply the default value. This effectively disables any trust configuration that may have previously been applied to the port.

The CoS value assigned by the switch can be changed on a port-by-port basis using this interface configuration command:

```
Switch(config-if)#mls qos cos override
```

After this command is applied, the switch rewrites the CoS value for all incoming frames to the configured default value, regardless of any existing CoS value.

Other platforms, such as those that employ CatOS, vary. You should always verify such a reference to the correct procedure by reviewing the relevant documentation at http://www.cisco.com. For example, the following is an overview of configuring prioritization, with a 6500 platform running CatOS between Cisco CallManager and IP phones and gateways using TCP ports 2000 to 2002. The sample commands classify all Skinny Protocol traffic from IP phones and gateways (VLAN 110) and Cisco CallManager (4/2) as DSCP AF31, which is backward-compatible with IPP 3.

With older implementations, several steps need to be performed (see Example 5-1):

Step 1   Enable switch-wide QoS.

Step 2   Create an ACL (ACL_IP-PHONES), marking all Skinny Client and Gateway Protocol traffic from the IP phones and from Skinny Protocol gateways with a DSCP value of AF31.

Step 3   Add to the ACL_IP-PHONE access list, trusting all DSCP markings from the IP phone so that the IP Prec = 5 RTP traffic is not rewritten.

Step 4   Create an ACL (ACL_VOIP_CONTROL), marking all Skinny Client and Gateway Protocol traffic from Cisco CallManager with a DSCP value of AF31.

Step 5   Accept incoming Layer 2 CoS classification.

Step 6   Inform the port that all QoS associated with the port will be done on a VLAN basis to simplify configuration.

Step 7   Instruct the IP phone to rewrite CoS from the PC to CoS=0 within the IP phone Ethernet ASIC.

Step 8   Inform Cisco CallManager port (4/2) that all QoS associated with the port will be done on a port basis.

Step 9   Write the ACL to hardware.

Step 10   Map the ACL_IP-PHONE ACL to the auxiliary VLAN.

Step 11 Map the ACL_VOIP_CONTROL ACL to the Cisco CallManager port.

Example 5-1 *Setup of a Catalyst Edge Switch (L2 Only)*

```
cat6k-access> (enable) set qos enable
cat6k-access> (enable) set qos acl ip ACL_IP-PHONES dscp 26 tcp any any range 2000
  2002
cat6k-access> (enable) set qos acl ip ACL_IP-PHONES trust-cos ip any any
cat6k-access> (enable) set qos acl ip ACL_VOIP_CONTROL dscp 26 tcp any any range
  2000 2002
cat6k-access> (enable) set port qos 5/1-48 trust trust-cos
cat6k-access> (enable) set port qos 5/1-48 vlan-based
cat6k-access> (enable) set port qos 5/1-48 trust-ext untrusted
cat6k-access> (enable) set port qos 4/2 port-based
cat6k-access> (enable) commit qos acl all
cat6k-access> (enable) set qos acl map ACL_IP-PHONES 110
cat6k-access> (enable) set qos acl map ACL_VOIP_CONTROL 4/2
```

Classifying Voice on the WAN Edge

A basic configuration of a WAN edge (CE) router is shown in Example 5-2 and defined further in this section. This applies the principles in base configuration terms, as discussed previously.

In this case, you apply a simple LLQ and CBWFQ policy to the router to support voice traffic. Voice traffic needs to be assigned to the LLQ, and voice-control traffic needs a minimum bandwidth guarantee.

Example 5-2 *Matching Voice and Voice Control*

```
ip cef
!
class-map match-all VOICE
  match ip dscp ef
!
class-map match-all VOICE-CONTROL
  match ip dscp cs3
  match ip dscp af31
!
!
policy-map WAN-EDGE
  class VOICE
    priority percent 33
  class VOICE-CONTROL
    bandwidth percent 5
  class class-default
    fair-queue
!
interface Serial0/0
 description WAN Link to CCT ID : 1234 :: SP-PE-1
 bandwidth 2048
 ip address 10.1.1.1 255.255.255.252
 service-policy output WAN-EDGE
```

The class map applied to VOICE and VOICE-CONTROL provides an example of matching against DSCP markings, which in this case are for the voice-bearer traffic and the voice signaling and control traffic. In this basic policy, you assume that no marking of traffic needs to happen directly on this box. Rather, it deals only with the outbound classification of the traffic.

In the policy map itself, in effect you assign three elements—those of prioritization for voice and specified as a percentage of the link bandwidth. This is an example of applying LLQ. Voice control specifies the allocation of 5 percent of link bandwidth for voice control, with the final classification being performed as class default, which uses the fair-queuing algorithm on the remaining traffic. In this case, it is assumed to be the default class.

The key to activating this policy is to attach the service-policy output to an interface—in this case, the output interface facing the SP PE. Thus, applying the classification actions as defined in the policy map WAN-EDGE to the output of the WAN serial interface provides this activation.

Classifying Video on the WAN Edge

In Example 5-3, videoconferencing traffic is assigned LLQ, and all nonvideo traffic is assigned to a default queue for WFQ.

Example 5-3 *Matching Video*

```
ip cef
!
class-map match-all VIDEO
  match ip dscp af41
!
!
policy-map WAN-EDGE
  class VIDEO-CONF
    priority 460
  class class-default
   fair-queue
!
interface Serial0/0
  description WAN Link to CCT ID : 1234 :: SP-PE-1
  bandwidth 2048
  ip address 10.1.1.1 255.255.255.252
  service-policy output WAN-EDGE
```

On the WAN edge, videoconferencing traffic should be assigned to an LLQ. The video stream minimum bandwidth guarantee should be the size of the stream plus 20 percent.

As before, this policy doesn't take effect until it is bound to an interface with a service-policy statement.

Classifying Data on the WAN Edge

Most enterprises have many applications that can be considered mission-critical (trans-actional). However, if too many applications are classified as mission-critical, they will contend among themselves for bandwidth, with the result of dampening QoS effectiveness. Taken to the extreme, a regular FIFO link (no QoS) is scheduled in the exact same manner as a link where every application is provisioned as mission-critical. Therefore, it is recommended that you classify no more than three applications as mission-critical (transactional).

These applications should be marked with different AF drop-preference values to distinguish them from each other. Such distinctions provide more granular visibility in managing and monitoring application traffic and aid in provisioning for future require-ments. Similar arguments are made for having no more than three applications in a guaranteed bandwidth (bulk data) class of applications and, likewise, marking these applications with different AF drop-preference values.

Default traffic is automatically marked as best-effort (DSCP 0). However, noncritical bandwidth-intensive traffic could (optionally) be marked as different so that adverse policies could be applied to control such traffic. These types of traffic can be described as "less-than-best-effort" or "scavenger" traffic.

It is imperative that DSCP classification be performed on all packets before they arrive at the WAN edges. In this manner, queuing and congestion avoidance can be performed at the WAN edge based strictly on DSCP markings.

NOTE   It's important to keep in mind that the default class map **match** setting is **match-all**. Therefore, when you attempt to classify mutually exclusive traffic flows (such as differing DSCP values), it is important to explicitly use the **match-any** qualifier when defining the class map. Another example could be through the use of multiple DSCPs on a single command line:

```
match ip dscp af11 af12 af13
```

The advantage of using multiple lines is that this triggers a separate counter in the class-based QoS Management Information Base (MIB) for each DSCP. (If they are matched all on the same line, only a single counter is triggered for all DSCPs.)

The Eight-Class Model introduces a dual-LLQ design: one for voice and another for interactive video. As pointed out earlier in this chapter, the LLQ has an implicit policer that allows for time-division multiplexing of the single priority queue. This implicit policer abstracts the fact that there is essentially a single LLQ within the algorithm and thus allows for the "provisioning" of multiple LLQs.

Interactive video (or IP videoconferencing, also called IP/VC) is recommended to be marked AF41 (which can be marked down to AF42 in the case of dual-rate policing at the campus access edge). It is recommended that you overprovision the LLQ by 20 percent of the IP/VC rate. This takes into account IP/UDP/RTP headers as well as Layer 2 overhead. Additionally, Cisco IOS Software automatically includes a 200-ms burst parameter (defined in bytes) as part of the priority command. On dual-T1 links, this has proven sufficient for protecting a single 384-kbps IP/VC stream. On higher-speed links (such as triple T1s), the default burst parameter has shown to be insufficient for protecting multiple IP/VC streams.

However, multiple-stream IP/VC quality tested well with the burst set to 30,000 bytes (for example, priority 920 30000). Our testing did not arrive at a clean formula for predicting the required size of the burst parameters as IP/VC streams continually were added. However, given the variable packet sizes and rates of these interactive-video streams, this is not surprising. The main point is that the default LLQ burst parameter might require tuning as multiple IP/VC streams are added (which likely will be a trial-and-error process).

Optionally, DSCP-based WRED can be enabled on the Interactive-Video class, but testing has shown negligible performance difference in doing so (because, as has been noted, WRED is more effective on TCP-based flows than UDP-based flows, such as interactive video). In these designs, WRED is not enabled on classes such as Call-Signaling, IP Routing, and Network-Management because WRED would take effect only if such classes were filling their queues nearly to their limits. Such conditions would indicate a provisioning problem that would be better addressed by increasing the class's minimum bandwidth allocation than by enabling WRED.

Additionally, the Eight-Class Model subdivides the preferential data class to separate control plane traffic (IP routing and network-management applications) from business-critical data traffic. IGP packets (such as RIP, EIGRP, OSPF, and IS-IS) are protected through the PAK_priority mechanism within the router. However, EGP protocols, such as BGP, do not get PAK_priority treatment and might need explicit bandwidth guarantees to ensure that peering sessions do not reset during periods of congestion. Additionally, administrators might want to protect network-management access to devices during periods of congestion.

The other class added to this model is for bulk traffic (the Bulk Data class), which is spun off of the Critical Data class. Because TCP continually increases its window sizes, which is especially noticeable in long sessions (such as large file transfers), constraining bulk data to its own class alleviates other data classes from being dominated by such large file transfers. Bulk data is identified by DSCP AF11 (or AF12 in the case of dual-rate policing at the campus access edges). DSCP-based WRED can be enabled on the Bulk Data class (and also on the Critical Data class). Example 5-4 shows the implementation of the Eight-Class Model for the WAN edge.

Example 5-4 *Eight-Class Model*

```
!
class-map match-all Voice
 match ip dscp ef ! IP Phones mark Voice to EF
class-map match-all Interactive Video
 match ip dscp af41 af42 ! Recommended markings for IP/VC
class-map match-any Call Signaling
 match ip dscp cs3 ! Future Call-Signaling marking
 match ip dscp af31 ! Current Call-Signaling marking
class-map match-any Network Control
 match ip dscp cs6 ! Routers mark Routing traffic to CS6
 match ip dscp cs2 ! Recommended marking for Network Management
class-map match-all Critical Data
 match ip dscp af21 af22 ! Recommended markings for Transactional-Data
class-map match-all Bulk Data
 match ip dscp af11 af12 ! Recommended markings for Bulk-Data
class-map match-all Scavenger
    match ip dscp cs1 ! Scavenger marking
!
policy-map WAN-EDGE
 class Voice
  priority percent 18 ! Voice gets 552 kbps of LLQ
 class Interactive Video
  priority percent 15 ! 384 kbps IP/VC needs 460 kbps of LLQ
 class Call Signaling
  bandwidth percent 5 ! BW guarantee for Call-Signaling
 class Network Control
  bandwidth percent 5 ! Routing and Network Management get min 5% Bandwidth
 class Critical Data
  bandwidth percent 27 ! Critical Data gets min 27% BW
  random-detect dscp-based ! Enables DSCP-WRED for Critical-Data class
 class Bulk Data
  bandwidth percent 4 ! Bulk Data gets min 4% BW guarantee
  random-detect dscp-based ! Enables DSCP-WRED for Bulk-Data class
 class Scavenger
  bandwidth percent 1 ! Scavenger class is throttled to 1% of bandwidth
 class class-default
  bandwidth percent 25 ! Fair-queuing is sacrificed for Bandwidth guarantee
  random-detect ! Enables WRED on class-default
!
```

This design is more efficient than strict policing, because these bandwidth-intensive noncritical applications can use additional bandwidth if it is available while ensuring protection for critical transactional data classes and real-time voice and video applications.

The development of this model is attributed to Tim Szigeti from the Cisco Enterprise Solutions Engineering Group.

For more information on this approach, go to http://www.cisco.com/application/pdf/en/us/ guest/netsol/ns432/c649/ccmigration_09186a008049b062.pdf.

Case Study: QoS in the Acme, Inc. Network

Acme, Inc. currently uses five different classes of service on the Acme network. For simplicity's sake, and because of the 3-bit resolution of some QoS technologies, such as 802.1p LAN CoS, MPLS EXP, and IP precedence, Acme IT limits its QoS to classes that can be identified in 3 bits. Traffic is classified at the WAN edge by matching IP precedence values—only the first 3 bits of the ToS byte, which cover 7 DSCP values each.

The policy template shown in Table 5-5 deals with policy marking of packets in Acme. It shows QoS policy for voice, video, and data classifications and their breakout assignments based on circuit speed, allocation per class as a percentage, and the classifications assigned.

Table 5-5   *Sample Policy Template Breakdown*

Policy Number	30	25	20	15	10	5
	Bandwidth at Interface Line Rate (in kbps)					
Class	622000	155000	45000 to 34000	34000 to 2048	2048 to 1024	1024 to 256
Management	2%	2%	2%	2%	2%	6%
Voice EF	10%	33%	33%	33%	33%	33%
Video AF4	5%	5%	8%	7%	10%	5%
Signaling AF3	5%	5%	5%	5%	5%	10%
Default BE	58%	45%	50%	43%	40%	36%
Scavenger CS1	20%	10%	10%	10%	10%	10%
Total	**100%**	**100%**	**100%**	**100%**	**100%**	**100%**

IP precedence values 6 and 7 are also used for network control traffic (routing protocols). Most of this traffic is link-local (CE-PE only), allowing an individual class of traffic to be set up for this traffic on a WAN port with minimum bandwidth. On the CE side of the CE-to-PE links, it is recommended that a separate class be used for management traffic. On the

PE side of the CE-to-PE link, this tends to vary with each provider. This traffic must, at a minimum, be mapped to a high-priority data class of service in the service provider cloud.

QoS for Low-Speed Links: 64 kbps to 1024 kbps

LFI allows large packets on a serial link to be divided into using MLP or Frame Relay encapsulation with FRF.12 fragmentation.

To determine the LFI fragment size, you must consider the packet flow through the router. Following the link fragmentation process and LLQ/CBWFQ's fragment ordering, fragments are placed on a transmit ring buffer or TX ring. The TX ring then queues packets onto the physical interface in a FIFO fashion.

Example 5-5 shows examples of applications using MLP and FRF.12.

Example 5-5 *LFI on MLP*

```
interface Multilink1                      Multilink bundle interface
bandwidtd XXX                             Enter Link bandwidth in kbps
 ip address 10.52.255.1 255.255.255.252
 no ip redirects
 no ip proxy-arp
 ip authentication mode eigrp 109 md5
 ip authentication key-chain eigrp 100 apple_key
 max-reserved-bandwidth 100
 service-policy output WAN-EDGE           Apply service policy outbound
 ppp multilink                            Configure Multilink
 ppp multilink fragment-delay 10          Set the max packet delay in ms
                                          (determines fragment size)
 ppp multilink interleave                 Enable LFI
 multilink-group 1                        Apply template to multilink group #1
 !
 !
interface Serial S:P
 description Multilink PPP group member
 bandwidth XXX                            Configure bandwidth equal to full line rate
 no ip address
 no ip redirects
 no ip proxy-arp
 encapsulation ppp
 fair-queue
 ppp multilink                            enable multilink on interface
 multilink-group 1                        Assign interface to multilink group 1
 !
interface Serial S:P                      Next I/F when MLP Bundling is required
 description Multilink PPP group member
 bandwidth XXX
```

Slow-Speed (768-kbps) Leased-Line Recommendation: Use MLP LFI and cRTP

For slow-speed leased lines, LFI is required to minimize serialization delay. Therefore, MLP is the only encapsulation option on slow-speed leased lines because MLP LFI is the only mechanism available for fragmentation and interleaving on such links. Optionally, cRTP can be enabled either as part of the modular QoS command-line interface (MQC) policy map or under the multilink interface (using the **ip rtp header-compression** command). Ensure that MLP LFI and cRTP, if enabled, are configured on both ends of the point-to-point link, as shown in Example 5-6.

Example 5-6   *Slow-Speed (768-kbps) Leased-Line QoS Design Example*

```
!
policy-map WAN-EDGE
class Voice
priority percent 33 ! Maximum recommended LLQ value
compress header ip rtp ! Enables Class-Based cRTP
class Call Signaling
bandwidth percent 5 ! BW guarantee for Call-Signaling
!
interface Multilink1
description 768 kbps Leased-Line to RBR-3745-Left
ip address 10.1.112.1 255.255.255.252
service-policy output WAN-EDGE ! Attaches the MQC policy to Mu1
ppp multilink
ppp multilink fragment delay 10 ! Limits serialization delay to 10 ms
ppp multilink interleave ! Enables interleaving of Voice with Data
ppp multilink group 1
!
…
!
interface Serial1/0
bandwidth 786
no ip address
encapsulation ppp
ppp multilink
ppp multilink group 1 ! Includes interface Ser1/0 into Mu1 group
!
```

These examples cover the application of the WAN-EDGE service policy discussed in Example 5-4. For more examples of configuring the WAN edge, refer to the Cisco QoS Solution Reference Network Design, http://www.cisco.com/application/pdf/en/us/guest/netsol/ns432/c649/ccmigration_09186a008049b062.pdf.

QoS Reporting

The service provider should offer a minimum level of QoS reporting to provide you with statistics on the QoS you are receiving. This reporting should include the following metrics:

- Observed traffic ratio for classes

- Number of packet drops per class as a number and percentage

- Average offered load per class

The network administrator may specify additional parameters as necessary to ensure the network's maintenance and operation.

You can use the Cisco IP SLA Response Time Reporter (RTR) feature in Cisco IOS to measure the response time between IP devices. A source router configured with IP SLA configured can measure the response time to a destination IP device that can be a router or an IP device. The response time can be measured between the source and the destination or for each hop along the path. Simple Network Management Protocol (SNMP) traps can be configured to alert management consoles if the response time exceeds the predefined thresholds.

Key areas that can be measured with IP SLA include

- Interpacket delay variance (jitter) of VoIP traffic

- Response time between endpoints for a specific QoS

- IP ToS bits

- Packet loss using IP SLA generated packets

You can configure the IP SLA feature on routers using the Cisco Internetwork Performance Monitor (IPM) application. The IP SLA/RTR is imbedded in many but not all feature sets of the Cisco IOS software. A release of the Cisco IOS software that supports IP SLA/RTR must be installed on the device that IPM uses to collect performance statistics.

Chapter 8, "Network Management, SLA, and Support Requirements," contains more information on reporting, monitoring, and managing QoS.

Summary

This chapter assessed the need for QoS and the implications for the enterprise when you use an MPLS VPN-based service. The conclusion is that the need for QoS is real in the LAN, WAN, and SP transit network in support of the move toward a converged network. You must understand the mechanisms that are available to solve the application of QoS in the network, how to take a rational and staged approach toward developing a scalable policy, and how to execute that policy.

QoS is not a silver bullet that creates bandwidth. It needs to be used as part of a well-defined capacity planning and overall application governance process that identifies current and future state evolutions. Ensuring that the network can support the enterprise developments in a productive and manageable form should be the aim of any policy development so that it remains manageable over time.

The common theme is planning, designing, implementing, and operating. Build on these themes to ensure that there is consistency in the QoS strategy from an end-to-end architecture perspective. As this technology evolves, there will be additional areas to explore, especially call admission control and resource reservation. Indeed, the recent implementation of "MLPP for Voice and Video in the Internet Protocol Suite," currently in the IETF Draft stage by F. Baker, et al., shows promise as to developing the right answers.

To more fully explore the vast topic of QoS, it is highly recommended that you read the Cisco Press book *End-to-End QoS Network Design: Quality of Service in LANs, WANs, and VPNs* by Tim Szigeti and Christina Hattingh.

References

RFC 2210, *The Use of RSVP with IETF Integrated Services*
http://www.faqs.org/rfcs/rfc2210.html

RFC 2309, *Recommendations on Queue Management and Congestion Avoidance in the Internet*
http://www.faqs.org/rfcs/rfc2309.html

RFC 2474, *Definition of the Differentiated Services Field (DS Field) in the IPv4 and IPv6 Headers*
http://www.faqs.org/rfcs/rfc2474.html

RFC 2475, *An Architecture for Differentiated Service*
http://www.faqs.org/rfcs/rfc2475.html

RFC 2547, *BGP/MPLS VPNs*
http://www.faqs.org/rfcs/rfc2547.html

RFC 3168, *The Addition of Explicit Congestion Notification (ECN) to IP*
http://www.faqs.org/rfcs/rfc3168.html

RFC 3270, *Multi-Protocol Label Switching (MPLS) Support of Differentiated Services*
http://www.faqs.org/rfcs/rfc3270.html

QoS Overview
http://www.cisco.com/univercd/cc/td/doc/cisintwk/ito_doc/qos.htm

Cisco IP Telephony Solution Reference Network Design Guide
http://www.cisco.com/warp/public/779/largeent/netpro/avvid/iptel_register.html

Cisco Solutions Reference Network Design (SRND) Guide for QoS
http://www.cisco.com/application/pdf/en/us/guest/netsol/ns17/c649/ccmigration_09186a00800d67ed.pdf

IP Videoconferencing Solution Reference Network Design Guide
http://www.cisco.com/warp/public/779/largeent/netpro/avvid/ipvc_register.html

Low Latency Queuing with Priority Percentage Support
http://www.cisco.com/univercd/cc/td/doc/product/software/ios122/122newft/122t/122t2/
ftllqpct.htm

Class-Based Marking
http://www.cisco.com/univercd/cc/td/doc/product/software/ios121/121newft/121t/121t5/
cbpmark2.htm

Configuring Frame Relay Traffic Shaping
http://www.cisco.com/univercd/cc/td/doc/product/software/ios122/122cgcr/fwan_c/
wcffrely.htm#xtocid27

Configuring Distributed Traffic Shaping
http://www.cisco.com/univercd/cc/td/doc/product/software/ios122/122cgcr/fqos_c/
fqcprt4/qcfdts.htm

Configuring ATM
http://www.cisco.com/univercd/cc/td/doc/product/software/ios122/122cgcr/fwan_c/
wcfatm.htm

IP Header Compression Enhancement—PPPoATM and PPPoFR Support
http://www.cisco.com/univercd/cc/td/doc/product/software/ios122/122relnt/xprn122t/
122tnewf.htm#xtocid274

Configuring Frame Relay-ATM Interworking
http://www.cisco.com/univercd/cc/td/doc/product/software/ios122/122cgcr/fwan_c/
wcffratm.htm

Classification in the Cisco IOS Quality of Service Solutions Configuration Guide, Release
12.3
http://www.cisco.com/univercd/cc/td/doc/product/software/ios123/123cgcr/qos_vcg.htm

Service Provider QoS Design Guide
http://www.cisco.com/en/US/netsol/ns341/ns396/ns172/ns103/
networking_solutions_white_paper09186a00801b1c5a.shtml

Network-Based Application Recognition
http://www.cisco.com/univercd/cc/td/doc/product/software/ios122/122cgcr/fqos_c/
fqcprt1/qcfclass.htm#xtocid24
http://www.cisco.com/univercd/cc/td/doc/product/software/ios122/122newft/122t/122t8/
dtnbarad.htm

Congestion Management in the Cisco IOS Quality of Service Solutions Configuration
Guide, Release 12.2
http://www.cisco.com/univercd/cc/td/doc/product/software/ios122/122cgcr/fqos_c/
fqcprt2/qcfconmg.htm

Congestion Avoidance in the Cisco IOS Quality of Service Solutions Configuration Guide, Release 12.3
http://www.cisco.com/univercd/cc/td/doc/product/software/ios123/123cgcr/
qos_vcg.htm#1000448

Policing and Shaping in the Cisco IOS Quality of Service Solutions Configuration Guide, Release 12.2
http://www.cisco.com/univercd/cc/td/doc/product/software/ios122/122cgcr/fqos_c/
fqcprt4/index.htm

Link Efficiency Mechanisms in the Cisco IOS Quality of Service Solutions Configuration Guide, Release 12.2
http://www.cisco.com/univercd/cc/td/doc/product/software/ios122/122cgcr/fqos_c/
fqcprt6/index.htm

Configuring Compressed Real-Time Protocol
http://www.cisco.com/univercd/cc/td/doc/product/software/ios122/122cgcr/fqos_c/
fqcprt6/qcfcrtp.htm

Modular Quality of Service Command-Line Interface in the Cisco IOS Quality of Service Solutions Configuration Guide, Release 12.2
http://www.cisco.com/univercd/cc/td/doc/product/software/ios122/122cgcr/fqos_c/
fqcprt8/index.htm

Traffic Policy as a QoS Policy (Hierarchical Traffic Policies) Example
http://www.cisco.com/univercd/cc/td/doc/product/software/ios122/122cgcr/fqos_c/
fqcprt8/qcfmcli2.htm#xtocid16

IP Telephony QoS Design Guide
http://www.cisco.com/univercd/cc/td/doc/product/voice/ip_tele/avvidqos/

Cisco Class-Based QoS Configuration and Statistics MIB
ftp://ftp.cisco.com/pub/mibs/v2/CISCO-CLASS-BASED-QOS-MIB.my

WRED, Explicit Congestion Notification (ECN)
http://www.cisco.com/univercd/cc/td/doc/product/software/ios122/122newft/122t/122t8/
ftwrdecn.htm

NetFlow
http://www.cisco.com/warp/public/732/Tech/nmp/netflow/netflow_learnabout.shtml

Voice Calculations
http://www.cisco.com/warp/public/788/pkt-voice-general/bwidth_consume.html

Video Calculations
http://www.cisco.com/warp/public/105/video-qos.html

H.323 Deployments
http://www.cisco.com/warp/public/cc/pd/iosw/ioft/mmcm/tech/h323_wp.htm

Cisco Products Quick Reference Guide: February 2002
http://www.cisco.com/warp/public/752/qrg/cpqrg2.htm

This chapter covers the following topics:

- Introduction to Multicast for the Enterprise MPLS VPN
- Mechanics of IP Multicast
- Multicast Deployment Models
- Multicast in an MPLS VPN Environment: Transparency
- Case Study: Implementing Multicast over MPLS for Acme
- What Happens When There Is No MVPN Support?

CHAPTER 6

Multicast in an MPLS VPN

This chapter's objectives are to define the options and technical implementations for the various IP Multicast routing options available to enterprises for typical IP virtual private network (VPN) deployments. Where routing is the cornerstone of every IP network, IP Multicast is the inverse. In other words, it's no longer the "where I'm going" world of routing, but now about "where I came from" in the multicast world.

This chapter looks at the requirements for supporting the converged world of Multiprotocol Label Switching (MPLS) VPNs and how the use of MPLS requires consideration of IP Multicast usage in the enterprise. The aim of this chapter is to provide a deployable set of policies that the enterprise can use as guidelines. You'll also see how to address these to the service provider. Specifically, the case study addresses the IP Multicast needs of Acme, Inc.

For further study of IP Multicast, read *Developing IP Multicast Networks* by Beau Williamson. It covers IP Multicast in depth.

Introduction to Multicast for the Enterprise MPLS VPN

Multicast is a method of efficiently transmitting content one-way across a network from a source to multiple receivers. The primary use of multicast within Acme, Inc. is to deliver TV-quality broadcasts of live events, such as the CEO year-end results. This delivery model is called "one-to-many." It lets a global company such as Acme deliver important content consistently and accurately to everyone in the company. Companies may have studios located in major offices, such as Acme's head office in San Jose. There, content is recorded and converted into a format that can be delivered to the network using Internet Protocol TV (IPTV) servers that can send video, voice, and Microsoft PowerPoint presentations. Users can view the multicast content live by using the viewer software that pulls a program schedule from a central IPTV Content Manager, which contains all the relevant details for a workstation to request, receive, and display content sent over multicast from the IPTV server.

The primary reason for using multicast to deliver multimedia content for live events is its scalability. In large enterprise networks, a live event can be viewed by thousands of users, and only a single multicast stream is required to deliver the content. If the content were delivered using a unicast stream, the stream would increase proportionally to the number of users watching it, as shown in Figure 6-1. The single multicast stream compared with X

unicast streams prevents networks from becoming saturated and source servers from becoming overloaded.

Figure 6-1   *Unicast Versus Multicast—Bandwidth Consumption*

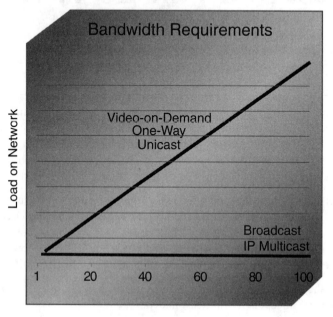

Other applications that use IP multicast within the Acme global enterprise network include reliable multicast protocol Pragmatic General Multicast (PGM) for Application and Content Networking System (ACNS) 5.x, multicast voice over IP (VoIP) application Hoot and Holler, CallManager application Multicast Music-on-Hold (M-MOH), and the multicast messaging application InformaCast.

Wider applications beyond communication content exist in the financial services world. IP Multicast in the trading and market data services arena uses multicast for delivery efficiency. Application middleware messaging such as TIBCO leverages IP Multicast. As such, the requirement to extend multicast infrastructure support to critical market applications over the WAN is increasing.

Multicast Considerations

IP Unicast relies on Layer 4 protocols, such as TCP for reliability. IP Multicast uses User Datagram Protocol (UDP) to provide best-effort delivery of packets, which can result in packet loss. UDP does not request retransmission of lost packets. Applications such as

IPTV viewer are designed to handle this problem. During transmission of a live event across the network, the impact of this packet loss is minimal. For example, a user watching the live event using IPTV viewer notices the video freezing, which is due to video frames or parts of the speech being lost. This is not a problem for the viewer if the packet loss is very small and happens only a couple of times during a broadcast. If the problem occurs continually during a broadcast, the viewer's experience will be very poor; therefore, it's critical that multicast be configured correctly on the network. Most streaming video applications allow for buffering, because they were originally designed for use over the public Internet, and therefore best-effort service. With the use for business purposes, the generous buffering allowances may be insufficient if the network has conditions causing loss leading that affect business services or key data systems.

Ideally, duplicate multicast packets should not be a problem. However, if workstations joining a specific group address receive duplicate packets, the application should be designed to handle this problem. Duplicate packets can be an issue over WAN links when you have limited bandwidth. The result could be saturated WAN links if a router sends more packets per multicast group address than the source originally sent.

Multicast traffic is delivered using UDP. Because of the nature of this connection, it does not react to congestion.

It is important that high bit rate content group addresses be blocked from traversing low-bandwidth WAN links; otherwise, the WAN link becomes congested. This congestion problem results in users at the remote site not being able to view the content sent using multicast due to the high number of dropped packets. Congestion caused by the high-quality (high quality equals high bandwidth demand) IPTV stream could also affect more critical traffic being transmitted over the WAN, such as VoIP calls. We will explore the mechanisms to properly control multicast over the WAN. You should ensure that quality of service (QoS), boundary access control list (ACL), and multicast rate limiting are configured on all WAN links to prevent congestion, as well as to ensure that bandwidth is conserved for more critical traffic, such as VoIP calls. The mechanisms that should be employed include administratively scoped multicast address ranges, assigning various bit-rate broadcasts to specific group addresses, boundary lists to give the various group addresses access to the network, and configuring group ranges on the broadcast server, such as IPTV Content Manager. The corresponding ACLs can be configured at the appropriate distribution switches connecting to the WAN gateways.

For on-demand content, rather than live streams, content can be distributed to localized caches or content engines for efficiency of access where bandwidth is limited. Operating under the "ships-in-the-night" concept of replicating offline content during the night or off-hours to the local content engines ensures that bandwidth-challenged locations can receive content that they would otherwise be unable to receive over their low-bandwidth WAN links. Multicast is often used to replicate efficiently to such local content engines.

When considering QoS for streaming video, the QoS baseline recommendation calls for streaming video (be it unicast video on demand or multicast) to be marked CS4 (DSCP 32).

This can be set on IPTV servers themselves, and the servers can be trusted by their access layer switches.

Mechanics of IP Multicast

IP Multicast can be broken into three categories to more easily explain how content is successfully delivered from a source server to multiple receivers:

- Multicast routing
- Host signaling
- Sourcing

Protocol-Independent Multicast sparse mode (PIM-SM) is the method used to facilitate the successful delivery of multicast traffic from source to destination through an enterprise network. The primary benefit of PIM-SM is that the protocol assumes that no host wants multicast traffic unless it specifically requests it. PIM is an independent routing protocol. Therefore, PIM uses the information in the unicast routing table to determine what happens to multicast traffic, regardless of the unicast routing protocol used on a router. The fundamental difference between multicast and unicast routing is that PIM determines the destination of multicast traffic by working with the source address rather than the destination address.

In unicast routing, traffic is routed through the network along a single path from the source to the destination host. A unicast router does not consider the source address; it considers only the destination address and how to forward the traffic toward that destination. The router scans its routing table for the destination address and then forwards a single copy of the unicast packet out the correct interface in the direction of the destination.

In multicast forwarding, the source sends traffic to an arbitrary group of hosts that are represented by a multicast group address. The multicast router must determine which direction is upstream (toward the source) and which is downstream . If there are multiple downstream paths, the router replicates the packet and forwards it down the appropriate downstream paths (best unicast route metric), which is not necessarily all paths. Forwarding multicast traffic away from the source, rather than to the receiver, is called Reverse Path Forwarding (RPF). RPF is described in the following section.

RPF

PIM uses the unicast routing information to create a distribution tree along the reverse path from the receivers toward the source. The multicast routers then forward packets along the distribution tree from the source to the receivers. RPF is a key concept in multicast forwarding. It lets routers correctly forward multicast traffic down the distribution tree. RPF makes use of the existing unicast routing table to determine the upstream and downstream neighbors. A router forwards a multicast packet only if it is received on the upstream interface. This RPF check helps guarantee that the distribution tree is loop-free.

RPF Check

When a multicast packet arrives at a router, the router performs an RPF check on the packet. If the RPF check succeeds, the packet is forwarded. Otherwise, it is dropped.

For traffic flowing down a source tree, the RPF check procedure works as follows:

Step 1   The router looks up the source address in the unicast routing table to determine if the packet has arrived on the interface that is on the reverse path back to the source.

Step 2   If the packet has arrived on the interface leading back to the source, the RPF check succeeds, and the packet is forwarded.

Step 3   If the RPF check in Step 2 fails, the packet is dropped.

Distribution trees are used to define the path that multicast traffic takes through the network. PIM uses shared trees and source distribution trees. Source trees may also be referred to as shortest-path trees (SPTs) because the tree uses the shortest path through the network. An SPT is represented on a router with the (S,G) notation, where S denotes the IP address of the source and G denotes the multicast group address. This is generally shortened to "S comma G" (S,G). Shared trees use a common point in the network called the rendezvous point (RP), which acts as the root of the multicast delivery tree. This tree is represented on a router with the (S, G) notation, where * denotes all sources and G denotes the multicast group address, which is shortened to "star comma G" (*,G).

Source Trees Versus Shared Trees

Both source trees and shared trees are loop-free. Messages are replicated only where the tree branches.

Members of multicast groups can join or leave at any time; therefore, the distribution trees must be dynamically updated. When all the active receivers on a particular branch stop requesting the traffic for a particular multicast group, the routers prune that branch from the distribution tree and stop forwarding traffic down that branch. If one receiver on that branch becomes active and requests the multicast traffic, the router dynamically modifies the distribution tree and starts forwarding traffic again.

Source trees have the advantage of creating the optimal path between the source and the receivers. This advantage guarantees the minimum amount of network latency for forwarding multicast traffic. However, this optimization comes at a cost: The routers must maintain path information for each source. In a network that has thousands of sources and thousands of groups, this overhead can quickly become a resource issue on the routers.

Memory consumption from the size of the multicast routing table is a factor that network designers must take into consideration.

Shared trees have the advantage of requiring the minimum amount of state in each router. This advantage lowers the overall memory requirements for a network that allows only shared trees. The disadvantage of shared trees is that under certain circumstances the paths between the source and receivers might not be the optimal paths, which might introduce some latency in packet delivery.

Protocol-Independent Multicast

Protocol-Independent Multicast (PIM) is IP routing protocol-independent and can leverage whichever unicast routing protocols are used to populate the unicast routing table, including Enhanced Interior Gateway Routing Protocol (EIGRP), Open Shortest Path First (OSPF), Border Gateway Protocol (BGP), and static routes. PIM uses this unicast routing information to perform the multicast forwarding function. Although PIM is called a multicast routing protocol, it actually uses the unicast routing table to perform the RPF check function instead of building a completely independent multicast routing table. Unlike other routing protocols, PIM does not send and receive routing updates between routers.

PIM forwarding modes are described in the next three sections.

PIM Dense Mode

PIM dense mode (PIM-DM) uses a push model to flood multicast traffic to every corner of the network. This push model is a brute-force method of delivering data to the receivers. This method would be efficient in certain deployments in which there are active receivers on every subnet in the network.

PIM-DM initially floods multicast traffic throughout the network. Routers that have no downstream neighbors prune the unwanted traffic. This process repeats every 3 minutes.

Routers accumulate state information by receiving data streams through the flood-and-prune mechanism. These data streams contain the source and group information so that downstream routers can build their multicast forwarding table. PIM-DM supports only source trees—that is, (S,G) entries. It cannot be used to build a shared distribution tree.

PIM Sparse Mode

PIM-SM uses a pull model to deliver multicast traffic. Only network segments with active receivers that have explicitly requested the data receive the traffic.

PIM-SM distributes information about active sources by forwarding data packets on the shared tree. Because PIM-SM uses shared trees (at least initially), it requires the use of an RP. The RP must be administratively configured in the network.

Sources register with the RP, and then data is forwarded down the shared tree to the receivers. The edge routers learn about a particular source when they receive data packets on the shared tree from that source through the RP. The edge router then sends PIM (S,G) join messages toward that source. Each router along the reverse path compares the unicast routing metric of the RP address to the metric of the source address. If the metric for the source address is better, the router forwards a PIM (S,G) join message toward the source. If the metric for the RP is the same or better, the PIM (S,G) join message is sent in the same direction as the RP. In this case, the shared tree and the source tree are considered congruent.

If the shared tree is not an optimal path between the source and the receiver, the routers dynamically create a source tree and stop traffic from flowing down the shared tree. This behavior is the default behavior in Cisco IOS. Network administrators can force traffic to stay on the shared tree by using the Cisco IOS **ip pim spt-threshold infinity** command.

PIM-SM was originally described in RFC 2362, *Protocol Independent Multicast-Sparse Mode (PIM-SM): Protocol Specification*. This RFC is being revised and is currently in draft form. The draft specification, *Protocol Independent Multicast-Sparse Mode (PIM-SM): Protocol Specification (Revised)*, can be found on the IETF website: http://www.ietf.org.

PIM-SM scales well to a network of any size, including those with WAN links. The explicit join mechanism prevents unwanted traffic from flooding the WAN links.

Bidirectional PIM (Bidir-PIM)

Bidirectional PIM (bidir-PIM) is an enhancement of the PIM protocol that was designed for efficient many-to-many communications within an individual PIM domain. Multicast groups in bidirectional mode can scale to an arbitrary number of sources with only a minimal amount of additional overhead.

The shared trees that are created in PIM sparse mode are unidirectional. This means that a source tree must be created to bring the data stream to the RP (the root of the shared tree). Then it can be forwarded down the branches to the receivers. Source data cannot flow up the shared tree toward the RP, which would be considered a bidirectional shared tree.

In bidirectional mode, traffic is routed only along a bidirectional shared tree that is rooted at the RP for the group. With bidir-PIM, the RP's IP address acts as the key to having all routers establish a loop-free spanning-tree topology rooted in that IP address. This IP address need not be a router address. It can be any unassigned IP address on a network that can be reached throughout the PIM domain.

Bidir-PIM is derived from the mechanisms of PIM sparse mode (PIM-SM) and shares many of the shared tree operations. Bidir-PIM also has unconditional forwarding of source traffic toward the RP upstream on the shared tree, but it has no registering process for sources as in PIM-SM. These modifications are necessary and sufficient to allow forwarding of traffic in all routers solely based on the (*,G) multicast routing entries. This feature eliminates any source-specific state and allows scaling capability to an arbitrary number of sources.

The current specification of bidir-PIM can be found in the IETF draft titled *Bi-Directional Protocol Independent Multicast (BIDIR-PIM)* on the IETF website (http://www.ietf.org).

Interdomain Multicast Protocols

The following three sections discuss interdomain multicast protocols—protocols that are used between multicast domains. Internet service providers (ISPs) also use these protocols to forward multicast traffic on the Internet.

Multiprotocol Border Gateway Protocol

Multiprotocol Border Gateway Protocol (MBGP) lets providers specify which route prefixes they will use to perform multicast RPF checks. The RPF check is the fundamental mechanism that routers use to determine the paths that multicast forwarding trees follow and to successfully deliver multicast content from sources to receivers. For more information, see the earlier section "RPF."

MBGP is described in RFC 2283, *Multiprotocol Extensions for BGP-4*. Because MBGP is an extension of BGP, it contains the administrative machinery that providers and customers require in their interdomain routing environment, including all the inter-AS tools to filter and control routing, such as route maps. Therefore, any network that uses internal BGP (iBGP) or external BGP (eBGP) can use MBGP to apply the multiple policy control knobs familiar in BGP to specify the routing policy (and thereby the forwarding policy) for multicast.

Two path attributes, MP_REACH_NLRI and MP_UNREACH_NLRI, were introduced in BGP-4. These new attributes create a simple way to carry two sets of routing information: one for unicast routing and the other for multicast routing. The routes associated with multicast routing are used for RPF checking at the interdomain borders.

The main advantage of MBGP is that an internetwork can support noncongruent unicast and multicast topologies. When the unicast and multicast topologies are congruent, MBGP can support different policies for each. Separate BGP routing tables are maintained for the Unicast Routing Information Base (U-RIB) and the Multicast Routing Information Base (M-RIB). The M-RIB is derived from the unicast routing table with the multicast policies applied. RPF checks and PIM forwarding events are performed based on the information in the M-RIB. MBGP provides a scalable policy-based interdomain routing protocol.

Multicast Source Discovery Protocol

In the PIM-SM model, the router closest to the sources or receivers registers with the RP. The RP knows about all the sources and receivers for any particular group. Network administrators may want to configure several RPs and create several PIM-SM domains. In each domain, RPs have no way of knowing about sources located in other domains. Multicast Source Discovery Protocol (MSDP) is an elegant way to solve this problem.

MSDP was developed for peering between ISPs. ISPs did not want to rely on an RP maintained by a competing ISP to provide service to their customers. MSDP allows each ISP to have its own local RP and still forward and receive multicast traffic to and from the Internet.

MSDP lets RPs share information about active sources. RPs know about the receivers in their local domain. When RPs in remote domains hear about the active sources, they can pass on that information to their local receivers, and multicast data can then be forwarded between the domains. A useful feature of MSDP is that it allows each domain to maintain an independent RP that does not rely on other domains. MSDP gives network administrators the option of selectively forwarding multicast traffic between domains or blocking particular groups or sources. PIM-SM is used to forward the traffic between the multicast domains.

The RP in each domain establishes an MSDP peering session using a TCP connection with the RPs in other domains or with border routers leading to the other domains. When the RP learns about a new multicast source within its own domain (through the normal PIM register mechanism), the RP encapsulates the first data packet in a Source-Active (SA) message and sends the SA to all MSDP peers. MSDP uses a modified RPF check to determine which peers should be forwarded the SA messages. This modified RPF check is done at an AS level instead of a hop-by-hop metric. The SA is forwarded by each receiving peer, also using the same modified RPF check, until the SA reaches every MSDP router in the internetwork—theoretically, the entire multicast Internet. If the receiving MSDP peer is an RP, and the RP has a (*,G) entry for the group in the SA (that is, there is an interested receiver), the RP creates (S,G) state for the source and joins to the shortest-path tree for the source. The encapsulated data is decapsulated and forwarded down the shared tree of that RP. When the receiver's last-hop router receives the packet, the last-hop router also may join the shortest-path tree to the source. The MSDP speaker periodically sends SAs that include all sources within the own domain of the RP.

Source-Specific Multicast

Source-Specific Multicast (SSM) is an extension of the PIM protocol that allows for an efficient data delivery mechanism in one-to-many communications. SSM allows a receiving client, after it has learned about a particular multicast source through a directory service, to then receive content directly from the source, rather than receiving it using a shared RP.

SSM removes the requirement of MSDP to discover the active sources in other PIM domains. An out-of-band service at the application level, such as a web server, can perform source discovery. It also removes the requirement for an RP.

In traditional multicast implementations, applications must "join" to an IP multicast group address, because traffic is distributed to an entire IP multicast group. If two applications with different sources and receivers use the same IP multicast group address, receivers of both applications receive traffic from the senders of both the applications. Even though the receivers, if programmed appropriately, can filter out the unwanted traffic, this situation still would likely generate noticeable levels of unwanted network traffic.

In an SSM-enhanced multicast network, the router closest to the receiver "sees" a request from the receiving application to join to a particular multicast source. The receiver application then can signal its intention to join a particular source by using Include mode in IGMPv3.

The multicast router can now send the request directly to the source rather than sending the request to a common RP as in PIM sparse mode. At this point, the source can send data directly to the receiver using the shortest path. In SSM, routing of multicast traffic is accomplished entirely with source trees. There are no shared trees, so an RP is not required.

The ability for SSM to explicitly include and exclude particular sources allows for a limited amount of security. Traffic from a source to a group that is not explicitly listed on the INCLUDE list is not forwarded to uninterested receivers.

SSM also solves IP multicast address collision issues associated with one-to-many-type applications. Routers running in SSM mode route data streams based on the full (S,G) address. Assuming that a source has a unique IP address to send on the Internet, any (S,G) from this source also would be unique.

Multicast Addressing

With the growing popularity of IP multicast applications, many users are considering deploying, or have already deployed, IP multicast in their networks. The design and documentation of an appropriate multicast addressing scheme are important components of a successful IP multicast deployment.

Here are some of the common issues you may encounter during IP multicast deployment:

- Simplify administration and troubleshooting of IP multicast.
- Control the distribution and use of IP multicast group addresses within an organization (such as between business units).
- Control the distribution and scope of multicast application data within an organization.
- Locate the rendezvous point with PIM sparse mode and determine which IP multicast groups each will serve.

- Control IP multicast traffic on WAN links so that high-rate groups cannot saturate low-speed links.
- Control who can send IP multicast and who can receive (security).
- Be ready to deploy next-generation IP multicast protocols (such as bidir-PIM and SSM).
- Link to the Internet for multicast.
- Allow for future requirements and expansion so that re-addressing does not have to occur at a later date.

A solid addressing policy is the key to solving or simplifying many of these issues. Without a correctly planned and scoped IP multicast addressing scheme, customers will encounter more complex configurations, which significantly decreases the control of IP multicast over the network and increases administration and support overhead.

The IPv4 multicast address space is handled differently than its unicast counterpart. Unlike unicast addresses, which are uniquely assigned to organizations by the Internet Assigned Numbers Authority (IANA), the multicast address space is openly available for use.

This openness could potentially create problems with address collisions, so steps have been taken to minimize this possibility. Mainly, the multicast address space has been divided into some well-known ranges to give guidance to network operators and to facilitate deployment of certain applications. The well-known group address ranges include the following:

- **Multicast address range**—224.0.0.0/4 (RFC 1112)
- **Local scoped range**—224.0.0.0/24 (http://www.iana.org/assignments/multicast-addresses)
- **IANA assigned range**—224.0.1.0/24 (http://www.iana.org/assignments/multicast-addresses)
- **SSM range**—232.0.0.0/8 (IETF: draft-ietf-ssm-arch-01.txt)
- **GLOP range**—233.0.0.0/8 (RFC 2770)
- **Administratively scoped range**—239.0.0.0/8 (RFC 2365)

Administratively Scoped Addresses

RFC 2365 provides guidelines on how the multicast address space can be divided and used privately by enterprises. The phrase "administratively scoped IPv4 multicast space" relates to the group address range 239.0.0.0 to 239.255.255.255. The key properties of administratively scoped IP multicast are that packets addressed to administratively scoped multicast addresses do not cross configured administrative boundaries. Administratively scoped multicast addresses are locally assigned, so they do not need to be unique across administrative boundaries. This range of multicast addresses was defined to give autonomous networks a set of private multicast addresses that could be used inside their networks without the fear of address collision from outside entities. It is the equivalent of unicast private addresses, as described in RFC 1918. To maintain the integrity of this address space and prevent leaks of control or data traffic into or out of this boundary, it needs to be scoped at the network edge.

A detailed document on IP multicast addressing and scoping can be found at http://ftp-eng.cisco.com.

Deploying the IP Multicast Service

The RP is a fundamental component in PIM sparse mode multicast networks. The RP is a common router in the network that senders and receivers use to learn about each other. Multicast sources are "registered" with the RP by their first-hop router, and receivers are "joined" to the shared tree (rooted at the RP) by their local designated router (DR).

The RP uses multicast to distribute the group RP mappings to all routers in the network, which is known as Auto-RP. All multicast-enabled routers in the network must be enabled for PIM sparse-dense mode to allow Auto-RP to propagate through the network in dense mode. These are the only groups that should operate in dense mode. PIM sparse-dense mode provides multicast-enabled routers with the information required to send joins for specific groups to build shared trees. With Auto-RP, you can configure the RPs themselves to announce their availability as an RP and as a mapping agent. The RPs send their announcements using the 224.0.1.39 IP address. The RP mapping agent listens to the announcement packets from the RPs and then sends RP-to-group mappings in a discovery message, which is sent to the 224.0.1.40 IP address. These discovery messages are automatically received by all routers configured for sparse-dense mode and are used to define their RP-to-group mapping information.

The RPs are configured with an anycast address, which is a method of configuring multiple devices on a network using the same IP address. The benefit of this approach is that if an RP fails, the unicast routing table still contains another reachable entry. Thus, shared trees are successfully built toward the next-closest RP. In Acme, the IP anycast address used is 192.168.1.1. It has been defined as the loopback1 address on all RP routers within Acme. For example, if the RP in New York fails, the RP in San Jose takes over, because it is the next reachable 192.168.1.1 IP address in the Interior Gateway Protocol (IGP) employed, which in this case is EIGRP.

MSDP is a method for RPs in different PIM-SM domains to peer and share information on active sources. It allows for interdomain streams sourced in San Jose to be viewed by users located in different PIM-SM domains, such as the Acme WAN, which has operations in Europe and Asia. Figure 6-2 is an overview of these concepts.

Figure 6-2   *Interdomain Multicast—Server to Receiver*

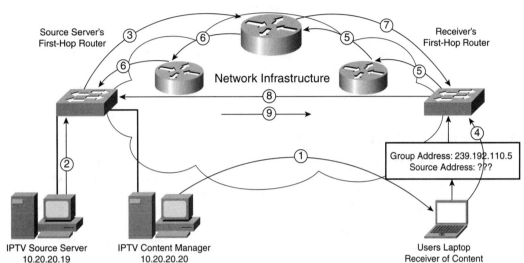

1. SDF file transferred from CM to user out-of-band (session info).
2. Source server sends multicast traffic onto local LAN.
3. Source servers first-hop DR registers source with RP.
4. Laptop sends request to become member of group address.
5. Users DR router sends (*,G) toward RP to build shared tree.
6. (S,G) state built from RP toward source server's DR.
7. Multicast traffic flows down the shared tree toward the receiver.
8. Switch over from shared tree to the shortest path once user's DR
   learns source servers IP address from first packets.
9. Multicast traffic flows down the shortest path tree.

When a multicast packet arrives at a router it performs the RPF check. It examines the source address to determine if the packet arrived at an interface that is on the reverse path back to the source. PIM performs the RPF check by looking up the unicast routing table to determine which interface would be used to reach the source IP address of the multicast packet. If the packet is sourced from the correct interface, it is forwarded. If it is not sourced from the correct interface, it is dropped.

Cisco IOS Software Releases 12.2.12, 12.2.12S, and 12.1.13E have a new command option on the **ip multicast boundary** interface command that can automatically filter RP-announce and RP-discovery messages based on the multicast groups the boundary command will allow to pass:

```
ip multicast boundary acl [filter-autorp]
```

This command is not enabled by default. When the new option is enabled, filtering for Auto-RP messages occurs in three cases:

- An RP-announce or RP-discovery packet is received from the interface.

- An RP-announce or RP-discovery packet received from another interface is forwarded to this interface.

- An internally generated RP-announce or RP-discovery packet is sent to the interface.

Default PIM Interface Configuration Mode

The recommended default PIM interface configuration mode is sparse mode. Additionally, a new command lets Auto-RP function with 224.0.1.40 and 224.0.1.39. It is fixed to operate in dense mode for the announcement and discovery of dynamic group RP mappings between all routers. This new command is

```
ip multicast auto-rp [listener]
```

This global configuration command lets the router have all its interfaces configured in sparse mode, thereby eliminating the potential for dense mode to flood across a topology. It still allows the two groups necessary for Auto-RP to function in dense mode for the dissemination of group RP mapping information and announcements.

Host Signaling

Before content can be delivered, the network infrastructure needs to be aware that users require content. Internet Group Management Protocol (IGMP) lets the end users in a network request delivery of multicast content. When a user requests delivery of multicast content, the workstation sends an IGMP join message to the LAN subnet. When two PIM-enabled multicast routers exist on the same LAN configured in a Hot Standby Router Protocol (HSRP) group, both track the IGMP messages by storing the multicast group address and the first host's source IP address. The router with the lowest IP address is selected as the IGMP querier router and is responsible for maintaining the IGMP table. A DR is also selected between the two PIM-enabled routers by the highest IP address. This router is responsible for sending (*,G) joins toward the RP (based on the IGMP table) and also for forwarding multicast traffic to the LAN. Figure 6-3 shows the IGMP operations in practice.

Figure 6-3   *IGMP Operation*

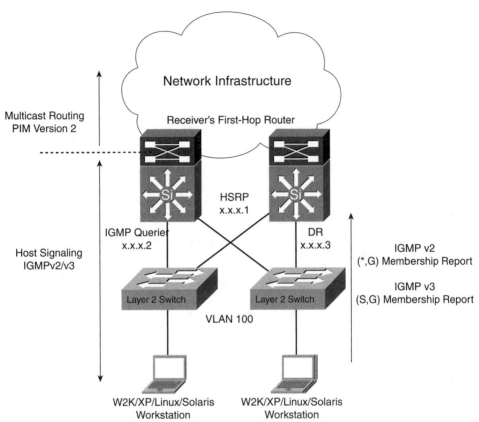

A control mechanism is required for Catalyst Layer 2 switches to make intelligent decisions about the delivery of multicast traffic. Otherwise, a Catalyst sends multicast traffic out all ports that are members of a specific virtual LAN (VLAN). IGMP Snooping or Cisco Group Management Protocol (CGMP) must be used to track the ports in the content-addressable memory (CAM) table that have hosts connected wanting to receive multicast traffic with a specific multicast MAC address.

IGMP controls messages transmitted onto the LAN by workstations and routers. Multicast packets are indistinguishable from multicast data at Layer 2. So the 65xx platform uses IGMP snooping to examine every data packet to determine if it contains any pertinent IGMP control information. The 65xx platform has special application-specific integrated circuits (ASICs) that can perform the IGMP checks in hardware. This results in a much more efficient method of delivering multicast traffic onto the user LAN segment. IGMP snooping implemented on a low-end switch with a slow CPU could have severe performance implications when data is sent at high rates. The solution is to use CGMP between the receiver's first-hop router and switch. CGMP is a client/server protocol that runs between the CGMP-capable switches and the multicast router. When the router receives an IGMP join or leave, it in turn sends a CGMP join or leave to the CGMP switches so that they can add ports to or remove ports from the multicast forwarding table. The router delivers CGMP traffic using multicast, which ensures that multiple catalysts receive the CGMP update. CGMP should be used only with legacy switches. For more information on the legacy switches, visit the following web pages:

- http://www.cisco.com/univercd/cc/td/doc/product/lan/cat2950/12122ea2/2950scg/swigmp.htm

- http://www.cisco.com/univercd/cc/td/doc/product/lan/cat2970/12225sea/2970scg/swigmp.htm

- http://www.cisco.com/univercd/cc/td/doc/product/lan/cat3550/12225seb/scg/swigmp.htm

- http://www.cisco.com/univercd/cc/td/doc/product/lan/cat3560/1225sea/3560scg/swigmp.htm

- http://www.cisco.com/univercd/cc/td/doc/product/lan/cat3750/12225sea/3750scg/swigmp.htm

- http://www.cisco.com/univercd/cc/td/doc/product/lan/cat4000/12_2_25a/conf/multi.htm

Sourcing

The IPTV servers stream live multimedia content to the local LAN segment as multicast traffic being delivered to a specific group address. The DR on the same LAN segment as the IPTV server takes this multicast traffic and determines the destination group address. It also checks the multicast routing table for (S,G) and (*,G) entries. The router adds an (S,G) entry in the mroute table, which causes an identical (*,G) route to be created automatically. The router now checks the source IP address and identifies whether the IP address is on a locally connected network. The router encapsulates the packets from the source server in register messages and then sends them to the RP router. An example is shown in Figure 6-4.

Figure 6-4   *RP Registration*

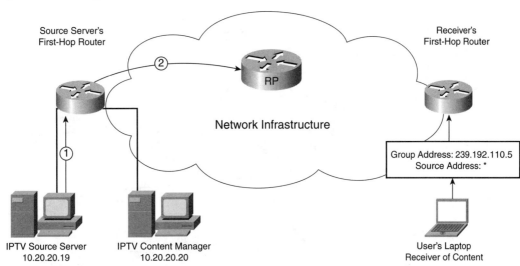

1 Source server sends multicast traffic onto local LAN.
2 Source server's first-hop DR registers source with RP.

Multicast Deployment Models

This section describes the multicast deployment and operation models available to the enterprise—the Any Source Multicast (ASM) solution and the SSM service.

Any-Source Multicast

The ASM solution is the most commonly deployed model for the IP Multicast infrastructure. The Acme case study predominantly uses this model, too. The Acme IPTV application uses it to deliver live content. A user's workstation sends a request (via the IPTV viewer software) to become a member of a specific multicast group address, which is learned from the scheduled programs listed in a content manager. The DR builds the shared tree toward the RP in an effort to pull content from the source server.

Meanwhile, the source server sends content to the DR on its local subnet, which is forwarded to the RP. The RP then sends the multicast traffic from the source server down the shared tree toward the user's workstation. As soon as the DR receives the content, it can determine the server's source IP address. These multicast packets arriving at the receiver's DR prompt the DR to cut over from the shared tree to the SPT. The DR can build an SPT toward the source now because it has the source server's IP address. As soon as this SPT is complete, content flows from the source server to the receivers. Figure 6-5 provides an overview of the global multicast domains employed by Acme.

Figure 6-5   *Global Deployment Model for Acme, Inc.*

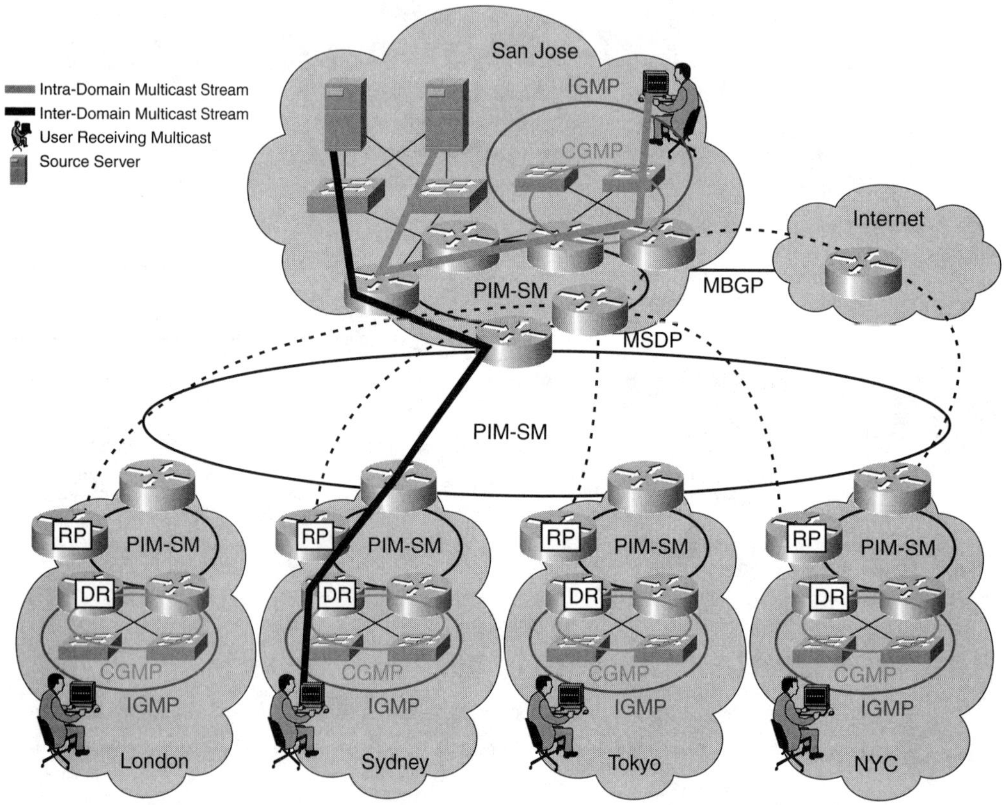

Source-Specific Multicast

SSM is a technology step that enhances the existing ASM routing solution. ASM will continue to be offered and supported while, in most cases, the transition to SSM support continues. This approach ensures support for all current applications and for new applications developed to take advantage of SSM. It is important to remember that the final goal of SSM is the same as the ASM model: to build a shortest-path distribution tree for content to flow from the source server to the receivers. To achieve this goal, the SSM routing model primarily changes at the edge of the network. The RP in the network is no longer responsible for tracking active sources; therefore, shared trees are not required, and sources don't have to register with the RP. The receiving workstation is now responsible for sending a request to the network to receive multicast traffic with a certain group address from a specific source server's IP address. This simplifies how SSM routing functions within the core of the enterprise network. In the SSM model, the IGMP membership reports sent by workstations contain specific details of the multicast group address and source server's IP address. Three host-signaling methods are IGMP v3, IGMP v3lite, and URL Rendezvous Directory (URD):

- **IGMP v3**—The SSM model requires workstations to use IGMP v3 because it lets workstations send membership reports with the group address and the source server's IP address. A host can signal that it wants to receive traffic from all sources sending to a group except some specific sources (called Exclude mode), or it can signal that it wants to receive traffic from only some specific sources sending to the group (called Include mode). IGMP v3 has challenges involving host stack support, which are detailed next. For more details, refer to http://www.cisco.com/en/US/products/sw/iosswrel/ps1829/products_feature_guide09186a008008702e.html.

- **IGMP v3lite** is a Cisco-developed transitional solution for application developers to immediately start programming SSM applications. It lets you write and run SSM applications on hosts that do not yet support IGMP v3 in their operating system kernel. Applications such as IPTV viewer 3.4 are compiled with the Host Side IGMP Library (HSIL) for IGMP v3lite. IGMP v3lite works by sending an IGMP v2 membership report and a UDP packet to port 465, which is sent to the all-multicast router IGMP 224.0.0.2 address. This interim solution requires receiver first-hop routers, workstations, and applications to support IGMP v3lite. Only Microsoft Windows 2000 workstations can leverage IGMP v3lite. Microsoft Windows XP supports IGMPv3.

- **URD** is a Cisco-developed transitional solution that allows existing IP multicast receiver applications to be used with SSM without the need to modify the application and change or add any software on the receiver host running the application. URD operates by passing a special URL from the web browser to the receiver's first-hop router. This URD intercept URL is encoded with the (S,G) channel subscription and has a format that allows the receiver's first-hop router to easily intercept it. As soon as the receiver's first-hop router knows about the (S,G) channel, it uses this to send an (S,G) join toward the source.

Using IGMP v3 or IGMP v3lite tells the receiver's first-hop routers about both the group address and the source server's IP address. Because the DR obtains the group and source server's IP address from the IGMP membership report, the DR does not need to build an SPT toward the RP. Instead, the DR immediately starts building an SPT toward the source server. The source server's first-hop router, which should be the DR router for the source server, does not register sources with the RP that fall within the SSM group address range— again eliminating the need for an RP.

You should pay attention to the implementation of IGMP in the enterprise. You must review the infrastructure's ability to support SSM, because IGMP v3 is required. For example, if IGMP v2 is deployed in the network, three main areas need to be addressed to ensure support for IGMP v3 and IGMP v3lite so that the SSM routing service can be used. The three main areas are explained in the following section.

Enabling SSM

As a starting point, you should review the IOS and any CatOS versions that are used. The following network components require consideration for SSM:

- **Receiver's Layer 2 switches**—The switches need to support IGMP v3. IGMP v3lite is not a concern because it uses IGMP v2 host signaling.

- **Receiver's first-hop router**—These routers need to support the interface level host-signaling protocols IGMP v3 and IGMP v3lite. The router must also support SSM.

- **Transit routers**—Transit routers are all other multicast-enabled routers within the global infrastructure network. All routers require support for SSM, but only the source server's first-hop router and the RP must have an IOS that supports SSM. None of the remaining transit routers require an IOS that supports SSM because the functionality of SSM within the core of an enterprise network is the same as with the ASM model.

The second important area is to consider host stack support available for all operating systems used within the Acme global enterprise network. If the workstations in the LAN will use IGMP v3, such as Microsoft Windows XP or Linux, special consideration is required on the receiver's first-hop router and switch (as detailed in the previous section) to avoid flooding multicast traffic. Acme's current global desktop operating standard on laptops is Windows 2000, which does not support IGMP v3; therefore, IGMP v3lite must be used. Linux has multiple host stacks that support IGMP v3. Sun currently does not support IGMP v3. Table 6-1 lists operating system support for IGMP.

Table 6-1   *Operating System Support for IGMP*

Operating System	ASM (IGMP v2)	SSM (IGMP v3lite)	SSM (IGMP v3)
Windows 2000	Yes	Yes (requires IPTV 3.4)	No support
Windows XP	Yes	Not required	Yes
Linux	Yes	No	Yes
Solaris	Yes	No	No support in version 8 or 9

In the third SSM area for consideration, a number of different workstation and server applications need to be considered when it comes to supporting an SSM environment. Table 6-2 shows the workstation and server application releases required to specifically support IGMP v3.

Table 6-2   *Viewer Support for IGMP*

Application	ASM (IGMP v2)	SSM (IGMP v3lite)	SSM (IGMP v3)
IPTV Viewer	3.1, 3.2, and 3.4	3.4	3.4
IPTV Content Manager	3.2 and 3.4	3.4 (bug)	3.4
IPTV Server	3.2 and 3.4	3.4	3.4
Real Server	Yes	No	Yes
Real Player	3.1, 3.2, and 3.4	No	No

Multicast in an MPLS VPN Environment: Transparency

A separate function is required to enable IP multicast over an MPLS VPN network, because MPLS has no native ability to support it. (However, it should be noted that native support is a work in progress and will be supported.) This is cause for concern, because the alternative to supporting multicast in such an environment is to employ generic routing encapsulation (GRE) tunneling to all sites connected to the VPN, which creates an $O[n]^2$ (where n is a variable) issue because of the huge amount of complexity in scaling relationships of any-to-any tunnels for the scaling of the implementation for the enterprise. For example, ten sites requiring any-to-any connectivity would require 100 GRE tunnels to deliver multicast over GRE between sites. Now picture the challenges when connectivity is required for 100 sites. Ten thousand tunnels would be required!

To get around this issue, multicast VPN (MVPN) was developed to enable the support of multicast in an MPLS environment, thus delivering the much-needed transparency and reduced complexity for the enterprise. The basic concept of MVPN is as follows:

1   The service provider has an IP network with its own unique IP multicast domain, such as a P network.

2   The MVPN customer has an IP network with its own unique IP multicast domain, such as a C network.

3   The service provider MVPN network forwards the customer IP multicast data to remote VPN sites.

To achieve this, customer traffic (C packets) is encapsulated at the service provider PE inside P packets. The encapsulated P packet is then forwarded to remote PE sites as native multicast inside the P network.

During this process, the P network has no knowledge of the C network traffic. The PE is the router that participates in both networks.

MVPN IP Multicast support for MPLS VPNs allows service providers to configure and support multicast traffic in an MPLS VPN environment. Because MPLS VPNs support only unicast traffic connectivity, deploying the MVPN feature in conjunction with MPLS

VPNs allows service providers to offer both unicast and multicast connectivity to MPLS VPN customers.

The MVPN feature supports routing and forwarding of multicast packets for each individual virtual routing/forwarding (VRF) instance. It also provides a mechanism to transport VPN multicast packets across the service provider backbone.

The MVPN feature in Cisco IOS Software provides the ability to support the multicast feature over a Layer 3 VPN. As enterprises extend the reach of their multicast applications, service providers can accommodate these enterprise needs over their MPLS core network. IP multicast is used to stream video, voice, and data through an MPLS VPN network core efficiently.

The MVPN solution allows Acme to transparently interconnect its private network across a service provider's network backbone. The use of an MVPN to interconnect an enterprise network in this way does not change how that enterprise network is administered, nor does it change general enterprise connectivity.

The major benefits of deploying with a service provider that supports MVPN are as follows:

- PIM adjacency with PE routers
- No customer edge (CE) overlay tunnels (GRE overlay)
- Multicast configuration changes are not required in customer networks
- The existing customer multicast deployment is unaffected
    - PIM modes
    - RP placement/discovery mechanisms

Multicast Routing Inside the VPN

A PE router in an MVPN has multiple multicast routing tables, as well as multiple instances of PIM, IGMP, and MSDP. There is one global table and a table per multicast VRF (MVRF).

Multicast domains are based on the principle of encapsulating multicast packets from a VPN to be routed in the core. Because multicast is used in the core network, PIM must be configured in the core.

PIM-SM, PIM-SSM (source specific multicast), and bidir-PIM are all supported inside the provider core for MVPN.

PIM-SM or PIM-SSM is the recommended PIM option in the provider core, because bidir-PIM is not yet supported by all platforms. PIM-SM, PIM-SSM, bidir-PIM, and PIM-DM are supported inside the MVPN.

MVPN supports the concept of Multicast Distribution Trees (MDTs). An MDT is sourced by a PE router and has a multicast destination address. PE routers that have sites for the same MVPN all source to a default MDT and also join to receive traffic on it.

The distinction between default MDTs and data MDTs is that a default MDT is a tree that is "always on." It transports PIM control traffic, dense-mode traffic, and RP tree (*,G) traffic. All PE routers configured with the same default MDT receive this traffic.

On the other hand, data MDTs are trees that are created on demand. They are joined only by the PE routers that have interested receivers for the traffic. They can be created by a traffic rate threshold and/or source-group pair. Default MDTs must have the same group address for all VRFs that comprise an MVPN. Data MDTs may have the same group address if PIM-SSM is used. If PIM-SM is used, they must have a different group address, because providing the same one could cause the PE router to receive unwanted traffic. This is a PIM-SM protocol issue, not an implementation issue.

Multicast domains (MDs) are the solution that Cisco Systems has adopted and integrated into Cisco IOS. An MD is essentially a set of VRFs that can send multicast traffic to each other. On the MVPN-enabled PE router, each MVRF has its own multicast routing table. Each PE router runs a number of instances of PIM-SM (as many as one per VRF) and, within each instance of PIM-SM, maintains a PIM adjacency with the CE router. The PE router also runs a "global" instance of PIM-SM, with which it forms adjacencies with each of its IGP neighbors, such as P (backbone SP) routers and/or other PE routers.

Each MVRF is assigned to an MD, and each MVRF MD is configured with a multicast group address belonging to the service provider PIM-SM instance. However, note that this MD group address must be unique in the service provider PIM domain, and it can overlap with group addresses in use by VPN customers. Figure 6-6 provides an overview of this concept.

For a more detailed view of how to build MVPN for MPLS VPN environments, see *MPLS and VPN Architectures*, Volume II, Chapter 7, "Multicast VPN." Or you can find the information online at http://www.ciscopress.com/title/1587051125.

Figure 6-6 *MVRF MD Overview*

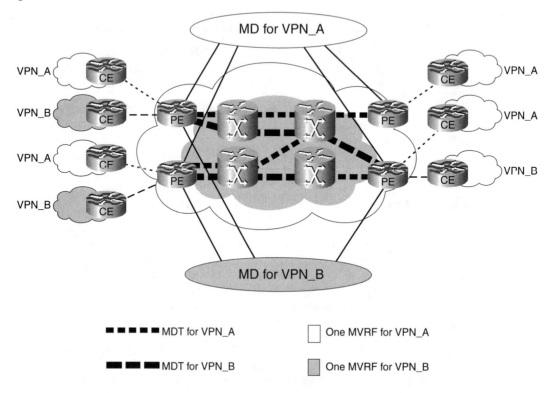

| ■ ■ ■ ■ ■ MDT for VPN_A | ☐ One MVRF for VPN_A |
| ■■ ■■ ■■ MDT for VPN_B | ▨ One MVRF for VPN_B |

Case Study: Implementing Multicast over MPLS for Acme

Acme and the service provider agreed that PE router interfaces would always be enabled for multicast, irrelevant of bandwidth. Acme would decide on the CE router WAN interface whether to enable multicast.

The configuration on the CE router to enable MVPN requires you to enable multicast on the CE router first. Then, to enable MVPN on the CE WAN interface connecting to the PE, you use the standard PIM sparse-dense mode command. You can use this command to enable multicast on a traditional WAN interface.

Multicast Addressing

A multicast group address is a destination IP address within an IP packet. The packet has no single destination within a network. An IP packet with a multicast group address has the destination of an arbitrary group of IP hosts that have joined the group and that want to receive the traffic sent to the group. The multicast group address range 224.0.0.0/8 (assigned by IANA) is broken into a number of smaller ranges for specific purposes, as shown in Table 6-3.

Table 6-3   *Multicast Group Addresses*

Group Address Range	Description
224.0.0.0–238.255.255.255	Multicast global range.
224.0.0.0–224.0.0.255	Link-local multicast addresses are local in scope. Routers do not forward them, regardless of the time-to-live (TTL).
224.0.1.0–224.0.1.255	Reserved range for network protocols or applications that are forwarded by routers.
232.0.0.0–232.255.255.255	Reserved for SSM.
239.0.0.0–239.255.255.255	Administratively scoped multicast addresses for use in a private multicast domain.

IANA has reserved the range of 239.0.0.0/8 as administratively scoped addresses for use in private multicast domains, as shown in Table 6-3. This address range is similar to RFC 1918, and IANA does not assign this to any other group or protocol. Table 6-4 shows the present multicast admin scope standard that allocates specific ranges of group addresses within 239.0.0.0/8 to be used for certain bit rate streams.

Table 6-4   *Assigning Bandwidth Streams to Group Address Ranges with Admin Scopes*

Multicast Group Address Range	Forwarding Mode	Bandwidth
239.192.0.0/21	PIM-SM	High bandwidth (700 Kbps +)
239.192.8.0/21	PIM-SM	Medium bandwidth (128 Kbps–699 Kbps)
239.192.16.0/21	PIM-SM	Low bandwidth (0 Kbps–127 Kbps)
239.192.248.0/22	PIM-SM	Special "high value" apps with dedicated RPs
239.192.255.0/24	PIM-SM	Satellite-based streams
239.232.0.0/21	SSM	High bandwidth (700 Kbps +)
239.232.8.0/21	SSM	Medium bandwidth (128 Kbps–699 Kbps)
239.232.16.0/21	SSM	Low bandwidth (0 Kbps–127 Kbps)
239.232.255.0/24	SSM	Satellite-based streams
239.255.0.0/16	Any	Special lab localization scope

Multicast Address Management

The key to allocating multicast group addresses is working with the teams sourcing multicast traffic and fully understanding their requirements. One of the main reasons it's important to work with teams using IP multicast is because no mechanisms exist today on the network to notify or alert operational network engineers or the team sourcing traffic that the wrong group addresses are being used or the wrong rate is being transmitted on the allocated addresses. For example, suppose an IPTV server starts sourcing 1 Mbps of IP multicast content using a group address from the low bit rate admin scope, and users at the remote office ask to receive this content. The 1 Mbps streams attempt to flow across the T1 or E1 (1.5 Mbps or 2 Mbps) WAN link connecting the remote site. The result of such an action would affect other multicast traffic unnecessarily by using more bandwidth than required, thus dropping IP multicast packets. Chances are, users will think that this is poor service. Therefore, it's important for network engineers to work closely with teams sourcing IP multicast to explain these potential issues and allocate IP multicast group addresses appropriately per the requirements. The IP multicast group addresses allocated must be reserved in the appropriate address management tool employed.

Predeployment Considerations

The primary IP multicast application using the MVPN service is IPTV. It generates 1480-byte packets because the default setting in the server's iptv.ini file is 1452. The IPTV server produces 1452-byte Routing Table Protocol (RTP) packets, which results in multicast packets of 1504 bytes from the following calculation: 1452 + 8 UDP + 20 IP + 24 GRE = 1504. The PE router needs to fragment the 1504-byte packets if a 1500-byte interface for PE-P and/or P-P links is used in the network. If the network has all WAN interfaces with a 4 Kbps maximum transmission unit (MTU), it's not an issue. Depending on the hardware and topology used, a service provider might be able to increase the MTU of all PE-P and/or P-P interfaces to be slightly more than 1500 bytes to account for the GRE overhead. Caution should be taken when changing the MTU, because it is a difficult-to-administer workaround.

As a result of fragmentation on the PE, the route processor must handle each of these packets. The Selective Packet Discard (SPD) punt limit is set to the default of 1 k pps. Thus, it does not take long before this threshold is exceeded and the PE router starts to discard packets to protect the route processor. The workaround for this problem is to lower the MTU from 1452 bytes to 1280 bytes on all Acme internal IPTV servers globally. The server administrator can change this figure in the IPTV server's iptv.ini file. 1280 bytes was chosen because it is the lowest supportable figure for IPv6. This solution is much more preferable than having the service provider manipulate the MTU setting it has set for the enterprise.

MVPN Configuration Needs on the CE

The first step of enabling multicast on a Layer 3 device is to enable multicast routing, which is not enabled by default. Enter the following command to enable multicast routing on a router:

```
router(config)#ip multicast-routing
```

For high-end routers, such as 75xx or 12xxx, that support distributed forwarding of multicast traffic, the following command should be used to enable multicast routing:

```
router(config)#ip multicast-routing distributed
```

Enabling the SSM range on a router defines the group address range that will be used to deliver SSM content. This is especially important on edge routers, known as the "source server's first-hop routers," which connect to the VLAN/subnet hosting the source server, and the "receiver's first-hop routers," connecting directly to the user's VLAN/subnet. Enabling SSM on the "source server's first-hop routers" prevents the router from forwarding the multicast traffic encapsulated in a unicast register to the RP. Enabling the SSM range on the "receiver's first-hop routers" prevents (*,G) joins from being sent by the DR toward the RP to build a shared tree when a new receiver wants to join a specific SSM group. The DR now realizes that this is an SSM group address and sends an (S,G) toward the source IP address:

```
router(config)#ip pim ssm range multicast_ssm_range
router(config)#ip access-list standard multicast_ssm_range
router(config-std)#REMARK ACL to define SSM admin range
router(config-std)#REMARK 232.0.0.0/8 IANA allocated SSM range
router(config-std)#permit 232.0.0.0 0.255.255.255
router(config-std)#REMARK 239.232.0.0/16 Internal SSM range
router(config-std)#permit 239.232.0.0 0.0.255.255
```

NOTE   The preceding SSM configuration should be applied to all multicast-enabled routers in the global transport network. Applying the commands to all multicast-enabled routers in the network has no detrimental effect, but instead keeps the configuration consistent. This approach also simplifies the multicast configuration being deployed rather than having only SSM applied where it's truly required, which is on the "receiver's first hop" routers.

The main requirement is to ensure that PIM sparse-dense mode is configured on the CE WAN interface connecting to the PE. PIM sparse-dense mode must also be configured on the WAN interface of the PE connecting toward the CE. While the PE is under the control of the SP, it serves as a useful troubleshooting reminder that this must be enabled on the local CE-PE interfaces to work properly. The commands required are as follows:

CE router:

```
router(config-if)#ip pim sparse-dense-mode
```

PE router:

```
router(config-if)#ip pim sparse-dense-mode
```

A carrier deploying an enterprise-wide MPLS VPN cloud should be instructed to enable **ip pim sparse-dense-mode** on all WAN interfaces of the PE connecting to the customer. This ensures that the control exists on the Acme side to determine if PIM should be enabled. This is especially important in regions that have WAN links less than 256 kbps.

Boundary ACL

When multicast is enabled in an enterprise network, the environment naturally consists of various WAN circuits of differing speeds. At Acme, content is primarily produced from central locations, and these source servers offer various quality multicast streams. The better-quality streams have a higher bit rate. Therefore, they can be delivered only over WAN circuits with sufficient bandwidth to handle that higher bit rate. A method is required to control the flow of multicast streams in this type of environment. You need to ensure that remote sites with slow WAN circuits can view only low-bit-rate streams. They must not be able to view a high-bit-rate stream that could saturate the WAN circuit and affect other traffic traversing the link. One method to control the flow of multicast traffic based on destination address and the feature is multicast boundaries. In Figure 6-7, the routers block medium- and high-bit-rate streams and allow the low-bit-rate stream to pass over the WAN circuit.

Figure 6-7 *Multicast Boundaries*

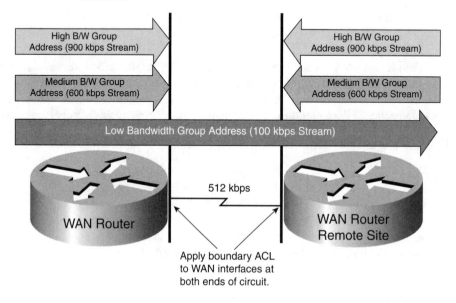

NOTE	Using boundaries to protect resources from high-bandwidth multicast is only an administrative boundary. If an IP multicast source server is connected to the network and it starts streaming 1 Mbps of IP multicast traffic using a group address that should be used for low bit rate, this could result in problems. Thus, it is very important that teams sourcing IP multicast traffic be educated on the importance of good IP multicast group address management.

Boundary ACLs must be configured on the WAN interfaces of the CE only. Each access list allows only a certain range of multicast destination addresses to pass while blocking other bit-rate streams. When an access list is applied to a router interface that allows only certain bit-rate streams to pass, this is known as defining a multicast boundary. At lower-speed sites, the application of the boundary ACLS should be applied on the local site's ingress interfaces, where distribution switches are downstream from the WAN edge. At such sites, processing of boundary ACLs could easily be employed on the distribution to offload processing of the boundary ACLs, allowing the ACLs to be processed in hardware.

The standard access list defining the multicast boundary should be applied to WAN circuits falling into specific bandwidth ranges. The access list allows only specific address groups to pass that are the destination addresses of multicast streams with a specific bit rate. Which standard access list should be applied to what bandwidth interface can be determined from Table 6-5.

Table 6-5   *Circuit Bandwidth Connecting Remote Sites*

		< 256 kbps	256 kbps – < T1/E1	T1/E1 and < 6 Mbps	> 6 Mbps
Multicast Stream Bit Rate	**0–127 kbps**	Do not apply multicast.	multicast_boundary_ lowbw	multicast_boundary_ medbw	No boundary required.
	128–699 kbps	Do not apply multicast.	Not allowed	multicast_boundary_m edbw	No boundary required.
	700 kbps	Do not apply multicast.	Not allowed	Not allowed	No boundary required.

T1 = 1.5 mbps and E1 = 2 Mbps

Positioning of Multicast Boundaries

Multicast boundaries should be deployed in the network at the CE aggregation routers and remote-site CE routers. The following sections explain the content of the standard access lists, where to locate them, and how to configure them on a router.

Using named ACLs benefits network engineers because it removes an element of uncertainty and confusion by documenting the bandwidth range covered by the ACL in the ACL title itself. Leading practice should be used in the form of the REMARK statement in the ACL to further enhance documentation.

The global multicast range is from 224.0.0.0 to 238.255.255.255, as highlighted in Table 6-3. Note that this boundary ACL blocks only 224.2.x.x because IPTV uses that range by default. To avoid any issues with IPTV servers being connected to the network at remote sites and using default addresses, this range is blocked to prevent the content from potentially affecting the WAN link.

NOTE   Care should be used to ensure that the blocking of global ranges does not potentially block Internet-based content or other applications. You are urged to confirm the use of the ranges to ensure that there is no impact on applications that are unintentionally using the global multicast range.

Configuration to Apply a Boundary Access List

To apply a multicast boundary to a router interface, use the following command, and associate it with one of the standard named access lists. It is also a best practice to apply multicast boundaries to the router interfaces at both ends of a WAN circuit. This keeps sources at the remote site from causing issues.

```
router(config-if)#ip multicast boundary acl-name
```

Two standard access lists have been developed for multicast boundaries: multicast_boundary_lowbw and multicast_boundary_medbw.

The ACL multicast_boundary_lowbw allows low-bandwidth streams, as shown in Example 6-1.

Example 6-1 *multicast_boundary_lowbw*

```
ip access-list standard  multicast_boundary_lowbw
REMARK Multicast boundary to allow 0-127K streams plus slidecast
REMARK This ACL is applied to WAN circuits > 256 kbps < T1/E1
!
REMARK 239.255.0.0/16 is a lab localization scope and should be denied
REMARK 239.255.255.255 is required for locally-scoped SDR/SAP announcements
!
permit 239.255.255.255
deny 239.255.0.0 0.0.255.255
!
REMARK 239.192.16.0/21 is assigned for "low-bandwidth" applications (0-127 Kbps)
REMARK This is for PIM-SM-based forwarding
!
permit 239.192.16.0 0.0.7.255
```

Example 6-1 *multicast_boundary_lowbw (Continued)*

```
deny 239.192.0.0 0.0.255.255
!
REMARK 239.232.16.0/21 is assigned for "low-bandwidth" applications (0-127 Kbps)
REMARK This is for SSM-based forwarding
!
permit 239.232.16.0 0.0.7.255
deny 239.232.0.0 0.0.255.255
!
REMARK 224.2.0.0/16 is the default range that IPTV uses for broadcasts; thus,
REMARK we need to block unauthorized IPTV streams using this range for low-
REMARK bandwidth broadcasts. Note that this also blocks many Internet-based
REMARK streams that use 224.2.0.0/16 as a default.
!
deny 224.2.0.0 0.0.255.255
permit 224.0.0.0 15.255.255.255
```

The ACL multicast_boundary_medbw allows bandwidth streams of less than 700 kbps, as shown in Example 6-2.

Example 6-2 *multicast_boundary_medbw*

```
ip access-list standard multicast_boundary_medbw
REMARK Multicast boundary to allow 0-700K streams plus slidecast
REMARK This ACL is applied on T1 - 6Mbps WAN circuits
!
REMARK 239.255.0.0/16 is a lab localization scope and should be denied
REMARK 239.255.255.255 is required for locally-scoped SDR/SAP announcements
!
permit 239.255.255.255
deny 239.255.0.0 0.0.255.255
!
REMARK 239.192.8.0/21 is assigned for "medium-bandwidth" applications (128-699
Kbps)
REMARK 239.192.16.0/21 is assigned for "low-bandwidth" applications (0-127 Kbps)
REMARK This is for PIM-SM-based forwarding
!
permit 239.192.8.0 0.0.7.255
permit 239.192.16.0 0.0.7.255
deny 239.192.0.0 0.0.255.255
!
REMARK 239.232.8.0/21 is assigned for "medium-bandwidth" applications (128-699
Kbps)
REMARK 239.232.16.0/21 is assigned for "low-bandwidth" applications (0-127 Kbps)
REMARK This is for SSM-based forwarding
!
permit 239.232.8.0 0.0.7.255
permit 239.232.16.0 0.0.7.255
deny 239.232.0.0 0.0.255.255
!
REMARK Default global permit
!
permit 224.0.0.0 15.255.255.255
```

Rate Limiting

Rate limiting should be applied to protect the bandwidth of a WAN circuit connecting a remote office to the corporate network. This is critical for lower-bandwidth circuits or when sending higher-bit-rate streams over midrange bandwidth, especially if multiple multicast streams are being transmitted over the WAN circuit.

The carrier may also implement the "mroute rate limit" feature to restrict the number of mroutes Acme, Inc. can advertise into the cloud. This is done to prevent the CE from advertising too many mroutes to the PE that would consume too much of the PE router's memory.

Table 6-6 is a simple guideline that can be used to help you determine if rate limiting should be applied. If rate limiting is to be applied, it's important to determine what percentage of available bandwidth should be made available to multicast. This list covers most of the circuit bandwidths currently used in Acme's internal network. This does not mean that the proposed rate limiting must be applied to higher-bandwidth circuits if the operational engineers deem it unnecessary. When applied, it rate-limits the multicast traffic. Table 6-6 shows the circuit bandwidth application of rate limits.

Table 6-6   *Circuit Bandwidth Application of Rate Limits*

Bandwidth	Rate Limiting	Description
< 256 kbps	Do not apply multicast.	Rate limiting is not an issue, because multicast should not be enabled.
256 kbps through T1/E1	Apply 50 percent rate limiting of circuit bandwidth.	0–127 kbps allowed over a link with this bandwidth, so a rate limit of 50 percent would allow a maximum of four concurrent 100 kbps streams on a T1 and six concurrent 100 kbps streams with an E1.
> T1/E1 and < 45 Mbps	Apply 50 percent rate limiting of circuit bandwidth.	128–699 kbps streams allowed over a link with this bandwidth, so a rate limit of 50 percent would allow one 100 kbps stream and one 500 kbps stream on a T1 and six concurrent 100 kbps streams plus two 500 kbps streams with a 6 Mbps circuit.
> 45 Mbps	Unnecessary.	—

The best approach to calculate the rate-limit figure that should be applied in your configuration is to first determine the bandwidth of the WAN circuit in question. Take the bandwidth figure from the first column of Table 6-6, and then determine the recommended percentage in the next column. If you feel the resulting figure is too high or too low due to facts such as current utilization figures or demand at the site, alter the percentage as you feel necessary. However, remember that this command must be applied in a manner to protect your WAN circuit bandwidth from being overrun by multicast traffic.

Take the percentage figure and calculate the kilobits per second (kbps) multicast rate limit from the circuit bandwidth that you want to apply. The best practice is to apply rate limiting to both interfaces at the A and B ends of a WAN circuit. This approach protects the circuit bandwidth if the remote site is hosting a multicast source. When working with smaller-bandwidth circuits, the minimum rate-limit figure should be 160 kbps to allow for a media bandwidth of one stream @ 100 kbps video + 16 kbps audio + burst.

NOTE   The example used would only apply to a link of 256 kbps. If you were to apply 50 percent to a circuit of this size (which results in 128 kbps available for multicast), you would fall below the minimum required figure of 160 kbps. Remember to use the figure of 160 kbps if 50 percent of the link bandwidth is less than 160 kbps.

Rate-Limiting Configuration

After you have calculated the kbps rate-limit figure that you want to apply, use the following configuration command to apply that to the router interface:

```
router(config-if)#ip multicast rate-limit out max-mcast-bw-in-kbps
```

MVPN Deployment Plan

The migration plan to MVPN requires several stages to ensure that the IPTV service can be supported through each phase of the core transition.

The following stages, including precutover testing, postproduction testing, and configuration preparation, are carried out to complete thorough testing:

Precutover Testing: Nonproduction

Step 1   Enable PIM on CE-PE routers.

Step 2   Set up the test IPTV server.

Step 3   Receiver testing from local gateways.

Step 4   Link failover testing.

Postproduction Testing

Step 1   Core site receiver testing

Step 2   Multiple-site user testing

Step 3   Detailed stream testing

Configuration Preparation

Step 1 (conf t)#**mls ip multicast**

Step 2 (conf t)#**no ip multicast cache**

Step 3 (interface x/x)#**ip mroute-cache** (hidden if enabled)

Preproduction User Test Sequence

The preceding test procedure was carried out during the preproduction checks with users in London, Amsterdam, and Brussels. This is to see if any packet duplication occurs when multiple joins are made.

Figure 6-8 depicts the test setup. As you can see, users are based in Brussels and Amsterdam. The rendezvous point is configured to point to Amsterdam. It also provides a view of the deployment scenario.

Figure 6-8 *Test Setup for Multicast over MPLS*

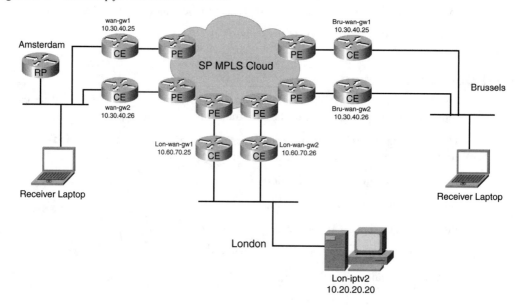

The preproduction test environment that is used is the closest to capturing the post-production setup before the cutover. This helps test IPMC behavior and the end-user scenarios.

The sequence of testing aims to thoroughly verify that no looping issues occur when join requests are made by users at each of the sites.

First, verify that few or no active streams in the network exist before cut testing.

1.0   Streaming from London

1.1   Configure lon-iptv2 as your Content Manager
- a) Stream "900 kbps Test Stream"
- b) Brussels joins
- c) Amsterdam joins
- d) London joins
- e) Brussels leaves
- f) London leaves
- g) Brussels joins

1.2   Stream "100 kbps Test Stream"
- a) Amsterdam joins
- b) Brussels joins
- c) London joins

1.3   Stream "900 kbps Test Stream" again
- a) London joins
- b) Brussels joins
- c) Amsterdam joins

Keep the 900 kbps stream active

2.0   Streaming from San Jose

2.1   Configure sanjose-cm as your Content Manager
- a) Stream "Acme 900 kbps Test Stream"
- b) Brussels joins
- c) London joins
- d) Amsterdam joins

2.2   Stream "Acme 500 kbps Test Stream"
- a) London joins
- b) Brussels joins
- c) Amsterdam joins

2.3   Stream "Acme 100 kbps Test Stream"
- a) Amsterdam joins
- b) Brussels joins
- c) London joins

3.0   Internet streams

3.1   Configure iptvhost.uoregon.edu as your Content Manager
- a) Stream "UO Natural resources"
- b) Amsterdam joins
- c) Brussels joins
- d) London joins

3.2 Stream "TV-BROADCAST" or other broadcast stream
   a) Brussels joins
   b) London joins
   c) Amsterdam joins

It is important to verify that users are not having any difficulty viewing streams in different locations. The following checks were made:

- Users in core sites (London, Brussels, and Amsterdam) could view the streams after the cutover.

- Users in hub and satellite sites could view streams.

The following testing was carried out to see if any issues were occurring:

- Per-site multiple-user testing.

- Check to see multiple join requests can be made.

- Stream quality is good.

- Gain feedback from users.

- Multiple-site testing.

- Verify that multiple sites can see the stream simultaneously.

- Gain feedback on any issues that may be affecting viewing.

The following test criteria were used to receive feedback from users on the quality of the test streams:

User feedback survey

IPTV multicast test plan and checklist

- Test 900 kbps test stream—ams-iptv2 Content Manager.

- Duplicate packets.

- Packet drops.

- Jitter.

- Short-term drop rate.

- Is stream visibility good?

- Any delays in viewing video?

- Is sound quality good?

- Are audio and video in sync?

Test 100 kbps test stream—lon-iptv2 Content Manager

- Duplicate packets.
- Packet drops.
- Jitter.
- Short-term drop rate.
- Is stream visibility good?
- Any delays in viewing video?
- Is sound quality good?
- Are audio and video in sync?

Test 900 kbps U.S. test stream—sj-cm Content Manager

- Duplicate packets.
- Packet drops.
- Jitter.
- Short-term drop rate.
- Is stream visibility good?
- Any delays in viewing video?
- Is sound quality good?
- Are audio and video in sync?

Test 500 kbps U.S. test stream—sanjose-cm Content Manager

- Duplicate packets.
- Packet drops.
- Jitter.
- Short-term drop rate.
- Is stream visibility good?
- Any delays in viewing video?
- Is sound quality good?
- Are audio and video in sync?

Test 100 kbps U.S. test stream—sj-cm Content Manager

- Duplicate packets.
- Packet drops.
- Jitter.
- Short-term drop rate.

- Is stream visibility good?
- Any delays in viewing video?
- Is sound quality good?
- Are audio and video in sync?

Internet: TV-broadcast stream

What Happens When There Is No MVPN Support?

In the event that the SP cannot support MVPN for MPLS, the following configuration is required for WAN links using MPLS VPN-based services where the MPLS carrier is unable to provide a native multicast solution, such as MVPN. This workaround solution provides multicast to sites connected with MPLS VPNs by creating a GRE tunnel dedicated to carrying multicast traffic between sites. Although MPLS VPN-based clouds typically support any-to-any communication within the cloud, tunnels must be set up in a point-to-point manner.

Example 6-3 shows that a tunnel configuration should be applied to both the hub site and remote-site routers terminating MPLS VPN-based connectivity.

Example 6-3 *Remote-Site Configuration*

```
! REMOTE SITE / SPOKE router configuration:
!
! Configure a tunnel to the hub site
!
interface Tunnel0
 description IP multicast tunnel for MPLS VPN
 ip address <tunnel-/30-address> 255.255.255.252
 ip pim sparse-dense-mode
 multicast boundary <acl name>
 ip multicast rate-limit out <max-mcast-bw-in-kbps>
 tunnel source <loopback0>
 tunnel destination <hubsite-router-loopback0-ip>
!
! Ensure that tunnel interface is not used for unicast routing
!
router eigrp 109
 passive-interface Tunnel0
!
! mroutes for local office networks must point to proper LAN interfaces
! to source multicast from remote site
! default mroute is set to point to the Tunnel interface
!
ip mroute <lan-subnet> <lan-mask> <lan-interface>
ip mroute 0.0.0.0 0.0.0.0 Tunnel0

Hub site Configuration
```

Example 6-3 *Remote-Site Configuration (Continued)*

```
! HUB SITE / HUB router configuration:
!
! Create a tunnel interface to each of the remote offices
!
interface Tunnel<tunnel#>
 description IP multicast tunnel for <remote-router-name>
 ip address <tunnel-/30-address> 255.255.255.252
 ip pim sparse-dense-mode
 multicast boundary <acl name>
 ip multicast rate-limit out <max-mcast-bw-in-kbps>
 tunnel source <loopback0>
 tunnel destination <remotesite-router-loopback0-ip>
!
! Ensure that tunnel interface is not used for unicast routing
!
router eigrp 109
 passive-interface Tunnel<tunnel#>
!
! Add a static mroute for each site's subnets pointing to the tunnel
! so that IP multicast will be directed to flow through the tunnel
!
ip mroute <remote-subnet> <remote-mask> Tunnel<tunnel#>
```

Other Considerations and Challenges

Acme and its service provider found a problem with MVPN and the MTU of multicast packets during implementation. To solve this problem, you must reduce the packet size on the IPTV servers from the default size of 1452 to 1280. The reasons for this decision are as follows:

PE routers running MVPN encapsulate multicast traffic in an MDT. This encapsulation technique can be either GRE or IP-in-IP. The default is GRE. Using GRE, you essentially add 24 bytes to the multicast packet. However, if you receive a multicast packet that is greater than 1476 bytes, by the time you have added the 24-byte GRE header, you have a packet greater than 1500 bytes. Service providers may use Gigabit Ethernet between the PE and player; hence, you need to fragment the packet.

Fragmentation is done on the route processor. In MVPN, a number of things also need to be handled by the route processor, such as PIM registers, asserts, state creation, and so on. SPD allows you to rate-limit the number of packets that are punted to the route processor from the VIP/PXF. The default is 1 kbps. The objective of SPD is simple—don't trash the route processor.

The issue the service provider identifies is that, by default, the IPTV application generates 1480-byte packets. Of course, by the time the PE adds the 24-byte GRE header, you need to fragment, which is done by the route processor. It will not take long before the SPD punt limit is reached and the PE starts to discard packets to protect the route processor.

The service provider found it has three options to address this problem:

1 Modify the MTU of the Ethernet interfaces on PE and P routers.

 Increasing the interface MTU of the Ethernet interfaces to 1524 bytes would resolve the problem. However, although Gigabit Ethernet cards support a 1524-byte interface MTU, the SP also uses 7200VXR (route reflector, sub-AS BGP border router) and 3600 (terminal server) that do not support this. Hence, they would start to lose IS-IS adjacencies and LSPs to these routers. So this option is not a viable solution.

2 Use IP-in-IP encapsulation for MDT.

 Using IP-in-IP encapsulation for the MDTs, the additional 20-byte header would mean that 1480-byte packets generated by IPTV would not require fragmentation. The problem with this approach is that currently IP-in-IP encapsulation is not done in distributed Cisco Express Forwarding (dCEF), but is fast-switched. Also, IP-in-IP would not solve the problem for packets that are 1481 bytes long. This is also not a viable option.

3 Reduce the size of packets sourced by IPTV.

 The last option is to reduce the packet size generated by IPTV source servers. Within the application, a file called iptv.ini allows you to configure the packet size that will be generated. By default, it is set to 1452 bytes. This allows for 20 bytes for the IP tunnel, 20 bytes for the IP header, and 8 bytes for UDP. So, excluding the 20-byte IP tunnel, the 1452-byte payload + 20-byte IP header + 8-byte UDP = 1480 bytes.

Summary

This chapter assessed the need for transparency of multicast support and discussed the implications for the enterprise when using an MPLS VPN-based service. The conclusion is that the need for IP multicast support is real in the LAN, WAN, and SP transit network in support of the move toward a converged network. You should understand the mechanisms that are available to solve the application of IP multicast in the network, how to take a rational and staged approach toward developing a scalable policy, and how to execute that policy.

You can see that IP multicast creates bandwidth efficiency and requires careful planning and overall application governance, which identifies current and future state evolutions for the enterprise. Ensuring that the network can support the enterprise developments in a productive and manageable form should be the aim of any policy development to ensure that it remains manageable over time.

The common theme is planning, design, implementation, and operation. Building on these ensures that there is consistency in the support of IP multicast within the enterprise and support by the service provider from an end-to-end architecture perspective. As this technology evolves, there will be additional areas to explore, especially SSM, because it lessens the complexity of the RP deployment.

References

Global Multicast Standards—Cisco Systems IT
Michael Anderson, Cisco Systems

RFC 2547, *BGP/MPLS VPNs*
http://www.faqs.org/rfcs/rfc2547.html

RFC 2917, *A Core MPLS IP VPN Architecture*
http://www.faqs.org/rfcs/rfc2917.html

RFC 3569, *An Overview of Source-Specific Multicast (SSM)*
http://www.faqs.org/rfcs/rfc3569.html

Multicast Overview
http://www.cisco.com/warp/public/732/Tech/multicast/
http://www.cisco.com/warp/public/614/17.html

Cisco Solutions Reference Network Design (SRND) Guide for IP Multicast
http://www.cisco.com/univercd/cc/td/doc/solution/esm/ipmcsrnd/multicast.pdf

Cisco Solutions—mVPN for MPLS VPN
http://www.cisco.com/warp/public/732/Tech/multicast/mvpn/

Cisco Products Quick Reference Guide: February 2002
http://www.cisco.com/warp/public/752/qrg/cpqrg2.htm

This chapter covers the following topics:

- Comparing an enterprise's security implications using provider-provisioned IP VPNs based on MPLS to traditional Frame Relay and ATM Layer 2 VPNs.

- Understanding the security issues raised in the provider network by using shared or private PEs.

- Understanding the cost and security trade-offs for different types of connectivity for connecting PEs to CEs.

- Understanding how to apply on your network security techniques such as filtering, tracing spoofed packets, remote-trigger black-hole filtering, loose and strict uRPF, sinkholes, and backscatter traceback.

- Understanding hacker tools such as bots, botnets, and worms and how to mitigate them.

- Learning how to prepare network operations to mitigate attacks by baselining via NetFlow and a NetFlow Collector, using Cisco Guard, plus defining team roles and procedures with available tools that are essential in maintaining an operational network in today's environment.

- Understanding the options implemented by our case study network group.

CHAPTER 7

Enterprise Security in an MPLS VPN Environment

This chapter examines the security issues to consider from the enterprise perspective when migrating from a WAN that's based on Layer 2 technologies such as Frame Relay and ATM to a Layer 3 IP virtual private network (VPN). The focus in this chapter is on infrastructure security rather than security of packet payload, which is covered in Chapter 9, "Off-Net Access to the VPN."

When an enterprise subscribes to an IP VPN service, IP routes are exchanged between the enterprise and service provider network. This process is new compared to the previous Layer 2 WAN. It provides knowledge of the enterprise network topology to an entity outside the enterprise. This additional knowledge of the enterprise infrastructure by an outside source causes some enterprise network managers to be concerned. It can be debated whether this is warranted, but the fact remains that when connecting at Layer 3, rather than at Layer 2, more information is exchanged between enterprise and provider about the enterprise network, and the first thing an attacker of networks needs is information.

In addition to this new Layer 3 exchange of information, one of the typical advantages of migrating to a Layer 3 service is that networks become more richly connected. This is driven by applications such as voice over IP (VoIP). However, along with the benefits of richer connection (in terms of more possible paths across the WAN) comes the challenge of tracking sources of attack in this environment.

In the case where a Layer 2 WAN provides a discrete number of connections to potential attack sources, the enterprise is faced with an anywhere-to-anywhere connection model that requires more effort to track attacks through.

Many of the techniques described in later sections, such as black-hole filtering, used to be considered applicable only to service provider networks, not enterprise networks. The reason for this was that enterprise networks were considered to have a low number of external peers and only a handful of points in the network where attacks could enter. For larger enterprise networks, this is no longer the case. The larger enterprises have multiple providers connected to their networks and have multiple extranet connections to business partners, and their networks now resemble provider networks. This chapter considers the issues related to securing the network infrastructure from attacks by miscreants.

NOTE   Detailed configuration recommendations for firewall and Intrusion Detection Systems (IDS) are outside the scope of this book. They are covered in several other Cisco Press books.

NOTE   The "References" section, which appears at the end of this chapter, contains extensive publicly available resources that detail the best recommendations for securing networks.

Setting the Playing Field

This introductory section enables you to set a level playing field with your colleagues when discussing various technologies and their implications for security. When discussing these issues with many network managers, the most challenging aspect of the meetings is answering questions about how enterprise security policies should change when moving from a Layer 2 WAN to a Layer 3 WAN. These types of questions can be difficult to answer because an "apples-to-apples" comparison is needed, in which everyone uses the same terminology. An example is comparing a WAN service over a Frame Relay network to a WAN service over a private IP network. This is different from comparing it to a WAN service over the public Internet. However, a VPN service over the public Internet requires encryption for most security concerns. It does not mean that encryption would be necessary over a private IP network to achieve the same level of security as a Frame Relay service.

The real interest is typically in making a security assessment of MPLS VPN networks compared to Frame Relay networks (in terms of exposure by the enterprise network). There are many parts to this analysis, so we'll start by comparing IP to Frame Relay. Then, we'll look at the difference that adding MPLS to the IP network makes. Studying these introductory topics will prepare you to compare MPLS VPN to Frame Relay security.

From a security perspective, the good thing about Frame Relay and other Layer 2 WAN technologies is that the WAN has no knowledge of the enterprise's IP addressing, which is the first thing an attacker needs to directly attack an enterprise. This information, however, has decreased in significance because attackers have moved their attention from attacking specific enterprises to attacking the provider network's infrastructure. This is a logical progression from the attacker perspective. If the aim is to cause disruption, attacking the provider infrastructure that affects many enterprises clearly gives a bigger bang for the attack performed.

Having said that, IP infrastructures are far more commonly the focus of intruder attacks than Frame Relay networks, because the number of IP technology students is far greater than the number of students who study Frame Relay infrastructures. If we look at the problem of susceptibility to attack for the provider WAN infrastructure, clearly many more people know how to send a packet to a given IP address than how to send something to a specific Frame Relay switch.

Frame Relay provides a defined path through the network from one endpoint to another, whereas IP networks facilitate any-to-any connectivity at Layer 3. Clearly, these have different design objectives. At first appearance, IP looks to be a protocol that helps attackers reach places and craft attacks. In part, this is true. On the public Internet, open connectivity is the goal, which gives attackers open access to public addresses. Comparing Frame Relay networks to the public Internet is not an apples-to-apples comparison. Comparing private IP networks run by providers with the express purpose of offering VPN service to Frame Relay networks is valid, however. The reason for the difference is that the controls a provider puts into place limit a user's access to only his VPN. For each technology that could be used to support VPN deployment, there are mechanisms for segregating the control (route information) and data plane (destinations accessible) operations of one customer from another. We will look at MPLS VPN mechanisms for performing those two functions later in this section. With direct Internet access, no such restrictions are in place. So clearly, it does not make sense to compare the security of a private Frame Relay to the security of the public Internet.

Similarly, comparing the security of a private Frame Relay network to a private IP network with no VPN mechanisms implemented on it is not an apples-to-apples comparison. However, it is valid to look at how effectively Frame Relay networks segregate user traffic and to compare that to MPLS VPN services.

The question of whether an IP network is public or private is not always straightforward. Service providers are motivated to reduce their operating expenses and put the same equipment to use in as many revenue-generating ways as possible. This often ends up in at least some parts of the provider infrastructure being shared between public and private services. This is not a new phenomenon. Even though Frame Relay services are considered private, in many service provider networks, public Internet traffic was carried over part of that Frame Relay infrastructure, segregated at Layer 2 from the private Frame Relay traffic. This did not cause concern because it's accepted that, if Internet traffic was on a separate data-link connection identifier (DLCI), it would not interfere with private Frame Relay traffic on another DLCI. The logical conclusion, then, is that having a separate header (in this case, the Frame Relay DLCI) is adequate to ensure separation of private and public traffic on the one infrastructure. At this level, the case for considering MPLS as secure as Frame Relay (at least in the data plane operation of forwarding traffic) is strong because, conceptually, there is little difference between a Frame Relay DLCI and an MPLS label; they are both connection identifiers appended to an IP packet. However, as previously stated, because MPLS devices are addressable via IP packets but Frame Relay switches typically are not, some further analysis is required to see whether MPLS devices can be reached from the Internet.

The first stage of this analysis is to look at how a plain MPLS network operates compared to an IP network. This refers to the single-label imposition of MPLS forwarding rather than to the two-label imposition of MPLS VPN. In a plain MPLS environment, MPLS-enabled routers assign a label to each prefix held in their routing table that is not from Border Gateway Protocol (BGP). Should a packet need to be forwarded to any of these non-BGP destinations, the label is appended to the packet and forwarded to the next hop (the reason for not supplying labels for BGP destinations will become apparent soon). As the packet traverses the MPLS-enabled portion of the network, the label value is examined and swapped at each hop, based on the label database.

Figure 7-1 shows this process. The values for labels at each hop are determined by the label distribution protocol. (The "References" section at the end of this chapter lists resources that further explain this operation.)

Figure 7-1 *Single-Label MPLS Imposition*

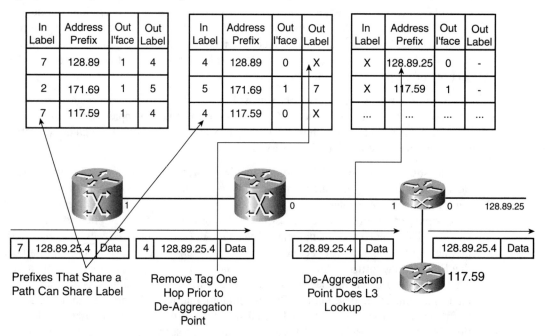

This single-label operation shows that within an MPLS core network, the mechanism of forwarding a packet is similar to the mechanism for forwarding in ATM or Frame Relay switches, and this is by design. One of the original drivers behind the development of MPLS was to find a way to leverage the cheap and fast Layer 2 switching paradigm employed by these switches for the benefit of IP traffic. However, by the time MPLS technologies were available in router products, IP forwarding based on ASIC technology (often called hardware-based forwarding, as compared to the original and slower software-based forwarding) had advanced in speed to match these label-switching approaches. For that reason, MPLS did not take off as a technology until the MPLS VPN service was defined.

The fact that switching in the core is based on MPLS labels rather than IP addresses has a nice benefit. For an infrastructure that supports public and private traffic, the core routers do not need to run BGP to be able to forward public Internet traffic. Figure 7-2 helps clarify this point.

Figure 7-2   *Getting BGP off Core Routers with MPLS*

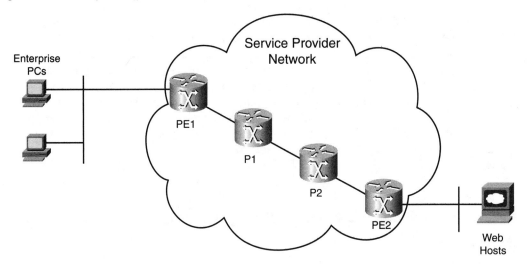

In Figure 7-2, the enterprise PCs want to contact the web hosts on the right. For the web hosts to be contacted, packets need to be sent to them addressed to their publicly routable Internet addresses. In normal IP forwarding, each hop looks up the destination address and makes a routing decision. This requires the provider to run BGP on each of the routers labeled P in Figure 7-2, because no internal routing protocols are designed to hold the number of routes that exist on the Internet.

To recap, P means provider core router and PE means provider edge router. P routers perform label switching, whereas PE routers perform label push and pop operations to add labels to or extract labels from an IP packet.

The provider no longer has to run BGP on the provider (P) routers, because the provider edge (PE) routers append a label based on the value of the BGP next hop, not the destination IP address. This BGP next-hop value is normally the /32 loopback address of the edge router that can reach the route advertised to the network by BGP. Because MPLS labels do not extend outside the provider network in this case, there is no need to define labels for each of the end customer networks. All that's needed is a label for the provider network's exit point. As soon as the packet arrives and the label is stripped, the PE router can perform an IP lookup to decide where to send the packet. So, by this mechanism, BGP is restricted to the edge routers, and clearly there is no need to define labels for BGP destinations in the MPLS-enabled part of the network.

What does all this mean for security? Well, the end result in a scenario like this is that the P routers end up looking a lot like Frame Relay switches from the perspective of forwarding traffic. The conclusion is that if the P routers do not hold Internet addresses, and no devices external to the provider network can send packets to the P routers, the security of the P router is similar to that of a Frame Relay or ATM switch.

The conclusion is that with MPLS, the core P routers can deliver secure transport to both private MPLS VPN and public Internet traffic. The remaining issue, however, is the PE routers. If they are addressable from the Internet, they are susceptible to denial of service (DoS) attacks from anywhere on the Internet. Therefore, they are a concern and need additional protection to offer secure service. Some providers go the extra mile and offer MPLS VPN service on separate PE routers to their Internet PE routers. In these cases, the enterprise can be fairly confident that security loopholes have been minimized. For enterprises considering service from providers that choose to have both Internet and private VPN customers on the same PE, some additional checks are required, as described in the section "Issues for Enterprises to Resolve When Connecting at Layer 3 to Provider Networks."

Comparing MPLS VPN Security to Frame Relay Networks

The preceding section gave an overview of how P routers can provide secure transport of packets in the simple MPLS topology. The more interesting case is considering the two-label imposition of MPLS VPN and how that compares to Frame Relay security.

In 2001, the network technology tester Meircom completed a report that analyzed the security characteristics of MPLS VPN networks compared to Frame Relay services. It concluded that security was equivalent. (You can locate this report at http://www.miercom.com/?url=reports/&v=16&tf=-3&st=v.)

This report validated the following:

- Address and routing separation between enterprise customers is maintained by provider-provisioned MPLS VPNs.
- Provider infrastructure is invisible to externally connected entities.
- Mechanisms (such as those described in this document, like black-holing traffic) exist to mitigate DoS attacks and are used in a similar way to that which is appropriate for Layer 2 WANs.

The approach used in the Meircom report is to define the components that allow an MPLS VPN to function and analyze the possibility for an attack on or intrusion to both components of the MPLS VPN. The two primary components are

- Virtual routing/forwarding instances (VRFs)
- Label-switched paths (LSPs)

VRF is a customer-specific routing table; think of it as a low-function virtual router for each customer within the PE router. Its purpose is purely to separate control traffic (route information) between multiple enterprise customers on the same PE. The abbreviated configuration shown in Example 7-1 identifies how these things are created in PE router devices.

Example 7-1 *VRF Configuration in PE Routers*

```
!
ip vrf Customer_1
  rd 300:300
  route-target export 200:2000
  route-target import 200:2000
!
interface Serial0/1
  ip vrf forwarding Customer_1
!
```

The first part of this configuration creates a VRF called Customer_1, and a route distinguisher (RD) of 300:300 is defined for this customer. This becomes the identifier for this customer's VPN routes within the provider network. MPLS VPNs are designed to allow for overlapping address space between multiple customers. The provider network differentiates between these similarly addressed networks by appending the RD to these routes and using multiprotocol BGP (MP-BGP) within its network to advertise these RD plus IPv4 routes to all other PE routers supporting the VPN. The combination of an RD and IPv4 address is called a VPNv4 address. This covers the control plane distribution of what were identical IP addresses in different customers but are now customer-unique addresses by the addition of the RD.

Forwarding, however, is a different story. No routing table holds VPNv4 addresses and performs lookups on them to determine forwarding decisions. Instead, MP-BGP distributes a label along with the VPNv4 route, which defines the label value for any other PE that wants to forward data to that destination. If that label value were the only value label for forwarding data to this VPN destination, all routers within the provider network would have to know about that set of VPN destinations. To avoid this, two labels are appended to any packets that are to be forwarded in an MPLS VPN network: one to take the packet to the next-hop PE router, and an inner label to identify where within that PE router the packet needs to end up. This means that no forwarding based on an IPv4 address happens within the provider network; therefore, IP addresses between customers can overlap.

Having created the VRF and defined the unique customer RD, routes are exported from the VRF to MP-BGP with the defined extended community value 200:2000. Next, routes with the same extended community value are imported to this VRF. This means that MP-BGP marks the routes from this VRF with the defined route-target value. Should any routes from other PE routers send an update that also have that extended community (this happens only if those PEs have also been configured with this route-target value, implying that they have connections to the same customer VPN), they are imported to this VRF.

It is possible to configure the RD and the route target to be the same value. However, the additional flexibility of configuring them to be different enables the possibility of extranet connectivity. Refer to Jim Guichard's book *MPLS and VPN Architectures* (ISBN 1587050811, published by Cisco Press) for further discussion of this topic.

The final part of Example 7-1 shows how specific enterprise-facing interfaces are associated with specific VRFs. In effect, the **ip vrf forwarding** configuration assigns a specific interface to the VRF virtual router.

Security Concerns Specific to MPLS VPNs

If everything is separated, where are the possible security compromises? Well, the first concern is that the P and PE routers within the provider network are secure themselves. At the most basic level, you would expect access control to the core routers from Telnet and Simple Network Management Protocol (SNMP) to be locked to specific source addresses via access control lists. There are concerns that potentially false routing information can be injected into the network. These concerns can be addressed by implementing Message Digest 5 (MD5) authentication on the network. MD5 is a method to ensure that only predefined routers can send routing information to a given P router.

The next security concern comes from looking at the forwarding path and analyzing the potential for inserting spoofed labeled packets into the network. This is actually impossible, because a potential attacker can gain access to a network interface only if he is a customer and has an interface on a PE router. These interfaces accept only IPv4 packets, so sending labeled packets to an MPLS VPN PE device just causes that PE device to drop the packet.

It is possible for a customer to send packets to the PE that will be dropped, with the intent of exhausting the PE router's CPU. However, those forms of attacks are naturally limited to the speed on the access link connecting the customer.

Given that each customer's control and data plane traffic is segregated in an MPLS VPN environment, what concerns are there? First, no customer can directly address core network routers on the network. One of the simplest ways to check if an MPLS VPN provider is hiding P router addresses from customer edge (CE) devices is to issue a traceroute from one CE to another CE on the VPN network. When the traceroute report comes back, no addresses of the P router devices should be viewable; the P router portion of the network should just appear as if it is one hop to the traceroute report. Providers can simply hide their P router addresses from VPN users by turning off time-to-live (TTL) propagation. Additionally, it is common practice for the provider to implement ACLs on the ingress to the PE devices to deny packets with destination addresses within the P portion of the network from entering the network.

NOTE   Chapter 9 discusses the options for the provider delivering Internet access as part of the MPLS VPN service. Implying that the PE device has Internet connectivity, this provides the greatest level of enterprise network simplification but opens the PE device to potential DoS attacks. Therefore, it presents a higher security risk. For the most secure service, separate VPN and Internet links are the best option. The next section addresses the generic issues of securing an interface connecting at Layer 3 to a third party.

The next concern is whether the MPLS VPN service can be denied by one customer who overwhelms the resources of the shared PE device. This customer can be either a valid customer or someone hijacking a PE-to-CE connection. The first generic recommendation for protecting the PE control plane to traffic generated by valid customers is to implement static routing between the PE and CE or to use MD5 authentication if a routing protocol is implemented on that link.

As well as MD5, it is possible to explicitly rate-limit any kind of traffic on the PE-to-CE link, including routing protocol traffic.

The second recommendation is to limit the number of routes any given PE accepts from a CE to protect PE resources should something catastrophic happen on one CE router (such as a software bug generating spurious route updates). In the case where spurious routes are sent to the PE, the route limit protects PE resources from being consumed. An enterprise can verify with its VPN provider that these and other provider-defined security features are implemented before signing up for the MPLS VPN service.

Figure 7-3 summarizes where these features should be implemented within the network. This gives the enterprise a checklist to confirm with potential providers concerning their security preparedness.

NOTE   Although Chapter 9 discusses some of the options for connecting the enterprise to the provider to enable Internet access, a fuller treatment of this subject is presented here. In this analysis, it is assumed that the core P routers support Internet connectivity, and different options for shared and dedicated PE routers, PE-to-CE links, and firewall locations are provided.

The safest option is to insist that the provider give VPN service that is delivered by a PE device not addressable from the Internet. This might cost more, because it costs the provider to supply a separate PE router dedicated to the two services and manage them separately. Additionally, a second access line at each location that needs Internet access is required, because each remote site has a separate connection for VPN access that does not have direct connectivity to the Internet. Each site that requires Internet access would look something like the topology shown in Figure 7-4.

Figure 7-3 *Securing the MPLS Core with Authentication for Routing and ACLs for the Data Plane*

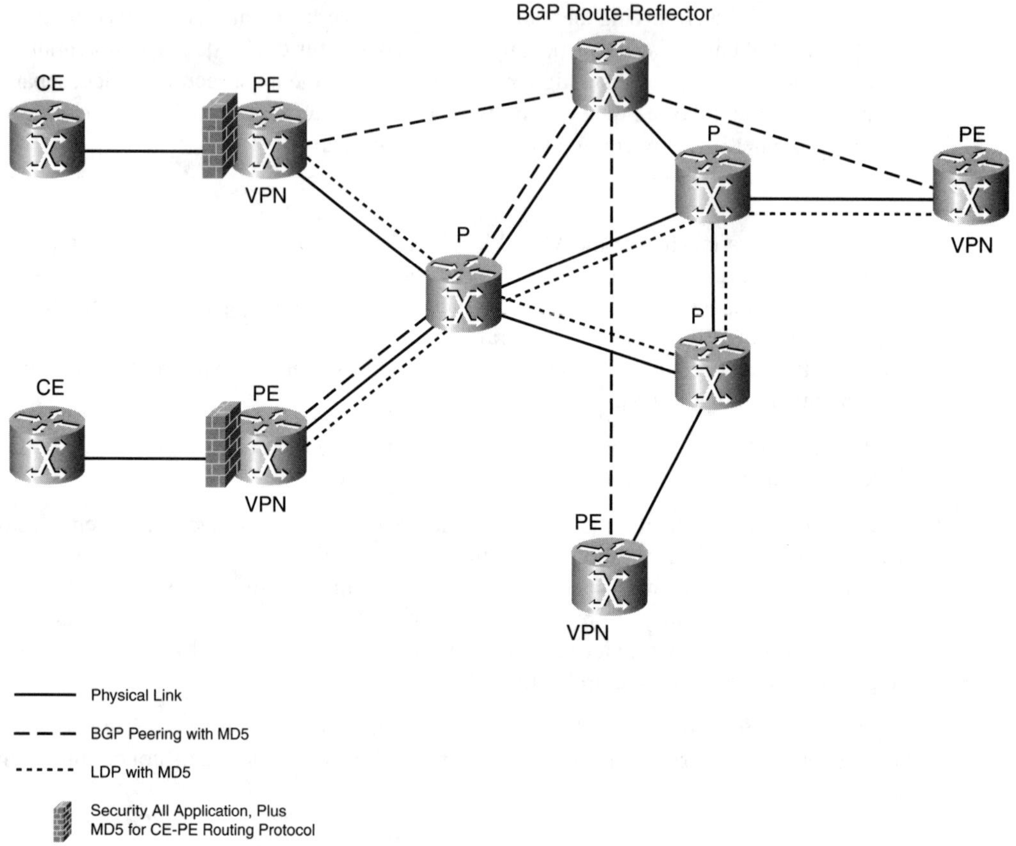

With this option, router 1 has full knowledge of VPN routes, plus a default route for accessing Internet locations. The default route, which directs traffic to the firewall/Network Address Translation (NAT) device, incurs substantial extra costs from both the provider and enterprise—not only in PE, CE, and PE-to-CE links, but also in firewall/NAT and IDS devices at each enterprise site because of this separate Internet access. However, this option provides the strongest separation between Internet and VPN services over the WAN and the strongest resistance from Internet DoS attacks.

A variation of this approach that does save some costs is to allow the PE device to carry Internet routes and therefore be reachable via the Internet, but still retain two links from the enterprise to the provider network. Essentially, the topology is the same as what's shown in Figure 7-4, except that PE1 and PE2 are combined, and the two PE-to-CE links terminate on this one combined PE router. Some cost savings for the provider can be passed on to the enterprise by having to supply only one PE; however, the trade-off is that a DoS attack from the Internet could affect the VPN service on this shared PE.

Figure 7-4   *Separate CE, PE, and PE-CE Links for Internet and VPN Access*

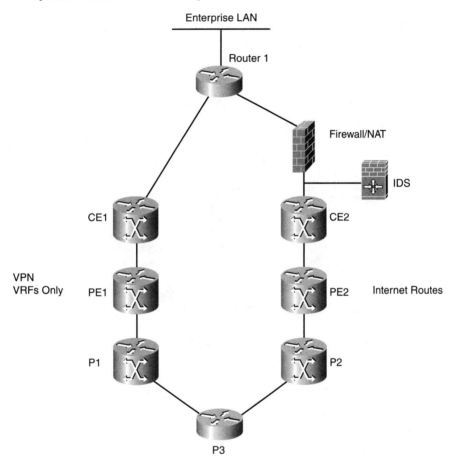

The next level of compromise in the choice between security and cost is reducing the number of CEs to one and consolidating the PE-to-CE link to one, as shown in Figure 7-5.

Figure 7-5 *Shared Access Line*

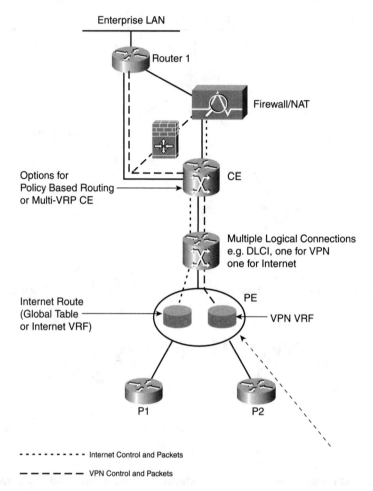

In this case, consider the enterprise VPN being addressed with the private 10.0.0.0 network. All interfaces on router 1, its connection to the CE, and the PE-to-CE link on the sub-interface connecting to the PE subinterface associated with the VPN VRF are all addressed on this private address space. Public Internet addresses are configured on the PE-to-CE link for the subinterface on the PE dedicated to Internet service, as on the CE, which also uses public addresses on the interfaces connecting the CE to the NAT device.

Routing is set up for outbound traffic such that router 1 knows about all VPN routes in the 10.0.0.0 space and a default to the firewall/NAT device for Internet connectivity. The same routing arrangement is configured for the CE device, with 10.0.0.0 routes for the internal VPN and a default for Internet routes. The only difference is that the CE also knows about the public addresses on the CE-to-firewall link so that packets arriving from the Internet are forwarded to the firewall device rather than back out to the Internet.

With a simple setup like this, routing operates acceptably. A modification to this basic setup is to use policy-based routing on the CE to force any traffic coming in from the Internet subinterface to go to the firewall/NAT device. The reason for this is just to add some extra protection for the internal network, at the cost of some additional processing by the CE router. This protection is useful if an attack or intrusion to the CE comes via the Internet connection, with addresses destined for the 10.0.0.0 network. Without policy-based routing, those packets would be forwarded directly to the internal network. With policy-based routing, the firewall/NAT device can stop those packets from making it into the internal network. This use of policy-based routing is highly recommended if, for example, the internal network has been addressed with publicly routable address space.

A design alternative to policy-based routing, which can have performance implications on some software-based platforms, is a feature called multi-VRF CE. This feature creates VRFs on a CE router and assigns interfaces to those VRFs to create multiple virtual routing instances within the one router. They segregate the control information and forwarding for different services, such as Internet and VPN, without the need for policy-based routing. In the example shown in Figure 7-5, two VRFs are created on the CE, with two interfaces assigned to each VRF. The Internet VRF has the CE-to-firewall/NAT device and the subinterface on the PE-to-CE link used for Internet traffic associated with it. Similarly, the VPN VRF has the CE-to-router 1 interface and VPN subinterface on the PE-to-CE link associated with it. The CE is not required to carry full Internet routes in its Internet VRF, just a default pointing toward the subinterface on the PE used to carry Internet traffic.

Clearly, these compromises save costs, and separation between the Internet and VPN traffic is maintained; however, the primary security concerns are that the PE is addressable from the Internet and therefore may be subject to a DoS attack. Additionally, the DoS attack may not incapacitate the PE but may saturate the PE-to-CE link, thus denying service for both VPN and Internet service to the enterprise.

If the enterprise wants to outsource the firewall and NAT responsibilities to the provider, the enterprise network manager must consider a number of options. Figure 7-6 shows the first and most simple option.

Figure 7-6   *Per-Customer Firewalls in the Provider Network*

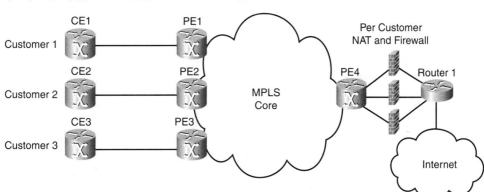

In this topology, each customer just needs its own VPN routes within its network and within its VRF in the provider PEs, along with a default route for Internet access. PE 4 has VRFs for all customers configured, with a single outbound interface toward the per-customer firewall/NAT device. This has many advantages from both the provider's and enterprise's perspectives:

- CE configurations are not changed to support Internet access.

- Different enterprises can select different security policies without affecting another enterprise's Internet access from the provider network.

- Different enterprises can even select different firewalls if the provider is willing to support that.

- Firewall management is centralized with the provider, so more resources are likely managing the security access.

The drawback to the provider, however, is that there is one firewall per customer, which could become a management headache for the provider and does not provide a backup in case of firewall failure.

A modification to this topology is to split the NAT and firewall responsibilities, moving NAT on a per-VRF basis to PE4. This is basically the same topology as shown in Figure 7-6, except that the customer NAT and firewall devices are replaced with one larger firewall device and NAT now operates on PE4. This also leaves the CEs untouched, which is simpler to provision and manage from the provider perspective. However, clearly, the enterprise can no longer select which firewall the provider delivers service on. One further modification to this is moving NAT to the CE devices. This has additional drawbacks to the NAT for each VRF implementation in that each CE needs to be configured, and they may or may not belong to the provider.

As soon as the connectivity to the MPLS VPN is chosen and placement of firewalls and so on is made, the next issue to consider is how such topologies can be attacked. From the enterprise perspective, there are two cases to consider:

- Can an intrusion occur? For example, can an unauthorized third party gain access to your VPN?

- What risk of DoS do you face?

The first concern is impossible in theory, because plain IP packets are restricted to each user's VPN by use of the VRF and LSPs created on the network, and MPLS-labeled packets are not allowed in from outside of the provider network. However, this does assume some fundamental conditions. It is assumed that the vendor implementation of these technologies does not provide some loopholes and that the provider operates the network correctly and does not misconfigure. No evidence to date suggests anything other than a correct implementation of MPLS VPN on Cisco equipment, meaning that there are no known cases of an implementation being responsible for an intrusion attack in the more than 200 provider networks where the technology has been deployed. Regarding misconfiguration, that is a matter between the provider and the enterprise and is a common concern for any technology—MPLS, Frame Relay, ATM, or anything else.

The more interesting security issue is the one of DoS attacks. Attackers use many approaches to achieve DoS; however, they are centered around achieving one of the following:

- Consuming memory on a network element to the extent that the ability to deliver service is affected.

- Occupying the CPU such that it is so busy processing attack information that it cannot process valid service packets.

- Consuming available bandwidth so that valid packets do not have a path through the network.

- Corrupting the routing information (by either injecting false information or denying valid route exchange) so that packets cannot be forwarded to the correct destination.

Within an MPLS VPN deployment, these issues are most pertinent to examine for the PE and CE devices. The P devices must be secure, just as they must be in any other technology for secure service to be offered. It is assumed that the techniques described in the next section have been applied to secure these P devices. Essentially, the CE-facing interfaces of the PEs are the only access points for any attacker to use on the network. It is assumed that core routers do not offer physical insertion points, because they are in secured facilities. Tapping into optical fibers at rates of up to OC-192, which connects these P routers, is not feasible.

The first question to answer is, can an attacker from outside a VPN reach one of your CEs? The answer is that if the network is operated without device misconfiguration, only if it is an Internet CE and has an Internet-routable address. Attackers cannot reach VPN-only CEs. If the CE can be reached from the Internet, security as described in the next section should be applied to it to minimize the possibility of attack. The same applies to accessibility of the PE-to-CE link: It is addressable only if it also carries Internet traffic. To protect the VPN service when it shares an access line with Internet traffic, VPN service can be maintained in the presence of a DOS attack if the Internet traffic is policed at the egress of the PE toward the CE. No matter what is sent, it cannot consume all the shared link bandwidth.

The next area of concern is whether another user of your shared PE can exhaust the PE resources by exhausting its resources. This is a matter for the provider. It must ensure protection against things such as too many updates being sent from a customer, too many SNMP queries, disabling the services of small servers, and so on.

The debate over security issues related specifically to MPLS VPN continues in the IETF mailing lists, with draft-behringer-mpls-security-05.txt cataloging the current thinking. As this document progresses, expect the 05 to change to 06 and so on if you search for this in the drafts section of http://www.ietf.org. A more general draft that identifies generic provider-supplied VPN security requirements is draft-ietf-l3vpn-security-framework-00.txt.

Issues for Enterprises to Resolve When Connecting at Layer 3 to Provider Networks

This section reviews some security mechanisms that are considered recommended practices when connecting at Layer 3 to any third-party network.

NOTE   Many references are listed at the end of this chapter to complement the overview provided in this section, because this topic is vast. The best places to start your research are http:// www.ispbook.com and http://www.nanog.org/ispsecurity.html.

History of IP Network Attacks

It's worth looking at the history of the most visible attacks on IP networks because it helps you understand the types of attacks that have existed in the past, and the direction that attacks are taking now, so that focus is applied to the current areas of concern.

DoS attacks can be considered as starting in 1999. The first major public awareness of this type of attack occurred with the February 2000 distributed DoS (DDoS) attack that denied service from Amazon, eBay, CNN, and E-Trade. The DDoS attack marked a new era in attacks, because it made feasible DoS attacks on major Internet locations by the generation of large amounts of traffic. In January 2001, attacks migrated from generating traffic to attacking routers. The most visible example was Microsoft websites being taken down by attacks on the routers that connected them to the Internet. This form of attack reached its most significant effects in January 2002, when the European service provider Cloud 9 went out of business because of persistent and successful DoS attacks on its infrastructure.

DoS attacks continue to gain in sophistication with the latest trends, such as the e-mail worm viruses that generate large amounts of traffic. These are not explicitly DoS attacks themselves, but they have a similar effect on the network. As these changes in attack types have occurred, their impact has changed from a local to global nature as the attacks have moved from attacking specific computers to network elements and finally to affecting the entire Internet, as we see with e-mail worms.

The number of attacks launched through the Internet is continually growing. The Internet provides much information about how routers work. Even conferences such as Blackhat (http://www.blackhat.com), Defcon (http://www.defcon.org), and Hivercon (http:// www.hivercon.com) provide details of router construction and routing protocol operations that some attackers find useful.

This section contains general references to types of attacks that have been seen, either on a widespread or limited basis, but precise details of the attacks are not given for obvious reasons. However, protection from different classes of attacks is defined. Initially, most of these techniques were viewed just as provider techniques. However, they are now just as relevant to large enterprise IP cores that now have Layer 3 connectivity to external networks. Enterprise network managers must be aware of the protection mechanisms identified here and ask prospective providers about what type of security protection mechanisms they implement. Enterprise network managers must also assess how secure their network is likely to be and what additional enterprise-based security measures are necessary to keep their network safe. Additionally, it is reasonable to assume that any technique to protect a P router is required because the router is exposed to Internet traffic. This must also be applied to enterprise routers that are similarly exposed to the Internet.

In this section, techniques such as tracing the source of DoS attacks used to be relevant to provider networks only. This is because enterprise networks typically had only one or two peering points to external networks, whereas provider networks had dozens, so it was more challenging to locate the source of attacks. However, with enterprises now having connectivity to multiple provider networks, extranet and external network-based data services, which are the sources of DoS attacks in an enterprise infrastructure, are increasing. This proliferation of external connections makes identifying the source of a DoS attack that appears on an enterprise network similar to the problem providers face by trying to identify the source of attacks.

Strong Password Protection

The most common and simple attack on infrastructure routers is via an insecure password. Attackers use tools that search for open Telnet ports and then send standard passwords through them to gain network access. From the enterprise's perspective, it is interesting to know if a provider implements some sort of central and secure password-management system, such as TACACS+. This increases the likelihood of secure passwords being used and reduces the possibility of operator error in setting secure passwords. In the world of hackers, identifying a weak password for a BGP-speaking router on the Internet is worth cash these days, because this could provide the launchpad for extensive DoS attacks.

Preparing for an Attack

The first step to prepare for an attack is to have one or more persons responsible for network security. In an enterprise, maybe not all the issues raised here need to be addressed directly; however, knowledge of what your provider can do for you during an attack and what needs to be done to complement that within the enterprise is an essential starting point. Too often, no security plans, procedures, or specific training or tools are in place, and learning tends to come on the job after an attack occurs. The person(s) responsible for security should follow these initial steps:

Step 1   Have a security contact for each network you peer with.

Step 2   Have contacts for security issues with the vendors.

Step 3   Document procedures for who is responsible for what during an attack.

Here are the primary phases to consider when creating a security policy:

Step 1 Prepare in terms of knowing your network and its normal traffic flows. Know the tools you have to identify, classify, and react to attacks. Participate in security groups. Additionally, use the security forums to keep up to date with new tools, techniques, and attack profiles.

Step 2 Know how to identify attacks by building baseline network activity logs and defining a procedure to detect anomalies.

Step 3 Know what you will do to classify the attack.

Step 4 Have a plan for tracing the source of the attack.

Step 5 Be prepared to react in multiple ways, depending on the nature of the attack, possibly rate-limiting, dropping, or capturing traffic for later analysis.

Step 6 Close the feedback loop by instigating a post mortem to learn from the attack and to see how your internal procedures can be optimized to deal with the attack.

NOTE   You might be interested in joining these primary forums to learn about security issues:

- **Operator meetings**—Your local one can be found at http://www.nanog.org/ orgs.html and http://www.first.org.

- **Security collection data**—Go to http://www.dshield.org and submit firewall logs.

Identifying an Attack

In preparing for an attack, the most important knowledge to have is to know how to identify attacks. NetFlow is the most valuable tool to use when you try to identify an attack that's in progress—where it's coming from, what it is targeting, and its nature. However, during an attack that generates significant amounts of traffic, analyzing all the NetFlow data can be infeasible for a human. You should use a type of NetFlow Collector, which sorts through the reams of NetFlow data, reports what is anomalous, and provides some intelligent sorting of that data for a security expert to digest and take action on.

The partner Cisco Systems works with on providing such a system is Arbor Networks. (Detailed information on Arbor products—Peakflow X for enterprises and Peakflow SP for providers—can be found at http://www.arbor.net.) When run properly, this system learns what is normal traffic for the network and reports anomalies for the security staff to investigate. What is most valuable from this system during times of attack is that the Peakflow system immediately identifies what is anomalous and what that anomalous traffic consists of in terms of source, destination, packet type, protocol, port range, packet size, and so on. All these things are essential to know to successfully block the attack.

Initial Precautions

The first line of defense against a network attack is a well-structured access control list (ACL) policy at the edge of the network and within the router. This section looks at ACLs applied to traffic that is destined for the router itself (either from a router that has an adjacency for exchange of routing information or management traffic) as well as transit traffic. These protection mechanisms need to be applied to all Internet-accessible routers, within both the provider and enterprise domain.

Simple ACLS are limited, though. For example, they were useless against the Code Red and Nimda viruses. For attacks like these, Network-Based Application Recognition and other higher-level filters must be applied.

Receiving ACLs

The first issue considered here is how you can protect the route processor of a router that is accessible from the public Internet. In today's hardware-based forwarding routers that form the backbone of provider networks, the linecards that are responsible for forwarding traffic can do so at the interface's line rate without difficulty. The only software part of the router that has constrained performance is the route processor, which is responsible for controlling traffic.

The primary means of protecting these route processors is to use receive ACLs. The basic concept is that a router receives two broad categories of traffic:

- Traffic that transits the router on its way to another destination (which constitutes the majority of traffic)

- Traffic such as Telnet, SNMP, or route information that is destined for the router itself and needs to be processed by the route processor on the router

In addition to these control packets, transit packets that the linecards cannot deal with directly are also sent to the route processor for special processing. Packets with certain options configured in the header or packets alerting the router to certain conditions on the network fall into this category.

A simple option for protecting the route processor is to limit the amount of traffic that a linecard allows into the router if the destination is the route processor itself. However, given that many routing adjacencies send updates to multicast addresses, this becomes cumbersome. Typically, this is implemented by an ACL with the destination address being the route processor IP address. This is a simplistic approach, because no differentiation between higher-priority routing protocol traffic and other lower-priority access-related traffic, such as Telnet, is possible. Receive ACLs provide this additional differentiation for traffic that enters a linecard and is destined for the route processor. The key implementation point is that the receive ACL itself is pushed to each linecard and is executed against traffic the linecard receives that is destined for the route processor, from what are termed receive adjacencies (basically peers exchanging route information) rather than being applied to the traffic that is transiting the router.

Figure 7-7 shows the location of these receive ACLs in a routing infrastructure.

Figure 7-7   *Receive ACL Location of Operation*

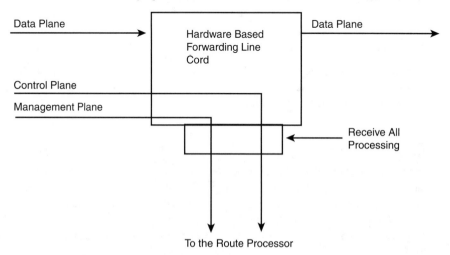

Traffic Types
   Data Plane = Transit Traffic to Destination Hosts
   Control Plane = Routing Protocol Traffic
   Management Plane = Telnet, SNMP, etc.

Infrastructure ACLs

The more traditional ACL protection falls under the category of infrastructure ACLs. *Infrastructure ACLs* are implemented to protect routers from receiving and processing packets that are not valid transit packets that need to be forwarded to customer hosts. Each infrastructure ACL is applied to protect the router from a specific type of packet. These protections need to be applied both to P routers and to enterprise routers connecting to the provider network—or, in fact, any third-party network.

NOTE   This section only introduces this topic; it covers the most basic issues. You can find more detailed information by visiting the URLs listed in the "References" section.

The first action of the infrastructure ACL is to ensure that no packets can enter the network from prefixes that should not be on the network. Things such as private addresses, like the 10.0.0.0 network and multicast addresses, clearly should not appear as source addresses of packets on the public Internet. Internet providers deny packets with these source addresses from entering their networks. Enterprises should also take the same precautions to deny packets with these source addresses from entering their network via Internet connections. The source for identifying these "banned" source addresses is the bogon list maintained by Team Cymru (http://www.cymru.com/). These source addresses are harmful because they are commonly the source addresses crafted into packets injected into the network for the purpose of a DoS attack.

Identifying the list of bogons (addresses considered bogus and not to be allowed) starts with the Internet Assigned Numbers Authority (IANA) allocation at http://www.iana.org/assignments/ipv4-address-space, which identifies all addresses not allocated to a valid user. If all the unallocated addresses are denied as either routes that can be injected into the network or as source addresses of packets, these bogon addresses are of no use to attackers. Of course, the issue arises of IANA allocating these address prefixes to valid users. For this, Team Cymru regularly updates the bogon list and provides a template for configuring IOS in a secure fashion, along with a secure BGP configuration. The following URLs provide preconfigured bogon lists and explanations of all the recommended configurations for border routers:

- http://www.cymru.com/Documents/secure-ios-template.html
- http://www.cymru.com/Documents/secure-bgp-template.html

One issue that is often not addressed when trying to protect either edge or core routers by using ACLs is the treatment of fragmented packets. The templates given in these URLs address denying ICMP fragments. This section explains why this is so important for ICMP and other protocols.

This issue with fragments is documented in RFC 1858 (http://www.ietf.org/rfc/rfc1858.txt). The bottom line is that unfragmented packets have Layer 3 and Layer 4 information in the header, which allows for identification and classification. Initial fragments have Layer 4 information, but subsequent fragments do not; they just have the destination IP address in their header. The issue then becomes how the router handles these noninitial fragments given that they have no Layer 4 data for application classification purposes.

The answer for Cisco equipment depends on what the ACL consists of and what type of packet is presented to the ACL for processing. The operation has changed for IOS starting with 12.1(2) and 12.0(11) onward.

These releases have six different types of ACL lines, and each has a specific processing action, depending on whether a packet does or does not match the ACL entry. When there is both Layer 3 and Layer 4 information in the ACL line and the **fragments** keyword is present, the ACL action for both **permit** and **deny** actions is defined as conservative. The definition of conservative for the permit case means it is assumed that the Layer 4 information in the packet, if available, matches the Layer 4 information in the ACL line. In the **deny** case, a noninitial fragment is not denied; instead, the next ACL entry is processed.

Specific examples of each of the possible cases are described at http://www.cisco.com/warp/public/105/acl_wp.html. However, just one example is useful here to illustrate the concept. In the following example, access list 100 illustrates the commands to invoke fragment processing. Clearly, denying all fragments to the router may break some operations. However, most uses of control traffic, such as ICMP and Telnet, do not have to send packets that cause MTUs to be exceeded, so fragment processing for these protocols may be turned on, as in the secure IOS template from Team Cymru:

```
access-list 100 deny ip any host 172.16.10.1 fragments
access-list 100 permit tcp any host 172.16.10.1 eq 80
access-list 100 deny ip any any
```

Access list 100 does not allow noninitial fragments through to the 172.16.10.1 address because of the first line. A noninitial fragment to the server is denied when it encounters the first ACL line because the Layer 3 information in the packet matches the Layer 3 information in the ACL line.

Initial or nonfragments to port 80 of packets destined for 172.16.10.1 also match the first line of the ACL for Layer 3 information, but because the **fragments** keyword is present, the next ACL entry (the second line) is processed. The second line of the ACL permits the initial or nonfragments because they match the ACL line for Layer 3 and Layer 4 information.

Noninitial fragments destined for the TCP ports of other hosts on the 171.16.23.0 network are blocked by this ACL. The Layer 3 information in these packets does not match the Layer 3 information in the first ACL line, so the next ACL line is processed. The Layer 3 information in these packets does not match the Layer 3 information in the second ACL line either, so the third ACL line is processed. The third line is implicit and denies all traffic.

Basic Attack Mitigation

Say that an attack gets past your ACL policy—what's next? Because the list of bogon addresses is being constantly updated with subsequent operational changes to security ACLs, how do you protect yourself when an attack is crafted using a new bogon address or one that has accidentally not been filtered? How can you track the source of an attack if the source address of the attack packets is bogus? In fact, filtering out these packets without first identifying their source may not be in the best interest of the network operator. Instead of hoping that the attack does not change to a different set of fake source addresses, a better option is to take the miscreant host off the network. For this reason, something more than plain security ACLs are necessary.

In a Cisco environment, Cisco Express Forwarding (CEF) and NetFlow provide the functionality required to track these attacks and identify the source host, because clearly relying on routing table information is not helpful when tracking a bogon source address:

- **CEF** provides the fastest packet-switching option available in Cisco routers.

- **NetFlow** provides an export of data that describes the traffic flows through the network. NetFlow is enabled on a per-interface basis with the **ip route-cache flow** command. NetFlow data can also be viewed on the router with commands such as **show ip cache flow**. This command displays information about things such as the IP packet distribution seen on the interface and the total number of flows used by each protocol on the interface. This information is useful when identifying a DoS attack, because the packet sizes tend to be fixed and also use a single protocol type.

As NetFlow logs flow information, it can tell you about source address information and is therefore most useful in tracking DDoS attacks using bogon addresses. Figure 7-8 shows a simple example of tracking spoofed source addresses through a network (with reference to the network).

Figure 7-8   *Tracking Packets with Spoofed Bogon Addresses*

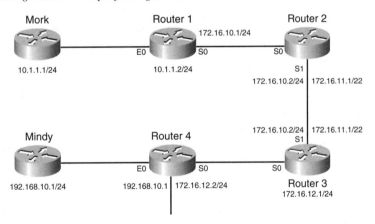

NOTE   A fuller description of the methodology described here, with links explaining the component technologies in more depth, can be found at http://www.cymru.com.

Assume that route information, either static or dynamically sourced, exists in each router. In Figure 7-8, an attacker resides on host Mindy and selects host Mork at the target of attack. The actual IP addresses are clearly not what would be found in a real situation; they are just for illustrative purposes. The attack could be of any form — lots of bogus UDP traffic, TCP connection request, anything. However, to avoid being caught, the attacker located on Mindy decides to spoof his address to be 96.170.4.8. The attacker knows that the entire 96/8 prefix is unassigned, so any packets destined for this network (being returned from Mork) do not arrive at an actual site.

The administrator of Mork is alerted to the attack by an unusually high CPU on Mork, or perhaps users complaining of a poor response or no response. A packet analyzer quickly identifies the source of the problem as excessive numbers of packets hitting server Mork with a source address of 96.170.4.8, the spoofed IP address. Clearly, examining the routing table to trace the source of the attack does not help, because that address block is not there. So the first action is to look at the NetFlow data on router 1 for information on this spoofed address, which shows something like the following:

```
router1#sh ip cache flow | include 96.120
Se0          96.120.2.2    Et0          10.1.1.1
```

This syntax asks router 1 to show NetFlow entries that include 96.120 in the address. The result is information that packets destined for 10.1.1.1 are coming in on Serial 0 with source address 96.120.2.2. We now follow the trail through the network. The next step is to use CEF to determine the active sources on serial 0:

```
router1#sh ip cef se0
Prefix              Next Hop            Interface
0.0.0.0/0           172.16.10.2         Serial0
172.16.10.0         attached            Serial0
```

This syntax tells us a few things. The router has a default route to 172.16.10.2, the subnet 172.16.10.0 is directly attached, and 172.16.10.2 is the only active source on that interface. This process of finding the interface receiving the packets with the spoofed source address and then using CEF to identify the active source on that interface can be followed all the way through the network to Router 4, which identifies host Mindy as sending the packets. Clearly, Mindy has a non-Cisco MAC address, and the network operator cannot access this device. Shutting off Ethernet 0 on router 4 will prove the source of the attack, assuming that spoofed packets to Mork stop appearing on the network. There are cases in which a router may have multiple active sources shown by CEF, as in the case where Ethernet connectivity is used. In this case, the resolution is to log on to all the routers listed as potential sources by CEF and enter the **sh ip cache flow | include 96.170** command to see if they are receiving traffic from the spoofed address. Should that command return no data, the potential source is not receiving packets with the spoofed source address. This narrows down the potential number of sources to one, and the hunt resumes.

This and similar techniques that are described in sources in the "References" section are most useful for attacks emanating from a single location. However, more and more attackers are leveraging techniques that initiate attacks from multiple sources. When that happens, it is usually the result of a compromised set of hosts, and the attack may be originating from hundreds of hosts (or more) using nonspoofed addresses. Clearly in these circumstances, a different approach is required. The following sections address some basic techniques to reduce the likelihood of these types of attacks, tell you how these types of attacks can be initiated, and show you how to deal with them when they arise.

Basic Security Techniques

This section examines five network techniques or capabilities that can be considered basic or required implementations for entry-level security for systems connected to today's Internet:

- Remote-triggered black-hole filtering
- Loose uRPF for source-based filtering
- Strict uRPF and source-address validation
- Sinkholes and anycast sinkholes
- Backscatter traceback

Remote-Triggered Black-Hole Filtering

The idea behind the remote-triggered black-hole filtering technique is to use a routing protocol to quickly disseminate a route to Null0, which essentially drops the traffic that is part of an attack. Here's a scenario: Imagine that an enterprise has a web server under attack. The attack's address is specific to the web server itself. Therefore, no matter what technique an attacker is using to conceal the attack's real source (or, indeed, using multiple compromised hosts to launch an attack from many locations), the destination is known and constant. The objective is to quickly disseminate to the edge of the network something that will instruct the edge routers to drop the attack packets. The result is that both attack and valid packets to the attack destination are dropped, so service is not restored to the attack host at this stage. However, the rest of the resources on the attacked network are available, such as web access, other servers, e-mail, and so on. This is so while the attack is going on, service may be denied to the entire network, either due to router resource exhaustion (if the attack consists of small packets) or bandwidth exhaustion (if the attack consists of large packets). However, without the attack packets, everything except the object of the attack can have service restored, and no collateral damage occurs.

NOTE The technique just discussed uses a routing protocol as a security tool. Let's digress and examine why this approach is superior to ACLs. It is tempting to rely on implementing an ACL scheme to block attack packets from entering a network while the attack is under way. However, consider the challenges of that approach in the case just defined. With a host under attack, the standard ACLs have failed. The attack is getting through. So to update the ACLs, the attack has to be identified and a new ACL created and pushed to all edge devices. This is a significant operational challenge. As the number of routers that need this new protection grows, so does the challenge of updating their ACL configuration.

So, if you were to look at ACLs as the solution to dropping these attack packets, you would have to be able to update the ACL configuration of 50, 100, or more routers within a minute or so, not have this make any impact on forwarding performance, and be able to use the feature in a consistent manner across all products. Providing ACL features to do this on hardware- and software-based forwarding systems simultaneously is not trivial. However, all platforms support BGP. They drop packets to null0, and the entire network is updated as quickly as BGP (or another routing protocol) updates the edge devices.

So how does this get done? Here's how:

1 Predefine a static route on each edge device that points to null0.

2 Set up a trigger router that is part of the routing protocol deployed (BGP is used in this example).

3 Send an update via the routing protocol to all devices for which the next hop for the host under attack is the address specified locally that routes to null0.

The first question that may arise is why not send an update directly to null0 for the attacked host to all edge routers? Well, the answer is that when advertising route updates, BGP needs to send an IP address as the next hop. It cannot send an interface as a next hop, so you must introduce this step.

How is this set up? First, the static route to null0 must be defined on each router that will be asked to drop packets destined for the attacked host. The IP address used in this static route must be one that you never expect to have to transit traffic for, or use within your network. A recommended address space is the one set aside for documentation, 192.0.2.0/24, so this would manifest itself as a static route on each router as follows:

```
ip route 192.0.2.1 255.255.255.255 null0 255
```

This sets the next hop for the 192.0.2.1/32 address to the null0 interface. Next, the trigger router has to be set up. It is most commonly set up as a route reflector client. The configuration on the router must achieve the following objectives:

• Send an update for the desired destination to be black-holed to have a next hop of 192.0.2.1.

• Use tags as a way to identify the route that needs to be black-holed.

• Set the next hop based on tag assignment.

So, the preattack configuration on the trigger router includes the following:

```
Router BGP 65534
!
redistribute static route-map black-hole
!
route-map black-hole permit 10
match tag 99
set ip next-hop 192.0.2.1
!
route-map black-hole permit 20
```

Here, the router is told to redistribute static routes if they have a tag of 99 and then to set the next hop to 192.0.2.1 for them. The entire process is triggered when you now enter a single static route, tagged to 99 on this router (in the following example, you want to black-hole traffic for 177.77.7.1):

```
ip route 177.77.7.1 255.255.255.255 null0 tag 99
```

The trigger black-holes traffic to 177.77.7.1 and, via BGP updates to the rest of the routers, tells them to do the same. After the trigger router has picked up the tagged route, an update for route 177.77.7.1 is sent with a next hop of 192.0.2.1. As soon as each edge router receives that, the recursive process of determining which interface to use for 177.77.7.1 begins, resulting in all traffic for 177.77.7.1 being sent to null0.

What has been done so far is a very quick way to eliminate that specific attack. The process of tracking this to the source can now begin, safe in the knowledge that collateral damage has been eliminated and all other services are up and running on the network that was under attack. After the source of the attack has been identified and removed, full service to the web server that was attacked can be provided.

There is one issue to consider before we move on to discuss how you can quickly eliminate attack traffic from specific sources (whether spoofed or not). Routing to null0 is fine for hardware-based forwarding devices (it merely takes the clearing of a hardware register), but this can be an issue for software-based forwarding. The reason for this is that the routing software is optimized to forward packets, not drop them. So for forwarding-based devices at the edge, it may be preferable to set the next-hop interface to a physical interface that has no other peers or hosts connected to it. This allows the router to continue forwarding packets optimally and sending attack packets to a destination that leads nowhere.

Loose uRPF for Source-Based Filtering

After the attack packets to the specific host under attack have been stopped, you have time to research the attack and determine its source. Using the Arbor system delivers that information in a timely fashion. As soon as the attack's source is identified, you need to drop packets coming from that source so that you can then allow packets destined for the attacked host to start flowing, safe in the knowledge that the attack packets have been stopped. To do this, you need to check source addresses at the network's ingress. That could be accomplished with ACLs with a lot of manual intervention during an attack. However, by using a feature called unicast Reverse Path Forwarding (uRPF) in conjunction with the remote-triggered black-hole filter technique described in the preceding section, it is possible to use the routing protocol to more quickly and intelligently block these unwanted packets.

---

uRPF and Its Origins

Reverse Path Forwarding (RPF) is a technique used in multicast to control the flooding of multicast packets and prevent loops. The algorithm is implemented as follows:

- If a router receives a datagram on an interface that it uses to send unicast packets to the source, the packet has arrived on the RPF interface.

- If the packet arrives on the RPF interface, a router forwards the packet out the interfaces that are present in the outgoing interface list of a multicast routing table entry.

- If the packet does not arrive on the RPF interface, the packet is silently discarded.

uRPF was created to provide similar functionality but for packets destined for a unicast address. uRPF exists in two forms, loose and strict. Strict was implemented to filter out packets using spoofed source addresses by dropping any packets whose source address does not match the IP address space allocated to it. Loose-mode uRPF was created to support source-based black-hole filtering (strict mode is discussed in the next section).

Although it is not essential to understand this technique to use it, loose uRPF checks to see if a route back to the source address exists in the forwarding information base (FIB) of the router performing uRPF. If a route does not exist, the packet is dropped. Likewise, if the packet is being forwarded to a next hop with a value of null 0, it is also dropped. This allows you to use exactly the same configuration that was used for destination-based black-hole filtering. However, the trigger route set up on the trigger router no longer is the destination you want to black-hole traffic for, but the sources you want to black-hole traffic from. The only extra piece of configuration needed to enable this technique is to set up loose-mode uRPF on each interface on the edge routers. This can be achieved by using the following interface-level command:

```
ip verify unicast source reachable-via any
```

Strict uRPF and Source Address Validation

Strict uRPF is a way to implement part of the filtering requirements defined in RFC 2827, *Network Ingress Filtering: Defeating Denial of Service Attacks Which Employ IP Source Address Spoofing*. This is called BCP0038. It defines ingress filtering to defeat DoS attacks using spoofed addresses. RFC 2827 recommends that an Internet service provider's (ISP's) customer should not send any packets to the Internet with a source address other than the address allocated to him or her by the ISP. This is a good goal, but the question is how to scale its implementation. This becomes operationally feasible if it can be implemented without the need for a unique ACL for each interface and if the filter can be dynamically updated to accommodate changes in address allocation.

uRPF can meet these goals with a single configuration for each interface. uRPF uses the CEF table for drop decisions, which is updated by routing protocols. uRPF works for all single-homed connections. Extra configuration may be necessary for some dual-homed configurations.

This feature is useful not only for ISPs to be assured that no customers are spoofing source addresses. It is also useful for enterprises to implement on their edge routers. Basically, no packets from the Internet should arrive with a source address in the range that's allocated to the enterprise. The typical implementation inserts the **ip verify unicast reverse-path** command under the interface configuration of the serial interface connecting the enterprise router to the provider. Figure 7-9 shows the two operations of uRPF.

Figure 7-9   *uRPF Strict and Loose Modes*

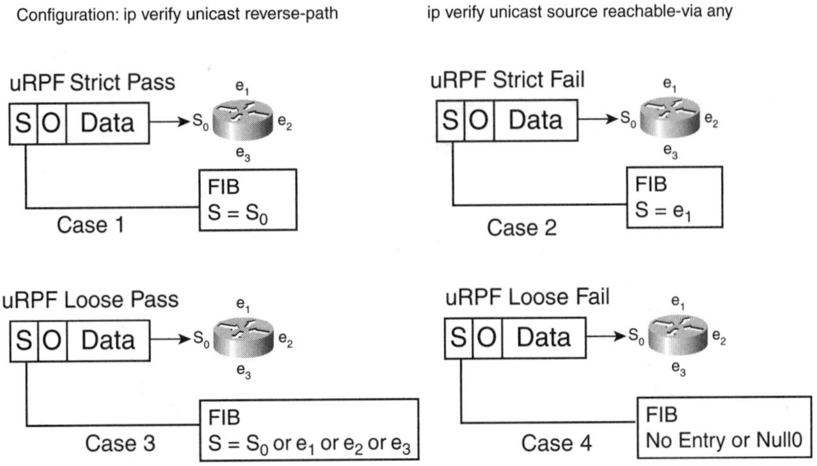

In Figure 7-9, Case 1 is where we implement strict uRPF and the packet entering the router on serial 0 passes the check. The pass is based on the source address of the packet matching an entry in the FIB for the interface the packet was received on. Case 2 is a situation in which the packet gets dropped, because the packet coming in to serial 0 has a source address that can be reached via Ethernet 1. This packet would be permitted in the uRPF check of Case 3, where the packet's source address can be any address that the router knows. Case 4 shows what causes uRPF loose to drop the packet. Either there is no FIB entry for the source, or the source address has a next hop of null0 (which is what we use to trigger black-holing).

With strict uRPF enabled, attacks like the smurf and its cousin, fraggle (which uses User Datagram Protocol [UDP] echo packets in the same fashion as ICMP echo packets), are not possible. The smurf attack, which is named after its exploit program, occurs when an attacker sends a large amount of ICMP echo (ping) traffic to an IP broadcast address. By sending traffic to the broadcast address, each host on that network (or subnet, more specifically) responds to the ping, amplifying what was a single packet sent into however many hosts there are on the subnet attacked (see Figure 7-10). There are two variants of this:

- A bogus spoofed address is sent, and the effect is merely to consume bandwidth and CPU at the site of the attacked location. Effectively, all the ICMP replies consume outbound bandwidth but are dropped further into the provider network when there is not a route to the spoofed address.

- The more aggressive mode of attack is to spoof a legitimate source address that belongs to a location you really want to attack. Basically, the ping is sent with a source address of the attack target to the broadcast address of an amplifier network. The attacked destination is overwhelmed with all the ping replies sent from all the hosts on the targeted subnet.

Figure 7-10 *Smurf Attack*

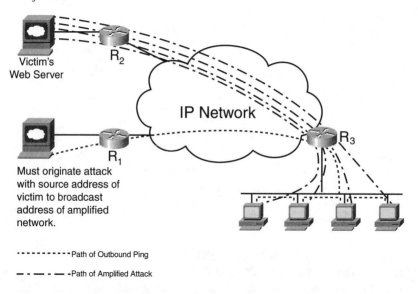

Clearly, an attacker cannot use this form of attack if strict uRPF is implemented on the ingress to the IP network shown in Figure 7-10. Whether the attacker spoofs with bogon source addresses or the source address of an intended victim, neither passes the uRPF check.

Sinkholes and Anycast Sinkholes

The concept of a sinkhole is simple: If a destination is under attack, divert the attack traffic to a safe place on the network, where the attack traffic no longer causes collateral damage and can be further analyzed, classified, and mitigated. Sinkholes are an essential piece of the security infrastructure. More uses for them are being created within the security community all the time. In fact, sinkholes typically are gainfully employed even when there is no attack alert. It is common practice to have a sinkhole router or UNIX machine advertise pieces of bogon addresses and dark IP space (which are IP addresses that were legitimately allocated but that are not in use by the owner) to see if anyone is probing to find an attack. In fact, sinkholes can get more sophisticated than just advertising bogon or dark IP addresses to lure attackers. They can also be set up with web servers to make attackers think that they have found something to exploit, while the source of the attack can be traced.

Sinkholes can be set up in one of two ways:

- **Unicast**—Unicast sinkholes use just a single source on the network to attract attack traffic, so they may require some re-architecting of the network to accommodate the extra traffic flow to that point.

- **Anycast**—Anycast sinkholes use the same technique employed by Domain Name System (DNS) servers. Multiple sinkholes are deployed around the network, advertising the same prefixes. Routers that are transiting attack traffic destined for one of the advertised prefixes just select the nearest sinkhole by the normal routing metrics process. No re-architecting of the network to accommodate a consolidated flow is necessary.

Sinkholes should be deployed in multiple layers of the IP network, in the service provider, in the demilitarized zone (DMZ) network, and within the enterprise. In fact, coupling a sinkhole with an analysis tool such as the Arbor Peak flow system provides an excellent tool for identifying, classifying, and mitigating many forms of DoS attack. One example is within the Cisco network, where this setup is common. During an attack, the sinkhole attracts traffic, and the Arbor system identifies it and creates a recommended ACL to stop the attack. This can then be brought in to something like CiscoWorks or a Perl script to distribute to the entire network. In some of these cases, the Arbor system picks up the scans that some worms deploy to proliferate. (More on worm behavior and mitigation appears in the section "Worm Mitigation.") For example, in the case of the Sapphire/Slammer worm, Arbor would have picked up the new activity on UDP port 1434 and created an ACL definition to block that traffic far quicker than any mechanism using human intervention.

NOTE   You can find more details on the Sapphire/Slammer worm at http://www.caida.org under the papers link.

Backscatter Traceback

Backscatter traceback is a quicker method of the hop-by-hop tracing technique. It uses several of the previously mentioned techniques in combination, so it had to be saved for last. The concept you want to realize is getting the edge routers to tell you which ingress interface the attack using spoofed source addresses is coming from. As you know from setting up destination-based black-hole filtering, if a host is under attack from a stream of packets with spoofed source addresses, you can push a route to null0 to the edge for the attacked host address. This causes the edge routers to drop the attack packets. From RFC 1812, you know that the router must generate a destination-unreachable ICMP message in response to dropping a packet being routed to null0. With the black-hole filtering discussed so far, there is no route back to the source originating this ICMP message, so the destination-unreachable messages go nowhere. However, what if you gave the router a place to send those unreachables and logged them for viewing? The result is that you would instantly be able to identify the edge router receiving the spoofed source address attack and the interface that router is receiving them on, because both would be identified in the unreachable message sent to the logging device.

So, the components are implemented in this fashion.

The sinkhole advertises large amounts of bogon and dark IP space, with the expectation that if an attack comes in, it uses random spoofed addresses, and some match the address space advertised by the sinkhole. An example of this is 96.0.0.0/6. The edge routers are set up with the usual static route of 192.0.2.1 to null0. The trigger router is ready to redistribute the route of the attacked host (picking 172.16.18.1 for this example) to have a next hop of 192.0.2.1. The trigger router that advertises the 96.0.0.0 space (of course, care must be taken not to advertise this outside your network by egress filtering) needs to be set up with an ACL to generate log messages for the ICMP unreachables it receives. The ACL is implemented inbound on the interface you expect the ICMP unreachables to reach the sinkhole router on. It would look something like this:

```
access-list 101 permit icmp any any unreachables log
access-list 101 permit ip any any
```

Figure 7-11 shows the complete process.

Figure 7-11 *ICMP Backscatter Traceback*

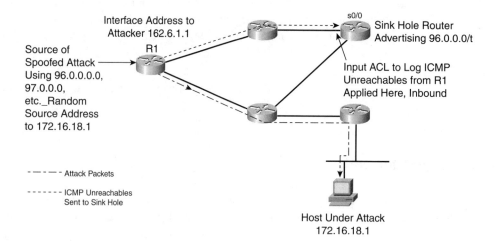

So, assuming that an attack is in progress on 172.16.18.1 and that one of the attack packets uses a spoofed source address of 96.0.0.1, what will be seen in the log of the sinkhole router?

The first thing to do is issue this command on the sinkhole router:

```
router2#show access-list 101
Extended IP access list 101
    permit icmp any any unreachable log (20000 matches)
    permit ip any any
```

This tells you that the sinkhole router is seeing lots of unreachables inbound on the interface the ACL was applied to. The next thing is to look at the log on the sinkhole router to get information on where all these unreachables are coming from. The output of the log on the sinkhole router looks something like this:

```
01:03:04: %SEC-6-IPACCESSLOGDP: list 101 permitted icmp 162.6.1.1 -> 96.0.0.1
   (3/1), 99 packets
```

Now you know where this is coming from. The router with customer-facing interface 162.6.1.1 is sourcing ICMP unreachables when it is trying to tell source 96.0.0.1 that it can no longer reach 172.16.18.1 (because 172.16.18.1, the target of the attack, has now been black-holed). The code 3/1 tells you that these are unreachable messages, because ICMP unreachable code 3 means destination unreachable and type 1 refers to a host address.

However, there are a few issues to consider. First, you must check that your equivalent to R1 in Figure 7-11 does in fact generate ICMP unreachables under these conditions. Also, generating large numbers of ICMP unreachables can cause CPU overload, depending on the hardware. The workaround for this is to implement ICMP rate limiting:

```
router(config)#ip icmp rate-limit unreachable n
```

n is the number of milliseconds between two consecutive ICMP unreachable packets. The default value is 500, which means that one ICMP unreachable packet is sent every 500 ms.

NOTE   Full details on this issue are available at http://www.cisco.com/en/US/products/ products_security_advisory09186a0080094250.shtml.

These techniques are applied with the enterprise network. They take on more significance when MPLS VPNs add richer connectivity to the WAN infrastructure. MPLS VPNs add any-to-any connectivity within the WAN to support applications, such as VoIP. In many cases, they enable quicker extranet connectivity. These business benefits are significant; however, they do come at a price—the additional effort needed to trace attacks and provide security in the new environment.

Cisco Guard

Cisco Guard is a relatively new product that automates some of the actions described here. It now forms a key part of the DDoS mitigation plan of many enterprises with large IP networks, as well as service providers.

Cisco Guard and Cisco Detector are two pieces of the anomaly detection and mitigation solution that are marketed by Cisco. Cisco Detector performs attack detection and identification. The Detector communicates with the Guard, which diverts specific traffic for on-demand protection. Placement of these devices is shown in Figures 7-12 and 7-13.

Figure 7-12 *Dynamic Diversion Architecture*

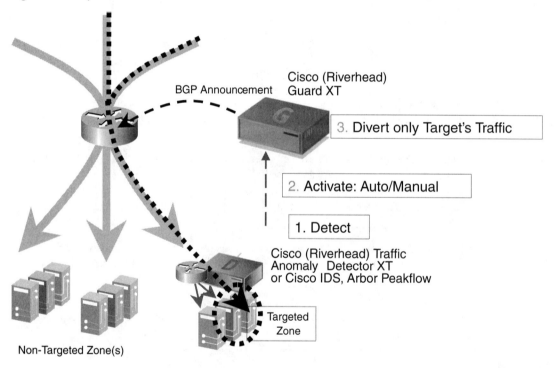

Figure 7-12 shows what happens when an attack occurs: attack traffic to the targeted zone passes freely. However, when this new attack traffic flows, it is detected by Cisco Detector, which notifies Cisco Guard automatically. Cisco Guard then uses BGP or another routing protocol to redirect attack traffic, as shown in Figure 7-13.

Figure 7-13 *Dynamic Diversion Architecture, Continued*

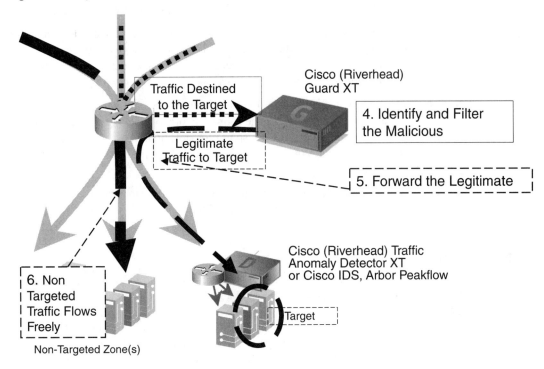

The primary benefit here is that the Guard and Detector can work in unison not only to detect the anomaly but also to implement a mitigation schema, all without human intervention. After the traffic is diverted, you can further inspect it to detect its source and remove it from the network.

As a matter of design, the Detector needs to be as close as possible to potential targets of attack, and the Guard has to be as far upstream as possible. In the case of an enterprise connecting to a provider, the enterprise cannot install the Guard any further upstream than the PE-to-CE link unless specific provisions are negotiated with the provider.

In that situation, the Guard can protect downstream resources from the attack but does not stop the attack from getting as far as the provider PE router. In that case, communication with the provider is necessary to stop the attack traffic.

Distributed DoS, Botnets, and Worms

This chapter has discussed some of the effects of attack activity and how to use some tools to identify and mitigate those attacks. In the spirit of Sun Tzu, however, you have to know your enemy to emerge victorious from battles. This section discusses some of the tools attackers use, which provides you with knowledge of how this enemy operates.

An attacker's goal is to disrupt normal network service, because he or she enjoys creating havoc. A common type of attack is the TCP SYN flood, which has grown in its variations and complexity. This attack seeks to tie up system resources by sending large numbers of connection requests, which the attacked host must deal with and reply to.

Attacks have changed focus from selected hosts to routers servicing multiple hosts to generating large amounts of traffic across the entire network to attacking routing protocols, management traffic, and the underlying transport protocols of all these higher-level protocols. In fact, all these types of attacks are continuously in progress on the Internet at any given moment.

This section examines some further DDoS attack techniques, how they can be implemented by attackers using botnets, and what worms are and their mitigation techniques.

Anatomy of a DDoS Attack

DDoS attacks can target (among other things) resources such as bandwidth (large packets), CPU (small packets), buffers, and protocol exhaustion (such as SYN floods and crafted packets to kill machine processes). These can be directed toward an enterprise, a provider, or the core of the Internet. As described previously, the attack can come in the form of spurious traffic generated by lots of compromised hosts, attacks on transport protocols such as TCP (SYN or RST attacks), internal buffers on routers, or any other part of the infrastructure.

NOTE   Cisco offers a feature called TCP Intercept to specifically address the SYN class of attacks. More details can be found at http://www.cisco.com/univercd/cc/td/doc/product/software/ios122/122cgcr/fsecur_c/ftrafwl/scfdenl.htm.

The effect of the DDoS attacks can be amplified by using multiple machines at differing locations, as shown in Figure 7-14.

Figure 7-14 *DDoS Architecture*

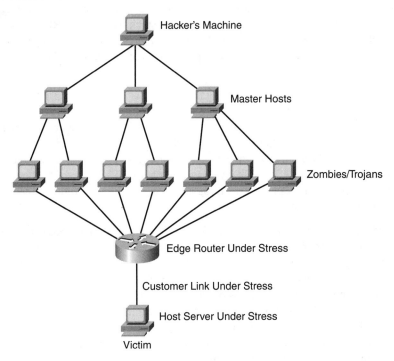

Hackers typically follow this type of process for a DDoS attack:

1 Crack a large number of unsuspecting hosts attached to the network using well-known vulnerabilities within the operating systems. Typically, these are unprotected home-user PCs that do not get regular security patches applied.

2 After the hacker recruits his army of compromised hosts, a Trojan (a program that runs as an invisible process on a compromised machine) is installed on each host with an apparently innocent control channel.

    The control channel can be something like commands to the Trojan that contain what look like ICMP packets, which can be used to initiate on-demand DDoS activity.

3 After this is all set up, the hacker can direct an attack from all these innocent host machines as desired.

One of the earliest forms of DDoS is described at http://www.cert.org/advisories/CA-1996-21.html. Although it's an early form, the process is still the same as that used by attacks today. It defines the use of multiple zombies to initiate TCP connections to a target host with the intention of exhausting kernel resources on the host machine. As soon as no response from the host requesting a TCP connection has been received for 120 seconds (because the zombies use spoofed source addresses), kernel resources are freed; however, this is a long time to wait. When the connection queue is full, no more connections are accepted, and the attacked host is out of service. Many more DDoS attack types are listed at CERT. Attack types now extend up the OSI stack to include URL-based attacks. These attacks are similar in concept to the TCP SYN attack, but they use repeated requests or refreshes from a random URL to tie up resources on the attacked host.

Botnets

From a hacker's perspective, the next question is how all this can be automated to ease the task of recruiting lots of unsuspecting machines to become zombies willing to receive commands and launch DDoS attacks on demand. The tool of choice has become the botnet. When you're constructing security schemes, it is worth understanding how botnets operate to keep your machines from becoming attack initiators, potentially allowing them to mitigate attacks from these entities.

Bots were created for valid reasons in the Internet Relay Chat (IRC) environment. http://www.irc101.org/ provides updates if you're interested in this service, which was originally defined in RFC 1459. The first bot, Eggdrop Bot (available at http://www.eggheads.org), was used to protect IRC channels in their owner's absence. To run IRC, you need an IRC client on the host, the IP address of the IRC server you want to connect to, and the IRC channel name. The first people on a channel became the channel operators, and they controlled the channel; however, because they would lose this status if they disconnected, bots were created to keep this connection open and preserve the channel's status even though the channel operator was absent.

Today, IRC is still the primary mechanism to distribute Trojans. It is true that e-mail attachments have become more popular recently, but there is still a long way to go for them to catch up with IRC as a distribution vehicle for these nefarious programs. Bots are really just a way of automating things to make life easier for the human user. The problems start when that human owner is a miscreant set on wreaking havoc on user services.

By grouping many IRC bots, a botnet is created. It can have one of the following architectures:

- **Hub/leaf architecture**—In this architecture, a single hub uses a specific channel to communicate with many leaf nodes. These architectures have been seen to scale to the thousands of leaf nodes.

- **Channel botnet**—A more scalable architecture that is controlled by posting commands to an IRC channel, which leverages the scaling properties of IRC itself.

The miscreant's goal is to create a botnet under his or her control that can launch attacks from many locations as desired. To do this, an attacker takes advantage of host vulnerabilities and installs bots on many machines, thus creating a botnet. Whether the miscreant uses IRC or mail to lure users to unwittingly install the bot, the process is the same. Human nature is exploited by advertising enticing material that, instead of delivering something of interest, infects the machine. Interestingly, after a miscreant compromises a host, the vulnerability is usually patched to stop other miscreants from accessing it. Two basic processes are followed to install the bot:

- Scan hosts for open ports that are associated with known vulnerabilities.
- Entice someone to download a self-installing bot.

NOTE   Miscreants tend to pick on Microsoft products more than other products purely because of their pervasiveness and because more miscreants are familiar with Microsoft product operation.

Either process can create a large botnet that can be used for things such as distributing pirated software and creating DDoS attacks. Or the botnet can be sold to other miscreants who want to enter into these illegal activities. The question network managers face is what to do about these things. Apart from the obvious solutions of applying patches to operating systems, closing nonessential ports, and having up-to-date virus-scanning software, a lot needs to be done. A new security loophole will always appear, so you must be prepared for how to mitigate it. It will, in all probability, get on your network. You may have the best edge security firewalls, IDS, and so on, but all it takes is for one laptop user to get infected from an unprotected Internet access point at home or at a coffee shop hotspot. You potentially have a compromised network when that machine is brought back to the network and connected inside the firewall/IDS protection.

The best process to protect your network is based on constant vigilance. There are tools to detect botnet activity on your network. There are also defense and reaction techniques, but all of them are based on having security personnel trained and in place. They must have knowledge of normal network activity and the ability to identify anomalous behavior, sinkholes, and black-hole filtering to let you restore partial service and investigate the attack further. The message is this: Botnets are real, and they evolve new ways to get installed all the time. The best defense is preparing yourself and your network to deal with DDoS attacks spawned from botnets when they occur.

Tools to Identify Botnets

Many tools exist to detect bots and remove them from your network. This way, you are not contributing to the spread of DDoS attacks. Here are the URLs to visit if you'd like to download these tools:

- **Spybot** — http://security.kolla.de/

- **Swat It** — http://www.swatit.org

- **TDS3, the Trojan Defense Suite** — http://tds.diamondcs.com.au/

- **TrojanHunter** — http://www.misec.net/trojanhunter

- **The Cleaner** — http://www.moosoft.com/

For a discussion of bot operation, ports used, and so on, visit http://www.swatit.org/bots/.

The next section looks at how to mitigate worm infection should a new infection break through your existing defenses.

Worm Mitigation

Similar to the concept of botnets and Trojan processes are Internet worms. Worms are programs that look for vulnerable machines on the network, install themselves on the vulnerable machines, and then use them as a base to seek out other vulnerable machines and replicate to them. It is like a combination a self-directed bot and a set of instructions for the bot to follow.

NOTE   The summer of 2003 marked a watershed in the pervasiveness of the Internet worm. Descriptions of the most high-profile worms launched (nachi, sobig, nimda, and so on) can be found at http://www.microsoft.com/technet/security/topics/virus/default.mspx.

In this case, our enemy uses a four-step process. It looks for a vulnerable host (for example, the Blaster worm scanned for an open TCP port 135), installs itself, propagates by the same means, and then executes a payload to steal data or launch attacks. It does all this without miscreant intervention after the worm is released. The question is how to prepare to mitigate this threat. The answer is to have a strong process that includes ongoing update work and utilization of security tools, such as those discussed in this chapter (NetFlow, blackhole filtering, and so on).

The first step to protecting your network from Internet worms is to limit the possible ways a worm can exploit a host by closing the known vulnerabilities. The Cisco solution for this is the Cisco Security Agent. This is a piece of software installed on each PC that monitors the activity of computer programs trying to install anything on the host and alerts the user to this activity.

Should that fail, or if you are under attack from traffic generated by infected hosts on connected networks, identifying abnormal traffic is the best solution. You must deploy NetFlow and a collector, such as the Arbor product, to analyze and report anomalous traffic on your network. The network should have a physical topology and network addressing scheme that makes it simple to compartmentalize the network during times of stress. This simplifies the implementation of containment filters applied after the worm activity is apparent.

NOTE	You can find resources that expand on these ideas at http://www.cisco.com/warp/public/707/21.html and http://www.cisco.com/go/SAFE/.

Dealing with worms is the same as dealing with any other attack. The only difference is that the number of sources is greater in worm-related infections. This can seriously affect your best tool for identifying and classifying these attacks—NetFlow. In many cases, worms randomize some part of the header, which creates a new NetFlow entry each time a new flow is detected, which can overwhelm some route processors. The way to mitigate this is to use sampled NetFlow. As long as NetFlow is not being used for other applications such as billing, this is perfectly acceptable.

Starting from the basis of having a security team in place with NetFlow, a NetFlow Collector, tools like a sinkhole, and the ability to black-hole filter, here is the recommended procedure to follow when you are infected with (or under attack from) a worm:

Step 1 **Identification and classification**—The baseline studies and anomaly detection tools are most useful. After you detect anomalous network behavior, you must identify the characteristics of the attack packets, such as protocol and port numbers used, packet characteristics of unique length, and so on.

Step 2 **Containment**—Things such as ACLs are used to keep clean areas of the network from being infected, so the outbreak of the worm is contained as much as possible.

Step 3 **Inoculation**—This is applied in parallel with subsequent phases. Inoculation means patching all systems to protect them from the vulnerability exploited by the worm. This does not stop the worm from operating; it just keeps cleaned hosts from being re-infected.

Step 4   **Quarantine**—Entails disconnecting infected hosts from the network while they are repaired.

Step 5   **Treatment**—Cleaning all the infected hosts.

Step 6   **Review**—Examine how the procedure worked and what could be improved for the next time.

Every person who is expected to participate in the mitigation of worm incidents needs to understand what is done in each phase, what tools and procedures are available in your network to deal with worms, and what his or her responsibility is. The precise nature of the activities in each phase varies from network to network and organization to organization, but the essential elements are the same.

Case Study Selections

Our case study network has security responsibilities assigned to specific IT team members. Each IT team participates in local security organization meetings and mailers and uses other resources identified in this chapter, such as NANOG. In terms of tools used, NetFlow is the centerpiece, with continual baselining of traffic so that any anomalous traffic pattern alerts the security team to potential issues. Cisco Guard has become a key piece of the infrastructure security program, and Cisco Secure Agent is installed on all PCs. Extensive use is made of black-hole filtering, backscatter traceback, and sinkholes. Specific security contacts are maintained for each provider and partner network connected to so that attacks can be effectively traced trough those networks should they be the source.

Summary

This chapter assessed the security implications of an enterprise using provider-provisioned IP VPNs based on MPLS, compared to traditional Frame Relay and ATM Layer 2 VPNs. The conclusion is that, in terms of technology, IP VPNs based on MPLS are as secure as Layer 2 VPNs. Security of the MPLS paradigm was further examined by looking at how MPLS can relieve core routers of supporting Internet routes in a provider environment. The objective is to analyze issues from an enterprise perspective so that reasoned choices can be made about the service selected from provider offerings.

The issue of shared or private PEs was also tackled, with the clear guidance that segregated PEs between VPN and Internet service are most secure form the enterprise perspective. Options for PE-to-CE connectivity were discussed, and the cost and security trade-offs were identified.

Security issues that used to be relevant only to provider networks are now relevant to larger enterprise networks as the number of third-party networks that enterprises connect to expands. Techniques such as filtering, tracing spoofed packets, remote trigger black-hole filtering, loose and strict uRPF, sinkholes, and backscatter traceback were all detailed. Insight was provided into hacker tools such as bots, botnets, and worms and how to mitigate them. The common theme is preparation, baselining via NetFlow and a NetFlow Collector. Additional security measures such as TCP Intercept, Cisco Guard, Cisco Security Agent, and more can be considered as part of the overall security plan. Regardless of what technical elements are deployed, defined team roles and practice with the available tools are essential to maintain an operational network in today's environment.

References

The following sections list publicly available resources that detail the best recommendations for securing networks. Barry Greene, a corporate consulting engineer at Cisco Systems and an Internet security expert, supplied many of these links.

Comparing MPLS VPN to Frame Relay Security

Mier Report on security comparison on MPLS VPN and Frame Relay networks

Cisco MPLS-based VPNs: Equivalent to the security of Frame Relay and ATM

http://www.miercom.com/?url=reports/&v=16&tf=-3&st=v

ACL Information

Cisco Reference for IP Receive ACLs
http://www.cisco.com/en/US/products/sw/iosswrel/ps1829/
products_feature_guide09186a00800a8531.html

Team CYMRU provides configuration templates, security templates, and other services to help make the Internet a safer place to network. These can be found at http://www.cymru.com/.

Miscellaneous Security Tools

Cisco reference for uRPF
http://www.cisco.com/en/US/products/sw/iosswrel/ps1835/
products_configuration_guide_chapter09186a00800ca7d4.html

Cisco Reference for MPLS Technology and Operation

http://www.cisco.com/pcgi-bin/Support/browse/index.pl?i=Technologies&f=3694

Cisco Reference for Cisco Express Forwarding

http://www.cisco.com/en/US/tech/tk827/tk831/tk102/tech_protocol_home.html

Public Online ISP Security Bootcamp

Singapore Summer 2003
http://palomar.getitmm.com/bootcamp/

Barry Raveendran Greene, Philip Smith. *Cisco ISP Essentials*. Cisco Press, 2002.

Tutorials, Workshops, and Bootcamps

ftp://ftp-eng.cisco.com/cons/

http://www.ispbook.com

Barry Raveendran Greene and Philip Smith. *Cisco ISP Essentials*. Cisco Press, 2002.

Original Backscatter Traceback and Customer-Triggered Remote-Triggered Black-Hole Techniques

http://www.secsup.org/Tracking/

http://www.secsup.org/CustomerBlackHole/

Source for Good Papers on Internet Technologies and Security

http://www.caida.org/

Security Work Definitions

What Is a BOTNET?
http://swatit.org/bots/index.html

Keeping track of vulnerabilities in network elements
http://www.securitytracker.com/startup/index.html

NANOG SP Security Seminars and Talks

Tutorial: Implementing a Secure Network Infrastructure (Part I)
http://www.nanog.org/mtg-0310/kaeo.html

Tutorial: ISP Security—Real World Techniques I: Remote Triggered Black Hole Filtering and Backscatter Traceback
http://www.nanog.org/mtg-0110/greene.html

Tutorial: ISP Security—Real World Techniques II: Secure the CPE Edge
http://www.nanog.org/mtg-0210/ispsecure.html

Tutorial: ISP Security: Deploying and Using Sinkholes
http://www.nanog.org/mtg-0306/sink.html

Tutorial: Deploying IP Anycast
http://www.nanog.org/mtg-0310/miller.html

Watching Your Router Configurations and Detecting Those Exciting Little Changes
http://www.nanog.org/mtg-0310/rancid.html

Building a Web of Trust
http://www.nanog.org/mtg-0310/abley.html

The Relationship Between Network Security and Spam
http://www.nanog.org/mtg-0310/spam.html

Simple Router Security: What Every ISP Router Engineer Should Know and Practice
http://www.nanog.org/mtg-0310/routersec.html

Flawed Routers Flood University of Wisconsin Internet Time Server
http://www.nanog.org/mtg-0310/plonka.html

Trends in Denial of Service Attack Technology
http://www.nanog.org/mtg-0110/cert.html

Recent Internet Worms: Who Are the Victims, and How Good Are We at Getting the Word Out?
http://www.nanog.org/mtg-0110/moore.html

DoS Attacks in the Real World
http://www.nanog.org/mtg-0110/irc.html

Diversion & Sieving Techniques to Defeat DDoS
http://www.nanog.org/mtg-0110/afek.html

DNS Damage—Measurements at a Root Server
http://www.nanog.org/mtg-0202/evi.html

Protecting the BGP Routes to Top Level DNS Servers
http://www.nanog.org/mtg-0206/bush.html

BGP Security Update
http://www.nanog.org/mtg-0206/barry.html

Industry/Government Infrastructure Vulnerability Assessment: Background and
Recommendations
http://www.nanog.org/mtg-0206/avi.html

A National Strategy to Secure Cyberspace
http://www.nanog.org/mtg-0210/sachs.html

How to Own the Internet in Your Spare Time
http://www.nanog.org/mtg-0210/vern.html

Birds of a Feather and General Security Discussion Sessions at NANOG

ISP Security BOF I
http://www.nanog.org/mtg-0210/securebof.html

The Spread of the Sapphire/Slammer Worm
http://www.nanog.org/mtg-0302/weaver.html

ISP Security BOF II
http://www.nanog.org/mtg-0302/securebof.html

The BGP TTL Security Hack
http://www.nanog.org/mtg-0302/hack.html

Security Considerations for Network Architecture
http://www.nanog.org/mtg-0302/avi.html

Lack of Priority Queuing on Route Processors Considered Harmful
http://www.nanog.org/mtg-0302/gill.html

Interception Technology: The Good, The Bad, and The Ugly!
http://www.nanog.org/mtg-0306/schiller.html

The NIAC Vulnerability Disclosure Framework and What It Might Mean to the ISP
Community
http://www.nanog.org/mtg-0306/duncan.html

Inter-Provider Coordination for Real-Time Tracebacks
http://www.nanog.org/mtg-0306/moriarity.html

ISP Security BOF III
http://www.nanog.org/mtg-0306/securitybof.html

S-BGP/soBGP Panel: What Do We Really Need and How Do We Architect a Compromise
to Get It?
http://www.nanog.org/mtg-0306/sbgp.html

BGP Vulnerability Testing: Separating Fact from FUD
http://www.nanog.org/mtg-0306/franz.html

BGP Attack Trees—Real World Examples
http://www.nanog.org/mtg-0306/hares.html

NRIC Best Practices for ISP Security
http://www.nanog.org/mtg-0306/callon.html

RIPE-46 BoF: NSP-SEC (Hank Nussbacher)
http://www.ripe.net/ripe/meetings/ripe-46/presentations/ripe46-nspbof-nsp-sec.pdf

IRT Object in the RIPE Database (Ulrich Kiermayr)
http://www.ripe.net/ripe/meetings/ripe-46/presentations/ripe46-nspbof-irt.pdf

Operational Security Requirements (George M. Jones)
http://www.ripe.net/ripe/meetings/ripe-46/presentations/ripe46-techsec-ops-security.pdf

Infrastructure Security (Nicholas Fischbach)
http://www.ripe.net/ripe/meetings/ripe-46/presentations/ripe46-nspbof-fischbach.pdf

Sean Convery. *Network Security Architectures*. Cisco Press, 2004.

Barry Greene. *Cisco ISP Essentials*. Cisco Press, 2002.

Saadat Malik. *Network Security Principles and Practices*. Cisco Press, 2002.

CCSP Study Guides by Cisco Press.

This chapter covers the following topics:

- Overview of the Main Implications for Network Management When an MPLS VPN Is Introduced
- Guidelines for the Enterprise in Evaluating Service Provider Management Capability
- Managing the VPN from an Enterprise Perspective
- Guidelines for the Service Provider on How to Meet and Exceed Enterprise Expectations
- Case Study: Troubleshooting a Problem with the Acme, Inc. VPN

CHAPTER **8**

MPLS VPN Network Management

So far, this book has concentrated on the technology and service offerings associated with Multiprotocol Label Switching (MPLS) virtual private networks (VPNs). All of this is of little value, however, if the service is not effectively managed from both enterprise and service provider perspectives. This chapter aims to educate both parties on the implications with network management when an MPLS VPN is introduced. As an introduction, it is useful to present an overview of network management before and after introducing the VPN.

In traditional WAN technologies, a VPN is created using what is termed the "overlay model" (see Figure 8-1). Branch offices and headquarters establish point-to-point links with one another. From a provisioning perspective, adding a new site typically involves experienced operators updating router-and-switch configurations at all other sites. This can be a time-consuming and error-prone process.

Figure 8-1 *Overlay VPN*

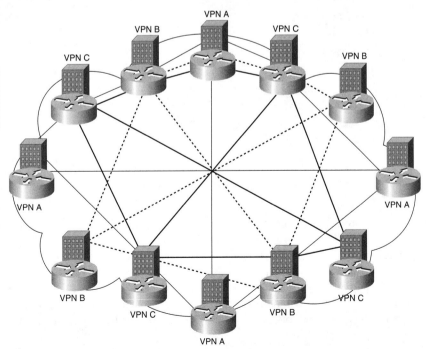

In contrast, MPLS-based VPNs use a peer model and Layer 3 connectionless architecture (see Figure 8-2). Provisioning a new site simply requires "peering" with a provider edge (PE) router as opposed to all other customer edge (CE) routers in the same VPN. In addition, the connectionless architecture allows for the creation of VPNs at Layer 3, eliminating the need for point-to-point tunnels or circuits.

Figure 8-2   *MPLS VPN*

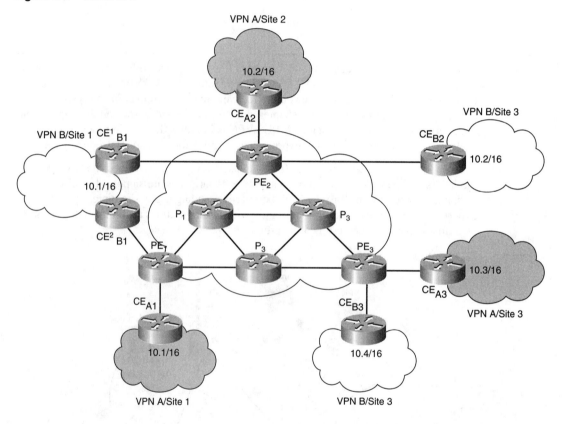

Although the newer service may still require some manual intervention, it is clearly a more scalable model.

From a performance management perspective, the main differences emanate from the service-level agreements (SLAs) that are defined, particularly if quality of service (QoS) is being employed. QoS in a fully meshed connectionless architecture introduces specific requirements because the enterprise no longer controls the potential bottlenecks—this is now the responsibility of the service provider. For example, the PE-CE links could become saturated with traffic, which ultimately leads to degraded performance for end-user applications. To avoid this and to ensure that specific traffic types, such as voice, receive priority treatment, the service provider must provision QoS on the PE-CE links, and the enterprise must map its traffic onto this QoS model. Both parties also require specific monitoring techniques to ensure that SLAs are being met.

Fault management is probably the area of greatest impact to the service provider (and hence should be of great concern to the enterprise). With overlay VPNs, the main consideration is circuit availability. This can be monitored using techniques provided in the Layer 2 technologies (such as ATM Operation, Administration, and Maintenance [OAM]). MPLS VPNs are built on IP, which is a connectionless technology. In addition, the (relative) lack of maturity of MPLS and configuration requirements of VPNs at the PEs increase the risk of connectivity problems. New developments within the MPLS protocol suite are pivotal for maximizing network uptime and must form part of the enterprise and service provider strategies.

The Enterprise: Evaluating Service Provider Management Capabilities

One of the most important parts of the Request for Proposal (RFP) should be a section on service provider network management. It is crucial that each applicant be vetted on the following:

- **Provisioning**—What is the service provider's process for provisioning the VPN and subsequently new sites within it?

- **SLA monitoring**—How does the service provider intend to monitor the SLAs?

- **Fault management**—Includes the tools, what faults are collected, and escalation procedures.

- **Reporting**—Accessibility, frequency, and content are most relevant.

- **Root-cause analysis (RCA)**—After a "severe" fault, what RCA policy does the service provider have?

Provisioning

This involves not only the configuration changes required to create the VPN, but also the process by which the enterprise is informed of progress and the level of involvement it requires. This differs, of course, depending on whether the service is managed or unmanaged.

For managed services, the idealized model is one of almost zero touch, where the enterprise simply "plugs in" the CE device and it automatically provisions itself.

This model has tremendous advantages for both parties:

- It reduces errors and operating expenditures (opex) while providing more centralized provisioning control.
- It automates an otherwise-manual process, allowing service providers to invest their scarce resources in producing new revenue-generating services rather than maintaining old ones.
- It helps service providers scale their limited technical resources by centralizing the configuration steps with a stored configuration.
- It lets service providers offer incremental services by remotely adding new configurations and managing the end customers' configuration.
- It reduces costs of warehousing, shipping, and manual intervention because CE devices can be drop-shipped directly to subscribers.
- It shortens time to billable services.

For unmanaged services, there is of course a requirement on the enterprise to supply and configure the CE devices after agreement with the service provider on aspects such as routing protocols and security. Even here, however, the service provider may be able to help the process by supplying part of the necessary configuration for the CE.

SLA Monitoring

It is crucial that, having signed a specific SLA, the enterprise has a high degree of confidence in the service provider's capability to satisfy it. To begin, the enterprise should ask the service provider how it would ideally like to monitor the SLAs.

The level of monitoring required varies depending on the types of applications that will be delivered across the network. For example, voice over IP (VoIP) traffic is highly sensitive to delay and packet loss. It is advisable for the enterprise to require the service provider to monitor adherence of VoIP traffic to well-defined standards, such as International Telecommunication Union (ITU) G.114. It specifies exact metrics for delay characteristics in voice networks.

Another assessment criterion is to inquire whether the service provider has attained any form of third-party "certification." An example is the Cisco-Powered Network QoS Certification. This specific example means that the service provider has met best practices and standards for QoS and real-time traffic in particular. Taking voice as an example, this certification means that the service provider has satisfied the following requirements:

- Maximum 150 ms one-way delay for voice/video packets
- Maximum one-way packet jitter of 30 ms for voice/video traffic
- Maximum voice/video packet loss of 1.0 percent

More information on this specific program can be found at http://www.cisco.com/en/US/netsol/ns465/net_value_proposition0900aecd8023c83f.html.

Other traffic types typically have their own QoS classes, as defined in the DiffServ model. The level of proactive monitoring expected of the service provider therefore should be negotiated for each class of traffic. For example, it might be that the enterprise specifies the following:

- A target for overall per-class packet delivery (less than 0.0001 percent packet loss, rising to higher percentages for non-drop-sensitive traffic or low-priority classes).
- Targets for delivery of interactive video AF4x class.
- Targets for delivery of signaling/high-priority data classes. These are usually marked with the DiffServ code points AF3x or CS3.

The service provider can employ specific tools and techniques to adhere to such requirements. These are discussed more fully in the section "The Service Provider: How to Meet and Exceed Customer Expectations."

Fault Management

The purpose of fault management is to detect, isolate, and correct malfunctions in the network. For assessment purposes, the three main questions are as follows:

- How does the service provider respond to faults after they are reported?
- What is the service provider's passive fault management strategy?
- What proactive fault monitoring techniques are used?

Handling Reported Faults

Sometimes, the enterprise detects faults with the VPN service and needs to report them to the service provider. These might range from serious outages to intermittent performance problems as experienced by some applications and end users.

In such scenarios, it is important to know what the processes, escalation, and reporting procedures are within the service provider. Here are some possible questions to ask:

- What are the contact options for reporting a fault?
- Is this 24/7?
- How is progress reported?
- What is the skill level of the Tier 1/help desk operator? For example, will he or she know the contracted service when a problem is reported? Will he or she be able to report the service's health within the service provider network?

- If an outage is reported, will the service provider verify that the connection is healthy from CE-CE (managed service) and from PE-CE (unmanaged)?

- What techniques will the service provider employ to determine reachability health?

- If a performance issue is reported, what techniques will the service provider employ to validate that its network is responding correctly to the type of traffic experiencing problems from the enterprise perspective?

- If a Tier 1 operator cannot provide immediate help on the problem, what are the escalation procedures? That is, to whom would a problem be assigned? How does this process continue, and what are the time frames? In other words, how long does a problem reside with one support person before being escalated?

Some of these issues are discussed from the service provider's perspective in the section "The Service Provider: How to Meet and Exceed Customer Expectations."

Passive Fault Management

Passive fault management can be further subdivided into monitoring network element-generated events and capturing and analyzing customer traffic.

Network Events

Events from network elements are usually obtained from Simple Network Management Protocol (SNMP) traps, Remote Monitoring (RMON) probes, and other, potentially proprietary messages (such as Syslog on Cisco equipment).

In terms of SNMP, the enterprise should ask if the service provider is monitoring notifications from the following Management Information Bases (MIBs):

- MIBs related to MPLS transport include LDP-MIB and LSR-MIB:

  - **LDP-MIB**—The Label Distribution Protocol (LDP) MIB allows a network management station to retrieve status and performance data. But probably most importantly, it provides notifications on the health of LDP sessions. For example, if an LDP session fails, an mplsLdpSessionDown notification is generated. Within the notification, the LDP peer (who the session was with) is specified. This allows the network management station to perform some correlation (by examining other events received in the same time frame) and affect analysis (is the LDP session over links carrying customer traffic?).

  - **LSR-MIB**—The label switch router (LSR) MIB allows the network management station to monitor the data plane characteristics of MPLS. From a fault-management perspective, the enterprise should inquire which parameters are retrieved, because the vendor may not support the notifications in the MIB definition. Care should be taken with excessive use of this

MIB because of scale implications. Tools starting to appear within vendor equipment will negate the need to poll for the existence and operational health of label-switched paths (LSPs). These are discussed later in this chapter.

- MIBs related to MPLS VPNs include MPLS-VPN-MIB and vendor-specific MIBs such as the Cisco BGPv4 MIB:

    — **MPLS-VPN-MIB**—This MIB allows the network management station to monitor the health and existence of VPN routing and forwarding interfaces. For example, if one of these interfaces fails, the network management station is informed and should be able to determine which customers and locations are affected.

    — **Vendor-specific MIBs**—An example is the Cisco BGPv4 MIB. This MIB in particular facilitates monitoring of the multiprotocol Border Gateway Protocol (MP-BGP) sessions that are vital to the exchange of route information within VPNs.

There are also standard and proprietary MIBs for Open Shortest Path First (OSPF) Interior Gateway Protocol (IGP).

Certain generic MIBs must be included in any effective fault-management strategy. This is not only because they provide important data relating to the health of the router and its functions, but also because they may help diagnose and correlate MPLS VPN problems. These MIBs allow the network manager to focus on the following categories:

- Hardware-related errors
- Environmental characteristics
- Resources and processes
- Interface problems

NOTE   Vendor-specific MIBs are almost always available to provide more useful events, but these are beyond the scope of this book. One point to stress, however, is that when no notifications are explicitly supported, it may still be possible to achieve monitoring through the use of the EVENT and EXPRESSION MIBs (provided that they are supported!). These MIBs allow data from other MIBs to be defined such that when certain thresholds are crossed, events are generated for the network management system (NMS). For example, a network manager could define a rule that says that when available free memory drops below 1 MB, a notification should be generated.

- **Hardware-related errors**—The most important of these are the reload, coldStart (SNMPv2-MIB), and linkup/linkDown (IF-MIB).

Several vendor-specific MIBs provide notifications related to the chassis inventory, such as within the OLD-CISCO-CHASSIS-MIB and CISCO-ENTITY-MIB family.

- **Environmental characteristics**—Most of these are from vendor-specific MIBs and allow attributes such as temperature, power supply, and voltage to be monitored. In Cisco devices, the notifications are defined in the CISCO-ENVMON-MIB family.

- **Resources and processes**—This covers aspects such as CPU and memory utilization. Again, this is mainly covered via vendor-specific MIBs such as the Cisco CISCO-PROCESS-MIB family.

The section "The Service Provider: How to Meet and Exceed Customer Expectations" has more details for service providers on SNMP usage and proprietary events.

Of course, such events need to be captured and responded to. The enterprise should ask the service provider what tool(s) it uses to capture events and how quickly the tools can be customized to deal with new ones. It may also be necessary to reconfigure how the fault-management system deals with specific events. For example, SNMP traps usually are translated into an alarm with a specific severity rating (Informational, Warning, Error, Critical, and so on). It may be necessary to change this, especially if the enterprise is experiencing problems in a certain area. Ideally, the service provider should be able to reconfigure the tool without involving the manufacturer/reseller.

Related to this are the procedures after the alarm is raised. The service provider may automatically alert an operator when certain important alarms occur. This might be done by e-mail, pager, Short Message Service (SMS), or fax. Other alarms may be handled manually. Either way, the enterprise should ask the service provider what its procedures are. Ideally, they should contain an element of automation.

Customer Traffic Monitoring

Why should the enterprise care about the service provider's ability to monitor customer traffic? Apart from the obvious billing implications, this becomes important if the enterprise starts to experience problems, particularly those of a performance nature. Possible performance problems include the following:

- End users start experiencing poor-quality voice calls.

- End users start experiencing poor-quality video feeds.

- Application responsiveness, such as e-mail and/or web access that is slow or degrading.

These performance problems are, of course, from an end user's perspective. The underlying causes are likely to be one or more of the following:

- The enterprise is marking traffic incorrectly, resulting in the wrong treatment in the service provider network.

- The enterprise is oversubscribing its classes of service (CoSs) and the VPN is (correctly) dropping or remarking the traffic.
- The service provider has incorrect QoS configurations, resulting in dropped packets.
- The service provider has reached bandwidth limits on certain links.
- The service provider has a performance bottleneck on a router.

Within an MPLS VPN, the enterprise shares the service provider's infrastructure with other organizations. In the event of a performance problem, it is important for the enterprise to know if the service provider can clearly identify its traffic, as well as answer the following questions:

1 Are enterprise QoS classifications being preserved through your network?

2 Is the bandwidth allocated to the enterprise as agreed in the SLA?

3 Is any enterprise traffic being dropped? If so, which type of packets (protocol, source, destination, and so on)?

From the service provider's perspective, when an issue is reported, it quickly wants to determine if the problem is within its network. To do this, the service provider needs to use a variety of techniques. It is likely (and recommended) that it will use synthetic traffic probing (such as Cisco IP SLA probes) to measure the connection's responsiveness. If this initial test seems to pass, it is essential that the service provider examine specific customer traffic flows to help answer the enterprise's questions. The techniques and tools that can be employed here are mostly vendor-specific. Here are some examples:

- Cisco NetFlow lets you identify traffic flows down to the protocol level.
- Cisco Network-Based Application Recognition (NBAR)—Classification at the application layer for subsequent QoS treatment.
- Specific MIBs, such as CISCO-CLASS-BASED-QOS-MIB.
- Specific command-line interface (CLI) commands for retrieving QoS, interface, and buffer data relating to customer traffic.

The section "The Service Provider: How to Meet and Exceed Customer Expectations" discusses in more detail these tools and how the service provider can use them.

Proactive Monitoring

One of the most important assessments the enterprise can make on the service provider is to ask what its proactive monitoring strategy is. For large VPNs, it is very difficult for the service provider to monitor every path, but the enterprise should at least expect the service provider to monitor the critical ones, such as from certain locations to the data center. In doing so, it is important to be able to distinguish between the control and data planes. It is fundamental that the service provider monitor at least part of the data plane in the enterprise connectivity path. This is because even though the control plane may appear healthy, the data plane may be broken. More information on this topic appears in the section "The Service Provider: How to Meet and Exceed Customer Expectations." For the moment, the following provides useful guidelines in forming questions in this area.

Figure 8-3 shows the areas within the service provider network where proactive fault monitoring can be employed.

Figure 8-3 *Proactive Monitoring Segments in an MPLS VPN Network*

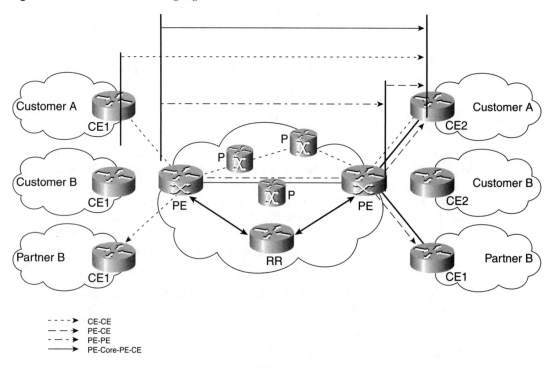

As shown, a number of segments and paths can be monitored:

- PE-CE (WAN) link
- PE-PE
- CE-CE
- Combinations, such as PE-Core-PE-CE

Each of these segments and paths are discussed in the following sections.

PE-CE

Layer 1 is traditionally monitored using the passive techniques already discussed, such as link up/down traps. However, depending on the vendor, it may be necessary to poll MIB variables. An example might be for subinterface status, where if a subinterface goes down, a trap generally is not generated. Subinterfaces are usually modeled as separate rows in the ifTable from the IF-MIB and hence have an associated ifOperStatus.

Layer 2 is heavily dependent on the WAN access technology being used. Point-to-point technologies such as serial, PPP, and high-level data link control (HDLC) do not have monitoring built in to the protocol. This situation is also true for broadcast technologies, such as Ethernet (although developments in various standards bodies will shortly address this, specifically in the area of Ethernet OAM).

The situation is somewhat different for connection-oriented technologies, such as ATM and Frame Relay. Both these technologies have native OAM capability, which should be fully enabled if possible.

At Layer 3, some data-plane monitoring functions are starting to appear in the various routing protocols. The most important of these is Bidirectional Forwarding Detection (BFD). The enterprise should ask the service provider if and when it plans to use this technology.

It is more likely, however, that the service provider will actively probe the PE-CE link. This is done either via a management application simply pinging from PE-CE or by using one of the vendor-specific tools, such as IP SLA from Cisco.

In the control plane, the service provider should have some capability to monitor route availability within the virtual routing/forwarding instance (VRF) on the PE. This would let the service provider detect when specific customer routes were withdrawn, hence facilitating some form of proactive troubleshooting. Unfortunately, no MIBs provide notifications for this, so the service provider has to inspect the routing tables periodically using a management application.

PE-PE

This segment introduces MPLS into the forwarding path. In this context, the enterprise should ask if the service provider would monitor the LSPs—in particular, LSPs being used to transport VPN traffic from PE-PE. An additional check would be the VPN path from PE-PE, which includes VPN label imposition/disposition. There may be some overlap in the latter case with SLA monitoring. For example, if the service provider is already monitoring PE-PE for delay/jitter data, ideally it would combine this with the availability requirement.

CE-CE

This option is only really available in a managed VPN service (unless the enterprise grants permission for the service provider to access its routers). In theory, this option offers the best monitoring solution, because it more closely follows the path of the customer's traffic. This option has some important caveats, however, as discussed in the section "The Service Provider: How to Meet and Exceed Customer Expectations."

The two main options are periodic pinging via a management application and using synthetic traffic from IP SLA probes. In both cases, the enterprise should ask what happens when a fault is detected. The expectation should be that an alarm is generated and fed into the central fault management system, from where troubleshooting can be initiated.

PE-Core-PE-CE

This option makes sense when the service provider wants to monitor as much of the customer path as possible but cannot access the CEs. The same techniques apply as for the CE-CE case.

Reporting

Enterprise customers should expect the service provider to offer a reporting facility for their VPN service. This normally takes the form of a web portal through which the enterprise network manager can log in and receive detailed metrics on the service's current state and performance. Figure 8-4 shows a performance-reporting portal.

Figure 8-4   *MPLS VPN Performance-Reporting Portal*

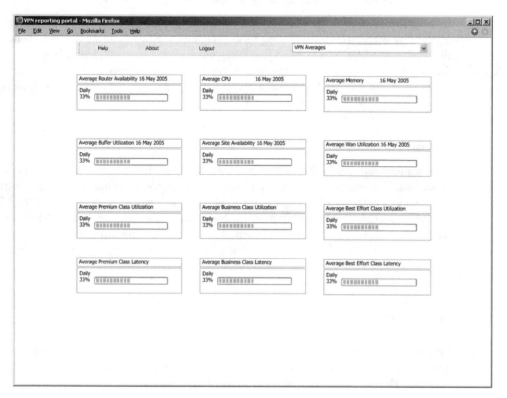

The following metrics should be supported:

- Utilization per CoS
- Packet loss
- Latency
- Jitter

If the service is managed, the reporting tool should also support CE-related data, such as memory, CPU, and buffer utilization.

Root Cause Analysis

Faults will occur in the service provider network. When they do, the enterprise should be informed as soon as possible. However, it is also important that when faults are rectified, the root cause be passed on. This allows the network manager to provide accountability information to his or her upper management and internal customers, as well as make ongoing assessments of the QoS he or she is receiving. For example, if outages related to maintenance occur, the enterprise might request more advance notice and specific details of the planned disruption.

Such data might take the form of a monthly report. The enterprise should look for the following data:

- Site availability (expressed as a percentage)
- Reliability
- Service glitches per router
- Defects encountered on vendor equipment, with tracking numbers
- Partner site availability and reliability (if applicable)
- Fault summary, including categorization (for example, configuration error, defect, weather, protocol, and so on)
- Planned changes

The Enterprise: Managing the VPN

This section focuses on providing the network manager with information and guidelines to help him or her prepare for the introduction and subsequent management of an MPLS VPN service.

Figure 8-5 shows a life-cycle model to be used for reference within this section.

Figure 8-5 *VPN Life-Cycle Model*

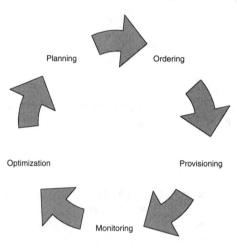

Planning

An important part of the network manager's responsibility is ensuring availability of network resources and performance to meet end-user needs. To do this, it is essential to establish a profile or baseline.

Another reason why a profile is useful is because it allows the network manager to plan a monitoring strategy between locations. It is good practice for enterprises to test reachability between key locations. This can be used to validate SLAs and also provide fast detection of connectivity problems. In a large enterprise with many sites, however, it may simply be impractical to monitor in a full-mesh style, as shown in Figure 8-6.

Figure 8-6 *Full-Mesh VPN Monitoring*

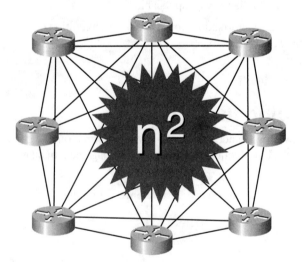

Nodes	Operation
2	1
3	3
4	6
5	10
6	15
7	21
8	28
...	...
100	4950

As shown, the number of probe operations increases proportionally to the square of the number of sites. This can be problematic from a management perspective, because it takes up resources on the CE routers and can be difficult to maintain as the network grows.

A better approach for large networks is a partial mesh, as shown in Figure 8-7.

Figure 8-7   *Partial-Mesh VPN Monitoring*

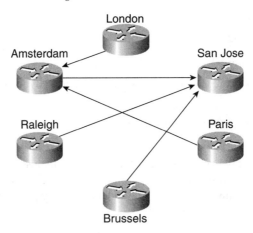

In this system, specific critical paths are monitored, such as branch office to headquarters or remote site to data centers. This can dramatically reduce the number of probes, as well as management and performance overhead.

Ordering

Evolving business requirements will require changes to the VPN service. Such changes might take the form of new sites, changes to routing tables/protocols, and decommissioning of sites and circuit upgrades.

It is good practice to agree to a moves/adds/changes/deletes (MACD) process with the service provider. A basic version of this might simply involve filling in a change request form and e-mailing it to the appropriate contact within the service provider, such as the account manager. A more sophisticated system might automatically request bandwidth upgrades.

Provisioning

The impact of the provisioning process varies according to whether the service is managed or unmanaged. The main difference is that in an unmanaged service, the enterprise is responsible for providing and configuring the CE routers, whereas in the managed service, this is largely transparent. In both cases, however, the enterprise should perform a number of tests during and after the provisioning process.

CE Provisioning

With unmanaged CEs, the enterprise is responsible for configuring the following:

- IP addresses
- Host name
- Domain name server
- Fault management (and time-stamp coordination by means of the Network Time Protocol)
- Collecting, archiving, and restoring CE configurations
- Access data, such as passwords and SNMP strings on the unmanaged CE

When the enterprise wants to manage the CE routers themselves, it must cooperate with the service provider to ensure that the devices are configured correctly. In addition, the service provider may require access to the CE routers to deploy probes and read-only access to the router configuration and SNMP MIBs.

The requirement to access SNMP MIB and CLI data introduces a security concern for the enterprise.

The service provider management systems require connectivity to the enterprise CE routers via the PE-CE connection. Access to the CE routers can be tightly controlled by access control lists (ACLs) or the equivalent with predefined source/destination addresses and protocols. Secured access can be implemented through the following mechanisms:

- An extended IP access list on the CE-PE interface of every CE router. The access list permits the service provider management system's subnets to communicate with the CE router loopback management interface using SNMP only. Any other packets sourced from the service provider management system's subnets are blocked.
- A standard IP access list to explicitly define service provider SNMP server systems that require read-only access to the CE routers.
- An SNMP community string and SNMP view to restrict the service provider read-only SNMP servers to a limited subset of MIBs required for reporting system and interface status, as well as traffic statistics.
- A further discrete standard IP access list to define service provider SNMP management server systems, which require SNMP write access to any MIBs required for active monitoring. An example might be the Cisco Round-Trip Time Monitoring (RTTMON) MIBs to configure IP SLA probes.
- A second SNMP community string and SNMP view to be configured restricting the service provider SNMP write access to the probe MIBs only.

- A second loopback interface to source probes because traffic sourced from loopback0 is directed to the highest class, prohibiting per-class reporting.

CE Management Access

The need to access CEs depends on whether the service being offered is managed or unmanaged. Both these scenarios are discussed.

Unmanaged CE Routers

If the CEs are unmanaged, the service provider can use IP version 4 (IPv4) connectivity for all management traffic.

Figure 8-8 shows a basic topology with unmanaged CEs. The network management subnet has a direct link to the service provider MPLS core network.

Figure 8-8   *Network Management of Unmanaged CEs*

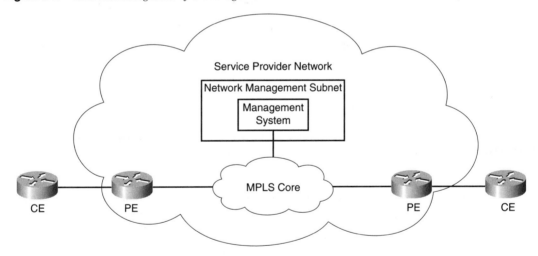

Managed CE Routers

In managed or hybrid (partially managed) scenarios, connectivity to the CEs from the service provider network is required. This is usually provided in the form of a network management subnet. However, as soon as a CE is in a VPN, it is no longer accessible by means of conventional IPv4 routing.

To enable IP connectivity between the service provider network management systems and enterprise-connected CE routers, you must configure a VRF instance on every PE router port connected to an enterprise location to import service provider management system routes. These routes are distributed within the VPN via a dedicated "management VPN" having a unique route target value. All customer-facing PE ports that connect to a service provider-managed CE router must be configured to import this specific route-target value, as shown in Figure 8-9.

Figure 8-9 *Using a Management VPN*

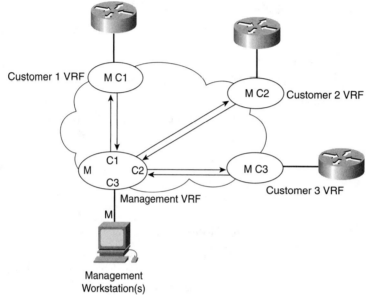

Management
Workstation(s)

Cisco Managed MPLS VPN Solution Guide, http://www.cisco.com/univercd/cc/td/doc/product/vpn/solution/man-mpls/overview/mmpls_ov.pdf

A network management VRF table contains the circuit addresses of all CE routes. The service provider management workstation(s) originate from this VRF.

Each customer VRF should contain the address of the service provider management workstation(s) to allow two-way communication between the management workstation and the CE router.

When a management VRF is created,

- All CE routers can be managed from a single location.

- Only routes that originate from the VRF are exported (by virtue of the transitivity rule). Routing separation is guaranteed between CE routers.

All CE routers are easily identified because they all use a circuit address from the same service provider-managed address space.

Example 8-1 shows a sample configuration of a customer VRF for use with a management VRF. This is an excerpt from the output obtained using the **show running-config** command.

Example 8-1 *Customer Management VRF Configuration*

```
ip vrf ACME
rd 6000:1
route-target export 6000:1
route target import 6000:1
!
! Export routes to the Management VRF
!
route-target export 100:1
!
! Import Management host(s) only
!
route-target import 100:10
```

Example 8-1 shows the use of two additional route targets:

- **route-target export 100:1** exports all routes from this VRF to the management VRF using the extended community attribute 100:1.

- **route-target import 100:10** imports any VPN-IPv4 addresses with the extended community attribute 100:10, which identifies any management host(s).

The management VRF is configured at the PE that connects to the service provider management subnet. Example 8-2 is a sample configuration (taken from the **show running-config** output).

Example 8-2 *Management VRF Configuration*

```
ip vrf VPN_Management
rd 1000:1
import map IN-Management
export map OUT-Management
route-target export 1000:1
route-target import 1000:1
!
! Only allow PE-CE circuit addresses into VRF
!
ip prefix-list PE-CE-Circuits seq 10 permit 8.1.1.0/16 ge 30
ip prefix-list PE-CE-Circuits seq 10 permit 9.1.1.0/16 ge 30
! continued for other circuits...
!
route-map IN-Management permit 10
match ip address prefix-list PE-CE-Circuits
!
! Set Management Workstation route to 1000:10
!
route-map OUT-Management permit 10
match ip address 20
```

(continues)

Example 8-2 *Management VRF Configuration (Continued)*

```
set extcommunity rt 1000:10
!
! Access List to identify management hosts (one line for each host)
!
access-list 20 permit 190.1.42.3 0.0.0.0
...
!
! Set a static route to Management workstation(s)
!
ip route vrf VPN_Management 190.1.42.0 255.255.255.0 next-hop IP address
!
! Enter other routes to Management hosts...
...
```

In Example 8-2, the VRF uses the service provider-specified route distinguisher (RD) and route target (RT) of 1000:1. In addition to the normal import/export route targets for the VRF, two route maps are specified: IN-Management and OUT-Management.

The IN-Management route map limits any imported addresses to those of the PE-CE circuit address space. In other words, the address prefix must be a /30 subnet beginning with 8.1.1.0, 9.1.1.0, and so on. This prevents all other routes in the customer VRFs from being imported.

Because the management VRF is connected to an interface, which originates many subnets, static routing is used to specify how to reach it. In this example, the management subnet is 190.1.42.0.

To guarantee that only the host addresses of management workstations are exported from the management VRF, static routes are used to identify each management address individually.

The OUT-Management route map then sets all management host addresses (those that match access list 0) to the extended-community attribute of 1000:10. They are then imported into the customer VRF with a corresponding import map.

Network Management Configuration Considerations

If the management host addresses in the preceding configuration are redistributed to a CE through a routing protocol such as Routing Information Protocol version 2 (RIPv2), the CE can readvertise the route back to the PE in a summarized form. This occurs even though split horizon (which does not send routes out an interface on which they were received) is enabled. For example, if the host route 190.1.42.3 255.255.255.255 is advertised to a CE with auto-summary enabled, that route is summarized to a B-class address of 190.1.0.0 255.255.0.0 and is advertised back to the PE. The split-horizon process lets the route pass because it is not the same as the route that was received.

There are two ways to avoid re-advertising routes back to the PE router:

- Turn off auto-summary at the CE.
- Use route distribution filtering at the PE.

Another useful technique is to configure CE devices with a loopback interface, the IP address of which is used as the management address of the CE router. The CE router must be configured to advertise this address with a 32-bit mask to the PE router. The PE router in turn exports only this loopback interface address with a 32-bit mask to the service provider management VPN using a second unique route target value (different from the import value previously mentioned). In this scheme, there should not be any requirement to export the PE-CE interface network address to the management VPN.

All other IP prefixes received by the PE router from the CE router are exported to the customer VPN only. No customer IP prefixes other than the CE router loopback address are advertised within the management VPN.

Acceptance Testing

It is highly recommended that the enterprise perform some form of formal acceptance testing of new circuits and sites. This typically consists of the following steps:

- **PE-CE link test**—This is a simple ping to the local PE device.
- **CE-CE test**—Again, a simple ping to a remote CE. An additional and useful extension is to ping a loopback address on the CE, because this validates that routes "behind" the CE can be reached.
- A more prolonged test to measure the performance characteristics of the path from the new site to others in the VPN. This is often called a "soak" test and is best implemented using IP SLA probes. Such a test might run for 12 or 24 hours.

TIP   Use an extended ping to test a range of packet sizes. This will help you discover failures that occur only near the 1500 maximum transmission unit (MTU) limit. Note that this requires the Do Not Fragment (DF) bit to be set in the header, as shown in Example 8-3.

Example 8-3 *Using Extended Ping to Test a Connection*

```
cl-12008-1#ping
Protocol [ip]:
Target IP address: 144.254.1.17
Repeat count [5]: 20
Datagram size [100]:
Timeout in seconds [2]:
Extended commands [n]: y
```

(continues)

Example 8-3   *Using Extended Ping to Test a Connection (Continued)*

```
Source address or interface:
Type of service [0]:
Set DF bit in IP header? [no]: yes
Validate reply data? [no]:
Data pattern [0xABCD]:
Loose, Strict, Record, Timestamp, Verbose[none]:
Sweep range of sizes [n]: y
Sweep min size [36]: 60
Sweep max size [18024]: 1510
Sweep interval [1]: 10
```

For QoS, a basic test can be performed using extended ping commands to insert QoS markings and validate that the service provider is handling them correctly by capturing appropriate statistics on the remote devices.

NOTE   Because extended ping allows the type of service (ToS) byte to be set, you must be careful to use correct values when mapping from Differentiated Services Code Point (DSCP). For example, if you intend to simulate voice, it has a DSCP value of 101110. However, the ToS byte needs to be set to 10111000 (decimal 184), not 5 as is sometimes assumed.

TIP   For best results, originate the tests from behind the CE devices to test firewall capability. It is also useful to perform these tests after the VPN goes live.

Monitoring

Even though the service provider may monitor its network for SLA purposes, it is highly recommended that the enterprise perform its own monitoring. There are several reasons for this:

- The enterprise should be able to monitor at a higher rate than the service provider.
- The enterprise should not assume that levels of QoS are being met.
- The enterprise has additional performance characteristics to be concerned with.

There are basically two relevant forms of monitoring: availability and performance or service degradation.

For availability, this may be a measurement at the host or site level or both. Because of network glitches and transient conditions, the monitoring solution should contain an element of "damping." This helps keep false alarms from being raised. An example might be a solution that pings hosts every 10 seconds but uses a sample period of several minutes to derive an availability measurement.

The second form of monitoring is for performance or service degradation. A relatively simple metric can be obtained using the same scheme as for availability, but taking into account round-trip times.

A more sophisticated scheme might involve dedicated probes. For example, the Cisco IOS IP SLA provides a mechanism to monitor performance for different classes and types of traffic over the same connection. This technology could be used to monitor the response time between a Cisco device and an HTTP server to retrieve a web page.

Optimization

The main objective of optimization is to increase application performance (because this can be directly correlated with productivity). An important part of optimization is calculating required bandwidth. Recent technologies have tried to simplify this whole process by providing bandwidth recommendations based on individual traffic classes. An example is bandwidth estimation within Cisco IOS. This technology produces a Corvil Bandwidth value, which is the minimum amount of bandwidth required to meet a specific QoS target. This technology is most applicable at the WAN interface point between enterprise and service provider networks.

NOTE   This feature is currently restricted to IOS 12.3(14)T and requires a special license. More information can be found at

http://www.cisco.com/en/US/tech/tk543/tk759/tech_brief0900aecd8024d5ff.html

and

http://www.cisco.com/univercd/cc/td/doc/product/software/ios123/123newft/123t/123t_14/gtcbandw.htm

---

Of course, increasing bandwidth may not always be an option. Other techniques include caching, compression, and increasing transmission/application speed. All of these require dedicated management system support, but the return on investment (ROI) would make such an investment worthwhile.

The Service Provider: How to Meet and Exceed Customer Expectations

This section discusses the implications of enterprise expectations on the service provider and how these translate into management functions and practices that help exceed them.

Provisioning

The provisioning function is heavily dependent on whether the service is managed or unmanaged, because a managed service adds the CE to the service provider's domain of responsibility.

Zero-Touch Deployment

For managed services, one of the most time-consuming and expensive tasks within the rollout or upgrade of the VPN is the provisioning of CE equipment. Vendors now provide solutions that can help automate this process. Figure 8-10 is a high-level example of how such a process might operate.

Figure 8-10 *Automated CE Provisioning*

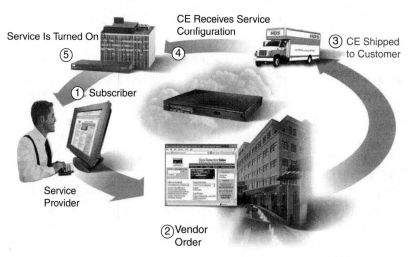

Cisco Configuration Express, http://www.cisco.com/cx

The steps are as follows:

Step 1   The subscriber orders managed service from the service provider.

Step 2   The service provider orders the subscriber CE from the vendor with the optional bootstrap configuration. Then it registers the CE with the configuration management application.

Step 3   The vendor ships the customer CE with the bootstrap configuration. The service provider can track the shipment online.

Step 4   The subscriber plugs in the CE and the device boots, pulls the service configuration, and validates.

Step 5   The device publishes "configuration success," indicating that service is on.

Of course, certain key technologies need to be in place from the vendor for such a system to be used. The key factor here is that this "zero-touch provisioning" system pushes intelligence down into the network. Devices require more advanced management functionality and cooperation with offline systems. A typical system might contain the following components:

- An online ordering system that supports the following functions:
  - A bootstrap configuration that lets the CE connect to the management system when it is powered up and connected at the customer site
  - A shipping address for the end customer
  - Interfaces with back-end manufacturing, which also results in a bootstrap configuration being created with chassis-specific details (such as MAC addresses and serial numbers)
  - Order tracking
  - Offline configuration management
- An offline configuration management system must support the following functions:
  - Inventory of CE devices
  - Initial configuration of CE devices and submodules
  - Secure communication with CE devices
  - Building and downloading service configurations when requested by CE devices
  - Progress, reporting, and status of CE communication
  - Embedded intelligence
- Embedded intelligence must support the following functions:
  - Automatically contacting the configuration management application on the bootstrap

— Providing inventory (physical and logical) to the management system

— Retrieval, checking, and loading of the configuration from the management system

— Publishing status events on this process to the management system

PE Configuration

Of course, provisioning the CE is only one of the tasks required in turning up a new circuit. The PE is where most of the configuration is required. Because of the relative complexity of this task, it is highly recommended that the service provider automate this task from a management provisioning system.

Most vendors supply such a system. In general, they take one of two approaches:

- **Element-focused**—This essentially means that the system supplies a GUI and/or a northbound application programming interface (API) to support the configuration of individual PEs. Such systems tend to be driven from a higher-order provisioning system, which has a wider, VPN-centric view. Their main benefit is to provide a clean, abstract API to the underlying vendor elements.

- **Network-focused**—These systems tend to model the VPN and related network properties, such as sites and service providers. They may also support element-specific APIs but have the additional use of allowing the whole provisioning operation to be driven entirely by the GUI. Such systems may be more suitable for Tier 2/3 service providers or those that have single-vendor networks.

Fault Monitoring

An effective fault-monitoring strategy should concentrate on ensuring that any potential service-affecting events generated by vendor equipment are collected first.

Enhancements can then be added to include functions such as impact analysis and correlation. Furthermore, a number of management products in this space provide specialized functions, such as route monitoring availability and correlation of control/data plane events. (For example, perhaps a connection was lost because a route was withdrawn, which in turn was caused by link failure in the network.)

MPLS-Related MIBs

MIBs are the primary source of fault-related events and data from the network elements, especially because "standard" MIBs are often implemented by different vendors, so they can simplify multivendor management.

This section discusses relevant MPLS MIBs and what features are most relevant within them.

Figure 8-11 shows the points in an MPLS VPN where the MIBs are applicable.

Figure 8-11 *MPLS MIB Applicability Points*

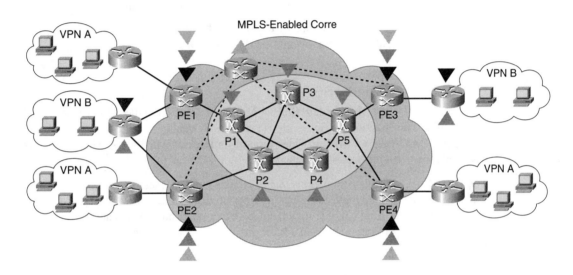

▲ PPVPN-MPLS-VPN MIB, SAA

▲ MPLS-LSR/TE/LDP/FTN/OSPF MIBs, Syslogs

▲ BGP MIBs

MPLS-VPN-MIB

The following notifications are useful for monitoring the health of the VRF interfaces when they are created and when they are removed:

mplsVRFIfUp/mplsVRFIfDown notifications

These are generated when

- The ifOperStatus of the interface associated with the VRF changes to up/down stat.
- The interface with ifOperStatus = up is (dis)associated with a VRF.

Problems can sometimes occur when a PE starts to exceed the available resources. For example, memory and the routes use up this resource. Therefore, it can be beneficial to set route limits that warn when specific thresholds are reached. Additionally, service providers might want to charge their customers in relation to the number of routes. The following notifications are useful for both of these purposes:

mplsNumVrfRouteMidThreshExceeded and mplsNumVrfRouteMaxThreshExceeded

These are generated when

- The number of routes in a given VRF exceeds mplsVrfMidRouteThreshold.
- The number of routes contained by the specified VRF reaches or attempts to exceed the maximum allowed value—mplsVrfMaxRouteThreshold.

BGPv4-MIB and Vendor BGP MIBs

In the context of VPNs, the standard BGPv4-MIB does not support the VPNv4 routes used by MP-BGP. This functionality currently is provided by vendor-specific MIBs. For example, CISCO-BGPV4-MIB provides support for tracking MP-BGP sessions, which is essential for successful operation of the VPN.

The Cisco MIB provides notifications that reflect the MP-BGP session Finite State Machine (FSM). For example, notifications are sent when the Border Gateway Protocol (BGP) FSM moves from a higher numbered state to a lower numbered state and when the prefix count for an address family on a BGP session has exceeded the configured threshold value.

MIBs related to MPLS transport:

- **LDP-MIB**—In particular, the label distribution protocol (LDP) session up/down traps
- **LSR-MIB**—Segment and cross-connect traps (if implemented by the vendor)

There are also standard and proprietary MIBs for the OSPF IGRP.

Resource Monitoring

To effectively monitor the network, the network manager should pay specific attention to resources on PEs. Because of their position and role in the VPN, they are particularly susceptible to problems caused by low memory and high CPU.

Some vendors may provide either MIBs or proprietary techniques to set thresholds on both these resources. However, it is recommended that baseline figures be obtained and alerts be generated should deviations occur.

The service provider should consult each vendor for the best way to extract memory and CPU utilization data, especially because this may vary across different platform types and architectures. Vendors should be able to recommend "safe" amounts of free memory. Often, this may have to be done via scripts that log in and retrieve the data via the CLI, but the ideal approach is to use a vendor Event Management Service (EMS) that is tuned to detect and troubleshoot resource problems.

The following factors might contribute to low resource levels:

- Memory:
    - Operating system image sizes
    - Route table size (the number of routes and their distribution)
    - BGP table size (paths, prefixes, and number of peers)
    - BGP configuration (soft reconfiguration and multipath)
    - IGP size (number of routes)
    - Any use of transient memory to send updates to linecards
    - Transient memory to send BGP updates to neighbors
- Main CPU:
    - BGP table size (number of routes)
    - BGP configuration (number of peers)
    - IGP size (number of routes and peers)
    - Routing protocol activity
    - Network-based interrupts (SNMP and Telnet)
- Linecard CPU:
    - Main factors contributing to higher resource usage
    - Rate of packets being switched by linecard CPU
    - Forwarding table updates
- Linecard memory:
    - Route memory
    - Forwarding table size
    - Any sampling processes that are running, such as Cisco NetFlow
- Hardware forwarding memory:
    - Forwarding table size
    - Number of labels
    - Number and size of access lists
    - Number of multicast entries
    - Type of routes in the forwarding table (IGP versus BGP versus BGP multipath)

OAM and Troubleshooting

It is inevitable that the service provider network will experience problems that affect enterprise VPN availability. When such situations occur, it is essential that the service provider have the optimal troubleshooting tool set at its disposal. Recent advancements in MPLS OAM in particular have the potential to provide this technology with carrier class OAM capability.

As discussed, fault management is a combination of proactive and reactive techniques. From the service provider perspective, proactive monitoring and subsequent trouble-shooting are ideal because they have the potential to detect problems before the end customer. The next section discusses both areas and recommends tools and strategies that the service provider can adopt. Legacy Layer 2 access technologies are beyond the scope of this book, the emphasis being very much on MPLS VPN.

Proactive Monitoring in Detail

The "Proactive Monitoring" section earlier in this chapter discussed the scope options a service provider has when monitoring the VPN for faults. Fundamentally, the techniques employed are either "off-box" (NMS-based) or "on-box" (probe-based). This section discusses these options in more detail and outlines the differences between them and the relative advantages and disadvantages of each. These approaches are illustrated in Figures 8-12 and 8-13.

Figure 8-12 *Off-Box Reachability Testing*

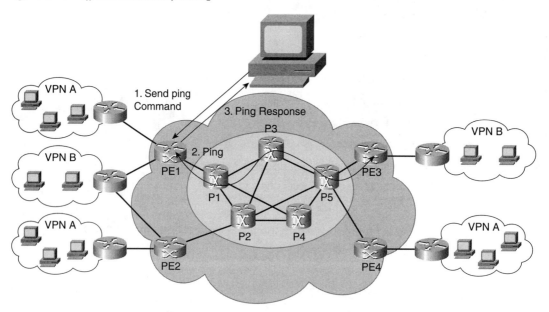

Figure 8-13 *On-Box Reachability Testing*

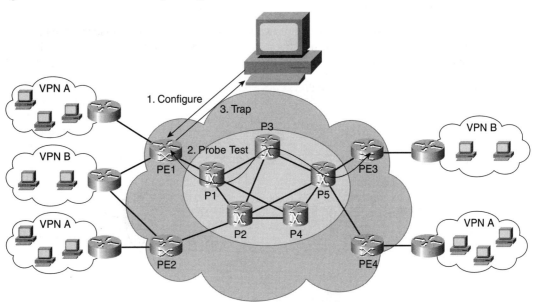

Active monitoring using intelligent probes is the idealized approach because it pushes the responsibility down into the network, limiting the amount of external configuration and traffic on the data communications network (DCN). However, there are several reasons why this might not always be chosen:

- Such probes are usually proprietary in nature and may not work well in a multivendor network. For example, if the network consists of multivendor PE devices, it may be that probes can be used with equipment from only one vendor, and this may complicate the management implementation.

- Due to the scale of some VPNs, the probes may consume too many resources on the routers.

- Probes must be maintained as the network grows.

- Probes might be unavailable on the software releases deployed on the routers.

In fact, often the best approach for the service provider is to employ a mixture of off-box and on-box testing to gain the required coverage.

The next section explores what on/off-box tools are available to the service provider.

VPN Layer

At this layer, the service provider monitors VPN reachability. As discussed earlier, the three main test path options are PE-PE, PE-core-PE-CE, and CE-CE. Each is basically a trade-off between accuracy and scalability, although logistics issues (such as CE access) might restrict what can be done.

PE-PE testing can be done in one of two ways. Either the service provider can build a dedicated "test VPN" or it can test within the customer VPN itself. These approaches are shown in Figures 8-14 and 8-15.

Figure 8-14 *PE-PE Monitoring Using a Test VPN*

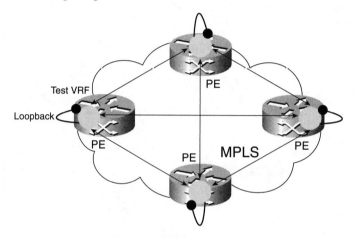

Figure 8-15 *PE-PE Monitoring Within Customer VPNs*

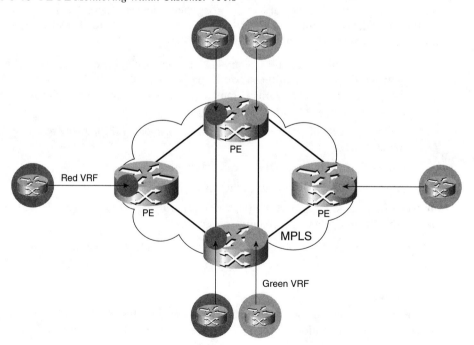

In the "test VPN," each PE tests reachability to all other PEs within the same route reflector domain, even though they may not have an explicit customer VPN relationship. This is still of the "*n* squared" magnitude discussed earlier. Service providers that use this technique therefore are more concerned that the PEs have basic VPN layer connectivity with one another.

In "customer VRF" testing, the service provider verifies specific customer VRF paths. This is more accurate because it closely mimics the customer traffic path, but it has scale implications. Because of the potential number of VRFs involved, the service provider is faced with the decision of which VRFs to monitor. This is usually influenced by specific customer SLAs. Figure 8-15 shows PE-PE testing, but the concept is similar to (and more accurate for) the other paths.

Off-Box Testing

In terms of the actual available instrumentation, off-box testing typically uses a "VRF-aware ping" that is supported by many vendors. This is essentially an Internet Control Message Protocol (ICMP) ping within the context of a VRF, using the VRF at the ingress/egress PEs and MPLS in the core to route the packet toward and back from the destination. If this ping succeeds, it provides strong validation that the PE-PE path is healthy. That is, the double label stack imposed as a result of using a VPN prefix is the correct one, the underlying MPLS transport is healthy, and the VRF route lookups and forwarding are correct. Here's an example of the VRF-aware ping:

```
cl-7206vxr-4#ping vrf red_vpn 8.1.1.2
Type escape sequence to abort.
Sending 5, 100-byte ICMP Echos to 8.1.1.2, timeout is 2 seconds:
!!!!!
Success rate is 100 percent (5/5), round-trip min/avg/max = 92/96/108 ms
cl-7206vxr-4#
```

On-Box Testing

This technique uses one of the proprietary probe tools available from vendors. A common deployment model for PE-PE testing is to use a separate, dedicated router attached to a PE to host the probes. This is commonly called a "shadow router." It has a number of advantages:

- In an unmanaged service, it allows CE emulation.
- If existing PEs are overloaded, it avoids placing an additional burden on them.
- If existing PEs are low on memory, it avoids further reduction.
- If the probes and/or the associated engine need to be updated, this can be performed without disturbing the existing network.

This scheme has two variations. The "shadow CE" is when the probe router is not VRF-aware and simply emulates one or more CEs. A problem with this approach is that it cannot deal with overlapping IP addresses that may be advertised by remote sites within different VPNs. An example using the Cisco IP SLA technology is shown in Figure 8-16.

Figure 8-16 *Shadow CE Scheme*

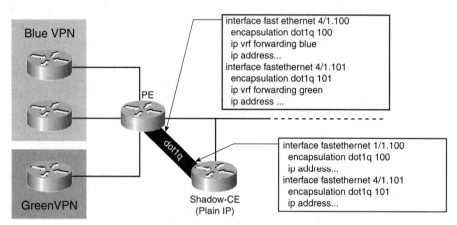

In the "shadow PE" model, the probe router is VRF-aware and is effectively a peer of the other PE routers. This solves the overlapping IP address problem, as shown in Figure 8-17.

Figure 8-17 *Shadow PE Scheme*

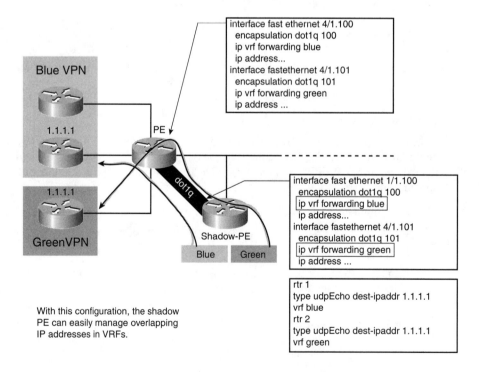

CE-CE monitoring seemingly is the optimal solution. Indeed, it's often used even in unmanaged services where the enterprise may grant access to the CE for probe deployment. The main problem with this approach is one of scale: As the VPN grows, so do the number of remote sites that have to be tested, and hence the number of probes. Given that CEs are typically low-end devices, this can present a performance problem. Another issue is the maintenance overhead on the management systems in terms of keeping up with adds/moves/changes and also tracking and correlating events from the CEs. In practice, the service provider should work with the equipment vendors to establish the performance profile for probing. Such a profile should include factors such as QoS and SLA metrics required. This can then be used to negotiate with each customer which sites will be monitored end to end. An example might be that customers get monitoring from certain key sites to the hubs or data centers.

Example 8-4 is a sample configuration taken from the Cisco IP SLA technology in the Cisco IOS. It shows a basic VRF-aware probe configuration.

Example 8-4 *VRF-Aware Probe Creation*

```
Router(config)#rtr 3
Router(config-rtr)#type udpEcho dest-ipaddr 172.16.1.1 dest-port 1213
Router(config-rtr)#vrf vpn1
Router(config)#rtr schedule 3 start now
```

Line 1 creates the probe.

Line 2 specifies that a User Datagram Protocol (UDP) echo test is required toward the destination address and port.

Line 3 specifies the VRF within which to execute the operation.

Line 4 instructs the probe to start sending immediately with the default frequency.

NOTE   IP SLA was originally called the "real-time responder." This is reflected in the CLI of older IOS versions, such as **rtr 3** in Example 8-4.

If such a probe were to detect a connectivity problem followed by restoration, the traps would look similar to Example 8-5.

Example 8-5 *IP SLA Connection Lost/Restored Traps*

```
rttMonConnectionChangeNotification notification received from: 10.49.157.202 at
  13/03/2003 15:32:14
  Time stamp: 0 days 08h:21m:01s.92th
  Agent address: 10.49.157.202 Port: 56806 Transport: IP/UDP Protocol: SNMPv2c
  Notification
  Manager address: 10.49.157.206 Port: 162 Transport: IP/UDP
```

(continues)

Example 8-5 *IP SLA Connection Lost/Restored Traps (Continued)*

```
Community: (zero-length)
Bindings (5)
  Binding #1: sysUpTime.0 *** (timeticks) 0 days 08h:21m:01s.92th
  Binding #2: snmpTrapOID.0 *** (oid) rttMonConnectionChangeNotification
  Binding #3: rttMonCtrlAdminTag.1 *** (octets) (zero-length) [ (hex)]
  Binding #4: rttMonHistoryCollectionAddress.1.0.0.0 *** (octets) AC.10.01.01 (hex)
  Binding #5: rttMonCtrlOperConnectionLostOccurred.1.0.0.0 *** (int32) true(1)
```

NOTE   This output can be obtained by using the **show logging** command with **debug snmp** switched on.

In Example 8-5, the line in bold shows the var bind that indicates the connection being lost.

```
rttMonConnectionChangeNotification notification received from: 10.49.157.202 at
  13/03/2003 15:41:29
  Time stamp: 0 days 08h:30m:17s.01th
  Agent address: 10.49.157.202 Port: 56806 Transport: IP/UDP Protocol: SNMPv2c
  Notification
  Manager address: 10.49.157.206 Port: 162 Transport: IP/UDP
  Community: (zero-length)
  Bindings (5)
    Binding #1: sysUpTime.0 *** (timeticks) 0 days 08h:30m:17s.01th
    Binding #2: snmpTrapOID.0 *** (oid) rttMonConnectionChangeNotification
    Binding #3: rttMonCtrlAdminTag.1 *** (octets) (zero-length) [ (hex)]
    Binding #4: rttMonHistoryCollectionAddress.1.0.0.0 *** (octets) AC.10.01.01
  (hex)
 Binding #5: rttMonCtrlOperConnectionLostOccurred.1.0.0.0 *** (int32) false(2)
```

The preceding line in bold shows the var bind that indicates the connection being restored.

MPLS Layer

The recent growth of MPLS as a transport technology has brought with it demand from network managers for OAM capabilities. Specifically, operators are asking for OAM features akin to those found in circuit-oriented technologies such as ATM and Frame Relay. Additionally, many service providers are used to basing services on highly resilient and fault-tolerant time-division multiplexing (TDM) networks. This has led to requirements being placed on MPLS to acquire built-in protocol operations to rapidly detect and respond to failure conditions.

The common requirement for such tools is an ability to test and troubleshoot the data plane. This is because the data and control planes may sometimes lose synchronization.

A key message for the service provider here is that it is not enough to simply monitor the control plane of an MPLS VPN. For example, even though routes may be installed in global and VRF tables, there is absolutely no guarantee that the data plane is operational. Only by testing the data plane does the service provider have confidence that customer traffic will be transported correctly across its network.

Various standards have been proposed to embellish MPLS with such technology. The next section concentrates on the main ones that are available or will be shortly.

LSP Ping/Traceroute

This tool set is currently an IETF draft, defined at http://www.ietf.org/internet-drafts/draft-ietf-mpls-lsp-ping-03.txt. The intent of these tools is to provide a mechanism to let operators and management systems test LSPs and help isolate problems. Conceptually, these tools mirror the same principles of traditional ICMP ping/trace: an echo request is sent down a specific path, and the receiver sends an echo reply. However, several differences are essential to ensuring the health of individual LSPs:

*   The echo request packet uses the same label stack as the LSP being tested.

*   The IP address destination of the echo request is a 127/8 address, and the content of the packet Type-Length-Value (TLV) carries the forward error correction (FEC) information. This is important, because if a broken LSP is encountered, a transit router punts the packet for local processing when it detects the 127/8 IP address, resulting in the packet's being dropped. In other words, IP doesn't forward the packet toward the destination if the LSP is broken.

*   If the packet reaches an egress router, a check is performed to see whether this is the correct router for the FEC being tested. In the Cisco implementation, the 127/8 address forces the packet to be processed by the route processor at the egress LSR.

Figure 8-18 illustrates the LSP ping.

Figure 8-18 *LSP Ping*

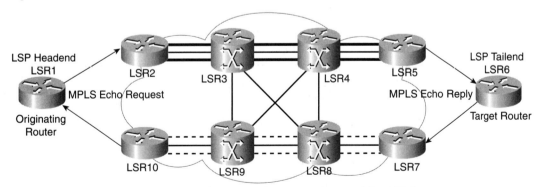

MPLS echo reply via IP, MPLS, or a combination of IP + MPLS.

LS Embedded Management LSP Ping/Traceroute and AToM VCCV, http://www.cisco.com/en/US/products/sw/iosswrel/ps1829/products_feature_guide09186a00801eb054.html

If you initiate an MPLS LSP ping request at LSR1 to a prefix at LSR6, the following sequence occurs:

Step 1   LSR1 initiates an MPLS LSP ping request for an FEC at the target router LSR6 and sends an MPLS echo request to LSR2.

Step 2   LSR2 receives the MPLS echo request packet and forwards it through transit routers LSR3 and LSR4 to the penultimate router, LSR5.

Step 3   LSR5 receives the MPLS echo request, pops the MPLS label, and forwards the packet to LSR6 as an IP packet.

Step 4   LSR6 receives the IP packet, processes the MPLS echo request, and then sends an MPLS echo reply to LSR1 through an alternative route.

Step 5   LSR7 to LSR10 receives the MPLS echo reply and forwards it back toward LSR1, the originating router.

Step 6   LSR1 receives the MPLS echo reply in response to its MPLS echo request.

The following is an example of using **lsp ping** via Cisco CLI. In this case, the LSP is broken, as revealed by the "R" return code (this means that the last LSR to reply is not the target egress router):

```
cl-12016-1#ping mpls ipv4 6.6.7.6/32
Sending 5, 100-byte MPLS Echos to 6.6.7.6/32,
      timeout is 2 seconds, send interval is 0 msec:

Codes: '!' - success, 'Q' - request not transmitted,
       '.' - timeout, 'U' - unreachable,
       'R' - downstream router but not target

Type escape sequence to abort.
RRRRR
Success rate is 0 percent (0/5)
```

A successful LSP ping looks something like this:

```
cl-12008-1#ping mpls ipv4 6.6.7.6/32
Sending 5, 100-byte MPLS Echos to 6.6.7.6/32,
      timeout is 2 seconds, send interval is 0 msec:

Codes: '!' - success, 'Q' - request not transmitted,
       '.' - timeout, 'U' - unreachable,
       'R' - downstream router but not target,
       'M' - malformed request

Type escape sequence to abort.
!!!!!
Success rate is 100 percent (5/5), round-trip min/avg/max = 1/2/4 ms
```

LSP traceroute provides hop-by-hop fault localization and uses TTL settings to force expiration of the TTL along an LSP. LSP traceroute incrementally increases the TTL value in its MPLS echo requests (TTL = 1, 2, 3, 4, and so on) to discover the downstream mapping of each successive hop. The success of the LSP traceroute depends on the transit router processing the MPLS echo request when it receives a labeled packet with TTL = 1. On Cisco routers, when the TTL expires, the packet is sent to the route processor (RP) for processing. The transit router returns an MPLS echo reply containing information about the transit hop in response to the TTL-expired MPLS packet.

The echo request and echo reply are UDP packets with source and destination ports set to 3503.

Figure 8-19 shows an MPLS LSP traceroute example with an LSP from LSR1 to LSR4.

Figure 8-19 *LSP Traceroute*

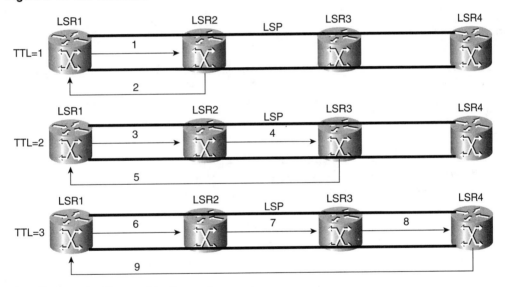

Cisco Configuration Express, http://www.cisco.com/cx

If you enter an LSP traceroute to an FEC at LSR4 from LSR1, the steps and actions shown in Table 8-1 occur.

Table 8-1   *LSP Traceroute Operation*

MPLS Packet Type and Description	Router Action
MPLS echo request with a target FEC pointing to LSR4 and to a downstream mapping	Sets the TTL of the label stack to 1. Sends the request to LSR2.
MPLS echo reply	Receives the packet with TTL = 1. Processes the UDP packet as an MPLS echo request. Finds a downstream mapping and replies to LSR1 with its own downstream mapping, based on the incoming label.
MPLS echo request with the same target FEC and the downstream mapping received in the echo reply from LSR2	Sets the TTL of the label stack to 2. Sends the request to LSR2.
MPLS echo request	Receives the packet with TTL = 2. Decrements the TTL. Forwards the echo request to LSR3.
MPLS reply packet	Receives the packet with TTL = 1. Processes the UDP packet as an MPLS echo request. Finds a downstream mapping and replies to LSR1 with its own downstream mapping based on the incoming label.
MPLS echo request with the same target FEC and the downstream mapping received in the echo reply from LSR3	Sets the packet's TTL to 3. Sends the request to LSR2.
MPLS echo request	Receives the packet with TTL = 3. Decrements the TTL. Forwards the echo request to LSR3.
MPLS echo request	Receives the packet with TTL = 2. Decrements the TTL. Forwards the echo request to LSR4.
MPLS echo reply	Receives the packet with TTL = 1. Processes the UDP packet as an MPLS echo request. Finds a downstream mapping and also finds that the router is the egress router for the target FEC. Replies to LSR1.

Here's a CLI example of a broken path:

```
cl-12016-1#traceroute mpls ipv4 6.6.7.4/32 ttl 10
Tracing MPLS Label Switched Path to 6.6.7.4/32, timeout is 2 seconds

Codes: '!' - success, 'Q' - request not transmitted,
       '.' - timeout, 'U' - unreachable,
       'R' - downstream router but not target

Type escape sequence to abort.
  0 6.6.1.1 MRU 1200 [Labels: 24 Exp: 0]
R 1 6.6.1.5 MRU 4474 [No Label] 1 ms
R 2 6.6.1.6 3 ms
R 3 6.6.1.6 4 ms
R 4 6.6.1.6 1 ms
R 5 6.6.1.6 2 ms
R 6 6.6.1.6 3 ms
R 7 6.6.1.6 4 ms
R 8 6.6.1.6 1 ms
R 9 6.6.1.6 3 ms
R 10 6.6.1.6 4 ms
```

In this case, the break occurs because the LSP segment on interface 6.6.1.5 sends an untagged packet.

By way of comparison, a successful traceroute looks something like this:

```
cl-12008-1#traceroute mpls ipv4 6.6.7.4/32
Tracing MPLS Label Switched Path to 6.6.7.4/32, timeout is 2 seconds
Codes: '!' - success, 'Q' - request not transmitted,
       '.' - timeout, 'U' - unreachable,
       'R' - downstream router but not target,
       'M' - malformed request

Type escape sequence to abort.
  0 6.6.1.25 MRU 1709 [implicit-null]
! 1 6.6.1.26 4 ms
```

The main difference here is that the successful traceroute ends with a ! as per regular IP ping.

As will be discussed shortly, these tools can be used as essential building blocks in a service provider's MPLS VPN troubleshooting strategy.

Proactive Monitoring of PE-PE LSPs

Although the LSP ping/trace tools provide invaluable troubleshooting capability, they are not designed for monitoring. Instead, they are of more use to an operator who wants to troubleshoot a reported problem or verify the health of some paths after network changes.

Vendors such as Cisco are developing probe-based techniques that use the LSP ping/trace mechanism, but in such a manner as to allow monitoring of a full-mesh PE-PE network.

The key to scalability of such probes is to test only those paths that are relevant to service delivery. In the context of an MPLS VPN, this means that from a given ingress PE, only LSPs that are used to carry VPN traffic are tested. This is important, because traffic in different VPNs that is destined for the same egress PE is essentially multiplexed onto the same transport LSP. This concept is shown in Figure 8-20.

Figure 8-20 *Intelligent LSP Probing*

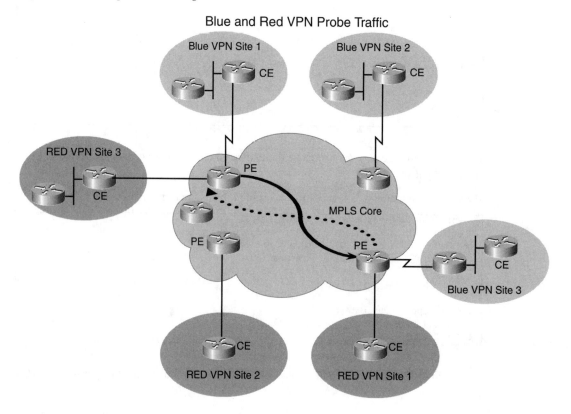

This figure shows that Blue VPN Site 1 and Red VPN Site 3 share the same transport LSP to reach Blue VPN Site 3 and Red VPN Site 1.

With such a mechanism in place, the service provider has the means to monitor LSPs at a high rate. Failure of an LSP results in an SNMP notification being sent to the NMS, whereupon service impact, correlation, and troubleshooting can begin.

One point to stress in such testing is the presence of Equal-Cost Multiple Paths (ECMP). Very often, ECMP is in use within a service provider core, meaning that multiple LSPs may be available to carry traffic from ingress to egress PE. Service providers therefore should ask vendors how both the reactive CLI and any probe-based tools will test available ECMPs. Equally important is that if a failure occurs, the notification sent to the NMS clearly identifies which one.

Performance Problems

This is perhaps the most difficult problem category for an operator to troubleshoot. Not only do these problems tend to be transient in nature, but they also are inherently more complex due to the many different network segments and features involved.

A typical example of a problem in this area is an enterprise customer reporting poor performance on one of his or her services, such as VoIP. Packet loss, delay, and jitter all adversely affect the quality of this service. How does the operator tackle such problems?

The first task is to identify the customer traffic at the VRF interface on the PE. Sampling tools such as Cisco NetFlow are extremely useful here. They identify flows of traffic (for example, based on source/destination IP addresses and ports) and cache statistics related to these flows, which can then be exported offline. An important piece of data is the ToS marking (IP Precedence or DSCP). If this can be done, the operator can answer one of the first questions: Is the customer's data being marked correctly?

Next, the QoS policies on the VRF interface can be analyzed to determine if any of the customer traffic is being dropped. The following example is from the Cisco modular QoS CLI (MQC) **show policy-map interface** command. It shows that 16 packets from the class (that is, traffic matching specific properties—the target traffic) have been dropped due to the policer's actions:

```
Service-policy output: ce_6cos_out_A_40M_21344K (1159)
    Class-map: ce_mgmt_bun_output (match-any) (1160/7)
       314997339 packets, 161278311131 bytes
       5 minute offered rate 952503000 bps, drop rate 943710000 bps
       Match: access-group 199 (1161)
          1 packets, 608 bytes
          5 minute rate 0 bps
       Match: access-group 198 (1162)
          0 packets, 0 bytes
          5 minute rate 0 bps
       Match: ip precedence 0  (1163)
          314997338 packets, 161278310523 bytes
          5 minute rate 952503000 bps
       bandwidth: 1955 kbps (EIR Weight 0%)
       police:
          8000 bps, 8000 limit, 8000 extended limit
       conformed 2580 packets, 1319729 bytes; rate 7000 bps; action:
  set-dscp-transmit 48
          exceeded 16 packets, 7968 bytes; rate 0 bps; action: drop
```

If traffic is being dropped, this might indicate that the customer is exceeding the allocated bandwidth (or bursting above agreed-on values), which may explain the problem.

If the ingress PE classification and QoS policy actions seem correct, the next stage is to analyze the remaining path across the service provider network. The first task is to find out exactly what that path is. From PE-PE, this can be obtained using the LSP traceroute feature described earlier. Then, for each interface in the path, the effects of any QoS policies are examined to ensure that no unexpected drops are occurring. In an MPLS core, this typically involves looking at any QoS congestion avoidance or management mechanisms. For example, traffic-engineered tunnels are becoming increasingly popular for guaranteeing bandwidth across the core network.

It may not always be possible to inspect the live customer traffic and associated network behavior. In these cases, synthetic probes are extremely useful because they allow an operator to probe the problem path for a certain time period. This reveals any major problems with the service provider network, such as wrong QoS classification/action, congestion, or bottlenecks. If these tests are positive, the problem is almost certainly with the customer traffic (incorrect marking or bandwidth being exceeded).

Fault Management

The previous sections have illustrated techniques for both the data and control planes of an MPLS VPN. This is of little value, however, if the service provider does not have adequate fault management systems and processes in place. If the service provider detects faults, they need to be acted on. More significantly, however, the enterprise customer often detects problems before the service provider does. The ability to test connectivity at higher frequencies is one factor in this. However, individual end users also report problems, mainly of a performance nature, to their own IT departments. Many enterprises can rule out their own networks and systems as the root cause and blame the service provider. At this point, a call is placed to the service provider's first-line support.

This section helps the service provider ensure that it has the correct reactive and proactive fault systems in place to deal with both scenarios.

Proactive Fault Management

Assume that a fault has been detected by the service provider's own monitoring system, within a VRF, from the PE across the MPLS core to the remote CE.

Traditionally, such a fault would be picked up by network operations in the network operations center (NOC), and the problem's severity would be assessed. Given that we are talking about a potential outage scenario, how should operations proceed in isolating, diagnosing, and repairing the fault?

This is in fact a multilayered problem that requires a systematic approach to troubleshooting.

The first area that the service provider should look at is recent events that have been collected from the network. Problems within the network may have resulted in events being generated and immediately explain why there is an outage. Examples include link up/down, contact loss with a router, and specific protocol issues such as LDP or BGP session losses. What is really needed is a means to correlate the data plane outage to the other events that have been collected from the network. Several systems in the market perform this task and immediately point to a possible root cause.

Furthermore, assume that there are no obvious reasons why the connection has failed. What is required is a means to identify what layer has the problem: VPN, IP, or MPLS. One approach is to rule out each one by performing data plane tests. If both the IP and MPLS data planes are correct, there is a problem with either VPN route availability or the VPN switching path, as shown in Figure 8-21.

Figure 8-21   *Troubleshooting a VPN Outage*

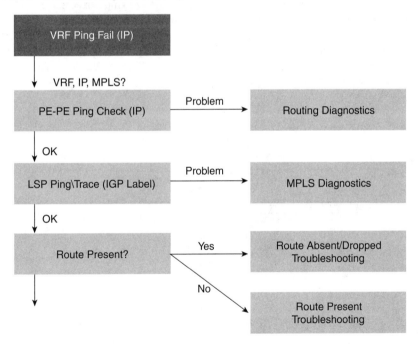

After the initial diagnosis has been made (control/data plane, VRF/MPLS/IP, and so on), further troubleshooting is required to isolate and then fully diagnose the problem.

Isolation within the data plane typically uses one of the traceroute tools discussed previously. You must be careful here, however, especially in heterogeneous networks. This is because not all boxes may support the OAM standards, and even if they do, some interoperability issues may exist. False negatives are the most obvious condition that may arise, such as one vendor's box failing to reply to an echo packet even though there is no problem. The service provider therefore should ask each vendor which draft version of the standard is supported and then conduct lab testing to identify any issues.

Another point worth stressing with the OAM isolation tools is that the last box returned in a trace output may not always be the failure point. For example, the fault may in fact lie with the next downstream router, but it cannot reply for some reason. Some intelligence is needed with this part of the process to rule out the last node in the trace output before inspecting (ideally automatically) those downstream.

Root cause identification requires inspecting the router's configuration, status, and forwarding engines. Although many issues are caused by misconfigurations and deterministic errors, defects within hardware or software are the most difficult to find and often are the most costly. Manual or automatic troubleshooting via management systems therefore should concentrate on ruling out obvious causes before looking for symptoms caused by defects in the data/control planes. A good illustration of the latter is label inconsistencies. For example, suppose an egress PE router receives a new route from a CE. BGP then allocates a label, installs the route and the label into the local forwarding tables, and propagates it to relevant ingress PE routers. Various things can go wrong here, such as allocation failures, local/remote installation problems, and propagation issues. These issues using Cisco CLI are shown in Figure 8-22.

Figure 8-22 *MPLS VPN Label Problem Areas*

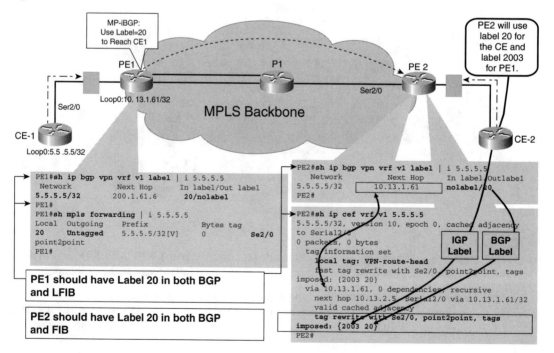

Problems within the control plane require inspection of individual routers to resolve problems. For example, if the ingress PE router loses a route (or never receives it in the first place), the egress router from which it should first be learned should be inspected first (to see if it was the route received, and if it was then propagated, and so on). LDP problems tend to manifest themselves as MPLS data plane problems and hence can be found using the same isolation/inspection technique previously described.

Hopefully, the picture being painted here is that MPLS VPN troubleshooting is not straight-forward. The real message, however, is that the service provider should ask some serious questions of the vendors in terms of what management support they provide to help automate the troubleshooting process. At the minimum, vendors should supply element management systems that check the health of MPLS and VPN data/control planes on a per-box basis. More useful are network-level systems that set up proactive monitoring and respond automatically to faults when detected. Such systems should employ the systematic techniques described in this section, as well as offer integration points into other Operation Systems Support (OSS) components.

Case Study: Troubleshooting a Problem with the Acme, Inc. VPN

It is useful to go through an example of troubleshooting an MPLS VPN connectivity problem within the Acme, Inc. VPN. This helps describe how the different tools fit together and how a service provider should prepare in the event that a fault is reported or detected.

In this scenario, assume that Acme, Inc. reports loss of connectivity between sites Glasgow and London, as shown in Figure 8-23.

Figure 8-23 *Connectivity Problem Between Glasgow and London*

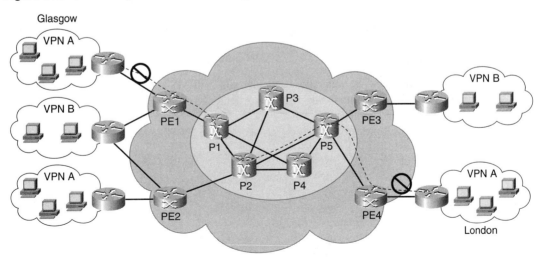

The problem is reported into first-line support, at which point an attempt is made to reproduce it within the service provider network. In an unmanaged service, this could be done by testing from the local PEs to the source and destination sites, as shown in Figure 8-24.

Figure 8-24 *Testing VPN Connectivity in the Service Provider Network*

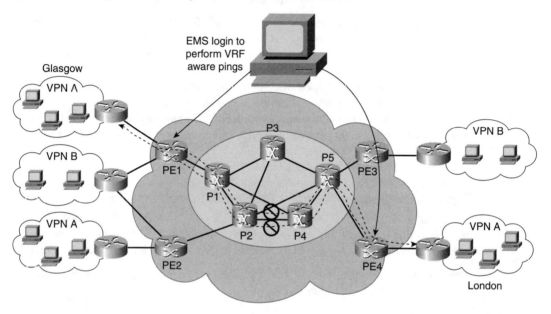

These tests fail in both directions. At this point, first-line support may choose to open a trouble ticket and escalate the problem. (This is very much dependent on the service provider support model.)

Assume that second-line support is now alerted. The EMS could be used to further narrow down the problem. It can do this by testing whether IP and LSP connectivity are valid in the core, as shown in Figure 8-25.

Figure 8-25 *Testing IP and MPLS Paths*

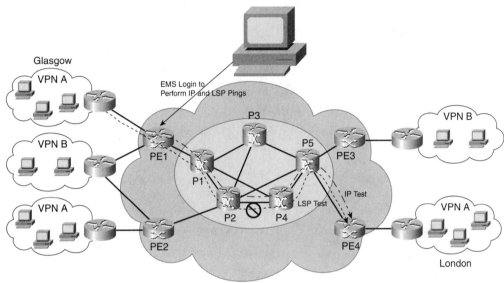

These tests reveal that basic IP connectivity is healthy but the transport LSP is broken.

The EMS now issues an LSP traceroute, as shown in Figure 8-26.

Figure 8-26 *Using LSP Trace to Help Isolate the Problem*

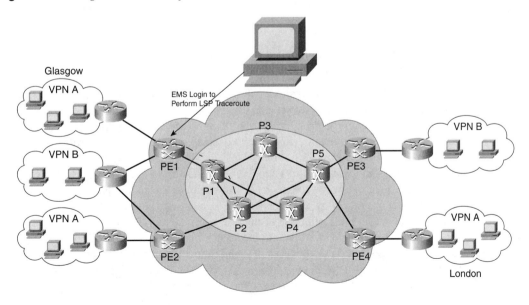

In this example, the traceroute gets as far as router P2. This router is now examined from both a control and data-plane perspective by the EMS, as illustrated in Figure 8-27.

Figure 8-27 *Diagnosing LSRs in a Broken Path*

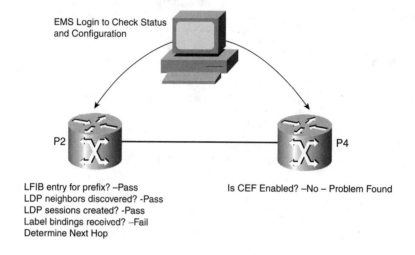

Notice that in this case, the actual failure point was not the last node returned from the trace output. Because of this, the next hop (LDP downstream neighbor) had to be calculated and inspected. This illustrates the value of having an automated management solution to help with troubleshooting.

Reactive Fault Management

Many of the same principles already discussed apply to reactive fault management. However, some subtle distinctions need to be observed.

First, in the scenario where a customer calls in to first-line support to report a problem, the service provider is looking for a management system that will help this part of the business, as well as link into the troubleshooting tools already discussed. An important aspect of handling customer-reported faults is to quickly be able to reproduce the problem, thereby verifying if the service provider or enterprise is the likely source. A second requirement is to deal with the varying skill sets of support personnel. Some service providers have good network knowledge. However, others have little or no understanding of an MPLS VPN. An ideal system is one that allows an inexperienced operator to simply enter the details of the customer and the source/destination of the problem. The tool then retrieves all necessary VPN and network-related data "behind the scenes" and attempts to verify the problem. If the problem exists, a report is generated, highlighting the nature of the problem and any other contextual data. This allows the operator to raise an appropriate trouble ticket and alert the necessary network engineers for further analysis.

Service providers might choose to build (or have built) the "front-office" applications themselves. However, at some point in the troubleshooting process, detailed knowledge of vendor equipment is required if the whole process is to be simplified to reduce opex and maximize service uptime. Service providers therefore should discuss the availability and integration of vendor MPLS VPN NMS/EMS systems into their OSS.

SLA Monitoring

Providing an excellent service is the primary goal of any service provider. Fundamental to this is adhering to the SLAs agreed to with end customers. But how do service providers know they are satisfying such SLAs, especially given the more stringent and complex ones associated with IP services delivered across an MPLS VPN?

The key to successful monitoring in an MPLS VPN is to ensure that the technology exists within vendor equipment to proactively monitor the network from a performance perspective. Next comes the OSS to allow configuration, detection, reporting, and troubleshooting related to such monitoring.

As has been stressed, the technology usually exists in the form of synthetic probing, because this provides the most accurate data. Such probes must support the following requirements to be useful in monitoring modern SLAs:

- How do the probes achieve their accuracy? How do they account for other activities that routers may be performing?

- There is an obvious overlap between probing for performance and probing for faults. If a path is broken, the SLA may be compromised. As will be discussed, the service provider might want to combine both strategies. But to do so, the probes used for SLA monitoring must also support basic detection and notification of unavailable paths.

- SLA monitoring requires probes that support QoS.

- Specialized voice quality support for codecs and quality measurements.

- Metrics such as packet loss, delay, jitter, and out-of-sequence packets should be supported, ideally within the context of a VRF.

- Thresholds should be supported that result in notifications being sent to proactively inform when certain parameters have been breached—for example, 500-ms jitter.

Accuracy

The service provider should ask the vendor serious questions about the accuracy of probe data. If there is any dispute over the SLA, it is crucial that the service provider rely on the data provided by the probes to prove or disprove any performance claims. Here are some specific questions that should be asked:

- What testing does the service provider perform, and on what platforms? For example, does the service provider test probes with known delays in the Unit Under Test (UUT) that can be independently verified?

- If the probes will be deployed on production routers carrying customer traffic (nonshadow model), are they suitably loaded with control/data traffic as per a live network?

- If basic ICMP ping figures were used as a performance metric, one of the major problems would be that ICMP traffic is generally treated as low-priority by the routers in the path. This naturally leads to inaccurate results, because the reply to test packets might be sitting in a low-priority queue, waiting to be processed. The service provider should therefore ask how such delays are accounted for in the vendor's probe measurements.

Probe Metric Support

To minimize overhead, the service provider should ideally have a probe technology that supports the basic metrics of delay, jitter, packet loss, and availability from within a single operation. This can then be combined with one of the core monitoring strategies outlined earlier to provide minimal SLA monitoring. For example, the Cisco IP SLA jitter probe supports these combined metrics. The following example shows how to configure such a probe that sends five packets every 20 ms at a frequency of once every 10 seconds with a packet size of 60 bytes:

```
(config)#rtr 1
(config-rtr)#type jitter dest-ip 10.51.20.105 dest-port 99
                      num-packets 5 interval 20
(config-rtr)#frequency 10
(config-rtr)#request-data-size 60
```

The metrics collected by this probe would then be obtained from the **show rtr operational-state command:**

```
red-vpn#sh rtr op 1
        Current Operational State
Entry Number: 1
Modification Time: 08:22:34.000 PDT Thu Aug 22 2002
Diagnostics Text:
Last Time this Entry was Reset: Never
Number of Octets in use by this Entry: 1594
Number of Operations Attempted: 1
Current Seconds Left in Life: 574
Operational State of Entry: active
Latest Operation Start Time: 08:22:34.000 PDT Thu Aug 22 2002
Latest Oper Sense: ok
```

```
RTT Values:
NumOfRTT: 997    RTTSum: 458111   RTTSum2: 238135973
Packet Loss Values:
PacketLossSD: 3 PacketLossDS: 0
PacketOutOfSequence: 0  PacketMIA: 0     PacketLateArrival: 0
InternalError: 0        Busies: 0

Jitter Values:
MinOfPositivesSD: 1        MaxOfPositivesSD: 249
NumOfPositivesSD: 197      SumOfPositivesSD: 8792    Sum2PositivesSD: 794884
MinOfNegativesSD: 1        MaxOfNegativesSD: 158
NumOfNegativesSD: 761      SumOfNegativesSD: 8811    Sum2NegativesSD: 139299
MinOfPositivesDS: 1        MaxOfPositivesDS: 273
NumOfPositivesDS: 317      SumOfPositivesDS: 7544    Sum2PositivesDS: 581458
<snip>
```

Here are some important points to note from this output (shown shaded):

- Three packets have been lost from approximately 1000 sent.

- The average round-trip time was 458,111/997 = 459 ms.

- Source-to-destination jitter fields are postfixed with "SD," such as NumOfPositivesSD.

- Destination-to-source jitter fields are postfixed with "DS," such as NumOfPositivesDS.

QoS Support

Enterprise customers typically require QoS markings to be preserved across the service provider network. This means that when the packets arrive at their destination, they should have the same QoS classification as when they entered. However, it is not practical or scalable for the service provider to create unique QoS classes for each customer. A common approach is for the service provider to offer a standard set of QoS classes onto which customer traffic is mapped, such as voice, business-class, and best-effort.

It then becomes essential that the service provider monitor how the network handles these classes. To do that, the probe technology needs to be able to set QoS in the packets. The following example shows how QoS is marked within the Cisco IP SLA technology. In this case, the ToS bits in the IP header are used (there is a standard mapping between ToS and DSCP). The following example shows how to configure a jitter probe to have a DSCP value of 101110 (ToS equivalent 0xB8), which is the recommended marking for voice traffic:

```
Router(config)#rtr 1
Router(config-rtr)#type jitter dest-ipaddr 10.52.130.68 dest-port 16384 \
  num-packets 1000 interval 20
Router(config-rtr)#tos 0xB8
Router(config-rtr)#frequency 60
Router(config-rtr)#request-data-size 200
Router(config)#rtr schedule 1 life forever start-time now
```

Specialized Voice Probes

Delay, jitter, and packet loss are the primary impairment factors with voice quality. Although it is essential that the service provider have access to detailed metrics around these properties, it can be complex to translate them into an instant assessment of voice quality. The service provider therefore should look to the vendor to provide voice quality "scores" as a guide. Two common examples are Mean Opinion Score (MOS) and International Calculated Planning Impairment Factor (ICPIF).

Additionally, it is important that common codecs be supported. This would ideally select the appropriate probe and packet formats required to more accurately test the network. Examples include G.711 mu-Law (g711ulaw), G.711 A-Law (g711alaw), and G.729A (g729a).

The following example shows how Cisco SAA (Cisco Service Assure Agent, renamed to IP SLA) has extended its jitter probe to support such features. This example simulates a G711u codec, 1000 packets, interval 20 ms, and frequency 1 minute:

```
Router(config)#rtr 2
Router(config-rtr)#type jitter dest-ipaddr 10.52.132.71 \
Router(config-rtr)#dest-port 16001 codec g711alaw
Router(config-rtr)#tos 0xB8
Router(config)#rtr schedule 2 life forever start-time now
```

Threshold Breach Notification

Expanding on the proactive fault management theme discussed earlier, probes ideally should support informing management stations when certain SLA conditions might be breached.

A further requirement is the concept of low and high watermarks, as shown in Figure 8-28.

Figure 8-28 *High and Low Watermark Thresholds*

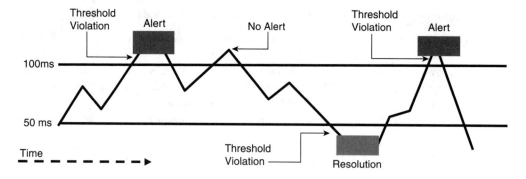

This minimizes notifications due to transient network behavior, resulting in events being sent only when the high watermark has been breached and thereafter only after the low watermark has been passed.

Again, the service provider should look for these features to be present in the probe technology because it allows proactive management of network performance to be put in place, hopefully alleviating any problems before the end customer detects them.

The following example shows how to configure high and low thresholds for a Cisco SAA jitter probe, with immediate generation of a trap:

```
(config)#rtr 1
(config-rtr)#threshold 100
(config)#rtr reaction-configuration 1
              threshold-type immediate
              action-type trapOnly
              threshold-falling 50
```

Reporting

A useful tool for the service provider to help support customer VPN reports is VPN-aware SNMP. If the vendor supports such a feature, it can help the service provider offer secure access to only the VPNs offered to a specific customer.

This feature works by allowing SNMP requests on any configured VRF and returning responses to the same VRF. A trap host can also be associated with a specific VRF. This allows the service provider to restrict the view that a given user on a given SNMP server has. When polling a device through a VRF for a given MIB, the user has restricted access/ view to specific tables of the MIBs. This concept is shown in Figure 8-29.

A service provider could also use this technique to offer partial information views to a peering service provider or third party in charge of measuring performance and service uptime for SLA verification purposes. Also, the protocol's VRF awareness allows for a management VRF to be used to communicate with a NOC.

Figure 8-29 *VPN-Aware SNMP*

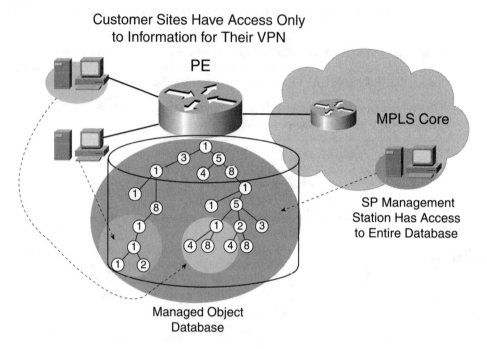

Summary

This chapter examined the network management implications for both the enterprise and a service provider when an MPLS VPN is introduced.

The conclusion is that from an enterprise perspective, management should be considerably simplified, mainly due to the connectionless nature of IP VPNs and the fact that site-to-site routing is accounted for by the service provider. However, because IP is now the end-to-end protocol, this brings in other considerations and requires changes to monitoring policies and traffic classification to ensure correct treatment throughout the service provider network.

From a service provider perspective, provisioning, fault, and performance management all require specific strategies and tools. A key point is the need to monitor the data plane of both the VPN and MPLS. To help achieve this, service providers should work closely with vendors to ensure that they provide the latest instrumentation in their equipment and building management systems to use and build on this capability.

References

DiffServ
http://www.ietf.org/html.charters/diffserv-charter.html

NetFlow
http://www.cisco.com/warp/public/732/Tech/nmp/netflow/index.shtml

NBAR
http://www.cisco.com/univercd/cc/td/doc/product/software/ios121/121newft/121t/121t5/
dtnbar.htm

BFD
http://www.ietf.org/html.charters/bfd-charter.html

ITU G.114
http://www.itu.int/itudoc/itu-t/aap/sg12aap/history/g.114/

Cisco IP Solution Center
http://www.cisco.com/en/US/products/sw/netmgtsw/ps4748/

IP SLA
http://www.cisco.com/en/US/products/ps6602/products_ios_protocol_group_home.html

This chapter covers the following topics:

- Remote Access to the Corporate Network via a Server that Is Separate from the Provider-Delivered VPN
- Remote-Access Server Configuration Examples
- L2TP Solutions that Identify the Different Components Owned and Managed by Both the Enterprise and Service Provider
- Specific DSL and Cable Connectivity Considerations
- Using IPsec for Remote Access, in Both the Roving User and Fixed-Site Off-Net Case
- Operation of Cisco Dynamic Multipoint VPN
- Considerations for Bandwidth Use by Encapsulating Multiservice Traffic in IPsec
- Access to Internet Destinations from Within a VPN
- Case Study Selections

CHAPTER 9

Off-Net Access to the VPN

This chapter's objectives are to define the options and technical implementations for the various types of off-net access required by enterprises for typical virtual private network (VPN) deployments. Off-net is defined as connectivity by users who are not directly connected to the provider VPN service via a private and permanent connection. This includes remote access for users who are part of the corporate VPN (via both unencrypted access and encrypted access with IPsec), access from and to the Internet, and extranet connectivity.

Several topics are covered in this chapter, as well as in Chapter 7, "Enterprise Security in an MPLS VPN Environment." IPsec and network security, for example, are often grouped. However, the split taken here places topics that relate to infrastructure security in Chapter 7 and topics that relate to security of packet payload in this chapter. This chapter details the various options you can select, from configuring separate remote-access servers to providing remote access as part of the provider-managed VPN service. Implementation considerations for IPsec and Internet traffic are detailed, along with the options selected for implementation as part of the ongoing Acme, Inc. case study.

Remote Access

This section defines remote access as access from a workstation that is not directly connected to a LAN served by the provider VPN. This can be dialup users, digital subscriber line (DSL), cable, or, increasingly, mobile wireless users. This chapter's intent is not to give a full treatment to these access methods, as would be needed by a provider planning to deploy DSL, cable, or wireless services. Rather, the intent is to provide enough information for the enterprise network manager to understand the issues as they relate to incorporating these services in an overall network architecture and to make the choices that best suit the requirements at hand. The choices are as follows:

- Do you want to treat all networks other than the provider you are connected to for your primary VPN as untrusted? (The question of whether the primary provider's network is trusted or untrusted is discussed in the "IPsec Access" section.)

- Do you want the provider to supply access for these users directly, or will you provide a separate connection for these remote users to gain access to your network?

These two questions have a total of four options: remote access via a provider's network, with or without encryption (implying that you place dialup users in your virtual routing/forwarding instance [VRF] within the provider network), and remote access via separate connections to your network, with or without encryption.

The choice of which option to select is based on the level of trust and the sensitivity of the data being transported. Additionally, the cost of support must not be ignored in this selection. The cost of support needs to include consideration for a separate connection to the corporate network if that option is selected, support of separate remote-access equipment, maintenance of IPsec encryption keys, and phone support for remote-access users whose connection difficulties take more time to troubleshoot.

As the use of remote-access technology has grown, the access methods preferred by network managers have changed. Initially, dialup access to a central number with Password Authentication Protocol (PAP) or Challenge Handshake Authentication Protocol (CHAP) authentication was deployed. As the need for greater footprint at a lower cost came along, Layer 2 Tunneling Protocol (L2TP) solutions started to appear from providers. Now, IPsec over many different access methodologies is prevalent. Each of the following subsections details a different access technology from the perspective of access via enterprise-owned equipment as well as provider-owned equipment. Provider-owned equipment typically adds to the complexity of mapping users to VRFs for the provider but simplifies the enterprise network management requirements.

Dial Access via RAS

Remote-access server (RAS) was the first method used for remote access in enterprises. The concept is simple. You place a remote-access server that can receive incoming dialup calls on the corporate LAN. Then anyone with dialup access can call over a plain old telephone service (POTS) line. The setup for these devices is fairly straightforward. It is reviewed here to set the scene for the solutions that are more commonplace today, because the more recent solutions build from this foundation.

Dialup access started off using Serial Line Internet Protocol (SLIP) but rapidly got replaced because of shortcomings, such as lack of support for address negotiation by PPP. A complete description of this protocol may be obtained from the link given in the "References" section at the end of this chapter, titled General PPP Information. You can find RFCs for PPP by searching for PPP at http://www.ietf.org/iesg/1rfc_index.txt.

As its name suggests, PPP handles the data link communication between two adjacent nodes. L2TP was created to extend PPP-based negotiation and data transport over packet-based networks. It is discussed in the next section as it pertains to enterprise networks.

Briefly, PPP supports asynchronous as well as synchronous communications, supports the running of multiple Layer 3 protocols over one link, allows dynamic address assignment, and handles authentication.

In a RAS environment where users are dialing in via POTS (or, equally possible, via ISDN), the process is for a workstation with dialer software to dial the RAS's number. PPP authenticates the user and gives her an IP address, and then she gains access to the network. The next section provides an overview of this process.

In PPP communications, the primary communication between the two ends consists of two parts: Link Control Protocol (LCP) and Network Control Packets (NCPs). LCP establishes and maintains the Layer 2 connection, whereas the NCPs are specific to each Layer 3 protocol.

The first phase of PPP negotiation is the exchange of LCP packets, which is the basic introduction of the two nodes that need to communicate. Here, each node agrees on general communications parameters, such as the maximum frame size and the use of compression. An optional phase checks line quality to see if the NCPs can be brought up. When the link negotiation is complete, an optional authentication process takes place via PAP or CHAP, which are defined in RFC 1334. This authentication needs to be configured into each node along with the username and password (or the location of the username and password).

PAP is simple to break into by using modem playback. The authentication performed by PAP sends a username and password from the dialer to the dialed node in clear text. This process continues until a connection is either granted or terminated. By capturing the tones sent by the modem down the phone line, an intruder without the username and password can play back those tones down the phone line and gain access. However, PAP is not used much any more, which makes this nearly a nonissue.

CHAP is a stronger authentication process. The LCP negotiates the link, and then the dialer receives a "challenge" from the dialed node. The peer responds with a value calculated by using a "one-way hash" function. The authenticator checks the response against its own calculation of the expected hash value. If the values match, the authentication is acknowledged; otherwise, the connection should be terminated. CHAP provides protection against playback attack through the use of an incrementally changing identifier and a variable challenge value. The use of repeated challenges is intended to limit the time of exposure to any single attack. The authenticator is in control of the frequency and timing of the challenges. This authentication method depends on a "secret" known only to the authenticator and that peer. The secret is not sent over the link. This method clearly defeats the modem playback security issue. Several different encryption methods may be employed to encrypt the username and password pair using the challenge key. Message Digest 5 (MD5) is the most common.

With authentication complete, the NCP negotiation can continue. Typical NCPs implemented are IP Control Protocol (IPCP) for IP and IPX Control Protocol (IPXCP) for Internetwork Packet Exchange (IPX). After the NCP negotiates the Layer 3 information, traffic can flow.

RAS Configuration

A basic configuration for a RAS port that is suitable for a dialer node connecting by either POTS or ISDN is as follows. (This is by no means the only way to do things, but it is a simple and proven method.) Typically, small RAS installations are supported by multiple POTS lines configured in a hunt group by the phone company so that dialer nodes can all be configured with the same access number. As this type of access grows within an enterprise, it is typically replaced with one or more PRI connections serviced by an 800 number to reduce costs.

Example 9-1 shows one way to configure each of the ports on the RAS.

Example 9-1 *RAS Port Configuration*

```
Interface async1
 Encapsulation ppp
 Async mode dedicated
 Ip tcp-compression on
 Ipunnumbered ethernet 0/0
 Async default ip address 10.1.1.1
 Ppp accm match match 000a0000
 Ppp authentication chap
 No ip route-cache
!
username chris password lewis
!
line 1
 txspeed 115200
 rxspeed 115200
 flowcontrol hardware
!
async-bootp dns-server 10.2.1.1
```

There are three sections to the relevant configuration commands for each async port: the asynchronous port configuration, the authentication username and password, and the line speed communication.

Clearly, the first line specifies PPP encapsulation. The second line places the port in dedicated mode (it can also be placed in interactive mode). Placing the port in interactive mode can be perceived as a security risk, because it presents the user with a prompt, which lets the user input a username and password.

The third line specifies the use of Van Jacobsen header compression. This is on by default, but it is good practice to ensure that it is enabled in the configuration in case it has been inadvertently turned off.

The **async default ip address** command defines the IP address that will be given to nodes dialing in and connecting to this port. The next line refers to the Asynchronous Control Character map. This is a configuration that tells the port to ignore certain control characters within the data stream. This is useful if you want to tell the port not to react to X/ON and

X/OFF signals within the data stream. The map given here defines the setting to ignore these well-known flow control signals.

CHAP is specified as the authentication method, and the interface is configured to do a lookup for each packet being sent so as not to have traffic coming from a high-speed LAN overrun the slow-speed async line with the **no ip route-cache** command. The next section identifies the username and password, with the line section specifying the line transmission features. The speed specified is the asynchronous data rate between the modem and the router port. It does not relate to the model train speed over the dialup link. The train speed is normally less than 56 kbps, depending on link quality. V.42b is used to detect common sequences of bits and create a dictionary of codes that represent larger sequences of these commonly transferred bits. By this means of using a short code to represent a longer string of data, V.42b modems can sustain transfer rates above 56 kbps, but it depends on the data constructs being transferred.

Finally, the Domain Name System (DNS) server for async clients is identified in the configuration.

As shown, there are many ways to configure this operation. The "References" section at the end of this chapter provides a link to a more scalable option that uses the interface group-async feature that simplifies configuration. It clones configurations between async ports and local pools of addresses to assign to incoming dialer nodes. As you examine ways a service provider can take some of the burden off the enterprise network through VPN services, ensure that the components are supported.

Dial Access via L2TP

This section covers the operation of L2TP-based services offered to enterprises. Enterprises should not have to maintain RASs, dial-in lines, and banks of modems themselves, especially when service providers already have existing equipment deployed and support staff that can take the burden of maintaining, upgrading, and supporting that environment.

Before L2TP-based dial solutions, enterprises had to provide a central RAS with a toll or 800 number or distribute RAS geographically throughout their network and face the burden of remote support for those devices. Now with L2TP, client software can be provided to enterprise users that gives them a local access number to call within most locations in the U.S. or international access points of presence (PoPs). So the users actually dial in to a service provider-maintained bank of modems. The dialed connection is then transported over the service provider infrastructure to the enterprise.

This is a straightforward concept, but some consideration needs to be given to authentication, adding new users, and so on. Additionally, if the enterprise is taking a Multiprotocol Label Switching (MPLS) VPN service from the provider, you have to decide whether the provider delivers these dial-in user connections via a separate link to the enterprise or uses intelligence within the network to place the user in the enterprise VRF and therefore does not require a separate connection to the enterprise network for remote-access users.

L2TP Components

There are several enabling component terms to define when a service provider delivers local dialup access numbers to an enterprise user base and then transports those dial-in user connections to the enterprise head office.

The L2TP terms L2TP Access Concentrator (LAC) and L2TP Network Server (LNS) are shown in Figure 9-1.

Figure 9-1 *L2TP Components*

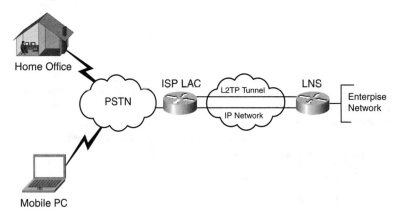

The LAC is the device that remote users dial in to. The LAC's role is to accept the incoming call and tunnel it over the packet network to the LNS at the enterprise where the determination of call completion or termination is made.

LNS is the server side of the L2TP process. It resides on the enterprise LAN and terminates both the L2TP tunnel from the LAC and the PPP sessions from the PCs dialing the LAC.

L2TP functionality is associated with Virtual Private Dialup Network (VPDN). Almost all of the operation should be transparent to the enterprise. However, it is valuable for the enterprise network manager to understand the service being purchased and the issues to consider when interfacing with the service provider.

L2TP Call Procedure

Understanding the call procedure is important when troubleshooting dialup issues, so you must know what the responsibility of the enterprise-provided equipment is, as well as what the responsibility of the provider equipment is. This is also useful when deciding whether you want the direct kind of VPDN deployment that terminates into an LNS on the enterprise premises or a service that terminates the remote users into your VRF in the provider network.

The call procedure starts with a PC using PPP to dial the LAC. Throughout the process, the PC is completely unaware that it is communicating with a VPDN system (other than the fact that it will use a domain name in the user ID). As soon as the call is placed, the first step the LAC takes is to challenge the PC, which responds with an e-mail address, such as lewis@enterprise.com. This e-mail address identifies the user and the domain name the user belongs to. At this stage, the LAC sees the domain name, which indicates to the LAC that this is a VPDN user. It then searches for an existing L2TP tunnel to enterprise.com. If none exists, one is created.

The primary concern from the enterprise perspective is that of username administration. It is clearly undesirable from both the enterprise and provider viewpoints to have the username list administered by the provider. Fortunately, this is not necessary. The service provider equipment can be configured to authenticate usernames against a RADIUS server administered by the enterprise. Configurations for this are given in the RADIUS reference at the end of this chapter. In this setup, the provider equipment is responsible for only identifying the domain name and then forwarding the authorization request to the appropriate RADIUS server for the domain name. The only additional concerns from the enterprise perspective are that the RADIUS server authenticating these user names must be both accessible from the provider network and secure from unauthorized users. The issue of securing an enterprise network from an attached provider network is addressed in Chapter 7.

L2TP is suitable not only for extending enterprise remote-access connectivity over a provider infrastructure. It also lets providers extend the reach of their networks over the infrastructure of other providers in the same manner. In fact, it is normal to see the same set of dialup numbers for a given location appear in the dial options from many different providers, because many have agreements to offer their dial services through other providers.

Connecting L2TP Solutions to VRFs

So far, the L2TP solutions presented require a separate connection (either logical or physical) between the provider and the enterprise to support remote users. The enterprise infrastructure can be further simplified by reducing this to a single connection if the provider takes on the burden of placing these remote-access users in the enterprise VRF within its network.

However, this introduces an additional level of complexity to the provider network operation. The complexity comes in terms of how a remote-access user is identified and placed within the VRF assigned to the enterprise by the provider.

From the perspective of the provider network, a remote user can connect anywhere in the network. The user needs to be authenticated and assigned an IP address for access to the enterprise network and to be transported from wherever he or she connects to the provider network to the enterprise.

Cisco has designed, tested, and deployed solutions that support this type of functionality for dialup, DSL, and cable users. The dialup and DSL solutions are quite similar. The cable solution leverages the Data over Cable Service Interface Specification (DOCSIS) standard to simplify VPN association.

Figure 9-2 shows the general architecture of service deployment for remote access to the MPLS VPN.

Figure 9-2   *MPLS VPN Remote-Access Architecture*

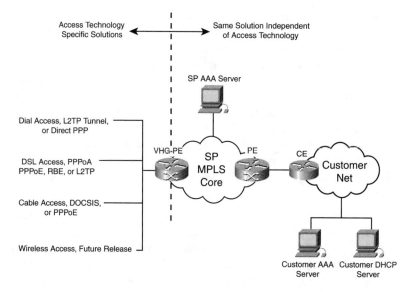

To better understand this architecture, you must first understand its components. The terms and definitions are as follows:

- **Home gateway (HG)**—A device that is owned and managed by a customer (enterprise network or Internet service provider [ISP]) to provide LNS functionality to remote-access users. In Figure 9-2, this is virtualized on the Virtual Home Gateway provider edge (VHG-PE), so the provider is offering an HG per customer on its PE.

- **Resource Pool Manager Server (RPMS)**—Provides an alternative method for a network access server (NAS) to acquire L2TP tunneling information for incoming PPP sessions. The RPMS can be configured to

  - Maintain all tunneling information (RADIUS servers no longer need to maintain such records)

  - Request tunneling information from RADIUS on behalf of the NASs

- **Virtual Home Gateway (VHG)**—LNS-owned and managed by the service provider on behalf of its customer to provide access to remote users of that customer's network. A single service provider device (router) may host multiple VHGs from different customers. A VHG may be dynamically brought up and down based on the access pattern of the remote users.

- **POP**—A protocol for servers that receive, store, and transmit e-mail.

- **PPP**—A protocol that provides router-to-router and host-to-network connections.

- **PPP over Ethernet (PPPoE)**—Providers prefer PPPoE because it lets them keep the billing and authorization mechanisms built in to their systems and deliver Ethernet service to a PC.

- **PPP over ATM (PPPoA)**—Used within the provider network to allow PPP to be transported over ATM infrastructure.

- **Routed Bridge Encapsulation (RBE)**—As defined in http://www.ietf.org/rfc/rfc1483.txt?number=1483 and superseded by http://www.ietf.org/rfc/rfc2684.txt?number=2684.

- **Service Selection Gateway (SSG)**—A Cisco IOS feature that permits remote users to select services using a web-based interface.

- **Service Selection Dashboard (SSD)**—A specialized web server that allows users to log on to and disconnect from specific services through a standard web browser.

- **Service identifier (SID)**—DOCSIS 1.0 has one SID per cable modem/router.

The VHG-PE is where the mapping and intelligence to take a remote-access user to the correct enterprise reside. With this architecture, the provider may elect to configure a number of different options, all of which should be transparent to the enterprise user:

- **Dial access**—L2TP tunnel or direct PPP

- **DSL access**—PPPoA, PPPoE, RBE, or L2TP

- **Cable access**—DOCSIS or PPPoE

Take a closer look at this dial case by examining the setup shown in Figure 9-3.

Figure 9-3 *End-to-End Architecture for Remote Access over an MPLS Service*

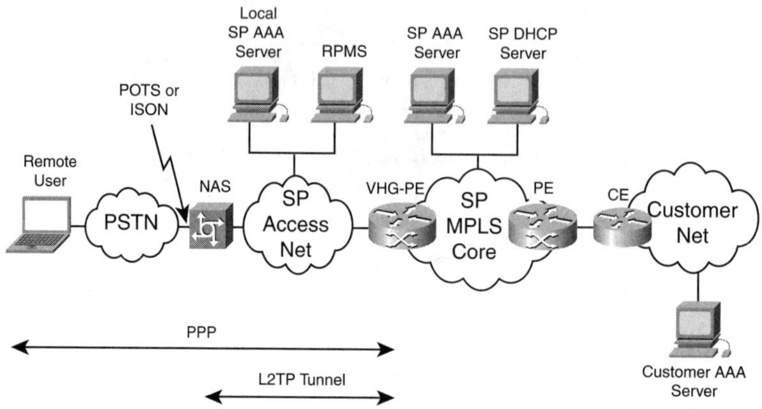

The following lists one possible sequence of events that must occur for a remote-access dial user to become part of its corporation's VPN:

1 The remote user initiates a PPP connection to the NAS using POTS or ISDN from his or her PC or remote router.

2 NAS accepts the connection, and a PPP link is established.

3 The NAS partially authenticates the user with PAP or CHAP. The domain name or dialed number identification service (DNIS) is used to determine whether the user is a VPN client. The NAS may resort directly to an authentication, authorization, and accounting (AAA) server to determine if the user is a VPN client. Alternatively, the NAS may query the RPMS for the tunneling information. If the user is not a VPN client (he or she is also using the service provider as an ISP), authentication continues on the NAS. If the user is a VPN client, the AAA server returns the address of a VHG-PE.

4 If an L2TP tunnel does not already exist, the NAS (LAC) initiates a tunnel to the VHG-PE (LNS). The NAS and the VHG-PE authenticate each other before any sessions are attempted within a tunnel. It is also possible for a VHG-PE to accept tunnel creation without any tunnel authentication of the NAS.

5 As soon as the tunnel exists, a session within the tunnel is created for the remote user, and the PPP connection is extended to terminate on the VHG-PE.

6 The NAS propagates all available PPP information (the LCP-negotiated options and the partially authenticated PAP/CHAP information) to the VHG-PE.

7 The VHG-PE associates the remote user with a specific customer MPLS VPN. The VPN's VRF (routing table and other information associated with a specific VPN) has already been instantiated on the VHG/PE.

8   The VHG-PE completes the remote user's authentication.

9   The VHG-PE obtains an IP address for the remote user.

The remote user is now part of the customer VPN. Packets can flow to and from the remote user.

The key issue for the enterprise to consider with this type of solution is maintaining the list of usernames requiring authentication and address pool management for the remote users to gain access to enterprise network resources.

A PE assigns addresses to remote users using local address pools, the service provider's RADIUS server, or the SP's DHCP server:

- **Local address pools**—With the "overlapping local address pools" features, the VHG-PE can associate a local pool with a specific VRF. Overlapping address pools are required because it is anticipated that multiple enterprises will use the same internal addressing number ranges.

- **Service provider's RADIUS server**—The SP-managed RADIUS server should be able to maintain overlapping address pools. It should have a separate pool per (VPN, VHG-PE) pair. The VHG/PE is identified by either the NAS-IP-Address attribute or by the NAS-Identifier attribute in the Access-Request. The enterprise's concern here is how the provider will reclaim IP address space as soon as it is no longer being used by a dial user. Specifically, it needs to know by which mechanism this is accomplished and by which event or amount of time is necessary for a previously used IP address to become available again. This is of interest for sizing the pools of addresses used by dial users. Clearly, if addresses can be reclaimed only once per day, more addresses need to be included in the pool than if addresses are made available within seconds of a dial user's terminating its session.

- **SP DHCP server**—This is supported either by DHCP servers that support per-VPN attributes or by a DHCP server per-enterprise customer.

DSL Considerations

Figure 9-4 shows the specifics of a DSL architecture using L2TP with DSL access.

Figure 9-4 *Architecture Incorporating PPPoE and PPPoA*

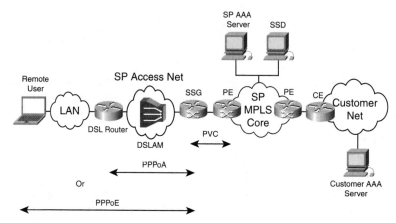

Incoming PPP over *X* (PPPo*X*) sessions, arriving at the LAC, are L2TP-tunneled to the VHG-PE that maps them to the corresponding VRF. The advantage of this solution for the provider is the ability to provide enhanced aggregation and route summarization at the edge of the MPLS VPN core. This solution is very similar to the dial RA in L2TP to MPLS VPN solution shown in Figure 9-3.

The following events occur when the remote user creates a PPPo*X* session over DSL in an attempt to access its corporate network or ISP (the customer network, as shown in Figure 9-4):

1 The remote user initiates a PPPoE session or the DSL router initiates a PPPoA session over the DSL access network.

2 The LAC accepts the PPPo*X* session.

3 The LAC partially authenticates the remote user with PAP or CHAP. The domain name is used to determine whether the user is a VPN client. The LAC queries an AAA server to determine if the user is a VPN client. If the user is not a VPN client (he or she is also using the DSL service provider as an ISP), authentication continues on the LAC. If the user is a VPN client, the AAA server returns the address of a VHG-PE and other L2TP tunnel information to the LAC.

4 If an L2TP tunnel does not already exist, the LAC initiates a tunnel to the VHG-PE (LNS).

5 As soon as the tunnel exists, a session within the tunnel is created for the remote user, and the PPP session is extended to terminate on the VHG-PE.

6 The LAC propagates all available PPP information (the LCP-negotiated options and the partially authenticated PAP/CHAP information) to the VHG-PE.

7 The VHG-PE associates the remote user with a specific customer MPLS VPN. The VPN's VRF (routing table and other information associated with a specific VPN) has already been preinstantiated on the VHG-PE.

8 The VHG-PE completes the remote user's authentication.

Cable Considerations

Figure 9-5 shows the components of a system to map cable users to specific VPNs.

Figure 9-5   *Architecture for Cable Remote Access*

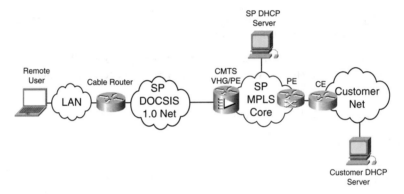

In DOCSIS 1.0, all traffic from a given cable router (or cable modem) carries the same SID. On the cable modem termination system (CMTS) VHG-PE, all traffic with the same SID value terminates on the same subinterface. At the CMTS VHG-PE, the subinterface is statically configured to map all traffic to a specific VRF. As a result, traffic from all customer premises equipment (CPE) behind a given cable router is mapped to the same VPN. This solution has no domain name-based remote user authorization or authentication. Address assignment is DHCP-based. Accounting is based on NetFlow.

The initial focus of cable solutions was to offer open access to ISPs, but using cable solutions to offer enterprise VPNs is entirely possible. A remote user can access a special web page and request to change his or her ISP/VPN. For such a change to take effect, both the cable router/modem and the PCs behind it must be reset, and SID-to-VRF mapping on the CMTS VHG-PE must be changed.

IPsec Access

Many enterprise managers decide to trust a provider's private VPN to securely transport their data, but they do not trust access networks that are open to any residence gaining network access. A common solution is to protect remote-access users with IPsec encryption over untrusted access networks. The enterprise manager must then decide whether the enterprise or provider network will manage the IPsec infrastructure.

With the release of the Cisco remote access-to-MPLS network solution, providers can offer a managed service whereby the provider manages all the IPsec infrastructure and delivers remote-access users to the corporation's VPN VRF.

The advantage here is that the access medium does not matter. Typically any access medium can be used as long as the user has connectivity to the Internet (or some other means of connecting it to the provider's network-based IPsec termination devices) and the provider-supplied VPN can be reached.

The alternative, of course, is to have a separate Internet connection to the enterprise and to manage the IPsec infrastructure from within the enterprise.

IPsec tunnels need not only be terminated into Layer 3 (L3) VPN VRFs for VPN remote access. There is no reason why IPsec tunnels cannot be terminated into Layer 2 (L2) VPN instances also.

Figure 9-6 shows the basic architectural components of this solution.

Figure 9-6   *IPsec-to-MPLS Access Architecture*

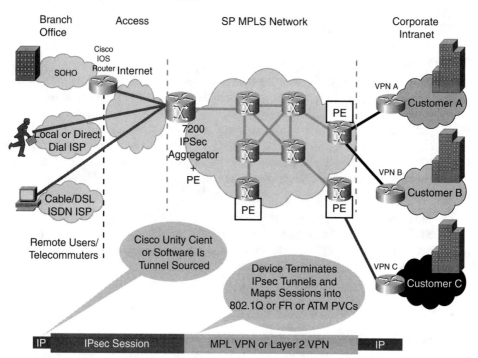

The goal is to take the IPsec tunnels connecting remote users (and possibly remote sites, too) into the VPN. The primary security services provided by IPsec are authentication, data integrity, and data confidentiality. Typically, only encryption or authentication are available. The most common deployments use encryption, which requires hardware acceleration within the IPsec terminating device to avoid performance issues.

An IPsec tunnel may directly encapsulate data traffic that is being sent between the two IPsec nodes, or it may encrypt all data flowing through other kinds of tunnels, such as L2TP, generic routing encapsulation (GRE), and IP-in-IP.

IPsec operates in two modes: transport and tunnel.

Transport mode protects the payload of an IP datagram. It is implemented by the insertion of a security protocol header (authentication header [AH] and/or Encapsulating Security Payload [ESP]) between the original IP datagram's header and its payload. Then, the appropriate cryptographic functions are performed. The "next protocol" in the IP header will be either AH or ESP, as appropriate. Transport mode can be set only for packets sourced by and destined for the IPsec endpoints (for example, an L2TP or GRE tunnel), meaning that the original IP header is preserved.

Tunnel mode fully encapsulates the original datagram with a new IP header, along with the appropriate AH and/or ESP headers. The original datagram is fully protected, including the original source and destination IP addresses.

NOTE   An IPsec tunnel, even one set up for tunnel mode, is not the same thing as a Cisco IOS tunnel interface. In Cisco IOS, IPsec is treated as a sequential function in the context of the physical and/or tunnel interface, conceptually similar to access control list (ACL) processing. A crypto map specifies the desired handling of packets—whether IPsec should protect them. Each packet that is sent out an interface is checked against the crypto map. The crypto map determines if the packet is to be protected, how to protect it, and the peer crypto endpoint.

Because IPsec packets are targeted directly at the IPsec endpoint, any of these packets targeted at the router that specifies a next protocol field of AH or ESP are sent to IPsec. The decapsulated packet is then handled as a regular IP packet.

During initial Internet Security Association and Key Management Protocol (ISAKMP) key exchange, extended authentication (XAUTH) extensions to ISAKMP may be used to allow the use of a RADIUS or other AAA server for authenticating the remote system.

ISAKMP may also use the mode configuration (MODECFG) extensions to set the IP address of the "inside" IP header when creating a tunnel mode IPsec tunnel. This address is (currently) taken from a single pool of addresses assigned to the router. This allows the client to be known to the internal network by a local address, instead of by a dynamically assigned address from a local ISP. When ISAKMP assigns an inside address to the client, it also installs a host route into the IP routing table so that the router can correctly route traffic to the interface supporting the IPsec endpoint.

Of course, should IPsec be deployed for a remote site, to bring that site into the enterprise VRF, it is expected that routing updates will be necessary between the device initiating the IPsec tunnel (the enterprise edge) and the terminating device (the provider edge device). This lets routing updates from the customer edge (CE) be tagged with the enterprise route distinguisher and imported to the provider's multiprotocol BGP (MP-BGP) and delivered to other remote sites.

IPsec does not support multicast or broadcast traffic. Therefore, transporting routing protocol updates from the enterprise to the provider edge requires a GRE overlay on the enterprise edge box. Conceivably, L2TP tunneling could be used, but this is not common. As soon as routing protocol updates are encapsulated within GRE, IPsec treats them just like any other unicast packet and encrypts them across the untrusted network. The issue of GRE tunnel creation is then decided by whether the enterprise edge box is managed by the provider or enterprise. Clearly, if the enterprise's goal is to outsource the management of the IPsec infrastructure and WAN connectivity, using a provider-managed enterprise edge box achieves the goal. This restricts the enterprise to relying on services, such as Cisco IOS upgrades for the edge device on the customer network, being operated on the provider's schedule. An upgrade schedule might need to be part of a service agreement if complete outsourcing is desired.

The challenge with this deployment scenario is for remote sites that can get access to the corporate network only through the Internet, and the enterprise wants to supply the CPE. This would require a compatible IPsec and GRE configuration to work with the provider's configuration, which would, of course, be a challenge to troubleshoot from both the enterprise and provider perspective. If the enterprise wants to manage its own GRE and IPsec implementation at the remote CPE, see the "GRE + IPsec" subsection of the "References" section for configuration examples for a deployment scenario including Network Address Translation (NAT). A simpler description is given in the next section to illustrate the use of GRE on the CPE not only for transport of nonunicast packets, but for resiliency, too.

GRE + IPsec on the CPE

IPsec is often configured in tunnel mode. However, doing so does not give you the benefits of other tunnel technologies, such as GRE and L2TP. Currently, no IPsec tunnel interfaces exist. The tunnel configuration of IPsec really just refers to the encapsulation. IPsec tunnels carry only unicast packets; they have no end-to-end interface management protocol. The approach here is to use IPsec in transport mode on top of a robust tunnel technology, such as GRE.

For VPN resilience, the remote site should be configured with two GRE tunnels—one to the primary headend VPN router and the other to the backup VPN router, as shown in Figure 9-7.

Figure 9-7   *VPN Resilience over Two Tunnels*

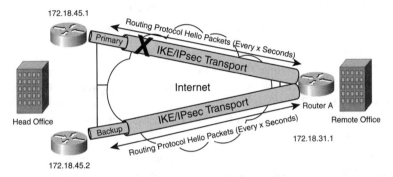

Both GRE tunnels are secured with IPsec. Each one has its own Internet Key Exchange (IKE) security association (SA) and a pair of IPsec SAs. Because GRE can carry multicast and broadcast traffic, it is possible and very desirable to configure a routing protocol for these virtual links. As soon as a routing protocol is configured, the failover mechanism comes automatically. The hello/keepalive packets sent by the routing protocol over the GRE tunnels provide a mechanism to detect loss of connectivity. In other words, if the primary GRE tunnel is lost, the remote site detect this event by the loss of the routing protocol hello packets.

It is conceded that relying on routing protocol hello packets to detect loss of connectivity can be slow, depending on the value of the timers used for hellos, but it is certainly a step up from having no detection. In the not-too-distant future, mechanisms such as Bidirectional Forwarding Detection (BFD) (http://www.ietf.org/internet-drafts/draft-katz-ward-bfd-02.txt) will enable faster detection of failed tunnels without the need to rely on routing protocol hello mechanisms.

As soon as virtual-link loss is detected, the routing protocol chooses the next-best route. Thus, Enhanced Interior Gateway Routing Protocol (EIGRP) chooses the feasible successor. In this case, the backup GRE tunnel is chosen. Because the backup GRE tunnel is already up and secured, the failover time is determined by the hello packet mechanism and the convergence time of the routing protocol.

Designing for GRE Resiliency

As just discussed, using GRE tunnels with IPsec in transport mode can provide a robust resiliency mechanism for hub-and-spoke connections. Network designers should be aware of the main issues to consider when using this feature:

- Cisco IOS configuration manageability for the headend router
- Overhead on the network and the router processor
- Scalability

In the case of the enterprise's using the provider network to terminate IPsec sessions into the enterprise VRF, the headend router is managed and owned by the provider, and potentially the CPE devices, too. In the case where the enterprise chooses to have a second connection for remote-access off-net users, the headend router is owned and managed by the enterprise.

In the resiliency design discussed, the GRE tunnels have a virtual interface as part of the Cisco IOS implementation and provide many of the features associated with physical interfaces. This is good, except when the headend router connects to thousands of remote sites.

Each headend router must have at least two GREs (one primary and one backup) for each remote site that terminates there. This could mean hundreds or even thousands of interfaces to configure (five lines in the configuration file for each interface) and manage for each router. There are no specific management tools for this type of configuration except for the Resource Manager Essentials (RME) product that is part of CiscoWorks. This management is a concern. You should think it through before implementation.

The benefits of implementing GRE tunnels for routing protocol update support and resiliency do come with some cost. GRE adds 24 bytes of overhead to each packet. However, when this is added to the bytes produced in IPsec transport mode and compared to the bytes increased by IPsec in tunnel mode, the network penalty of the GRE mechanism is only 4 bytes per packet. In addition to network overhead, GRE adds overhead to the processor. Performance testing on a 7200 router with NPE-G1 has shown that 1000 GRE tunnels add 10 to 16 percent of overhead to the CPU compared to running the same traffic over a serial interface. This overhead is associated with the extra network-level encapsulation and the extra routing decisions.

However, you can expect a GRE tunnel implementation to provide better scalability and performance than IPsec tunnels alone. This is because Cisco IOS routers are optimized for making routing decisions as opposed to making decisions about which IPsec SAs need to be used at the one physical interface.

Configuring GRE Resiliency

The configuration for router A that is shown in Figure 9-7 is listed in Example 9-2. It is simple to find the meaning of each command-line configuration on Cisco.com using the search facility.

Example 9-2 *Remote Office Router Configuration*

```
crypto isakmp policy 10
authentication pre-share
!
!
crypto isakmp key cisco123 address 172.18.45.1
crypto isakmp key cisco123 address 172.18.45.2
!
!
crypto IPSec transform-set one esp-des esp-md5-hmac
 mode transport
!
!
crypto map gre 10 IPSec-isakmp
 set peer 172.18.45.1
 set transform-set one
 match address gre1
 crypto map gre 20 IPSec-isakmp
 set peer 172.18.45.2
 set transform-set one
 match address gre2
!
!
interface Tunnel0
 ip address 10.4.1.1 255.255.255.0
 tunnel source 172.18.31.1
 tunnel destination 172.18.45.1
 crypto map gre
!
!
interface Tunnel1
 ip address 10.4.2.1 255.255.255.0
 tunnel source 172.18.31.1
 tunnel destination 172.18.45.2
 crypto map gre
!
!
interface Ethernet0
 ip address 10.2.1.1 255.255.255.0
!
interface Serial0
 ip address 172.18.31.1 255.255.255.0
 crypto map gre
!
interface Serial1
 no ip address
 shutdown
```

continues

Example 9-2   *Remote Office Router Configuration (Continued)*

```
!
ip classless
ip route 172.18.0.0 255.255.0.0 serial0
ip eigrp 100
 network 10.0.0.0
!
!
ip access-list extended gre1
 permit gre host 172.18.31.1 host 172.18.45.1
!
ip access-list extended gre2
 permit gre host 172.18.31.1 host 172.18.45.2
```

CE-to-CE IPsec

Alternative approaches to MPLS VPN solutions by service providers have been deployed for supporting L3 VPNs. Some providers offer secure any-to-any communication by installing a CPE router that is IPsec-enabled and configuring a full mesh of IPsec tunnels between all the VPN's sites. From the enterprise perspective, this provides a service similar to MPLS VPNs, in that the enterprise edge router sees a single provider router as its IP next-hop destination for all other sites. In addition, the connectivity seen by the enterprise edge is seen as any-to-any communication.

The downside is provisioning a full mesh at the CPE. Its maintenance can result in large configuration files, and additional CPU is needed to support IPsec operations. However, all these things are the service provider's concern. They aren't management issues for the enterprise. To help scale these implementations, it has become common practice to use IPsec purely as a tunneling technology and not to encrypt data.

Where the issue of providing IPsec encryption has become an area of concern for the enterprise is when the enterprise must, for regulatory or other security issues, encrypt its own data before handing it to a third party. In fact, it can be argued that if an enterprise cares enough about security to want IPsec encryption, it should care enough to manage its own IPsec infrastructure, because handing that off to a third party does not secure the data from that third party.

Looking at the case where the enterprise decides it needs to encrypt data before handing it off from its own infrastructure, the first concern is how to set up all the SAs—whether a full-mesh, partial-mesh, or hub-and-spoke topology is required. If the enterprise decides that the benefits of Layer 3 IP VPNs previously described are what it wants, but it also requires IPsec encryption, an issue needs to be addressed. One of the primary benefits of L3 VPNs is the ability to add a site to the VPN and make that a local matter between the enterprise edge and provider edge connecting to that enterprise router. The mechanics of the L3 VPN then propagate that information to where it needs to go. Any-to-any communication is provided without any configuration overhead on the part of the enterprise. If this needs to have an overlay of IPsec tunnels created for encryption, the enterprise is right back to the issue of having to decide between site-to-site topology and maintaining a full mesh of tunnels itself, which thereby negates the benefits of L3 VPN.

For these situations, a solution is required that supports dynamic creation of IPsec tunnels on demand and minimizes the amount of configuration needed to create IPsec associations on the CE device. In addition, by making the IPsec relationships on-demand and as-needed, you ease the scaling issues related to the numbers of SAs to be created.

Cisco provides a solution that meets these goals—Dynamic Multipoint VPN (DMVPN). This solution can be used to support a dynamic IPsec overlay for an enterprise that requires IPsec encryption on top of a provider-provisioned L3 VPN. It also can provide simple any-to-any communication for off-net sites of its intranet. Further details appear in the next section.

DMVPN Overview

DMVPN started as a way to help scale the deployment of very large IPsec networks. The primary topology for IPsec deployments was hub and spoke. This had some advantages in that the only sites that needed a provisioning action when a new site was added were the new spoke and the hub site itself. However, this could result in unwieldy hub configurations and extra work to make dynamic routing protocols behave as desired. Also, any spoke-to-spoke traffic would likely follow a suboptimal route via the hub. Full mesh was sometimes considered because it provides optimal routing. However, it adds more restrictions to deployment. All nodes require a provisioning action to add a single node, unwieldy configurations are required on all nodes, and the many logical interfaces stress Interior Gateway Protocol (IGP) operation on spoke routers and the available memory/CPU, limiting the size of the VPN with small routers at the spokes.

DMVPN was created to resolve most of these issues. It had the following goals:

- Reduce the preconfiguration in a spoke that is necessary to bring it into service to knowledge of a single hub site.
- Support any-to-any IPsec relationships on an as-needed basis.
- Automatically add new sites to the dynamic full mesh without any manual configuration of existing sites.
- Support routers with small amounts of memory and CPU at the spoke, allowing them to participate in very large VPNs.

Achieving these goals requires autodiscovery, mapping peers to each other, and dynamic authentication. For mapping peers, you must consider mapping an IP infrastructure address to a VPN layer address. The VPN layer address can be thought of as the endpoints that exist in the CE routers at the end of each IPsec tunnel. The IP infrastructure addresses are the addresses that exist in the IP network connecting the two CE router endpoints.

There are two ways of providing the required mapping in a dynamic fashion. The first is Tunnel Endpoint Discovery (TED). TED uses a discovery probe, sent from the initiator, to determine which IPsec peer is responsible for a specific host or subnet. After the address of that peer is learned, the initiator proceeds with IKE main mode in the normal way. For TED to function, each LAN must have Internet-routable IP addresses, but this is often not the case. If a private IP address space is used, such as the 10.0.0.0 network, the TED probes cannot locate the other VPN peer across the Internet.

The other option is to use Next-Hop Resolution Protocol (NHRP), which also supports the use of multipoint GRE (mGRE) to encapsulate routing protocol traffic for transmission over the IPsec tunnel. mGRE is discussed in more detail in the next section.

Before we look at how these technologies work together to enable DMVPN functionality, it is useful to have an overall view of what happens within the DMVPN. Each DMVPN site is preconfigured with the address of a hub site. This is the only VPN-specific address or SA configuration in the CE router before it is provisioned. With this configuration, a permanent IPsec tunnel to the hub is created that acts as a routing neighbor and next-hop server (NHS). Each spoke CE router registers itself with the hub, and all control data (routing protocol exchanges) flows through encrypted tunnels to the hub. However, via the operation of NHRP, spoke CE routers can query the hub site for the address of other spoke routers belonging to the same VPN and dynamically build IPsec tunnels directly from spoke to spoke. Basically, the spoke asks the hub router for the Internet-routable IP address it needs to build a tunnel to for a specific inside address it needs to tunnel and route a packet for. As soon as this dynamic spoke-to-spoke tunnel is available, spoke-to-spoke traffic has no impact on the hub site. The spoke-to-spoke tunnel is created via the mGRE tunnel interface (one per CE). Detailed and complete device configurations can be obtained from the link listed in the "References" section for DMVPN and therefore, are not replicated here. However, the following sections briefly explain the configuration elements for completeness.

mGRE for Tunneling

The only difference between multipoint GRE and regular GRE is that the destination end of the tunnel does not check the source address. This makes mGRE operate as a multipoint-to-point technology, meaning that any source can send to a specific destination. This functionality is useful in two contexts. First, if DMVPN is being used just to simplify the configuration and deployment of a hub-and-spoke topology, or indeed for a migration phase from hub and spoke to full DMVPN, the hub site has an mGRE tunnel, whereas the spokes have point-to-point GRE. For dynamic spoke-to-spoke communication, the spokes also require their tunnel interfaces to be mGRE.

To modify a tunnel interface at the hub to use mGRE, the commands shown in Example 9-3 are entered under the tunnel interface.

Example 9-3 *Configuration for mGRE*

```
interface Tunnel0
        Tunnel mode gre multipoint
        Tunnel key 100000
```

The tunnel key needs to be the same on all the spokes that want to communicate with this hub.

NHRP for Address Resolution

Nonbroadcast multiaccess (NBMA) NHRP is specified in http://www.ietf.org/rfc/rfc2332.txt?number=2332. It is designed to resolve IP-to-NBMA address mappings for routers directly connected to an NBMA. In this case, the mesh of tunnels of an IPsec VPN exhibits behavior similar to an NBMA, such as Frame Relay. The result of NHRP operation in this case is that a shortcut route is identified for a spoke to contact a spoke directly, without needing to communicate with the hub in the data path first. However, note that data packets do flow via the hub site until the spoke-to-spoke connection becomes available.

To make NHRP operational, the hub site is configured as the NHS, and the spoke sites are configured as next-hop clients.

On the hub sites, the configuration looks like the configuration shown in Example 9-4 under the tunnel interface.

Example 9-4 *NHRP Hub Configuration*

```
ip nhrp authentication test
ip nhrp map multicast dynamic
ip nhrp network-id 100000
ip nhrp holdtime 360
```

The **ip nhrp authentication test** command, along with the **ip nhrp network-id** command and the matching **tunnel key** entry, are used to map the tunnel packets and the NHRP packets to the correct multipoint GRE tunnel interface. The **ip nhrp map multicast dynamic** command lets NHRP automatically add spoke routers to multicast NHRP mappings when spoke routers initiate the mGRE + IPsec tunnel to register unicast NHRP mappings. This allows dynamic routing protocols to work over the mGRE + IPsec tunnels between the hub and spokes. Without this command, the hub router would need to have a separate configuration line for a multicast mapping to each spoke.

For the spokes, the NHRP configuration is basically the same, with the addition of the two configuration lines shown in Example 9-5.

Example 9-5 *NHRP Spoke Configuration*

```
ip nhrp map 10.0.0.1 172.17.0.1
ip nhrp nhs 10.0.0.1
```

Routing Protocol Concerns

The primary issue here is that the hub is still the central point of collection and distribution for control data, such as routing protocol updates. It is important to configure the hub to not identify itself as the IP next hop for the routes it receives from spokes and sends out to other spokes. This is achieved for EIGRP with the configuration command **no ip next-hop-self eigrp 1** that is inserted in the tunnel interface's configuration.

This has the effect of the hub advertising routes with the original IP next hop from the update received from the spoke again.

In addition, the **no ip split-horizon eigrp 1** command must be entered to allow an EIGRP hub to send received updates out the same tunnel interface and update spokes with each other's routes.

For Routing Information Protocol (RIP), you must turn off split horizon on the mGRE tunnel interface on the hub. Otherwise, no routes learned via that tunnel interface will be advertised back out. The **no ip split-horizon** command under the mGRE tunnel interface section achieves this behavior for RIP. No other changes are necessary. RIP automatically uses the original IP next hop on routes that it advertises back out the same interface where it learned these routes.

Open Shortest Path First (OSPF) has no split-horizon rules because it is a link-state protocol. However, adjustments are necessary in terms of network type and support for multicast or unicast hello transmission.

Given that the mGRE tunnel interface being configured is a multipoint interface, the normal OSPF network type is multipoint. However, this causes OSPF to add host routes to the routing table on the spoke routers. These host routes cause packets destined for networks behind other spoke routers to be forwarded via the hub, rather than forwarded directly to the other spoke. The resolution is to configure the **ip ospf network broadcast** command under the tunnel interface.

You also need to make sure that the hub router will be the designated router (DR) for the IPsec + mGRE network. You do this by setting the OSPF priority to greater than 1 on the hub (because 1 is the default priority). However, a better solution is often to reduce all the spokes to priority 0, because this prevents the spokes from ever becoming a designated router.

> Hub: **ip ospf priority 2**
> Spoke: **ip ospf priority 0**

Given the two-level hierarchy of VPN address and infrastructure address, resolved together in this case by the NHRP, the routing tables for both the hub and spokes are worth examining.

In the routing table for a DMVPN system, the infrastructure addresses (those that identify the physical interfaces on the public infrastructure) become known via the physical interface that connects the spoke to the public infrastructure. Other addresses are learned via tunnel interfaces. All destinations appear reachable by the single multipoint GRE tunnel interface. The multipoint GRE tunnel interface does not actually go anywhere by itself. It can be thought of as a gateway to access the destinations that IPsec protects. Each spoke creates SAs as needed with the hub site for routing information exchange, and other spoke sites for passing traffic on an as-needed basis.

IPsec Profiles for Data Protection

A full explanation of IPsec operation is not given here. However, references to publicly available documentation on Cisco.com are given at the end of this chapter. In addition, the book *IPSec VPN Design* by Vijay Bollapragada, Mohamed Khalid, and Scott Wainner (ISBN 1587051117, published by Cisco Press) is an excellent reference for this protocol. However, having said that, a brief description is given here of the configuration relevant to IPsec when using the DMVPN solution.

The DMVPN solution directly addresses the following issues with respect to the method of implementing static IPsec for traditional CPE-to-CPE VPN applications:

- To define what traffic is interesting to IPsec and therefore what IPsec encrypts for transport over a VPN connection, ACLs are implemented. So, in the case where a new network is added to a site located behind an IPsec VPN CPE router, that router's ACL configuration must change on both the hub-and-spoke routers to encrypt traffic from that new network or subnetwork. If the CPE is a managed service, the enterprise needs to coordinate with the provider to make this happen, a time-consuming and operationally expensive exercise.

- With large hub-and-spoke networks, the configuration file on the hub can become unwieldy, leading to long boot times and complex troubleshooting procedures. Typically, 200 to 300 sites create a hub configuration of several thousand lines. This is not only troublesome to navigate, but it consumes significant memory resources.

- Should spoke-to-spoke communication be required, such as in voice over IP (VoIP) applications, either inefficient routing via the hub site or an increasing configuration file on the spoke sites to communicate with all other spokes is required. This drives up the size of the CPE router and hence the cost of the overall solution.

Let's take a look at what is configured in the more traditional hub-and-spoke or mesh IPsec VPNs and illustrate how this is dramatically simplified with DMVPN.

Looking at a standard IPsec VPN configured on CPE devices, the following elements are configured on a hub-and-spoke router, as shown in Example 9-6. The only addition on the hub router is that it has a crypto map for each of the peers established.

Example 9-6   *IPsec VPN Configuration*

```
crypto isakmp policy 10
  authentication pre-share
 crypto isakmp key cx3H456 address 0.0.0.0
  !
 crypto IPSecIPSec transform-set trans1 esp-md5-hmac
  mode transport
  !
 crypto map map1 local-address Ethernet0
 crypto map map1 10 IPSecIPSec-isakmp
  set peer 180.20.1.1
  set transform-set trans1
  match address 101
 !
 !
 interface Ethernet0
  ip address 172.17.0.1 255.255.255.0
  crypto map map1
 !
 !
 access-list 101 permit gre host 192.17.0.1 host 180.20.1.1
```

The **crypto isakmp policy 10** command creates an IKE policy with sequence 10. When a
router peers with another IKE device, it negotiates an IKE transform set. During this
negotiation, it checks the peer transform sets according to this sequence number until a
match is found. In this case, the 0.0.0.0 indicates that the same key is used with multiple
destinations. The **authentication pre-share** command dictates that the transform set use
preshared keys for authentication. This is a less scalable solution than using certificates, but
it is simpler in terms of single device configuration and is used here for that simplicity.

The **crypto isakmp key** command identifies the preshared key value for the peer in
question. The **crypto IPSec transform-set** command defines an acceptable combination of
security protocols and encryptions to use. The **crypto map** entries identify the peer, the
transform set to use with that peer, and the ACL that defines which traffic is interesting and
needs to be encrypted. This map is then applied to an interface with another **crypto map**
entry.

The ACL defined only needs to match the GRE tunnel IP packets. No matter how the
networks change at either end, the GRE IP tunnel packets will not change, so this ACL need
not change.

NOTE   When using Cisco IOS Software versions earlier than 12.2(13)T, you must apply the **crypto
map map1** configuration command to both the GRE tunnel interfaces and the physical
interface. With Cisco IOS version 12.2(13)T and later, you apply the **crypto map map1**
configuration command to only the physical interface (in this case, Ethernet0).

With DMVPN implemented, the configuration for both hub and spoke sites transfers to having the global **crypto** entries, plus a single tunnel specification with all the NHRP and tunnel definition elements.

Summary of DMVPN Operation

The following is an overall description of what happens in the DMVPN setup, which is illustrated in Figure 9-8.

Figure 9-8 *Dynamic Multipoint VPN Architecture*

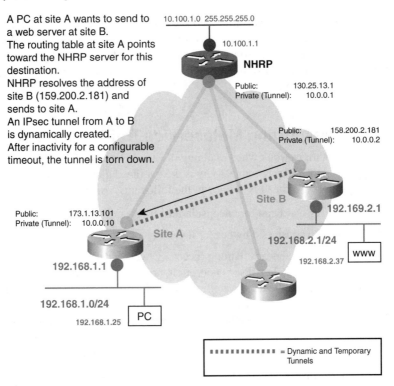

In this case, a PC (192.168.1.25) at site A wants to connect to the web server at 192.168.2.37 that is behind the spoke router at site B. The router at site A consults its routing table and determines that the 192.168.2.0 network (obtained by whatever routing protocol is in effect within the corporation) can be reached via an IP next hop of 10.0.0.2 via the tunnel0 interface. This is the mGRE tunnel interface that gives access to VPN destinations. In this case, you are configuring dynamic spoke-to-spoke communication. The router at site A then looks at the NHRP mapping table and finds that an entry for 10.0.0.2 does not exist. The next step therefore is to request a mapping from the NHS. The

NHS resolves 10.0.0.2 to a public address of 158.200.2.181 and sends that information to the router at site A. On receipt, this information is stored in the NHRP table in site A's router. This event triggers an IPsec tunnel to be created from site A's public address to 158.200.2.181. Now that a tunnel has been built, traffic can pass from site A to site B through the newly created IPsec tunnel.

However, what about return traffic from site B to site A? When the web server wants to send traffic back to the PC, the same steps are necessary to form a mapping from site B to site A, with the slight modification that when site B has the NHRP mapping for site A, the response can be sent directly to site A because a tunnel already exists. After a programmable time, the NHRP entries age out, causing the IPsec tunnel to be torn down.

DMVPN improves the scalability of IPsec deployments. However, not all issues are resolved when you look at it from the provider's point of view that offers this as a managed service. For the managed service offering, a Cisco solution called Dynamic Group VPNs offloads much of the IPsec work from the enterprise network to the provider network in a more scalable fashion.

The Impact of Transporting Multiservice Traffic over IPsec

One issue not to overlook when planning the use of IPsec or GRE tunnel implementations to support remote-access connectivity is the overhead that these technologies place on router systems. Overhead is defined in the following terms:

- Processing overhead for encapsulation, encryption, and fragmentation
- Bandwidth consumed by header layering

Considering first the encapsulation processing overhead, the effect is somewhat dependent on router capabilities. For IPsec encryption, hardware acceleration modules generally are available to mitigate the negative effects on CPU utilization of encrypting payload traffic. The effects of GRE encapsulation and fragmentation, however, are not so easily overcome. Whether GRE is process-switched or switched via Cisco Express Forwarding (CEF) depends on the platform and release implemented. Clearly, process switching can add overhead and delay to router processing, depending on router load.

Another performance effect to consider is fragmentation of oversized frames, primarily due to the addition of an IPsec and GRE header to a maximally sized Ethernet frame. When a packet is nearly the size of the maximum transmission unit (MTU) of the outbound link of the router performing encryption, and it is encapsulated with IPsec headers, it exceeds the MTU of the outbound interface. This causes packet fragmentation after encryption, which means the decrypting router at the other end of the IPsec tunnel has to reassemble in the process path. Prefragmentation for IPsec VPNs increases the decrypting router's performance by allowing it to operate in the high-performance CEF path instead of the process path.

Prefragmentation for IPsec VPNs lets the encrypting router calculate what the IPsec encapsulated frame size will be from information obtained from the transform set (such as ESP header or not, AH header or not). If the result of this calculation finds that the packet will exceed the MTU of the output interface, the packet is fragmented before encryption. The advantage is that this avoids process-level reassembly before decryption, which helps improve decryption performance and overall IPsec traffic throughput.

There are some restrictions on the use of this feature. They are specified in detail in the "Prefragmentation" section at the end of this chapter. This feature is on by default.

The effects of header layering have an impact on the amount of useable service that such an encrypted link can support. This effect is most pronounced when considering a G.729 codec, which produces 12-byte voice payloads every 20 milliseconds. Figure 9-9 shows how the layering of headers increases the number of bytes that need to be transported from the original 20 bytes of voice, all the way up to 140 bytes, for each voice packet, when all the headers are layered on.

Figure 9-9 *Effects of Encapsulating G.729 Voice Packets into IPsec Encrypted Tunnels*

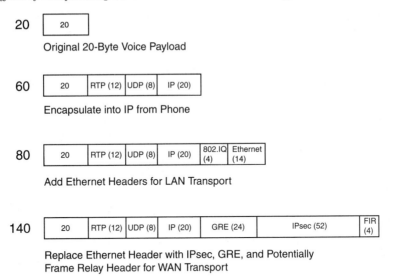

This has the following effects when you're considering bandwidth provisioning for service:

- The size of the packet for calculating the serialization delay component of the overall delay budget for a voice service
- The actual WAN bandwidth consumed for a given profile of LAN traffic
- The number of voice calls that can be supported on a given link

The increased latency imposed by encryption is not a concern if hardware modules are used for encryption. However, the interaction of IPsec with quality of service (QoS) mechanisms is worthy of further discussion.

There is a belief that as soon as a packet has been encrypted with IPsec, the original QoS marking contained in the Differentiated Services Code Point (DSCP) bits is lost, because the original IP header is encrypted in tunnel mode. However, this is untrue. IPsec's standard operation is to copy the value of the DSCP bits from the original IP header to the new IPsec tunnel header so that externally viewable QoS markings are preserved. Also, concerns have been raised that IPsec orders packets in sequence, whereas QoS mechanisms by their nature reorder packets depending on priority. However, this is not a concern, because QoS mechanisms do not reorder packets within any given flow. Although it is true that a voice packet may be put at the head of a queue of data packets by a priority queue implementation, for example, the sequence of IPsec from one host to another within a single flow is unaffected by this operation. A deeper examination of this topic is available at http://www.cisco.com/application/pdf/en/us/guest/netsol/ns241/c649/ccmigration_09186a00801ea79c.pdf.

Returning to the three concerns of delay budget, bandwidth consumption, and number of calls supported, the following is known.

The access links from the CE to the PE tend to have the greatest impact on delay budget consumption when designing packet networks to support voice. Because the CE-to-PE links tend to be lower-bandwidth, serialization delay is the most significant factor in packet delay (assuming that a priority queue is implemented and that the voice packet always rises to the top of the outbound queue). Serialization clearly depends on the clock speed of the access line and the size of the packet. Clearly, when calculating serialization delay for voice packets, the full size of the encrypted packet (in this case, 140 bytes, as shown in Figure 9-9) must be used rather than 20 bytes or some other figure.

Regarding bandwidth consumption, different bandwidths are consumed for each call, depending on the codec used. Some of the most popular voice codecs are described in the following list. It compares the bandwidth consumed by these codecs per voice call over traditional WANs to IPsec and IPsec + GRE encapsulation:

- **G.729a at 33 packets per second**—Over Frame Relay, one call consumes 21 kbps. With IPsec, 33 kbps is consumed. Adding GRE takes this codec to 39 kbps.

- **G.729a at 50 packets per second**—Over Frame Relay, one call consumes 28 kbps. With IPsec, 47 kbps is consumed. Adding GRE takes this codec to 56 kbps.

- **G.711 at 33 packets per second**—Over Frame Relay, one call consumes 77 kbps. With IPsec, 80 kbps is consumed. Adding GRE takes this codec to 86 kbps.

- **G.711 at 50 packets per second**—Over Frame Relay, one call consumes 84 kbps. With IPsec, 104 kbps is consumed. Adding GRE takes this codec to 114 kbps.

The last question remaining is how many calls can be supported on a given link size. This problem has many parts. First, how much of the access link bandwidth can be dedicated to the priority queue? A general guideline that has been used in many different network deployments is 33 percent. This figure is not absolute; it is just a safe figure for a number of different scenarios. The concern with making the priority queue bandwidth too high is that having a packet be in the priority means less and less in terms of guaranteeing latency. Clearly, the deeper the priority queue can get, the greater the potential latency a priority queue packet can experience. So for simplicity, taking the 33 percent recommendation as a rule of thumb, it is possible to make some assumptions about call usage and derive a bandwidth figure required per site depending on the number of users. Limiting the priority queue to 33 percent ensures a more predictable response from the data applications using the link.

First, consider a site with 10 users. If you assume a 3:1 ratio for simultaneous calls, there are not likely to be more than three active voice calls at any time. Using a G.729 codec at 50 pps gives you 3×56 kbps = 168 kbps for voice. If that represents 33 percent of the link bandwidth, the link needs to be 512 kbps, with the remaining bandwidth used for data applications.

A similar analysis can be performed for a site with, say, 35 employees. In this case, for a call ratio of 4:1, you get nine simultaneous calls. With G.729, the calls consume 504 kbps, which is approximately 33 percent of a T1 link.

Split Tunneling in IPsec

This refers to a feature within the VPN client residing on the hosts of remote-access users. It can also be found on hardware VPN clients that are used to encrypt all site-to-site traffic in DMVPN setups. Split tunneling is there to direct traffic destined for corporate hosts over the secured IPsec tunnels, and traffic for the public Internet, directly to the public Internet. This presupposes that the remote user or remote site is using the Internet in the first place to gain connectivity to the corporate network. Clearly, the advantage is that traffic destined for the public Internet does not have to go through the corporate Internet connection and consume bandwidth on that shared resource.

The disadvantage of split tunneling is a potential opening of security holes to the end hosts. The concern is that a host can be compromised by an attacker on the Internet, and when that host then gains access to the corporate network, the attacker can also do so.

A corporation's decision of whether to use split tunneling can go either way, depending on the security procedures that can be implemented within that corporation. It's inadvisable to merely implement split tunneling without considering how its potential security issues should be addressed. A reference for configuring split tunneling is given at the end of this chapter. Also, the "Case Study Selections" section identifies the security procedures that our Acme enterprise implemented to allow the use of split tunneling in some cases.

Supporting Internet Access in IP VPNs

Earlier in this chapter, the subject of providing access from the Internet to the corporate VPN was discussed. Similar issues occur when you look at providing access to Internet resources to VPN users, whether they're located at a central or remote site. An additional issue to consider that affects network design is which part of the WAN you want traffic destined for the Internet to traverse. This is best shown in Figure 9-10.

Figure 9-10 *Enterprise with a Backbone Linking Spoke Sites in San Francisco, Chicago, and New York*

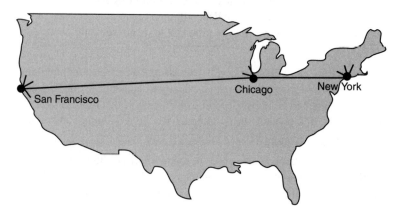

This enterprise has numerous sites located around hub locations in New York, Chicago, and San Francisco. Before being converted to an MPLS VPN WAN, the enterprise had an Internet access point in each of the hubs. By route control mechanisms (that is, manually configuring default routes and not propagating a default route throughout the network), the sites near New York had a 0.0.0.0 route pointing toward the New York hub, the sites near Chicago had a 0.0.0.0 pointing toward the Chicago hub, and the sites near San Francisco had a 0.0.0.0 pointing toward that hub site.

The enterprise chose this option instead of having a single Internet access point in, say, Chicago and backhauling all Internet traffic across its WAN. The enterprise has therefore decided to manage three different Internet access points and keep Internet traffic off the backbone connecting the hubs. When the enterprise now migrates toward an MPLS VPN, some new decisions about this arrangement have to be made. The issues to consider are as follows:

- Does the enterprise maintain its three Internet access points separate from the MPLS VPN service in contracts from its provider?

- With an MPLS VPN, no WAN backbone connects hubs that the enterprise owns and manages. Should the enterprise decommission its own Internet access points and have Internet access provided as part of the MPLS VPN service?

- If the enterprise chooses to use Internet access via the provider-provisioned MPLS VPN, will it also outsource the NAT, firewall, and potentially web cache functions to the provider?

The first decision is whether to keep the existing three Internet access points. Typically, the primary reasons for enterprises electing to use this type of setup are to preserve interhub WAN backbone bandwidth and to provide some resiliency, in that if one access point goes offline, not all users are affected. Both of these reasons are fairly well negated by migration to an MPLS VPN. First, as has been stated, because there are no dedicated interhub backbone links when all sites are connected to an MPLS VPN, there is no reason to try to conserve it! Second, presenting a single default route to the enterprise does not mean that a single Internet access point within the service provider network is used to deliver service. Providers typically have mechanisms to load-balance connections across multiple Internet access gateways. Generally, they can provide better service continuity characteristics to the enterprise user base by providing a single default for Internet access than an enterprise can by statically directing groups of sites to different hub sites.

If the enterprise wants to maintain its own three distinct Internet access points while implementing the MPLS VPN, there is a new problem to consider. As each site of the enterprise exchanges routes with the provider PE VRF for that VPN, and then those routes are propagated to that VPN's VRF for all other PEs that have sites in that VPN, the ability to have sites in the San Francisco region use the San Francisco hub and the Chicago sites use the Chicago hub is lost for a plain-vanilla MPLS VPN implementation. The reason is that the enterprise edge router just sees the provider PE as a single next-hop router. As soon as a packet routed out the enterprise edge router via a default route entry reaches the PE VRF, a single 0.0.0.0 is in the PE VRF for that VPN, and that 0.0.0.0 is the same in the enterprise VRF in all PEs.

A workaround is possible if the CE router at a site connects to the PE via an encapsulation that supports subinterfaces, such as Frame Relay. In this case, the CE router can have one subinterface for the regular MPLS VPN define a 0.0.0.0 route pointing toward a second subinterface that goes to a separate VRF on the PE router. There can be a second VRF that is present only for sites in the San Francisco area, a different VRF that is used on PEs that connect sites in the Chicago area, and a third VRF that exists only on PEs connecting sites in the New York area. Each of these three additional (and regional) VRFs will have routes from the enterprise within it, but each will have a separate destination for the 0.0.0.0 default route in it.

From the enterprise perspective, it appears to be just one VPN, with the exception that the default route for the sites surrounding each regional hub leads to that hub.

As soon as the routing design to get access to the Internet is defined, the question of providing firewall, NAT, and cache services comes into play. Clearly, this is related to the decision of how Internet access is provided as part of the new MPLS VPN-supported WAN. If the option is selected to maintain one or more Internet access points within the corporation, clearly these services will continue to be managed by the enterprise.

However, there are options for the provider to manage and bill for these services. Now, there is the question of security ownership. If an enterprise is concerned enough about its security to demand a firewall, NAT, or something else to conceal and protect its internal infrastructure, does the enterprise get the security desired by handing over management of those services to a third party? The answer generally comes down to the resources available within the enterprise. Typically, larger enterprises have the resources to manage their own security, and they get added peace of mind knowing that no third party has control over it. However, smaller and medium businesses do not have the expertise to keep up to date with security issues. Also, outsourcing security to a provider may be suboptimal, in that complete trust must be placed in the provider. The real level of security delivered is likely to be better.

The issues that the enterprise must understand about the purchase of these security services relate to where NAT is performed. If the provider has a single NAT gateway on its network to access the global Internet, either enterprise customers must have unique address schemes or the PE or CE has to perform NAT to ensure uniqueness by the time packets reach the Internet gateway.

Some providers have chosen to provide a separate Internet gateway for each customer to get around this restriction. The separate gateway per customer can be logical or physical, depending on preference. With multiple logical or physical NAT Internet gateways, all the provider's customers can use the same address space without restriction.

When the provider offers the single shared implementation, it is important for the enterprise to check that no access from one customer's network to another is possible via the default routes existing in the multiple NAT/Internet gateways on the provider network. This can occur by using the single Internet gateway as an interconnect between customer VPNs. To avoid this problem, policy-based routing needs to be implemented on all customer traffic to the gateway. The effect is that all traffic from the VPN toward the Internet gateway can only be forwarded to the Internet, not back toward any VPN on the provider network (something like a split-horizon rule for traffic).

So far, the options discussed for Internet access delivered by the provider have been on the basis of a default route in the VRF pointing toward a central gateway within the provider cloud. Another option is to use the global routing table within the PE router to access an Internet gateway. The PE has multiple customer-specific VRF routing tables. It also has one global routing table that generally contains the provider-specific infrastructure addresses and potentially Internet routes, too. The approach here is to have the default route within the customer-specific VRF point to the public address of the Internet gateway. This static route must be configured by the provider with the **global** keyword to direct the VRF routing process to inspect the global routing table to find the route information. Likewise, the global routing table needs a route to point back to the enterprise edge router for return traffic. Clearly, the restriction with this method is that the enterprise uses a globally unique address space that can exist in the provider's global routing table.

Case Study Selections

In this section, Acme, Inc. has to decide how, out of all the available options, to handle the following:

- **Remote user access**—Does Acme own and operate its own RAS, use L2TP solutions, provide direct remote access over private infrastructure, or use the Internet?

- **Internet connections**—Does Acme maintain direct Internet access on one or more of its main sites or obtain Internet access as part of a VPN service?

- **User access to the Internet**—Is this provided as part of the VPN or kept separate?

- **Off-net sites**—How are they made part of the corporate network and given access to the Internet?

Two primary decisions based on Acme's business model and costs drive further decision-making. Internet access is integral to Acme's operation, both for customer intimacy in terms of delivering service and for customers to place orders. As such, Acme decides that Internet access is mission-critical and needs to be directly under the enterprise's control, with resources immediately available to resolve issues and plan business continuity. Outsourcing this to a third party and relying on SLAs to ensure Internet access service is untenable at this stage.

The second decision is to use an outsourced model for dial access. This is based purely on the cost benefits of doing so, both in terms of avoiding the purchase and maintenance of RAS devices and eliminating costly 800-number toll charges. The model is that a provider will offer access to its public dial access numbers, offering widespread access to local phone numbers in most regions. Client software on user hosts will dial those local access numbers and be authenticated via the shared L2TP procedures described in this chapter. Once access to the provider's public Internet has been given, the IPsec VPN client is initiated on the user host to the nearest IPsec termination device on the Acme network for access to the intranet. Several IPsec concentrators are located around the globe for remote-access users to connect to. This model is also used for cable and DSL subscribers, providing a uniform access model regardless of remote-access media. As such, the option to have the provider deliver DSL or cable users into the corporate VRF was not selected.

The next issues to consider are Internet access and connecting off-net sites. Given that Acme has elected to maintain its own Internet connections, it does not make sense to also provide Internet access as part of the provider-provisioned VPN. The access is already part of the intranet.

For off-net sites, a DMVPN solution has been chosen. The remote sites connect directly to the main network's Internet connections to improve the operation of VoIP solutions.

The open question is the use of split tunneling for the remote-access users and off-net sites. Acme has a set of criteria that define under what conditions the use of split tunneling is acceptable. The result of observing these conditions is that split tunneling is not configured for dial users, whereas it may be configured for off-net sites that have a hardware IPsec VPN client.

These conditions can be summarized as follows:

- Split tunneling is enabled only for sites that have a hardware IPsec client between the host PCs and the Internet service. Any PCs that require just Internet access are to be placed on the Internet side of the hardware VPN client so that unsecured hosts do not have corporate intranet access.

- A stateful, enforced, and permanent firewall capability must be enabled between the Internet connectivity and any hosts that have direct reachability to the ACME network. Cisco IOS Context-Based Access Control (CBAC) is acceptable for this requirement.

- An Intrusion Detection System (IDS) capability must be implemented between the Internet connectivity and any hosts that have direct reachability to ACME network. This matter and other products are discussed further in Chapter 7.

- There also are a number of operational issues to consider for IDS implementation. These include ensuring a very low percentage of "false alarms" and using configurable intrusion signatures that do not require system images to add new signatures.

With these caveats, split tunneling benefits can be realized in a limited fashion on the Acme network while still maintaining adequate security.

Summary

This chapter covered the topics you should consider when adding remote access for both fixed and mobile users to an enterprise network subscribing to a provider-provisioned VPN service.

The basics of configuring remote-access servers were examined. You saw how many enterprises leverage provider infrastructure by various L2TP mechanisms. This chapter also covered what is necessary for a provider to offer remote access as part of the VPN service, in terms of placing remote-access users in the VPN VRF.

Special consideration was given to IPsec access, in terms of both traditional configuration of static IPsec (including support for routing protocol traffic) and the use of DMVPN for on-demand IPsec connections. Options for designing Internet access to the VPN were defined, including the use of split tunneling within IPsec deployments.

Finally, the options chosen for implementation in the case study were explained.

References

General PPP Information

http://www.cisco.com/en/US/tech/tk801/
tech_topology_and_network_serv_and_protocol_suite_home.html

Configuring Dial-In Ports

http://www.cisco.com/en/US/products/hw/modules/ps2797/
products_configuration_example09186a00800e0dcd.shtml

L2TP

http://www.cisco.com/en/US/tech/tk827/tk369/
technologies_design_guide_book09186a00800d8e3c.html

Layer 2 Tunnel Protocol Fact Sheet

http://www.cisco.com/warp/public/cc/pd/iosw/prodlit/l2tun_ds.htm

Layer 2 Tunnel Protocol

http://www.cisco.com/univercd/cc/td/doc/product/software/ios120/120newft/120t/120t1/
l2tpt.htm

VPDN Configuration Guide

http://www.cisco.com/warp/customer/131/5.html

VPDN Configuration and Troubleshooting

http://www-tac.cisco.com/Support_Library/Internetworking/VPDN/vpdn_config.0.html

Security Configuration Guide

http://www.cisco.com/univercd/cc/td/doc/product/software/ios113ed/113ed_cr/secur_c/
index.htm

RADIUS Configuration Guide

http://www.cisco.com/univercd/cc/td/doc/product/software/ios113ed/113ed_cr/secur_c/scprt2/index.htm

Broadband Aggregation to MPLS VPN

http://www.cisco.com/en/US/products/hw/routers/ps133/products_configuration_guide_chapter09186a008017513d.html

Remote Access to MPLS VPN

http://www.cisco.com/en/US/netsol/ns341/ns396/ns172/ns126/networking_solutions_package.html

Network-Based IPsec VPN Solutions

http://www.cisco.com/en/US/netsol/ns341/ns396/ns172/ns334/networking_solutions_package.html

IPsec

http://www.cisco.com/warp/public/732/Tech/security/IPSec/

http://www.cisco.com/en/US/netsol/ns340/ns394/ns171/ns142/networking_solutions_white_paper09186a0080117919.shtml

GRE + IPsec

http://www.cisco.com/en/US/tech/tk583/tk372/technologies_configuration_example09186a0080094bff.shtml

DMVPN

http://www.cisco.com/warp/customer/105/dmvpn.html

http://www.cisco.com/en/US/products/sw/iosswrel/ps1839/products_feature_guide09186a0080110ba1.html

Split Tunneling

http://www.cisco.com/en/US/netsol/ns340/ns394/ns171/ns27/
networking_solutions_white_paper09186a008018914d.shtml

Prefragmentation

http://www.cisco.com/en/US/products/sw/iosswrel/ps1833/
products_feature_guide09186a008009c92c.html

This chapter covers the following topics:

- Topics to consider for inclusion in RFP documents
- Turning the RFP into a joint planning document for implementation with selected vendors
- Defining the SLAs
- Training network operations staff on the new network
- Planning site installation
- Site handover requirements
- Case study selections

CHAPTER 10

Migration Strategies

Having examined the options available for implementing provider-provisioned Layer 3 virtual private networks (VPNs) and how the technology affects the enterprise network after it's implemented, we now consider how migrating from a traditional WAN to a Layer 3 VPN WAN can be managed. The procedures, mechanisms, and forms provided in this chapter are very similar to those used to successfully migrate the Cisco internal network from Frame Relay connectivity to a Layer 3 VPN with only the planned outages affecting end user service.

Network Planning

Assuming that the decision has been made (based on business, technical, and operational considerations, as outlined in previous chapters) to migrate to a Layer 3 VPN, planning is required to successfully implement that migration. This section examines the issues of writing Request for Proposal (RFP) documents, issues to discuss with the selected provider(s) and how these relate to service-level agreements (SLAs), training operators in the new network, and recommendations for how to project-manage the migration.

Writing the RFP

After the decision to implement a Layer 3 VPN has been made, the provider currently delivering WAN connectivity should be assessed to determine whether that provider has the service model, geographic coverage, SLA commitment, support infrastructure, and track record necessary to deliver the new network. In many cases, having an existing relationship with a provider may count against that provider. Undoubtedly, there will have been service issues in the past, and other providers won't have that baggage associated with them. In other respects, the attitude of "better the devil you know than the one you don't" prevails. Neither option is completely objective, so actually writing down the requirements and evaluating all potential providers equally is the best course of action.

The first job is to select a short list of potential providers for supplying WAN connectivity that you will invest time into, send an RFP to them, and fully evaluate their responses. You should send RFPs to a reasonable number to make sure that you are getting a good feel for what is competitive in the market at that time. What that number is will vary depending on requirements, but between 5 and 15 is reasonable.

The first thing to consider is what type of information will be put into the RFP. You can base your RFP on this comprehensive table of contents:

1	Introduction
2	Scope and objectives
3	Nondisclosure agreement
4	Company contact information
5	Applicable law
6	General RFP conditions
6.1	RFP conditions
6.2	Timescale
6.3	Delivery of the proposal
6.4	Questions and answers
6.5	Evaluation criteria
7.	Service provider introduction
7.1	RFP contact details
7.2	Customers/sales information
7.3	Reference accounts/customers
8	Architecture fundamentals
8.1	Quality of service (QoS) considerations
8.1.1	QoS technologies
8.1.2	QoS mapping
8.1.3	MPLS/IP VPN QoS architecture
8.1.4	MPLS/IP VPN routing protocol support
8.1.5	MPLS/IP VPN multicast support
8.2	Core locations
8.2.1	Core circuits
8.2.2	Internet Data Center (IDC) facilities
8.2.3	Higher rates or lambda services coverage
8.2.4	MPLS/IP VPN service coverage
8.2.5	MPLS/IP VPN service road map
8.3	Hub locations
8.3.1	IDC facilities
8.3.2	Higher rates or lambda services coverage
8.3.3	MPLS/IP VPN service coverage
8.3.4	MPLS/IP VPN service road map
8.3.5	Reposition of hub locations
8.4	Regional satellite locations
8.4.1	Reposition of satellite-to-hub connectivity
8.4.2	Engineering sites coverage
8.4.3	Large satellite sites coverage

This table of contents is only a guideline; some elements may not apply to all networks. However, it is a good starting point for the things to consider that will be important to your network. For each of the technical issues previously described in this book, this framework allows you to identify what you want as a solution to fit your corporation's needs and how you want the providers to respond to those needs.

NOTE It is worthwhile to decide ahead of time how you will rate the providers' responses by allocating some sort of marking or weighting scheme that places more importance on your corporate network needs than issues that are not so important. For example, you may determine that, because of operational reasons, you need the provider edge-customer edge (PE-CE) protocol to be Enhanced Interior Gateway Routing Protocol (EIGRP) rather than any alternative, so the marks awarded for offering this functionality may be greater than, say, multicast support if you do not make extensive use of multicast applications.

Architecture and Design Planning with the Service Providers

With the RFP written, responses gathered, and a selection made, a detailed design document must be created that documents the technical definition for the future WAN topology and services in the new network. This document forms the basis of the future design based on a peer-to-peer network architecture provided for by the new Layer 3 MPLS IP VPNs. This is a working document for both the VPN provider and those managing the network migration so that a common understanding of the technical requirements can be achieved. Clearly, this will closely resemble the requirements defined in the RFP. However, because compromises are always required in accepting proposals to RFPs, different trade-offs will be required when evaluating each provider's offerings. After the provider(s) are selected, this document replaces the RFP as a source of technical description and takes into account what the chosen provider(s) can actually offer and how that will be implemented in the enterprise network to deliver the desired service. The following is a sample of a table of contents for a design document:

Detailed design objective
    QoS
    IP multicast
    Routing integration
    Using two independent IP/MPLS networks
    Key design elements
    Network today
Roles and responsibilities
WAN RFP design implications
WAN carriers
    SP1
    SP2
Next-generation network (NGN) network topology overview
    Current network topology
    New network topology
    Core/IDC site topology
    Core sites
Regional hub site topology—IP VPN
    Satellite site topology—type 1
    Satellite site topology—type 2
    Satellite site topology—type 3
    Satellite site topology—type 4
    Satellite site topology—type 6
    Partner sites
IDCs/co-location connectivity
    IDC overview
    Infrastructure requirements

Cabling specifications
Environmental conditions
Power requirements
Security requirements
Access control to the IDC rooms
On-site assistance
IDC and circuit topology
MPLS IP VPN architecture and theory
Routing over IP VPNs
IPV4 address/routing hierarchy
Routing overview
Default routing
BGP weight attribute change
Mechanisms to avoid routing anomalies
Network management subnets
BGP configuration for CE gateways
QoS
Edge-to-edge SLA
Latency
Jitter
Loss
Number of service provider classes of service
Per-class admission criteria (DSCP/IPP)
Policing treatment (per-class markdown or drop)
Enterprise-to-SP mapping model
Remarking requirements (CE to PE)
MPLS/DiffServ tunneling mode in use (Uniform/Pipe/Short Pipe)
Remarking requirements (CE from PE)
MPLS traffic engineering
MPLS DiffServ traffic engineering
Multicast
Network management
Enterprise monitor
Router real-time monitor
Router latency monitor
Traps and syslogs
SLAs
Address management
Addressing schema
Security
Hardware and software specifications
CE device for connectivity greater than STM-1
For connectivity less than E3 (0–multiple E1s)
Core router backbone switches

> Out-of-band routers
> Core site metro gateways
> Hub site metro gateways
> Port adaptors
>
> Software specifications
> Lab testing
> Future considerations

This list only suggests topics to consider for the working document that defines how the network will be designed and how it will operate. The implementation teams from both the provider and the corporation need intimate working knowledge of the network's design and operations.

Should a systems integrator be used to manage the transition from frame-to-MPLS VPN connectivity, the systems integrator should be able to demonstrate to you a good understanding of these topics. Beyond basic understanding, a good systems integrator will be able to tell you about how different options that exist within each of these topics will affect your network after they are implemented.

Project Management

Converting a network from a Layer 1 time-division multiplexer (TDM), or from a Layer 2 offering, to a Layer 3 IP VPN is a significant task for any corporation. To successfully manage that transition, some minimal project management is advisable. Many project-management methods are available. A suitable one can efficiently do the following:

- Define the order process.
- Track orders against delivery dates.
- Track changes to designs and contractual commitments.
- Maintain reporting on risks to project success and provide an escalation path when needed.
- Provide an updated Gantt chart of planned activities and resource allocation.
- Track contracted to actual performance and keep track of project budgets.

SLAs with the Service Providers

This is one of the most contentious topics in negotiation between providers and their customers. It is natural that a customer paying for a service will want the delivered service to be measured against what is being paid for and will want a penalty to be in effect if the delivered service does not match what he paid for. With point-to-point Layer 2 connections, this is relatively simple. It's relatively easy to measure the path's availability and the delivered capacity on that path. However, after the any-to-any connectivity of an IP VPN is delivered, with support for multiple classes of service (CoSs), the situation is more complex.

The typical service provider SLA defines the loss latency and jitter that the provider's network will deliver between PE points of presence (POPs) in its network. In almost all cases, this is an average figure, so POPs near each other compensate for the more remote POPs in terms of latency contribution. Some providers also offer different loss/latency/jitter for different CoSs. Again, this is normally for traffic between provider POPs. What is of interest to enterprise applications, and hence to enterprise network managers, is the service's end-to-end performance, not just the bit in the middle. Specifically, the majority of latency and jitter (most commonly loss, too) is introduced on the access circuits because of the circuits' constrained bandwidth and slower serialization times.

To solve this problem, you need SLAs that reflect the service required by the applications. By this, I mean that latency and jitter can be controlled by implementing a priority queuing (PQ) mechanism. For a PQ system, a loss of this kind is a function of the amount of traffic a user places in the queue, which the provider cannot control. For classes using something like the Cisco class-based weighted fair queuing (CBWFQ), the latency and jitter are a function of the load offered to the queuing mechanism. This is not surprising, because this mechanism is designed to allocate bandwidth to specific classes of traffic, not necessarily to deliver latency or jitter guarantees.

Some providers have signed up to deliver the Cisco Powered Network (CPN) IP Multiservice SLA, which provides 60-ms edge-to-edge latency, 20-ms jitter, and 0.5 percent loss between PE devices. With this strict delivery assured, designing the edge connectivity to meet end-to-end requirements is simplified.

With advances to the Cisco IP SLA, it will be possible to link the measuring of latency and jitter to class load. It is then reasonable for a provider to offer delay guarantees for CBWFQ classes, provided that the offered load is less than 100 percent of the class bandwidth. This then puts the CBWFQ's latency and jitter performance under the enterprise's control. If the enterprise does not overload the class, good latency and jitter should be experienced; however, if the class is overloaded, that will not be the case.

There should be more to an SLA than loss, latency, and jitter characteristics. The SLA should define the metrics for each service delivered, the process each side should follow to deliver the service, and what remedies and penalties are available. Here is a suggested table of contents to consider when crafting an SLA with a provider:

Performance characteristics
Loss/latency/jitter for PQ traffic
Loss/latency/jitter for business data traffic
Loss/latency/jitter for best-effort traffic
Availability
Mean time to repair (MTTR)
Installation and upgrade performance

It is worth discussing each element in more detail. It is important to base performance characteristics on the requirements of the application being supported and to consider them from the point of view of end-to-end performance. Starting with PQ service, which will be used for voice, see Figure 10-1, which shows the results of ITU G.114 testing for voice quality performance. The E-model rating is simply a term given to a set of tests used to assess user satisfaction with the quality of a telephone call.

Figure 10-1 *SLA Metrics: One-Way Delay (VoIP)*

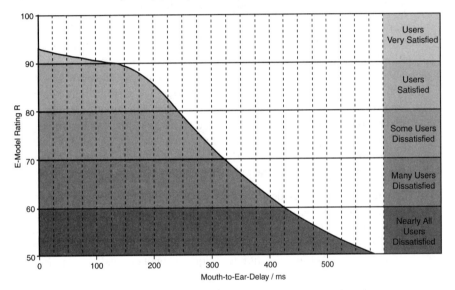

ITU G.114 Determination of the effects of absolute delay by the E-model

If you select a mouth-to-ear delay budget of 150 ms, you may determine that the codec and LAN delay may account for 50 ms, for example (this varies from network to network), leaving you 100 ms for the VPN. If the provider is managing the service to the CE, this is the performance statistic. However, if the provider is managing the service only to the PE, perhaps only 30 ms is acceptable to stay within the end-to-end budget. This more stringent requirement comes from the serialization times of the access link speed (for maximum-sized fragments), the PQ's queue depth, and the size of the first in, first out (FIFO) transmit ring on the routers in use as a PE, all taking up 35 ms for the ingress link and 35 ms for the egress link.

Whether the provider manages from CE to CE or PE to PE, targets must be set for the connection type, and reports need to be delivered against contracted performance. From the enterprise perspective, it's simplest to have the provider measure and report on performance from CE to CE; however, that does come with a drawback. To do so, the provider must be able to control the CE for the purposes of setting up IP SLA probes to measure the CE-to-CE performance and collect statistics. This is generally done by having the provider manage the CE device. However, not all enterprises want the IOS revision on the CE to be controlled by the provider, because the enterprise might want to upgrade its routers to take advantage of a new IOS feature. Clearly, this needs to be negotiated between the provider and enterprise to reach the optimum solution for the network in question.

For the data class, some research suggests that, for a user to retain his train of thought when using an application, the application needs to respond within one second (see Jakob Nielsen's *Usability Engineering*, published by Morgan Kaufmann, 1994). To reach this, it is reasonable to budget 700 ms for server-side processing and to require the end-to-end round-trip time to be less than 300 ms for the data classes.

Jitter, or delay variation, is a concern for real-time applications. With today's newest IP phones, adaptive jitter buffers compensate for jitter within the network and automatically optimize their settings. This is done by effectively turning a variable delay into a fixed delay by having the buffer delay all packets for a length of time that allows the buffer to smooth out any variations in packet delivery. This reduces the need for tight bounds on jitter to be specified, as long as the fixed delays plus the variable delays are less than the overall delay budget. However, for older jitter buffers, the effects of jitter above 30 or 35 ms can be catastrophic in terms of meeting user expectations for voice or other real-time applications. Clearly, knowledge of your network's ability to deal with jitter is required to define appropriate performance characteristics for the WAN.

The effects of loss are evident in both real-time and CBWFQ classes. For real time, it is possible for jitter buffers to use packet interpolation techniques to conceal the loss of 30 ms of voice samples. Given that a typical sample rate for voice is 20 ms, this tells you that a loss of two consecutive samples or more will cause a blip to be heard in the voice conversation that packet interpolation techniques cannot conceal. Assuming a random-drop distribution within a single voice flow, a 0.25-percent packet drop rate within the real-time class results in a loss every 53 minutes that cannot be concealed. The enterprise must decide whether this is acceptable or whether tighter, or less tight, loss characteristics are required.

For the data classes, loss affects the attainable TCP throughput, as shown in Figure 10-2.

In Figure 10-2, you can see the maximum attainable TCP throughput for different packet-loss probabilities given different round-trip time characteristics. As long as the throughput per class, loss, and round-trip time fall within the performance envelopes illustrated, the network should perform as required. The primary reporting concern with the data classes is how well they perform for delay and throughput, which depends almost entirely on the load offered to them by the enterprise. Should the enterprise send more than what is contracted for and set up within a data class, the loss and delay grow exponentially, and the provider can't control this. Realistically, some sort of cooperative model between the provider and enterprise is required to ensure that data classes are not overloaded, or, if they are, that performance guarantees are expected only when the class is less than 100 percent utilized.

Figure 10-2 *TCP Throughput*

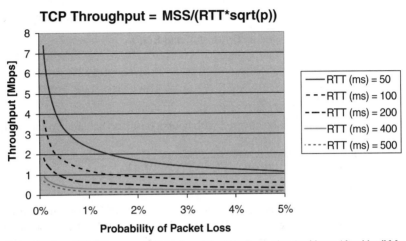

Graph created based on information from "The Macroscopic Behavior of the TCP Congestion Avoidance Algorithm," Matthew Mathis, Computer Communication Review, July 1997.

Other subjects listed in the SLA are more straightforward. Availability, MTTR, and installation and upgrade performance are mostly self-explanatory:

- **Availability**—Defines the hours that the service should be available and the percentage of time within that availability window that the service must be available without the provider's incurring penalties.

- **MTTR**—Refers to how quickly the provider will repair faults within the network and restore service.

- **Installations and upgrade performance**—Tells the provider how long it has to get a new site operational after the order has been delivered by the enterprise, or how long it has to upgrade facilities should the enterprise order that.

Network Operations Training

Clearly, with a new infrastructure to support, system administrators need appropriate training in the technology itself, the procedures to use to turn up or troubleshoot new sites, and the tools they will have to assist them in their responsibilities. The question of whether to train the enterprise operations staff in the operation of MPLS VPNs (with respect to the service operation within the provider's network) is open. Some enterprises may decide that, because no MPLS encapsulation or MPLS protocols will be seen by the enterprise network operators, no training is necessary for this technology. However, experience to date has shown that when you troubleshoot issues with service provider staff, knowledge of MPLS VPN operation is helpful.

The following high-level topics were taught to a large enterprise that successfully migrated network operations to a provider-delivered MPLS VPN service. These topics can be used as a template to evaluate training offerings to see if all necessary topics are covered:

- Routing protocols (PE-to-CE and BGP)
- MPLS
- QoS
- Multicast

These topics can be covered with course outlines that are similar to the following:

Course 1: Routing on MPLS VPN Networks

Course Description

This course offers an integrated view of the PE-to-CE routing protocol and its interaction with the provider MPLS VPN, BGP, and basic MPLS/VPN operation. Both theory and hands-on practice are used to allow participants to configure, troubleshoot, and maintain networks using those protocols.

Prerequisite

Basic knowledge of TCP/IP, routing, and addressing schemes

Content

Routing (assuming EIGRP as the PE-to-CE protocol)

> EIGRP introduction
> EIGRP concepts and technology
> EIGRP scalability
> BGP route filtering and route selection
> Transit autonomous systems
> BGP route reflectors
> BGP confederations
> Local preference
> Multiexit discriminator
> AS-path prepending
> BGP communities
> Route flap dampening
> MBGP

MPLS VPN technology

> Terminology
> MPLS VPN configuration on IOS platforms
> CE-PE relations
> BGP

> OSPF
> RIP
> Static
> Running EIGRP in an MPLS VPN environment
>
> ### Course 2: QoS in MPLS VPNs
>
> #### Course Description
>
> This course covers the QoS issues encountered when connecting campus networks to MPLS VPN WANs.
>
> #### Prerequisites
>
> A good understanding of generic QoS tools and their utility
>
> Basic knowledge of MPLS and IP
>
> #### Content
>
> Overview
>
> Modular QoS command-line interface (MQC) classification and marking
>
> CBWFQ
>
> Low-latency queuing (LLQ) (both fall into the broader category of congestion management)
>
> Scaling QoS
>
> QoS tunnel modes in MPLS VPN networks
>
> Monitoring QoS performance
>
> ### Course 3: Multicast
>
> #### Course Description
>
> This course describes basic multicast applications, the challenges and resolution of implementing multicast over an MPLS VPN, and basic troubleshooting of that environment.
>
> #### Prerequisites
>
> A good understanding of multicast use and configuration
>
> Basic understanding of MPLS/VPN networks
>
> #### Content
>
> Multicast operation
>
> > PIM sparse mode
> > SSM

IPv6
 Host-router interaction
 Multicast on MPLS/VPN
     Multicast Distribution Tree (MDT)
     Default MDT
     Data MDT
     Deployment considerations

Implementation Planning

To ensure a smooth transition to the new network service, each site requires careful planning. The following is provided as an example of how to identify tasks, assign owners, and track the progress of actual versus planned activities. This is offered as a starting point for when you consider what activities are necessary to ensure a proper working installation at each site. This documentation exists for the following phases of the network transition:

- **Phase 1**—Pre-cutover to ensure that all planning documents are complete and distributed

- **Phase 2**—Connecting major sites to the new network

- **Phase 3**—Cutover on a site-by-site basis

- **Phase 4**—Post-cutover activities and sign-off

Phase 1

Phase 1 contains documentation that resembles Table 10-1.

Table 10-1   *Typical Phase 1 Implementation Planning Tasks*

Sequence	Due (by EoB)	Owner	Action
1	1/27/2006	Adam	Team approval that all risks have been identified.
2	1/27/2006	Samantha	Create a plan for Tuesday the 31st to introduce core IDCs into production.
3	1/31/2006	Michael	Operations approves IDC connectivity.
4	1/31/2006	Adam	Routing team approves documentation.
5	1/31/2006	Michael	QoS team approves documentation.
6	1/31/2006	Samantha	Multicast team approves documentation.
7	1/31/2006	Mo	Documentation approved by providers.
8	1/31/2006	Samantha	Support document for engaging provider's support groups.

Phase 2

Phase 2, which is the stage of planning a major site (such as an IDC) connection to the new production network, must be completed. This could be monitored via a document like that shown in Table 10-2.

Table 10-2   *Typical Phase 2 Implementation Planning Tasks*

Sequence	Due (By EoB)	Owner	Action
1	1/31/2006	Team 1	Check out-of-bound access/dial for all IDCs.
2	1/31/2006	Team 1	Shut and make passive all Gigabit Ethernet links to the corporate network from the respective MAN gateways connecting to IDCs.
3	1/31/2006	Team 1	Ensure that the MPLS cloud learns only expected routes, such as core IDCs.
4	1/31/2006	Team 1	Issue **no shut** and **no passive** commands on one Gigabit Ethernet link to leak the corporate address into the new MPLS network.
5	1/31/2006	Team 1	Ensure that the MPLS cloud learns only expected routes, such as core IDCs and corporate routes.
6	1/31/2006	Team 1	Check that internal support can reach all devices (monitor at P6).
7	1/31/2006	Team 1	Commence operations to drive cleanup and accept configs.
8	1/31/2006	Team 1	Tweak metrics for MPLS cutover so that routing works as expected during the transition.
9	1/31/2006	Team 1	Document and report change/variance (including the procedure to isolate the core).
10	1/31/2006	Team 1	Conduct a team status meeting to discuss the success so far. Assign remedial actions to address any issues that may be apparent.
11	1/31/2006	Team 1	Decide whether to proceed with the current plan or amend it.
12	2/1/2006	Team 1	Perform a health check of the network during a maintenance window.

Phase 3

Phase 3 involves rolling out the network implementation to all locations. There may be many sets of procedures for sites of differing sizes and complexity; however, the aim is to produce a reasonable set of procedures that can be replicated in each site with similar requirements. Some suggested details for this phase appear in the section "On-Site Implementation."

Phase 4

Phase 4, the final phase, defines the activities to be completed post-cutover and includes the items covered in Table 10-3. This phase should be executed as a rolling activity because the installation progresses through all geographies and sites the new network will reach.

Table 10-3 *Typical Phase 4 Implementation Planning Tasks*

Sequence	Due (by EoB)	Owner	Action
1	2/15/2006	Team 2	Routing team verifies operation and signs off.
2	2/15/2006	Team 2	QoS team verifies operation and signs off.
3	2/15/2006	Team 2	Multicast team verifies operation and signs off.
4	2/15/2006	Team 2	Network management team verifies operation and signs off.
5.	2/14/2006	Team 1	Conduct a daily/weekly technical review with service providers.
6	2/15/2006	Team 2	Document and summary report from each technology team lead (assess whether more time is needed).
6.1	2/15/2006	Team 1	Conduct a network performance call with the provider.
7	2/15/2006	Team 1	Compile a migration report and assess the migration strategy with respect to moving forward.
8	2/16/2006	Team 2	Health check by the operations team.
9	2/16/2006	Team 2	Outstanding testing that may be required.

On-Site Implementation

This section discusses the required tasks to survey a site ahead of installation and lists the tasks for a circuit activation check. Clearly, after all the communications testing and as soon as the new links and routers can be monitored by network management systems, a final check is required that checks all applications from the user's perspective.

The site survey is important to plan what needs to be done during the installation for each site. The investment in a properly executed pre-installation survey is well worth the payback in terms of a smooth installation experience. Table 10-4 shows a list of things to consider.

Table 10-4   *Typical Site Survey Requirements*

Site Location: Site 1	Status
1.0 Site address and contact information	Names, phone numbers, hours of access, and out-of-hours contact information.
2.0 Environmental	Cabling, power supply type, and cabinet space.
3.0 Electrical	AC or DC power, power receptacle type, and location of power outlets to equipment.
4.0 Cabling	Under the floor or overhead, restrictions, cable labeling scheme, and the kind of cabling required.
5.0 Telco interface	Location of wallboard/demarc, interface type, who can terminate cables to the demarc, circuit type, ID and in-service date.
6.0 Data applications	List applications to be available at this site, such as Frame Relay, asynchronous, optical connections, and so on.
7.0 Voice applications	Specify PBX and signaling types.
8.0 Network management	Are console terminals available? Will there be a maintenance printer? Where will the dial-in modem be connected?

After all this information is gathered and analyzed and has resulted in the appropriate orders and shipping of equipment, it's time to install the equipment and verify its operation. Typically, the provider installs at least up to the demarc point, with likely installation of the routers themselves and the channel service unit/digital service unit (CSU/DSU) if it is not already built into the router.

The following addresses concepts for verifying circuit and communications activation. As stated previously, as soon as all communications are verified, a final user test of all applications' operation is required before the site is considered complete in terms of migration and is accepted by the enterprise.

By whatever means the enterprise is comfortable using, the circuit must be deemed to be clean, which means that error rates on the line are within design limits. Typically, this is achieved by performing a Bit Error Rate Test (BERT) for several hours. A BERT ensures that the circuit is working properly by testing for the following:

- Packet loss across the carrier backbone must be what was contracted for all data classes.

- Latency characteristics, as defined in the SLA, must be met.

- New links need to deliver the expected bandwidth paid for.

In the event of a link or PVC failure of the new circuit, restoration has to be provided within the contracted guidelines via an alternative path within the provider's network (if available).

Case Study Selections

For the case study used throughout this book, the forms and processes defined are close to those used by Acme. The RFP, detailed design document, site planning, and site completion milestones were the primary checkpoints in monitoring the migration progress.

The primary selection made during the early stages that affected the network design directly was when different providers were used in different geographies. In those situations, Acme decided to place its own router between the two providers to handle IP connectivity.

Interprovider solutions would allow multiple providers to collaborate and provide seamless service without requiring this additional handoff, but political issues seem to be the cause of preventing that from happening at this point.

Summary

Based on the information in this chapter, you now have a good idea of what to write up as a table of contents for your RFP, and you know how that relates to the SLAs you require for network, installation, and repair performance. You now also understand that, after vendors are selected, the critical document is the detailed design that specifies how both you and the service provider will deliver the end service. Finally, you understand the training requirements for operations, and you have the suggested site planning and completion forms.

Appendix

This appendix covers the following topics:

- Coverage and topology
- Customer edge router management
- Network access, resiliency, and load balancing
- QoS capability
- Multicast capability
- Routing protocol capability
- Security
- Software deployment processes
- Interprovider IP/VPN
- IPv6
- MTU considerations
- Hosting capability
- IP telephony PSTN integration
- IP telephony hosted call agent
- Remote and dial access
- Internet access
- Other network services

Questions to Ask Your Provider Regarding Layer 3 IP/MPLS VPN Capability

After you digest all the material in this book, and assuming that you decide to migrate to a Layer 3 virtual private network (VPN) service from a service provider, you need to give some thought to the sorts of questions you will ask about the service offering and what responses will most closely match your needs as an enterprise.

Migrating from a Layer 1 or Layer 2 private WAN to a Layer 3 IP/MPLS VPN should provide all the functionality of a privately built network on top of a service provider's shared intelligent infrastructure. This VPN service should be capable of routing customer IP traffic in an optimal, any-to-any fashion aligned with the physical underlying infrastructure of the provider's network without the need to provision or maintain a full mesh or near-full mesh of individual permanent virtual circuits (PVCs). This eliminates the enterprise's need to perform time-consuming research to determine best points and routes for hub interconnection. In addition, the enterprise needs to perform capacity planning only on a per-port basis, not a per-VC basis.

"Transparency" of the service is a key theme: You should expect any Layer 3 IP/MPLS VPN service to be a "drop-in" replacement of existing network functionality, without significant reengineering of the network. Depending on how the provider has implemented its VPN service, the amount of network reengineering required varies. Typically, the key areas to focus on are as follows:

- **Routing protocol support**—Does the provider offer connectivity using your Interior Gateway Protocol (IGP), or does it require Border Gateway Protocol (BGP) to be supported to its edge devices?

- **Multicast support**—Can the provider's network handle multicast replication, or will generic routing encapsulation (GRE) tunnels need to be created by the enterprise to transport that traffic?

- **QoS**—Can the provider map quality of service (QoS) classes to the existing QoS scheme without loss of original marking? Some remarking may be necessary under certain circumstances, but you need to know what they are when planning a migration.

- **Encryption**—What encryption services are offered as part of the VPN service?

When assessing service provider's capabilities, the following sections are a good collection of questions to consider. It is worth marking absolute requirements for your network in a separate color, such as red, to emphasize their importance. You also should request a full explanation and road map details for any requirement that cannot be fully met today.

Coverage and Topology

Preference should be given to providers that can offer provider edge (PE) devices in the majority of the vicinities where you have site locations. The reason for this is that latency over the high-speed networks that connect PE devices is much lower than the latency of lower-speed links connecting enterprise edge routers to the PE. The more PEs in the vicinity of your site locations, the less backhaul over low-speed networks that is required.

When considering extranet capability, it is likely that the sites on your network that you want to be visible to a partner remain limited in scope, meaning that the partner is not simply made part of the any-to-any VPN. Therefore, you should determine if the provider can support one of these scenarios for extranet connectivity:

- A Layer 2 VPN service between your enterprise and an extranet partner site, terminating in a separate data-link connection identifier (DLCI), virtual circuit (VC), or VLAN for each partner site.

- A separate virtual routing/forwarding instance (VRF) per extranet partner site, delivered via a separate DLCI, VC, or VLAN to the CE router.

These issues could be addressed by questions such as the following:

- **PE coverage**—Please provide the global locations (cities) where you locate your PE routers, owned and operated by you, for customer connections.

- **Partners' PE coverage and interconnects**—If you leverage partners to provide local access, please give the global locations (cities) where your partners provide PE routers. Please provide the global locations (cities) where you interconnect with the partners' networks. Please also provide details on the Cisco Powered Network (CPN) designations and use of Cisco equipment in each partner's network.

- **Extranet connectivity**—Can you offer an Layer 2 VPN service between a Cisco extranet partner site and Cisco, terminating in a separate DLCI, VC, or VLAN for each partner site at a Cisco location? Can you offer a separate Layer 3 VRF for each extranet partner site, terminating on the Cisco customer edge (CE) router in a separate DLCI, VC, or VLAN?

Customer Edge Router Management

Enterprises have to choose whether they want the CE managed by themselves or the provider. If managed by the enterprise, this is called an unmanaged service, and it has the following benefits.

It allows the enterprise to manage other information technology (IT) infrastructure services on the CEs, such as public switched telephone network (PSTN) gateway functionality or content distribution functionality.

Many new features are applicable primarily at the WAN/VPN edge, where more advanced functionality is needed to offer the level of service for enterprise applications. Such an example is advanced QoS functionality.

When the CEs are accessible from the enterprise network, the enterprise can observe and communicate the state of the WAN interfaces upon circuit or equipment failure to assist in troubleshooting, rather than first forcing a service provider's dispatch to look at the equipment.

This permits the enterprise to deploy enterprise security capabilities, such as encryption, directly on the CE instead of having to provide a second router to interface with a service provider's managed router.

The following may be considered suitable questions to cover these issues:

- **Unmanaged/managed CE service**—Do you offer an unmanaged CE service where the enterprise maintains ownership of the router's configurations?
- **Intelligent intermediary devices**—Do you use intelligent intermediary devices to monitor link status and performance?

Network Access, Resiliency, and Load Balancing

To ensure QoS, and for ease of configuration, an enterprise should prefer the use of "direct" access technologies between the CE and PE routers. That is, Cisco prefers the use of time-division multiplexing (TDM)-based (HDLC/PPP) access.

If indirect or shared access is used, such as Frame Relay or ATM, the enterprise needs to be assured that the proper QoS will be applied to support its jitter and committed bandwidth requirements. Frame Relay and ATM circuits must be provisioned such that the committed bandwidth rate is equal to the port rate specified on the PE routers. Any packets sent by a CE or PE over an Frame Relay or ATM-based access network must be guaranteed delivery by that access, because the CE and PE routers represent the primary IP QoS control points in the network. Because the Layer 2 parameters are defined this way, the drop and queuing decisions are maintained by devices with Layer 3 intelligence, and the Layer 2 connections are essentially straight pipes. For example, for Frame Relay, it is normally preferable for Layer 3 VPN deployments to configure the Frame Relay committed information rate (CIR) to be equal to the **frame-relay mincir** value in the map class. This means that no backward explicit congestion notifications (BECNs) should be generated and no drop decisions are made at Layer 2. Drop decisions are made by the application-aware IP mechanisms.

In addition, if ATM is used, the service provider should understand that the enterprise specifies link speeds in terms of IP bandwidth required. The ATM bandwidth required to carry that amount of IP bandwidth must account for the "cell tax," typically 40 percent over the IP bandwidth required. A single PVC should be used to deliver all IP traffic, conforming to jitter requirements.

For example, if the enterprise specifies that a site needs 2 Mbps of IP bandwidth, and the service provider can only offer ATM access, the service provider must provision a minimum of 2.8 Mbps of (sustained cell rate) bandwidth to support the IP bandwidth requirement.

In any case, where the PE port's speed exceeds the site's total committed bandwidth rate, which is likely in the case of Metro Ethernet, ATM, or FR, the PE routers must be capable of shaping all traffic to the committed bandwidth rate and providing the appropriate QoS into that shaped output queue.

In some cases, the enterprise provisions network access through two redundant access circuits between two different pairs of routers. The capability to load-balance traffic across these links for a larger aggregate capacity is required.

The following are examples of the types of questions to ask to obtain the provider capabilities just discussed:

- **Access technologies**—What access technologies do you support? If access technologies differ based on location, please explain the differences between location types (such as tier 1, 2, and 3 sites) and what those mean in terms of access technology and speeds available. Should the access technologies differ significantly from the existing connections for your locations, the cost of new interface hardware may add significantly to the project's overall cost.

- **Shaping capability**—In access technologies where the circuit speed is more than the committed bandwidth rate for a site, can you perform shaping for total output bandwidth? Can you also provide proper QoS handling for your classes of service into the shaped output queue?

- **Load balancing**—In the case of redundant connections between two different PE routers and two different CE routers, does your network architecture permit equal-cost load balancing over them through the use of dual route distinguishers and eiBGP multipath?

QoS Capability

Table A-1 provides a fictitious allocation of traffic types to packet-marking values. Each enterprise is likely to have a different scheme; this table is provided for illustrative purposes only.

Table A-1   *QoS Classes of Service*

CoS/IP Precedence	Forwarding Method	Description
6	CBWFQ min-bw	Network control and management
5	LLQ	Voice bearer traffic
4	CBWFQ min-bw	Videoconferencing bearer traffic
3	CBWFQ min-bw	Call signaling and high-priority data applications
2	CBWFQ min-bw	Interactive traffic
1	CBWFQ min-bw	"Scavenger"—Bulk traffic dropped first during congestion
0	FBWFQ	Default class—All other traffic

The provider doesn't need to match these classes exactly. However, the provider must provide a number of classes that match or exceed the required QoS of each of these traffic types and be able to map these markings to those classes transparently. Assuming that the provider offers three classes, the lowest-priority CoS typically needs a 99.9 percent packet delivery rate, as detailed in Table A-2.

Table A-2   *Required Service Provider Classes of Service*

CoS/IP Precedence	Forwarding Method	Packet Delivery Rate
Low-latency/ priority queue	LLQ	99.995 percent
High-priority data	CBWFQ	99.990 percent
Normal-priority data	CBWFQ	99.900 percent

To ensure that the enterprise can recover and revert to its own QoS markings for its seven classes at the opposite end of the IP/VPN service, it is a requirement for "subclasses" within each primary CoS whose IP Differentiated Services Code Point (DSCP) values remain consistent upon arrival at the remote CE node. For example, a service provider may offer three CoS levels. These may be "silver" and "bronze" based on IP DiffServ's "assured forwarding" per-hop behavior and "gold" based on IP DiffServ's "expedited forwarding" per-hop behavior. There must be a mechanism by which the enterprise can map its CoS values 6, 4, 3, and 2 (from Table A-1) into the "silver" CoS (perhaps as IP DSCP values CS4, AF41, AF42, and AF43) and have them retained such that this mapping can be reversed into the original seven CoS values for the enterprise's network. In provider networks where this capability is not present, complex reclassification for traffic reentering the enterprise network from the provider network is necessary.

Low-speed links may need to use Link Fragmentation and Interleaving (LFI) to support the enterprise's end-to-end jitter requirements. Low speed is typically defined as less than 768 kbps. Typically, it is required that jitter as measured from CE to CE be no more than 30 ms, based on the capability of end device jitter buffers to compensate for this effect. Service providers are required to have the capability to use LFI for low-speed links (1 Mbps and less) to meet this jitter requirement.

These issues can be captured in the following questions:

- **Number of classes of service**—How many classes of service are available for use within your IP/VPN service, and which type of service is offered with each class (low-latency queuing, minimum-bandwidth, or best-effort)?

- **QoS transparency**—Is your network configured to preserve the IP DSCP values sent from the CE router throughout your network until it reaches the remote CE router?

- **Number of QoS "subclasses" that can be used in any given class of service**—How many different "subclasses" or DSCP markings can be used in each of your classes of service, and what (if any) special handling is applied (such as greater drop precedence)?

- **Traffic engineering**—Do you perform any traffic engineering, which may place traffic in a lower CoS on a different path than the highest CoS?

- **LFI**—Do you provide LFI capability on the PE router for all low-speed links? If so, please explain the type(s) of LFI used for each access method where committed bandwidth would be 1 Mbps or less.

- **cRTP**—What support for Compressed Real-Time Protocol (cRTP) is available, and in what locations?

Multicast Capability

An increasingly popular design is to use two multicast models on the enterprise network:

- **Any Source Multicast (ASM)**—Originally introduced in 1990, ASM is a legacy form of Source-Specific Multicast (SSM) in which the host cannot specify the source it wants.

  The standard protocol set in support of ASM is IGMPv2 or IGMPv3.

- **SSM**—Used to replicate one-to-many traffic streams containing audio, video, and software distribution.

This requires that the network be able to interface with a service provider network natively with Protocol-Independent Multicast (PIM) for multicast. In this case, interfaces within the enterprise network are configured with PIM sparse-dense mode. All multicast groups carrying data operate in sparse mode, and the Auto-RP group (for distribution of PIM rendezvous point [RP] information) operates in dense mode. In the case that per-VPN limits are set up for multicast group counts or source counts, the enterprise requires SPs to be able to provision for up to 3000 potential source and group (S,G) entries as a typical figure for a large corporate network.

The optimum solution from an enterprise perspective is for the provider to support multicast VPN (MVPN) to obviate the need for the enterprise to create tunnels for the multicast traffic itself. Here are two typical questions to pose to providers:

- **MVPN capability**—Do you support MVPN functionality such that the enterprise can use native PIM sparse mode (PIM-SM) to interface with your network?

- **MVPN limits**—Do you configure a maximum number of multicast groups or source and group entries per VPN? Can you support up to 3000 (S,G) entries?

Routing Protocol Capability

An enterprise of any size uses an IGP—most commonly Enhanced Interior Gateway Routing Protocol (EIGRP) or Open Shortest Path First (OSPF). This discussion assumes the use of EIGRP; however, the principles also apply to other IGPs. In an effort to reduce the amount of reengineering that would take place to implement an IP/VPN network architecture, the enterprise requires a service provider to support EIGRP between the CE and PE routers. The enterprise requires that EIGRP metric information be propagated through the service provider VPN service and redistributed into EIGRP on the remote side of the VPN service. This preserves route types and metrics across the VPN service. When per-VPN limits are set up for unicast route entries, the enterprise requires providers to provision for up to 3000 potential routes in the VPN. On a per-site basis, one or two key hub sites may introduce up to 10,000 routes to the VPN, depending on the amount of global infrastructure connected behind these key sites.

The following questions address some of the detail requirements for IGP support to the PE:

- **Routing protocol support**—Do you support EIGRP as a CE-to-PE routing protocol with redistribution of metric information?

- **EIGRP site-of-origin support**—If EIGRP is supported as a CE-to-PE routing protocol, do you support site-of-origin support to prevent the re-advertisement of routes learned from another site back to the VPN cloud?

- **Routing protocol convergence time, CE to CE**—From the perspective of a CE, and given a common failure scenario of an access link failing between remote CE and PE routers, what is the maximum time expected for routing protocol convergence?

- **Unicast route limits**—Do you configure a maximum number of unicast route entries per VPN? Do you configure a maximum number of unicast route entries per site? Can you support up to 3000 routes in the VPN, with the potential for up to 2000 being announced from core hub locations?

Similar questions could be created for OSPF if that applies. However, the use of sham link within OSPF may be required for your migration and therefore needs to be specified. Sham link enables routes across the Multiprotocol Label Switching (MPLS) VPN and routes within the enterprise campus to coexist and both be used to transport packets to remote destinations.

SLA Measurement and Monitoring Capability

An enterprise requires regular reports on the network's performance compared to the contracted service-level agreement (SLA). Regular measurements of latency, jitter, and per-queue packet delivery should be made available. It is preferable to have per-queue latency and jitter metrics.

The enterprise should specify that the SLA be compared to a measurement of latency and jitter for every site's CE-to-PE router link. The PE-to-PE measurements should be reported separately. Additionally, this should be reported giving average figures over 5-minute intervals, not averaged over a month.

The following questions can address these issues with providers:

- **Latency measurements**—Can you offer a regular report on latency between enterprise sites, measured from CE to CE router? The addition of latency measurements from local CE to PE, PE to PE, and remote PE to CE is sufficient.

- **Per-queue latency**—Can you offer per-queue latency statistics?

- **Jitter measurements**—Can you offer a regular report on jitter between enterprise sites, measured from CE to CE router? The addition of jitter measurements from local CE to PE, PE to PE, and remote PE to CE is sufficient.

- **Per-queue jitter**—Can you offer per-queue jitter statistics?

- **Per-queue packet delivery**—Can you offer per-queue packet delivery statistics, detailing packet drops? Reports for each local CE to PE, PE to PE, and remote PE to CE are sufficient.

SLA Details

As mentioned in the section "QoS Capability," an enterprise network is engineered so that its latency is constrained only by the physical topology of the network's underlying fiber paths. An enterprise needs to understand two different latency metrics:

- Observed nominal latency expected when the network is operating normally (without fault)

- Contractual maximum latency in the form of a contractual commitment (taking into account the possibility of a network fault)

Availability, as used here, is defined as service availability, including the local loop, the IP routing information exchange, and the reachability of all other enterprise sites on the cloud. For example, an enterprise considers a site to be unavailable if the access circuit is up and routing protocol information is being exchanged but the local site cannot reach several other sites on the VPN service.

The following list provides questions to pose to providers on this matter:

- **Average latencies**—For each pair in the following list of sites, please detail the nominal (95th through 99th percentile) latencies expected between CEs located in each site: Sydney, Singapore, Hong Kong, Tokyo, Beijing, Bangalore, Dubai, San Francisco, Chicago, Dallas, New York, Amsterdam, London, Brussels, Madrid, Munich, and Milan. (It is expected that this list will be replaced with locations specific to the enterprise network locations.) This is intended to capture the usual network latency expected.

- **Maximum expected latencies**—For each pair in the following list of sites, please detail the maximum expected latencies you would commit to between CEs located in each site: Sydney, Singapore, Hong Kong, Tokyo, Beijing, Bangalore, Dubai, San Francisco, Chicago, Dallas, New York, Amsterdam, London, Brussels, Madrid, Munich, and Milan. This is intended to capture the contractual maximum latency observed in the fault of an underlying network element.

- **Jitter**—Can you commit to a maximum of 30 ms jitter as measured from CE to CE when properly configured with appropriate LFI configurations?

- **Packet delivery**—Can you meet the packet delivery requirements for each required CoS, as detailed in the section "QoS Capability"?

- **Availability**—What percentage of availability can you commit to for your service, including the local loops?

Security

The primary concern here is to establish the teams, tools, and procedures to be in place and utilized in the event of a security advisory from an equipment vendor, or when an actual attack takes place.

The following questions can be used when assessing security issues with providers:

- **Internet traffic (non-VPN)**—If Internet traffic rides across the same infrastructure as shared MPLS VPN traffic, please detail the architecture used to carry general Internet traffic. For instance, is the Internet traffic in its own VPN? Are the routes in the default VRF?

- **Management access**—Please detail how management access to the network infrastructure is controlled, for engineer troubleshooting access as well as Operation Systems Support (OSS) system access.

- **Security team**—Who are the security contacts within your organization, what attack-tracing tools does that group use, and what will happen if our or your network is the object of a denial of service (DoS) attack?

Software Deployment Processes

One of the focuses of many corporate IT departments is the adoption of new technology. Enterprises expect their service providers to be aware of new technology developments. SPs should be able to implement new functionality for the enterprise use of their VPN services in a "leading-edge" manner. This means that the network operating system of devices within the provider network should be no more than two or three releases behind the latest available from the equipment vendor.

One question worth posing to providers is, assuming a business case exists for you to deploy a particular feature on your infrastructure, how long would it take to introduce the technology on your network from the time the equipment vendor made production releases of code available?

Inter-Provider IP/VPN

Although it is expected that enterprises will manage the handoff between providers in different geographic regions for some time, ultimately an interprovider solution is attractive from the enterprise perspective. The provider should answer this question: Are you considering any partnerships with other service providers that would use "peering points" to interconnect IP/VPN clouds? If so, please provide details of the partners, locations where you are considering interprovider exchanges, and an overview of the interprovider IP/VPN implementation (including whether the capabilities discussed here would be supported, such as multicast, routing protocol type and metric preservation, and so on). Please also provide details about the customer engagement for this type of partnership.

IPv6

Depending on the enterprise's location, IPv6 either will be important or not. Even if IPv6 is not important today, it is highly likely that, at some point in the future, it will become relevant to the enterprise network.

Ask the provider about support for IPv6: Do you support IPv6 encapsulation natively across your network (using 6PE or something similar)? If not, do you have a road map for doing so? If such a road map exists, please detail the time frames in which you expect IPv6 support to be available.

MTU Considerations

An enterprise requires the service provider network to be able to carry IP packets of up to 1500 bytes presented to the service provider's PE router by the enterprise CE router. Network performance should not degrade for large numbers of 1500-byte packets.

It is desirable that the service provider network be able to support larger maximum transmission units (MTUs) than 1500 bytes presented by the CE to support encryption of IP traffic. IP GRE and IPsec tunnel mode encapsulations to support encryption add an additional 76 bytes to packets traveling through the network. Service providers' ability to handle 1580- to 1600-byte packets is desirable and should be investigated.

It is noted that the use of MVPN prepends an IP/GRE header to the multicast packet sent across the infrastructure, which may cause a different maximum IP MTU that could be used for multicast traffic. This extra header must be taken into consideration.

Here are some questions to ask the provider on this issue:

- **Unicast MTU 1500**—Can you carry 1500-byte packets presented by the CE router across your network?
- **Unicast maximum MTU**—What is the maximum IP MTU of a packet presented by the CE router that can be carried across your network?
- **Multicast/MVPN MTU**—What is the maximum IP MTU of a multicast packet presented by the CE router that can be carried across your network?

Hosting Capability

In some locations where the enterprise does not have data center-quality facilities, the enterprise may need to use service provider hosting facilities such as Internet Data Centers (IDCs). These IDCs are expected to deliver data center-quality environmental features (power, enhanced security, and air conditioning) for the hosting of hosts and applications.

The following should be determined about provider capabilities for this issue: Detail the locations in which you have IDCs that can host enterprise hosts and applications. Please also detail whether access to the IP/VPN infrastructure from that location is local (on-site) or remote (via access circuit).

IP Telephony PSTN Integration

Many enterprises are investigating the convergence of their voice PSTN access with their IP/VPN data access so that the enterprise does not have to manage PSTN gateways at each of its offices except for emergency calls.

To determine provider capabilities on this issue, ask the following questions:

- **IP PSTN service outbound**—Do you offer, or plan to offer, an IP PSTN service for calls outbound to the PSTN from VPN sites? If planned, please provide a timeline.

- **IP PSTN service inbound**—Does your IP PSTN service also support inbound calls from the PSTN? If planned, please provide a timeline.

- **IP PSTN protocol support**—If you support either outbound or inbound PSTN service, what IP telephony protocols do you support in your PSTN access service (H.323, SIP, MGCP, and so on)?

- **IP PSTN platform**—What technology platform is your IP PSTN service provided on?

- **IP PSTN number portability**—Where do you have the ability to redirect existing PTT/ILEC allocated direct inward dial (DID) numbers to your inbound PSTN service so that the enterprise will not have to provide new telephone numbers to its offices and employees?

- **Emergency calling (IP PSTN)**—Does your IP PSTN service make any provisions for emergency service (for example, 911)? What special handling, if any, is required for such capability?

IP Telephony Hosted Call Agent

Another service that enterprises investigate for some remote offices is a hosted IP telephony call agent (IP Centrex). The enterprise assumes that this service will be coupled with an IP PSTN service (as discussed in the preceding section) to provide access for telephone calls to and from the PSTN.

Ask your provider the following:

- **IP telephony hosted call agent**—Do you offer, or plan to offer, such a hosted call agent service? If planned, please provide a timeline.

- **Call agent type**—What technology platform is your IP hosted call agent service provided on?

- **Administration**—How is the service administered? What type of administrative interface is provided for visibility into a user's configuration?

- **Service management APIs**—Do you provide any APIs for automated provisioning, dial plan management, and so on from the Cisco Enterprise Management tools?

- **Enterprise telephony integration**—Does your service permit integration with other enterprise telephony infrastructure? If so, can your service be configured to accept an arbitrary dial plan, such as pressing 8 plus a three-digit global site code plus a four-digit extension?

- **Enterprise voice mail integration**—Can your service integrate with an enterprise-operated voice mail or unified messaging system such as Cisco Unity? Does your service provide its own voice mail or unified messaging service? If so, what provisions are available for its integration with an enterprise voice mail network, such as Cisco Unity?

- **IP phone application deployment**—If this service is supported on Cisco CallManager, do you allow the enterprise to configure or update applications for use by the IP phone?

- **SRST capability**—Is your call agent service compatible with the Cisco Survivable Remote Site Telephony (SRST) in case of WAN failure?

- **Emergency calling (call agent)**—Does your IP PSTN service make any provisions for emergency service (for example, a local PSTN gateway with a handful of analog lines)? What special handling, if any, is required for such capability?

Remote and Dial Access

This section raises the questions you should ask your provider that relate to remote access and dial modem access to the sites on the IP/VPN service:

- **Remote Internet VPN access**—Can you provide Internet-based VPN access to your IP/VPN service?

- **Remote VPN access technology platform**—What technology platform(s) does your remote access/dial access service use?

- **Internet VPN access interconnect points of presence (PoPs)**—In which locations do you provide access from the Internet to an IP/VPN service?

- **Dial access**—Can you provide local dial-modem access to the Internet for the use of this Internet VPN access capability through your facilities or through partner facilities? If so, please detail the locations where you have dialup access points and modem speed support (V.92, V.90, and so on).

Internet Access

This section raises the questions you should ask your provider that relate to receiving Internet access from IP/VPN-connected sites:

- **Internet access from IP/VPN sites**—Can you provide Internet access service to enterprise sites in conjunction with your IP/VPN offering via a separate DLCI, VC, or VLAN?

- **Internet access technology platform**—What technology platform(s) does your Internet access service use?

- **QoS of Internet access**—How is QoS handled on your Internet access service when provided via IP/VPN service?

- **Security capability**—Please provide details of any security capabilities you have in ensuring the security of Internet access to IP/VPN sites.

- **Internet DoS protection**—Do you provide any advanced DoS or anomaly detection, alerting, and mitigation capabilities for Internet attacks?

Other Network Services

What other IP services are you in the process of planning for your IP/VPN network? Examples may include content distribution, advanced security services, and so on.

INDEX

Numerics

802.1p bits, 156

A

acceptance testing, 297–298
access
    as server provider selection criteria, 28
access technologies
    ATM, 57
        QoS characteristics, 57
    ATM PVC from CE to PE, 59
    dedicated circuit from CE to PE, 58
    Frame Relay, 57
    Frame Relay PVC from CE to PE, 60
    metro Ethernet, 60–61
ACLs
    boundary ACLs, 215
        configuring, 216–217
    effectiveness against attacks, 247
    infrastructure ACLs, 248–250
    receive ACLs, 247
Acme
    backbone WAN, 12
    global span, 10
    IT applications base, 10
    IT communications infrastructure, 11
    management's business needs, 10
    new technology considerations, 13
        Layer 2 IP/MPLS VPN services, 18, 20–21
        Layer 3 IP/MPLS VPN services, 13, 16–18
    regional WANs, 12
Acme, Inc. case studies
    remote user access, 369
Acme, Inc. case study
    analysing service requirements, 75–77, 79
        congestion, 80, 82–83
        delay, 79–80
        evaluation tools, 83–84
        load testing, 80, 82–83
        post-transition results, 86–87
        routing convergence, 79
        TCCP, 84

        transition issues, 86
        vendor knowledge, 83
    QoS for low-speed links, 179, 181
activing
    QoS on switch devices, 171–173
address resolution
    NHRP, configuring, 357
addressing, 113
addressing schemes for multicast
    administratively scoped addresses, 197
    well-known group address ranges, 197
administratively scoped multicast addresses, 197
anatomy of DDoS attacks, 264, 266
anycast address, 198
anycast sinkholes, 259
application trust, 155
applying
    multicast boundaries to router interface,
        216–217
    QoS to backup WAN circuits, 156
architecture of botnets, 266
areas, 96
**ASICs (application-specific integrated circuits),
    201**
ASM (Any Source Multicast), 402
ASM (Any-Source Multicast), 203
assigning
    metrics, 98
async default ip address command, 338
ATM, 57
    QoS characteristics, 57
ATM PVC from CE to PE, 59
attacks
    automating with botnets, 266–267
    DDoS
        anatomy of, 264, 266
    identifying, 246
    mitigating, 250
    mitigation techniques
        backscatter traceback, 259, 261
        Cisco Guard, 262
        loose uRPF for source-based filtering,
            255–256
        remote-triggered black-hole filtering,
            253–255

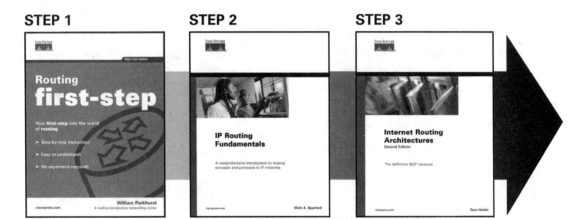

CISCO SYSTEMS

Cisco Press

FUNDAMENTALS SERIES
ESSENTIAL EXPLANATIONS AND SOLUTIONS

1-57870-168-6

When you need an authoritative introduction to a key networking topic, **reach for a Cisco Press Fundamentals book**. Learn about network topologies, deployment concepts, protocols, and management techniques and **master essential networking concepts and solutions**.

Look for Fundamentals titles at your favorite bookseller

802.11 Wireless LAN Fundamentals
ISBN: 1-58705-077-3

**Cisco CallManager Fundamentals:
A Cisco AVVID Solution**
ISBN: 1-58705-008-0

Cisco LAN Switching Fundamentals
ISBN: 1-58705-089-7

Cisco Unity Fundamentals
ISBN: 1-58705-098-6

Data Center Fundamentals
ISBN: 1-58705-023-4

IP Addressing Fundamentals
ISBN: 1-58705-067-6

IP Routing Fundamentals
ISBN: 1-57870-071-X

Network Security Fundamentals
ISBN: 1-58705-167-2

Storage Networking Fundamentals
ISBN: 1-58705-162-1

Voice over IP Fundamentals
ISBN: 1-57870-168-6

Coming in Fall 2005

**Cisco CallManager Fundamentals:
A Cisco AVVID Solution**, Second Edition
ISBN: 1-58705-192-3

Visit **www.ciscopress.com/series** for details about the Fundamentals series and a complete list of titles.

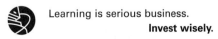

Safari ®
BOOKS ONLINE
ENABLED

THIS BOOK IS SAFARI ENABLED

INCLUDES FREE 45-DAY ACCESS TO THE ONLINE EDITION

The Safari® Enabled icon on the cover of your favorite technology book means the book is available through Safari Bookshelf. When you buy this book, you get free access to the online edition for 45 days.

Safari Bookshelf is an electronic reference library that lets you easily search thousands of technical books, find code samples, download chapters, and access technical information whenever and wherever you need it.

TO GAIN 45-DAY SAFARI ENABLED ACCESS TO THIS BOOK:

- Go to **http://www.ciscopress.com/safarienabled**

- Complete the brief registration form

- Enter the coupon code found in the front of this book before the "Contents at a Glance" page

If you have difficulty registering on Safari Bookshelf or accessing the online edition, please e-mail customer-service@safaribooksonline.com.